The Gospel of the Prophet Mani

Edited and almost wholly Newly Translated from many languages
of original Manichean Texts and of Excerpts by others,
for the first time in English, With a Life of the Prophet,
an Outline of Manichean History, and other Introductions,
Explanatory Commentary, Full Annotations
and an Illuminating Appendix

BY

DUNCAN GREENLEES, M. A. (OXON.)

THE BOOK TREE
San Diego, California

Originally published
1956
by The Theosophical Publishing House
Adyar, Madras, India

New material, revisions and cover
© 2007
The Book Tree
All rights reserved

ISBN 978-1-58509-502-5

Cover layout and design
by Atulya Berube

Published by
The Book Tree
P.O. Box 16476
San Diego, CA 92176
www.thebooktree.com

We provide fascinating and educational products to help awaken the public to new ideas and information that would not be available otherwise.
Call 1 (800) 700-8733 for our *FREE BOOK TREE CATALOG*.

THE WORLD GOSPEL SERIES

Gather us in, Thou Love that fillest all;
Gather our rival faiths within Thy fold;
Rend each man's temple-veil and bid it fall
That we may know that Thou hast been of old.
Gather us in; we worship only Thee:
In varied names we stretch a common hand;
In diverse forms a common Soul we see,
In many Ships we seek one Spirit-Land.
Each sees one colour of Thy rainbow light;
Each looks upon one tint and calls it heaven;
Thou art the Fullness of our partial sight—
We are not perfect till we find the seven.

G. MATHESON

Apart from a few scholars and devotees, the modern public are unwilling to spend time on reading through the whole of the lengthy Scriptures of the world. This little Series is planned to offer them in a cheap, handy and attractive form the essence of all the world's great Scriptures, translated and edited by one who has a deep and living sympathy for each of them.

It is based on the inevitable conclusion of any fair student that all the great Religions and their Scriptures come from one Divine Source, in varying degrees of purity of transmission, and according to the needs and capacities of those to whom they came—the authentic Word of God to man.

The Publishers hope to issue two volumes yearly, each of about 300 pages, with short notes or running commentary, and a brief introduction to point out the significance of the book in the history of world thought. This is Volume Twelve.

When the Series is completed, it will form a useful little reference library of the world's religious literature, which has done so much to mould the thought and culture of today, even though few individuals in each of the communities have perhaps been able to reach the ideal laid down in them.[1]

DUNCAN GREENLEES.

---

[1] Yet, as this is, an objective study, aiming at a fair presentation of the Manichean view, it is obvious that the writer does **not** thereby pronounce his own personal convictions or religious faith.

THE GOSPEL OF THE PROPHET MANI[1]

LIGHT and Dark, Good and Evil, are the two opposite and coeternal Sources of all that is. They were mingled together when the ambition of Evil to possess the Light had to be countered by God sending a Light-Spark from Himself, the conscious Soul, down into Matter to uplift and purify the Light therein entangled everywhere. Manifested in five-fold Potencies, or 'Sons', perfectly reflected in the five aspects of the human mind, God's 'Living Spirit' fashioned the universe as a means to separate gradually these primal Sources. This story of the One Soul is repeated by every individual Soul aspiring to return to its lost Kingdom of the Light near God, and aided thereto by Divine Outpourings and the human Messengers of the Light who found religions.

[1] Both vowels are long, as *Maa-nee*.

These Saviours free the Soul held in the corrupting bonds of Matter by awakening her memory of heavenly origin and continuing divinity. She co-operates thenceforth with the work of self-purifying by her prayer and fasting, alms and chastity, together with her practice of the twelve Virtues of the Zodiacal Signs which overcome the horoscope enslaving her to recurring births in Matter. So she rises through the mystical body of the Church or 'Perfect Man' to union with the human Teacher and the Lord, and so at last comes for evermore to blissful enjoyment of God's presence in the Gardens of the Light.

The organs of the human body closely correspond with the outer universe, as do the powers and functions of the Light and Darkness, Spirit and Matter. The one has to be gradually transmuted by faith and works to the other, thus liberating the Soul. The fivefold hierarchy of the Church aids mightily in this spiritual alchemy. As the Light-Sparks are everywhere imprisoned in dark Matter, a total harmlessness and a universal reverence are implicit in this Faith, and its ethical standards are among the highest ever known.

The loving gratitude and passionate devotion given equally to Mani and his predecessors foreshadow the universalism of modern Theosophy, while Mani himself aimed to unite the creeds in a single worldwide Faith that shared the noblest elements found in each.

The sufferings demanded by that Faith led its devotees to regard Death with joyful eagerness as a final release from the miseries of embodiment—the overthrow of Darkness and the source of Evil in their life, the open doorway to eternal glory in the boundless Light. At that hour the Liberator came to them to drive away all gloom and ignorance, and to escort them to the adorable Father's lovely realm of Wisdom where the Soul is espoused to God.

When all the Light-Sparks have thus been freed, the world of physical gross Matter will cease to be, and the powers of Darkness will be finally overthrown; then will the Light be supreme for evermore, and all freed Souls will enter on the endless life of perfect love.

FOREWORD

For many centuries Manicheism was a powerful and far-reaching religion, rivaled only by Christianity in its scope, but today it is virtually unheard of. It was more dualistic, Gnostic and spiritual so became the arch rival of Christianity and was ultimately stamped out. Every effort has been made to remove it from the memory of humankind and, for the most part, these efforts were a success. Today, however, there is a resurgence of interest in Gnostic thought and teachings. This book will contribute a wealth of new information that would otherwise be lost to history. There is without question no better book on the subject. The author has assembled every known lost fragment of the faith that could possibly be found in order to accurately reassemble its doctrines and teachings. The information is presented factually, without a bias in either direction, to document this movement and its history accurately. He lets the teachings speak for themselves, which allows the reader to make an independent assessment regarding its veracity.

From an historical point of view the book is valuable because it both broadens and clarifies our view of religious history, showing what Christianity was truly up against and why Manicheism remained so popular for so long. There is no doubt that the prophet Mani was a great spiritual teacher - he had to be for the religion to flourish for so long. It lasted for over one thousand years in one form or another. Many of the holy books written by Mani have been lost or destroyed, only fragments remain, while has followers were killed and persecuted for centuries. What has been recovered has been painstakingly pieced together in this important work for the benefit of scholars, religious researchers and those interested in alternative spiritual paths.

Paul Tice

PREFACE

IN 1942 I used a good deal of unwanted leisure to enquire into the reality of the spiritual experiences said to underlie Religion, and so was led to investigate the shadowy history of Christian origins. This soon confronted me with a passionate prejudice that recalled our present-day mutual hatreds of Catholic and Communist—the furious antipathy for what the orthodox called 'Manichean'; those doughty bigots found words inadequate to express their loathing, and dark and shameful deeds were done against the followers of Mānī and their books.

What exactly caused this savage hatred? Was it simply an insane ignorance, such as has made in many lands and times the life of Jew and Negro a panic fever? Or was it rather the jealous fear of a worthy rival, an economic motive, or a question of prestige and power, which prompted this lunatic behaviour among men who called themselves followers of the God of Love and His gracious Christ?

I began to read everything on Mānī and his teachings I could find, and to copy every fragment of material I met which could throw light on this baffling problem of social terroristic injustice. At this time

Jackson's splendid book came to my hand and, as the idea of the WORLD GOSPEL SERIES was then beginning to dawn, I copied a great part of it, together with the translated Chinese Manichean Text and the Hymns in the British Museum. Step by step, I reduced my materials from various languages to one common factor —English.

When the time to study Mānī for this Series drew near, I obtained the magnificent 'Kephalaia' and 'Psalms' in Coptic, and so was able to delve into a vast treasury of original literature in the 'original' tongue used by Manicheans. The courtesy of St. Mary's College, Kurseong, Bengal (a seminary of the Society of Jesus), put in my reach Migne's colossal edition of the Christian authorities, as well as the otherwise unobtainable Coptic 'Homilies' and the Syriac text of bar Khoni's 'Scholia'. I copied nearly the whole of these valuable source-texts, and then felt myself ready to prepare for this volume. An Adyar friend, Sri K. Kunjanni Raja, had in 1947 got for me the Arabic text of AnNadim, and I found elsewhere the Turkish of the interesting 'Khuastuanift'; one of my earliest discoveries. Pehlevi, Soghdian, and other Turkish fragments came in from various books and journals. Where, as in the case of Chinese, the original (?) language is beyond my powers, I feel no hesitation in confidently relying on translations by such great scholars as Pelliot, Henning, Bang and Widengren, or on the discretion of quoters like Alfaric and Reitzenstein.

The first obstacle in studying Mānī and his system is the savage thoroughness with which his books were hunted out and destroyed. So far as we know, only a few fragments in his own Syriac still survive. But happily the great love and reverence of the Manicheans for their books assure us that we have in fact, in our early Coptic works, and even in the much later Turkish and Chinese literature, a reliable picture of what Mānī actually taught. This is confirmed even by the hostile accounts of Christian, Parsi, Muslim and Confucian witnesses. Reliance on such apostolic and sub-apostolic material will not lead us far astray; and the factual and restrained story of Mānī's sufferings and death gives us full confidence in its exact historicity.

Another obstacle is that this study calls, not only for a trained religionist but also for a linguist of unusual breadth and powers. To go really to their sources, the materials used in this volume demand a working knowledge of Coptic, Syriac, Arabic, Pehlevi, Soghdian, Old Turkish, Chinese, Greek, and Latin—besides the usual facility in French and German, in English and even Russian. Though I cannot pretend to meet all these demands, I have made shift with what the many years of life have brought to me, and as the bulk of this 'Gospel' comes from Coptic I am fairly safe on my own ground.

Why should we trouble at all to resurrect this perished religion, so often falsely dubbed a mere 'heresy'? Certainly it is for no futile evangelistic dream. A faith so largely built on a myth beyond investigation, and making so high demand on morality and gentleness, would have small hope to compete with its rivals in our age of intensifying sensuality and violence. Rather is it to delight the pure historic sense—to restore to its proper place in the story of human thought about the universe and man's part therein, a religion long denied a just realisation of its importance, and to fill in a gap made in human knowledge by the insensate vandalism of sectarian violence long ago. Whatever has concerned Man in the past or present is Man's proper study. And it is a peculiar joy to recover the shattered fragments of what was once a beautiful vase to hold a great man's message, even if to our taste it seem bizarre. It is a delight also to rediscover for our contemporaries the personality and experience of one of the great Religious Founders like Jesus, the Buddha, Zarathushtra, Muhammed—a Founder whose name has so long been hidden by the dust and clouds of conflict.

As we rejoice to read the lives and teachings of Mānī's great Brethren, who came from the same One Source of Light with messages of doctrine and ethics, each to his own age and its successors, so let us also delight in the labours and pleasing personality of Mānī himself and of his first successors Sisin and Innai. Let us consecrate his memory in the holy Shrine of humanity's Ideals; let us yearly honour the great dates of his proclamation, 9th April, and of his martyrdom for righteousness and the freedom of human thought, the 26th February.

xv

To these three, to the others who gave us the lovely 'Psalms' which captivated Egypt's ascetics 1600 years ago, to Kushtai the faithful secretary to whom we probably owe the 'Kephalaia' and the eyewitness story of the Master's sufferings, to Salmai the humble devotee and mourner, to Amu the Apostle who planted the Faith firmly in its Central Asian fastness, to those nameless heroes and heroines who died that at least fragments of the holy books might reach our day, to the one who hid away his little library in that box beneath his Fayum hut, to all those whose kindly sympathy have helped me in gathering and understanding materials—I offer reverent and grateful thanks.

May the happier future of which some of those once dreamed (cf. GPM 47) come soon to this our lovely tortured world! May it replace our gloomy clouds of jealous hatred, cruel contempt and unthinking violence with the bright sunshine of truth and loving comradeship! And may all who read this book come at last to the Kingdom of the Light, and there meet the blessed Mānī and all his Brethren, the Teachers of the World who have led it step by step upon the road "from Darkness to the Light, from Death to Immortality"![1]

---

[1] In this volume, words and phrases which are in italics have been speculatively restored by me from indications of parallel texts and the space left by words destroyed in our manuscripts.

As the usual practice is in this Series, words which for the sake of grammatical sequence I have substituted for those in the text have been printed in a heavy type.

INTRODUCTION

1. The Third Century

IT was an age of death, of new birth, of bitter conflict between the two, between the old and the new—an age of transition, of soaring hopes and of vain attempts to reawaken perished ideals.

Political. The twin empires of Rome and Persia swayed uneasily on the balance-point of Mesopotamia; at times the one moved on to the territories of the other, and then fell back again beyond its starting-point. The great Emperors of Rome had given place to military kinglets, who held the shadow-titles that had once glorified Augustus, Tiberius, Trajan, but now had little meaning any more for the two or three months of rule that each might hope to enjoy—and many faced equally powerful rival kinglets in other provinces. Even when for a spell one of these might establish himself in real power at Rome itself, his death soon restored the usual confusion of the 'thirty tyrants'. At such a time it was easy enough for the new Persian dynasty that replaced the vanquished Parthians to seat themselves firmly on the Eastern throne, so that they could not be overthrown even by the few Roman Emperors who dared attempt the feat. The great and wealthy plain of Mesopotamia was often ravaged by these frequent futile wars, and was gradually sinking into the wretched, and partly sand-covered, state in which it remained till our own days.

Further east, India was a tangle of petty states, free at the moment from all central control but under the general leadership of Kushans in the north and Pāndyas in the south; China was a great and settled empire shut off within its boundaries from the restless movements of the west; while, in between, Central Asia was the home of the widespread ancient Scythian tribes, partly Iranized, with Turks and Mongols on one border, and the shamanistic Tibetans on the other. None of these elements seemed likely to grow into a world power which could change and mould the future.

Religious. The old State cults of the Mediterranean basin had become decrepit, and few any longer believed in the great Gods on whose names myth and epic had been built. In their place had arisen the pagan 'Mysteries' and the Soteric cults—Hermes, Isis, Attis, Mithra had held their sway awhile and were now following Zeus, Amenre', Hercules and Mars into oblivion. The philosophies of Plato, Epicurus and the Stoics were the dry crusts education offered to thinking men, who as yet hardly cared to notice the crazy worship of a crucified Jew. When Christians made themselves more unpopular than usual by refusing the easy formal worship and State service which oiled the machinery of society in that age, they brought on themselves a brief but brutal persecution, here and there, and sometimes for several years on end. For the rest, they were left to enjoy their lugubrious rites in dark caves and catacombs, while their few real scholars were famous only within their own community.

Persia had forcibly restored Zarathustra's Mazdeism as the State religion. But this restoration was imposed from above; being based on the power of the rich and mighty, and overburdened with purificatory rites and monetary penalties for each offence, it awoke scant response of love in the people's heart. Nor could it ever hope now to extend its sway and to unite a world which Persia's monarchs, following the steps of Darius and Xerxes, could now dream once more of conquering.

In Babylonia the old Chaldean paganism was dying out, along with its Western compeers, and in its place many Gnostic sects throve, more or less Christian in form, and all of them analogous to the Hermeticism still prominent in Egypt though slowly yielding to the Christian teachers from Alexandria. Beside these sects —whereof the Marcionites and Bardesanians seem to have been the chief—was the young Mandean religion taught in prehistoric days—so it claimed—by the Prophet Seth-el, son of Adam, and more recently by John the Baptist in the Palestinian homeland. Filled with memories of the Chaldean myths that paralleled the Jewish 'Genesis' and the warm mysticism of Chaldean esotericism, it was destined to sink lower and lower into the magic, sorcery and spiritism which the motherland of astrology had retained from its pagan antiquity; it too could never aspire to become a religion for the seeking world.

India was still, as always, a welter of competing but mutually tolerant faiths—the people being divided between the timeless Hinduism and the vigorous and, mainly, non-violent reformist faiths of Buddhism and the Jains. The interplay between these was already profoundly modifying each of them, and the Mahāyāna taught by Aśvaghoṣa and Nāgārjuna later on was already in its primal glory; the Upanishads had prepared the ground for a great revival of personal love and devotion to God, along with a realisation by experience of the universal Unity.

In Central Asia spiritism in various shamanistic forms, together with the cults of local and nature deities, as in the Bön of Tibet and the Shinto of Japan, seems to have been prevailing; China was divided between the traditional conservative philosophy of Confucius (Khung-fu-tsü) and his followers, the mysticism of Lao-tsü's 'Tao', and the slowly infiltrating Buddhism that predominated already on Persia's eastern frontiers.

Taking a broad view of the known world at the time, one can easily see how Mānī felt that a genius combining the ethics, ideals of purity, and devotion of existing great religions, with the popular if grotesque myths of the masses, could create a universal Faith and unite the nations in a single body of aspiration and of righteousness.

The growing Christianity, with its close involvement in the unpopular Jewish cult, was too exclusive, too fanatical, and in that age too lost in verbal hair-splitting over the elaboration of a Law to replace the lost Temple and Holy Land; it did not seem to many outside its own communion as fitted to form such a world religion. It lacked the gentle tolerance and understanding which India's contact gave to Mānī's Faith; it also lacked the serene patience which naturally stems from a belief in reincarnation; it lacked the culture which could see that Infinite Truth must have an infinity of facets, and can be approached upon an infinity of paths, not one of which can be proclaimed as the only right, not one denounced as wrong. Yet all these elements were already in the world, waiting for the new Messenger of the Light to utilise, to weave into the wondrous garment of radiant wisdom which he came to give the world. These, and other coloured threads as well, Mānī wove into the fabric of his thought, which he dyed with the crimson of his own heart's blood.

2. Mani, the Messenger of the Light

1. The Parents of a Prophet

Like many of his great Brethren, Mānī came of royal blood. His father Pattiq, or Fattaq Bābak, was the son of Abu Barzām, so AnNadim tells us, of the Ḥaskānīya family, living in Ecbatana, then the summer capital of the Parthian Empire. Schraeder takes this name to be a corruption of 'Khaskaniya', the family name of the royal Arsacid line which ruled Persia from B.C. 250 to A.D. 226.

This Pattiq married a girl named Mais or Ūtākhīm, evidently of the same royal line, for the *Tashi-tripitaka*, 2141 a, says she belonged to the 'family of Kamsargān' and lived at 'the royal abode of Buʻattiei (Pattiq) her husband'—her own name being given here as 'Muānyām', a corruption of the Syrian name 'Mar-Maryam', or Mary the holy. Christian writers gave her the name 'Karossa', of which there is no other trace; it may derive from the family name 'Kamsar' or be a corruption of the well-known name 'Atossa', which could stand for any unnamed Persian lady.

Though all but deified by his followers while still alive, Mānī himself nowhere claims to be the Son of God the Heavenly King; the frequent calling him 'Son of the Ruler, or Rulers' in Turfan texts seems to refer to this descent from the fallen dynasty of Parthians. He himself loved to call mankind his 'brethren', his 'beloved', or his 'limbs'.

2. Birth and Childhood

For some reason Pattiq and his wife left their Ecbatana home and settled at Ctesiphon [1] in Babylonia. Here he used to attend the local pagan temple, along with his neighbours. One day he heard a voice crying from the idol-sanctuary: "O Pattiq, eat no meat,

[1] Called Sou-lin in Chinese, Sūristan in Persian, and Mada'in in Arabic. It is an hour's run by car south of Baghdad.

drink no wine, and touch no woman!" When this happened on three successive days, Pattiq resolved to obey. He left Ctesiphon, went to Maisān or Characene on the Lower Tigris and joined the Mandean sect [1] which was numerous there. He seems to have taught his fellows the value of an ascetic and celibate life, and it has even been suggested he may have written a part of the Mandean scripture called '*Ginzā*', 'the Treasure'.

Mais was bearing a child just before this time, and as we nowhere hear of mortal brothers or sisters, it was probably the only one. While Mānī was in the womb, she used to enjoy pleasant dreams and, so AnNadim tells us, she would on waking see an Angel carry the unborn child up to heaven and then return him to the womb after, sometimes, a day or two.

The child was ultimately born (possibly during the southward journey) at the village of Baromiā, or Mardinu, near the Kuthā Canal, just south of the modern Baghdad. It was on the 7th or 25th April, A.D. 215—the year the Roman Caracalla overthrew Vologeses V and brought his brother Artaban IV (215-226) to the throne as the last Parthian King in Persia. Mani himself tells us in Keph. I that Artaban was already reigning at his birth.

His personal name may have been Shuraiq (Cubricus), but every Manichean source knows him

---

[1] *i.e.*, the socalled 'Baptists of St. John', a few of whom still exist thereabouts in the midst of their Muslim neighbours. See Lady Drower's books.

only as 'Mānī' or 'Manichaios'. Bar Khoni thinks the name derives from *mānā*, illustrious, or vessel, but the Persian books know the form '*mānīhī*' from which seems to come the usual form in Greek and Coptic 'Manichaios'; there is also a chance that it may connect with with the Semitic '*Mnāhīm*', the 'Comforter' or 'Paraclete'—a title later assumed by the Prophet himself (Jn. 14 : 26). His own native Syriac always calls him 'Mānī', the form we use throughout in this volume. The playful malice of his Christian opponents saw in the name a reference to the 'mania' of his doctrines—a typical piece of false etymology and polemic propaganda!

For twelve years in Maisān Pattiq taught his little son his own religion, with its background of mingled Chaldean myth, asceticism, and Christianized Gnosis. AnNadim tells us that even when extremely young Mani used to utter 'words of wisdom'. He seems to have been trained as an artist—his skill in painting even gave the word *mānī* significance as 'painter' in later Persian. He had talents also in poetry, and an imagination of amazing and unbridled power—as shown by his moulding into a living whole of the myths long treasured in his native land.

3. The Call to the Ministry (A. D. 228)

When Mani was just twelve, the Parthian dynasty was overthrown by the Persian Sassanids; Ardashir I (226-240), claiming to be a scion of the great Darius and Xerxes of old, led a national revolt, and took the throne of Iran, driving the fallen dynasty into Armenia.[1] In those days Mani had a vision of the 'Twin' (Syr: *Tôm*; Ar: *etTawam*), or the 'Paraclete', a godlike Angel who came from " the High God, King of the Gardens of Light". According to AnNadim, this glorious messenger thus addressed him: " Withdraw from this sect, for none of its people belong to you; your concern is with purifying the soul and abandoning the passions. But (the time for) your public appearance has not yet come, for you are still too young." He should observe perfect celibacy and wait for a second call in twelve years' time.

Mani himself tells the story in his own way (Keph. I): " In the same year that Ardashir was *about to receive* the crown (*i.e.*, March 228-April 229), then the Living Paraclete came down *to me and* spoke with me. He revealed to me the hidden Mystery which was concealed before the worlds and generations, the Mystery of the Deep and the Height; he revealed to me the Mystery of the Light and the Darkness, the Mystery of the struggle, fight and great war which the Darkness waged. After that he showed me also how through their mingling the Light has *interpenetrated* the

---

[1] Taqizadeh points out that though Ctesiphon fell late in March 227, Ardashir was already 'King of Iran' by 223/4; the war broke out when he founded a Fire-temple and palace at Gor, his provincial capital, and there were battles at Ispahan, Ahwaz and Meisan. It was his grandfather Pabhagh who took Istaghir in Pars, slew the local King Gochihr about A.D. 213, and overthrew the Bāzrangian dynasty there, of which his mother was a member. Ardashir succeeded his father Shapur after a brief reign, and by 208, at the age of about 28, he began to attack neighbouring Kings, and soon became Commander-in-Chief.

Darkness, and how this world was founded. Thereon he also taught me how the Ships were established, so that the *Powers* of Light could let themselves down in them, so as to refine the Light *out of* creation, *throwing* the dregs and refuse *into the* Abyss; the Mystery of the creation of Adam the First Man; also the Mystery of the Messengers who are sent into the world to choose out the churches; the Mystery of the Elect *and their* precepts; the Mystery of the Hearers, their helpers, and *their* rules; the Mystery of the Sinners and their deeds, and the punishment which draws near to them. Thus through the Paraclete everything that exists and will exist was revealed to me; ... all that the eye sees and ear hears, the mind thinks and *the heart desires*—I have learnt all through Him. Through Him I have seen the Whole, and become One Body and One Spirit (therewith)."

When the end of his life drew near, Mani insisted (§19) before the persecuting King Bahram that he had no human teacher but received his whole doctrine from the God-sent Angel, his 'Twin' or Higher Self, whose presence and help throughout life he warmly attested in M 49. There is not the slightest reason to doubt the total sincerity of this story; it is the experience of every Messenger from God in all nations and every age. Yet of course the materials, woven afresh in a new pattern by the inspiration of the Prophet, were certainly drawn from his own background—in Mani's case, from the dualism of Zarathushtra, the esotericism and the asceticism of Gnostic Christianity, the legends of Chaldean paganism and Mandean ritual, the harmlessness of Jain and Buddhist, the lofty ethic of the Sermon on the Mount.

4. Hidden Years (A. D. 228-240)

Of those twelve years of waiting little is known. Probably Mani lived in comparative obscurity because Ardashir restored Mazdeism as the State religion of the Empire and exterminated most of the old royal house, to which Mani himself apparently belonged. They were years of war, for Ardashir demanded all the lands lost to Rome; but his eleven years of fighting proved fruitless, the war restored the *status quo*.

Doubtless Mani gave his time to the study of earlier religions, incorporating suitable elements from them into the eclectic synthesis of his own Message. He may even have come into contact with the then active propaganda of Mahayana Buddhism, and with the Hermetic Gnosis then freely circulating through Egypt, Syria and much of the Hellenistic world, spread largely by Stoics and Platonists. He was well informed of Christian doctrine, specially honouring the Gospels of Matthew, John and Luke, and the Epistles of Paul; in addition he shows clear knowledge of the Leucian Acts of the Five Apostles and several apocryphal Gospels. Tradition connects his name with those of Marcion and Bardaisan; surviving fragments show very close parallels with the 'Hymn of the Soul' and other Gnostic poems now embedded in the Acts of John and Thomas.

Bar Hebræus tells us that Mani lived for some time at Ahwāz, the capital of Susiana, as a 'priest', but it is most unlikely that he was in any sense a *Christian* priest. Even as a lad he may have been regarded as a 'holy man', being filled with 'words of wisdom', and Alfaric quotes a source as saying that he began to teach in Maisan where he grew up. It is likely that he may even have gathered his first few disciples in those very early days.

Even his bitterest enemies never ventured on any slander against his personal character or alleged that he fell away from the strictest celibacy at any time in his life. He moved later in royal courts, but even then such was his simplicity of life that he was called a 'beggar' and 'an insignificant man'. The surviving writings of his personal followers show us a most lovable person, faithfully doing God's will on earth as he saw it, treating all men with gentleness and kindly affection, and winning from those who knew him best a passionate love and boundless adoration, which could be satisfied only by conferring titles of divinity.

5. The Prophet is Proclaimed (A.D. 240-242)

At the age of twenty-four, apparently on 12th April 240, though some calculate it as 31st March 241, Mani again saw his Angel-Teacher, who said to him: "Now the time has come for you to go out and proclaim your authority (as God's Prophet). Peace be on you, Mani, from myself and from the Lord who sent me to you and who has chosen you for His Message. He has now bidden you to invite (people) to your Truth, and to proclaim the good news of the Truth (*i.e.*, the True Gospel) from before Him, and to persevere in that with all your zeal." Mani himself tells us in the Kephalaia that " he moved out in order to preach . . . at the end of King Ardashir's years ".

It was the second Sunday after Easter, 20th March 242, though some count it as 9th April 243, when the new King Shapur I, now about 43 years old, was crowned at his capital on the auspicious eve of the Mīhrakān festival. On the same day Mani proclaimed himself God's Prophet, apparently in the royal city, though he does not seem then to have met the King. Two disciples, Zakwā (Zakkouas) and Shamʿōn by name, were with him there, and AnNadim tells us that his father Pattiq also stood by " to watch what would come of his mission ". At first nothing very much seemed to come of it at all. The people were more interested in the crowning of the secular King than in lectures about an unseen spiritual King of the Light.

But someone evidently warned King Shapur that this move on the part of a scion of the old house endangered the new; Mani found it desirable almost immediately to flee the country and to seek shelter in what was then almost the ends of the earth. He " took ship to the land of the Indians " and sailed on the first of his great missionary journeys. (Keph. 76).

6. The Mission to India (A.D. 243)

We may never know why Mani selected India; perhaps he knew of the tolerance to be expected there, which caused the welcome given four centuries later to the Parsi refugees ; possibly some friend was about to go there for trade and took him along with him. His companions seem to have been Pattiq (his father?) and Amu (Ammōs), later the Apostle to Central Asia.

He himself tells us (Keph. 76) that he " preached to them the Hope of Life and there chose out a good selection" of disciples. He roused some interest and established his first churches in Sind, then largely Buddhist and Jain in faith. There too, " in the land of the Brahman ", he wrote his first book, the ' Shapurāqān ', in the Persian language in delicate flattery of the Persian King. Probably by this use of, to him, a foreign tongue he hoped to assure Shapur of his political loyalty; in due course this book reached the King's hands and seems to have made a fair impression on him.

For a short while all went well in Sind, but apparently his teaching of celibacy was found " too strict" by the people, brought up to a more usual view of family life. There was a swift reaction, and they rejected Mani's message; he says: " At that hour I ceased to find Light, I ceased to speak freely with the Voice that is this Truth sojourning with me "— an interesting psychological reaction to resistance (Cf. Mk. 6 : 5)!

With a few of his disciples Mani took ship westwards. It was probably on this voyage occurred the quaint incident narrated in MH. 91. They were in mid-sea when a porpoise (?) lifted its head from the water and cried to Mani for help; but he bade it go on its way. The creature came again crying with pain from a head wound, and so Mani was able to explain how while plants have to suffer in silence animals can let us know of their pains and move away from their cause. Evidently the extreme kindliness of his ethic was already established, possibly by Jain contacts in Sind.

7. To Khorassan (A.D. 243-244)

The little party landed on the Mekran coast and immediately proceeded inland to Khorassan, the homeland of Mani's Parthian ancestors. While in the desert another incident occurred, which Amu later related to the King: " We were on our way, while our Father (*i.e.*, Mani) sat on the *mule*. Then a big lion came down *to meet us, with an arrow in its side*, weeping. So our Father bade that it *keep still* while he removed it. Then he spoke to us again: ' You see this. That was Pilate, who once condemned Jesus; but in his favour he uttered one word, namely: *Lo, my hands are pure from the blood of this Righteous One. On that account has he received forgiveness of (his) sins* ' (MH. 91)." Indian teachers even now often tell such stories to illustrate their doctrines of karma and reincarnation—*e.g.*, Ramana Maharshi about the cow Lakshmi.

We hear little of Mani's mission to Khorassan, but it must have been successful, for in later years this always proved a safe refuge for persecuted Manicheans. At this time Tabari (1 : 833) tells us: "When Ardashir died and Shapur became ruler, the latter appointed his own son Hormizd to the Governorship of Khorassan." This prince may soon have been recalled, but the contact with Mani there may have led to his conversion, perhaps later, while the Prophet was at the court of his father. The Governor was now Ferōz, King Shapur's brother. We have in M 47 the interesting story of his meeting with the Prophet: "Now the King of Kings had two brothers with names Mēṣwan the lord and Mīhrṣāh—and he was the implacable enemy of the Messenger's Religion. He had planted a garden very splendid and wonderfully planned, having no equal. When the hour of salvation had come to him, the Messenger appeared there before Mīhrṣāh who was joyfully banqueting in the garden . . . Then the King asked the Messenger, ' In the Paradise you speak of (?) could there be a garden like this garden of mine?' Then the Messenger punished this scoffing word; immediately through his power he showed him the Paradise of Lights, with all Gods and deities, and the imperishable Wind of Life, and the garden altogether . . . and another . . . Thus he remained unconscious for three hours while he pondered in the heart what he had seen. Then the Messenger laid a hand on his head, and he returned to consciousness. When he stood up, he fell at the Messenger's feet and took his right hand (*i.e.*, took him as his teacher)."

By this conversion of a princely Governor Mani was set firmly on the road that led him first to royal favour and then to exile and martyrdom.

8. Early Travels (A.D. 244-245)

Mani then " went *through all* the land of Persia and her towns, *preaching* in the living Truth which *was* with *him, according* to the light of the *license* to preach *given him by* the Powers and Authorities ", so he tells us. Prince Feroz seems to have encouraged this open propaganda for a while, though local jealousies soon led to a demand for its cessation.

Then he moved over the great plateau and down to the green plains of his own homeland; for some time he taught at Maisān, at that time a large and busy market city. Here too he established his Church on a strong organised basis, but here too the people as a whole rejected him; they found his teaching harder to bear even the alternating tyrannies of Roman and Persian Emperors over them, together with the petty extortions of their countless subordinate officials. Perhaps this was when Mani had his discussion with a 'Nasorean', or Mandean, about God's justice and declared that even earthly judges are cruel only to the wicked and uphold righteousness; his own later experiences probably forced him to revise this naive estimate (Keph. 89).

He travelled northwards over Mesopotamia to Babylon, which he here calls 'the land of the Assyrians'. Here also he founded his Church and for some time preached to good effect. Probably this was when he had the discussion with a Babylonian about the origin of humanity narrated in Keph. 57. But at last the local rulers here too rose against him, incited by the 'sects'—probably various kinds of Christians and Chaldean pagans. He assures us that only God's protection enabled him to pass even a single day longer in their land, and wonders how the people there could patiently endure all their worldly tyrants while they could not bear the sweet yoke of righteousness he would lay upon them, but hindered him all they could.

He left Babylon, and went further north into the hills of Media and Armenia. Here the same story repeated itself. Mani made a few disciples everywhere —disciples who clung to the Faith through centuries of bitter persecution—but most of the people were unconvinced and unattracted.

The 'Parthia' to which he next turned was probably the Caspian coastland of Mazendaran, for we next find Mani at the royal city of Jund-i-Shapur in south-west Persia not far from the ancient Susa, and a great garrison fort commanding the road towards the heart of the Persian Empire.

9. Mani at King Shapur's Court (A.D. 245-255)

Evidently Prince Feroz reported to the King, his brother, that Mani had no political ambitions but was concerned with giving the Empire a religion that could unify its varied peoples. For about this time Shapur invited the Prophet to live at his court.

When Mani entered the royal presence a wonder manifested itself, so AnNadim tells us: "Upon his shoulders was the likeness of two torches of light, and when Shapur saw it he esteemed it greatly and it was important in his eyes. He had formerly thought to scourge and kill him, but when he made his acquaintance veneration arose and he rejoiced in him. He asked Mani why he entered, and then gave hopes that he would turn to him (as a convert)." In his 'Chronology', p. 191, Biruni tells us: "King Shapur began to believe in him when he had been raised on high with him and supported with him in the air between heaven and earth"—which recalls the story of how an Angel used to raise the unborn Mani himself, and the story of Simon's levitation before the Roman Emperor, found in the Clementines and books of similar provenance. Certain Manicheans told Biruni that Mani often used to go up thus to Heaven for several days to avoid his followers, while others denied all such miraculous tales.

AnNadim goes on: "So Mani asked him a host of needs, among them that his followers be respected in the country and in all the towns of his kingdom, and that they might enter any of the towns they wished." This request evidently stemmed from Mani's rather discouraging reception hitherto; a letter of royal support would prevent at least open opposition.

We learn that " then Shapur agreed (to give) him the whole of what he asked ". On Mani's request he wrote letters to all the Governors, nobles and royal kinsmen, telling them not to hinder the Prophet in any way.

Mani gives a laconic account of this event, saying merely: " I appeared before Shapur the King; he received me with great honour and allowed me to move about in *his realm and* to preach the Word of Life " (Keph. 1). Later on, he testified to Bahram I: " King Shapur looked after me, he wrote letters about me to all people to this effect: ' Protect him and support him, so that no one should offend and sin *against him* ' " (MH 48).

It is said that Shapur for ten years adhered to Mani's religion; it is to this period we may assign the several incidents of his life at Court narrated in the ' Kephalaia '—an all-but contemporary story written down at Mani's own request by eyewitnesses, to preserve a record of his day-to-day teachings. In Keph. 1 he himself says: " I spent further years . . . *with him* in the *royal* retinue: many years in Persia, in the land of the Parthians, as far as Adiabene (Kurdistan) and the frontier adjoining the territory of the Roman Empire."

10. Two Manis or One

This little story, so happily saved for us in Keph. 76 out of the general wreckage of Manichean sources, runs thus: " Once it happened as our Lord and Luminary Mani sat in the *city of* Ctesiphon, King

xxxvii

Shapur asked about him and had him called; then our Lord got ready and went to Shapur the King. Then *he returned* and re-entered his Church. When he had passed a short time sitting there, then King Shapur again enquired for him . . . and sent to call him. So Mani returned and went again to King Shapur, spoke with him, and preached God's Word to him. Again he came back and entered the church. Yet a third time did King Shapur ask after and summon him; then he once more returned to him.

"Then one of his disciples named Auradēs son of Kapēlos answered and said to our Luminary: 'O please, our Lord, give us two Manis who resemble thyself and come down like thee! Good and serene and kind *must* they be *and then* the disciples *will walk* in righteousness like thyself. . . . While (one) Mani will stay with us like thee, (the other) Mani *can go to* Shapur the King, while his *mind* is being convinced *by the preaching of the Truth* to him!'

"When our Luminary heard these words from that disciple, he nodded his head and said to him: 'See I, a single Mani, have come to the world to preach the Word of *God* therein, and in it *do* the good Will which has been given *me to do*. *Now* look, (though) I am only a single Mani, they have not given *me* a chance to speak freely in the world, for I have *striven hard* to find opportunity and to carry out the good Will that is entrusted to me; yet have I in *living* truth done the work of the Mystery I preach. So I have gone *everywhere* to do the Will of the *Light and to spread* abroad this truth as I have been given (it). And see, the world resists me in *every way, heaping calumnies* upon me through its Sects. They give me therein no place to *speak*, even while I am (only) a single Mani. . . . If we had done just as you have said to us, what should we do then? Of what sort would *the result* be? Well, this is *how I answer* you, and I proclaim it to you!'"

Mani then related his experiences in India, Persia, Chaldea, Assyria, Media and ' Parthia'; everywhere opposition to his teaching had soon forced him to withdraw. Men were ready to submit to any amount of oppression from political, bureaucratic and military tyrants, but would not accept the sweet burden of God's Law.

The story goes on: " Then the Messenger said to this disciple: ' When I, a single Mani, came to the world, all the world's cities were stirred and hesitated, they would not accept me unless I (first) subdued their rebellion. *I set truth* in the *hearts* (?), I tamed their powers, I brought out all the *impurity* (?) which was therein; I planted therein the *Tree of Wisdom*. I sowed the seed of Life, I chose one by one (disciples) out of the multitudes. . . . I, a single Mani, came into the world and *spoke;* all the powers of the world have been moved and confusion has *arisen* before me. If now two Manis had *come* to the world, where would they be able to bear them, or *which land* would be able to welcome them?

"' I, a single Mani, have come, and I walk on tiptoe *cautiously;* there has been *no chance* for me to stand in it *firmly* on the fullness of my feet, *that I might walk on the earth* like everyone (else) and do in it the *will of God entrusted to me.* . . . But you, do you all pray to God that He may *bring* to the end *of his mission* this one Mani who is *among you this* day, so that whatever may happen *to his flesh-body* he shall do the will of the Living One *in the* holy *Church.* And you, hail to you if you strengthen yourselves in the Truth I have given you, so that you may thereby *stand firm* in the Life which endures for ever and ever.'

" Thereupon, when that disciple had heard this, he said to the Messenger: 'Hail to the Lord of me and of all my brethren, who hear these great things from thee! We know that we are all of us in the Living One, but we have lived in that thou hast come to us; we have found the Truth more than all men who are in the world. Which of us could fully repay to thee the good thou hast done to us, O Father, save the Father who has sent thee? He can fully recompense thee for the pains, for the reward which thou desirest from the God who sent thee is this: Every prayer which thou prayest the Father, He should grant thee thy prayer and thy *request.*' "

This little story gives us a happy glimpse into the personal relationship between Mani and his followers, and into the charming sense of humour shown by the Prophet: When men cannot put up with even one Mani, what on earth will they do with two?

The talk with the 'Nasorean' already referred to gives us another such glimpse. It begins: " Again it once happened that a Nasorean came before the Messenger and said to him: 'I will ask thee in one word; do thou thyself convince me with a single word, but not with many words.'

"Then the Messenger said to him: 'If thou canst utter to me a single word, then will I also say (only) a single word to thee. But if thou askest me many (things), then I too shall utter a crowd to thee!'

"*Then* that Nasorean said to the Messenger: 'Thy God to whom thou prayest, is He good or evil?'

"Then said the Messenger to that Nasorean: 'Now then, look out! *See, thou hast* not *asked me* one single word, but thou hast asked a *crowd of words!*' *Then* the Messenger said to him: 'My God is a Judge.'" The discussion then proceeded to show that every Judge upholds good and represses evil; so also God.

11. The Ugly Saint

A story in Keph. 83 shows us something of Mani's personal kindness which is very pleasing. There was once a great gathering of all the élite and nobility of a certain city, and Mani sat down in their midst. Presently came one of the most faithful and pious of his Elect, deeply learned in the doctrine and perfect in his holy righteousness—but outwardly very ugly to look at.

The story goes on: "When he had entered he threw himself down on the ground and bowed lovingly before the Messenger. Then the crowd of men, nobles and free women, looked and they saw how that Elect cried out, called much and prayed in his joy. When they looked at him and saw how ugly he was in his body, being ungainly (?) and fat (?), they all laughed at him and made fun of him. They talked about him with one another with laughter and scorn. . . . But that laughter did not embarrass that *Elect, who prostrated* continually while praising *the beloved Master*.

"Whereas *the Messenger*, the Glorious One, stood *up on* the dais whereon he sat; he drew him to himself, took him close, and pressed him on his body (*i.e.*, back, in embrace), while he was being kissed by that Elect, and (then) he sat down. . . . He seated himself upon his dais before *the Elect* and the whole assembly of the nobles and the free women who sat before him. He asked them: ' Why do you laugh at this man in whom dwell the Light-Mind and the Faith?' "

He went on to show that it is the Soul which matters, that God sends the Messengers to rescue the beautiful Soul out of its ungainly prison, the material body. As the diver takes the shining pearl out of the ugly oyster shell and then offers it to the King, so too the righteous Soul is presented to the King of Light to enjoy the endless bliss of Heaven. There is some indication in the broken text that this wise teaching was accepted and that the crowd showed respect to the ugly Saint after hearing the Master's reproof of their foolish levity.

12. The Tigris Flood

The following story in Keph. 61 shows how Mani used incidents in daily life to explain his teaching.

xlii

"Again when once the Messenger entered in before Shapur the King, then he kissed him, he greeted (?) him, and he went out again from before King Shapur. He seated himself upon a dyke which had at that time been built up on the bank of the great Tigris River. It was the month of Pharmuthi (Feb.-Mar.); the Tigris River was then very full with much water, it foamed (?), bubbled up, it roared under the great flood that the waters had poured down. It streamed through the city gates while they only *collapsed*, and the waters entered into the centre (?) of the town until they flooded the market-place of the city—the other little markets (?) of the city *also* went *under water because of the violence* of its onrush. Also its government stood there in great alarm because of the fullness of the flood of this water.

"The Messenger then stood there on the dyke, while with him were also standing three of his disciples, Leaders of his Church. They gazed at the River full of so many waters, and saw how this water rose up against the city walls and even poured inside the walls. Then one of his disciples spoke to the Messenger, saying; 'How great is the strength of the Garment of Water! How big it is to come in raging flood filling the River Tigris with its volume like a great sea! It has hurled waves from bank to bank and reached from wall to wall! How vast must be the source that pours out all these waters, that they come every year at their proper time!'

"Then the Messenger said to him: 'Why do you wonder at the volume of the Tigris water, or why be astounded at its flood? Now listen to this that I shall tell you, and wonder indeed at the flood which was in this first age! . . .'" Then he went on in his own way to tell of the mighty Element of Water, sacrificed by the Divine First Man to the Powers of Darkness, narrated in his own 'Great Gospel'—where we need not follow him. He closed with the remark that God must be infinitely greater than His own creature.

13. Sunrise and Cloud

Keph. 65 tells us of this incident: "Again, when once the Messenger sat there in the assembly of his disciples, the Sun then rose. He began to teach his disciples of the Sun's greatness and divinity, how it was patterned on the fashion of the First Greatness (*i.e.*, Supreme God). He revealed (truth) to them and said: 'It is the Gate of Life and the Vehicle of Peace for this great Aeon of the *Light for ever* (*i.e.*, of this world). But then Satan knew that it is the door for the souls' escape, so he put a strong injunction in his Law that none should honour it, saying: He who honours it shall die (cf. Job 31:26-27, Ezek. 8:16-17). He has also named it the corruptible Light, thereby preventing the Souls from merely turning their faces towards the Light, and has caused them to deny the Light of their being.'"

Mani then went on with a beautiful account of the Sun's value to us in its seven 'good deeds': (i) it gives light and vision to all, (ii) it destroys the fears lurking in darkness, (iii) it wakens us from sleep, (iv) it gives life and sweetness to trees, fruits and flowers, (v) it drives snakes and vermin from our path, (vi) it reduces the pain of wounds and sickness, and (vii) reveals to us the wonders of all creation. Thus its five great gifts to us are Light, Beauty, Joy, Life and Strength. Should we not then be grateful to it for this? Mani ended with comparing the Sun to the Messenger of the Light himself, and its work with the spiritual mission of God's Prophets to men.

The last chapter (95) of the same precious 'Kephalaia' gives us another spontaneous little address. This begins thus: "While the Messenger again sat in the assembly of his disciples—the sky was clouded on that day—then he raised his eyes and saw these clouds on that day. He said to his disciples: 'This cloud which is visible to you, which you see, I shall show you and make clear to you how it has come up. . . .'" He then entered on an involved account of the different kinds of clouds derived respectively from the five Elements of Fire, Water, Wind, Light and Air—which need not detain us here; it is highly mythological in content.

14. Alienation from King Shapur (A.D. 255)

During those ten years Mani seems to have stayed at the King's side, teaching his doctrines and trying to wean from violence and vainglory a monarch of a dynasty devoted more than most to war, hunting, and display. No doubt, during those years he must have travelled widely in the royal retinue, from as far east as the limits of Khorassan to the western boundaries of the Empire in South Armenia.

He can have found little time for writing during this busy period, but some of his lost Epistles may well date back to it. The 'Great Epistle to Pattiq', of which AnNadim tells us—No. 7 in his list—and which is probably the 'Fundamental Epistle' of St. Augustine and Euodius, resembles in style what we know of the 'Shāpur-āqān'. The lost volume of Mani's Epistles may well have been bound in almost chronological order, for Nos. 1, 2, 4 and 5 seem to be on topics which must have demanded early treatment, and Nos. 3, 6, 8 and 10 are addressed to places visited in the early years—India, Babylonia, Armenia and Ctesiphon.

But this comparatively quiet time was now to end. Kings are notoriously fickle, and the new Sassanid dynasty founded its power on a claim that it restored the religion taught of old by Zarathushtra and held by the glorious line of ancient Persian Emperors—Cyrus, Darius and Xerxes. We can well understand how a senate dominated by the orthodox Magi must view with strong disfavour a King who was all but a convert to some new religion—and that one pacifist and non-violent! This smouldering resentment was undermining the throne, and it is not strange that a man like Shapur should place his own power and titles above loyalty to a mere vagrant Prophet.

So we learn that under the influence of the Magi Shapur the King broke with Mani, reverted to orthodoxy, and sent the Prophet into exile—though he does not seem to have cancelled his earlier letters to the provinces that he should not be molested.

This left the King free to indulge in the warlike adventures so dear to his people. Taking advantage of the Roman Emperor's absence, his armies overran much of Syria and even captured Antioch. Valerian hurried back to deal with this serious invasion and retook Antioch, but unwisely following Shapur over the Euphrates was captured with most of his army near Edessa in A.D. 260. Persia recovered much of the lost provinces, adding Antioch, Tarsus and Cesarea, Shapur's victorious army being checked only outside the walls of Palmyra. Meanwhile the wretched Valerian was kept prisoner till he died; then the body was crucified, stuffed with straw, and hung up in a Babylonian temple—a tragic foreshadowing of Mani's own fate seventeen years later.

15. Mani's 'Twelve Apostles'

Like his predecessor Jesus, Mani seems to have called out a special group of inner disciples who, after his own departure, were to carry on his work as 'Apostles' in the Church—one of them to succeed him as the Leader, or *Arkhēgos*, of the Religion. Several of these seem to have usually gone with him on his travels, while the others stayed in various provinces to organise the Church there, awaiting their turn to share the burdens of travelling with the Master. It is clear from Keph. 85 that this organisation was in fact developed during the Prophet's own lifetime.

We have no single list of these 'Twelve Apostles' and are left to speculate about the identity of some; but among the number we have authority for including most of the following names.

Sisin (Sisinnios), destined later to succeed Mani, seems to have been a constant companion, and so he was the accredited biographer of the 'Memorabilia'— a book which survived for at least eight or nine centuries and was known to Hegemonius. He may also have written our 'Kephalaia of the Sage'. But Mani sent him several letters, which at least suggests a period of physical separation. He was a man of intense sincerity and boundless courage, worthy to be the 'St. Peter' of the new Church. He was known to the Chinese as *Mo-szu-hsin*, the 'holy King of the Law', and two of his psalms survive in the Chinese book now in the British Museum (BM), one on the Impermanence of the Body, and the other on the glory of the Ascended Mani.

Innai (Innaeus), probably at this time a mere youth, but devoted to his Master. He later became Sisin's successor and appears likely to have been the first author of the pathetic story of Mani's suffering and death, which leaves off at a point when Innai himself was still alive.

Kushtai (Custaeus) was Mani's personal secretary and the author of the apocalyptic book 'The Great War', which shows affinity with the Jewish apocalypses of Elijah and Zephaniah, probably of the 2nd century (cf. GY 95-98).

Salmai (Salam, Salmaeus) was the author of the moving 'Threnody' in MH, which shows him to have been a passionate devotee of the Lord.

Amū (Ammōs, Wei-Mao) established the Faith in Turkestan; a book of his Acts, recalling Christian apocrypha, seems to have related many interesting experiences; several fragments survive, besides the hymn in BM describing the Land of Light.

Addai, said to have been later the Apostle to the East, *i.e.*, to Khorassan. He may be the 'Adimantus' who carried the Faith to Africa and supplied in his 'The Bushel' the epitome of five Scriptures now known to us in Chinese as the 'CMT'; 'The Doctrine of Addai' may not directly relate to him.

Zakwā (Zakū, Zakouas) taught the Faith in Syria and South Palestine in A.D. 274, even while his Master was still alive.

Paapi (Pappos) the Egyptian, to whom Epistle 20 was sent. About A.D. 295 he was opposed in Egypt by Alexander of Lycopolis.

Gavriavi (Gabriabios) is probably the 'Khabara' of a Turfan fragment and the 'Khabarhat' of Epistles 14, 15 and 18. He seems to have taken over authority for some time during the persecution on Mani's death.

Bahraya (Baraias), named in Epistles 85 and 38.

To these ten we may add the semi-mythical *Thomas*, whom Mani sent to Egypt and Syria, the author by A.D. 290 of a group of splendid Psalms in MP. But it is quite possible that the real author, 'Thōm', as the Coptic calls him, is the 'Twin' (cf. §3), Mani's inspiring Angel—the Psalms being then ascribed, as so often in literature of the age, to the inner source of their inspiration.

The name of *Pattiq*, who was with Mani on the Indian mission and again during his last journey on earth, may or may not refer to Mani's own father. If it was he, by A.D. 280, when Pattiq carried the Faith to Rome itself, he must have by then attained a great age. To him in Egypt between A.D. 244 and 251, we learn, the 'Fundamental Epistle' was sent.

The mysterious '*Lord Syrus*' who hastened to the scene of his Master's death soon after it happened, and who told of it in MP. 14-20, may also have been an 'Apostle', or the name may simply refer to some 'Syrian Saint', *i.e.*, perhaps Zakwā. Of '*Ozeos*' (the Susianese) we know almost nothing, unless he were the same as 'Addai'. Quoting *Mani-Fund*, p. 15. Alberry tells us (MP. p. 97) that *Herakleides*, writer of some of the loveliest Psalms, was also one of the Twelve Apostles.

16. Into Central Asia (A. D. 255 - 273)

Mani took to the road again. Faced with the seeming failure of his efforts to win royal support, his courage was at least justified by the thought of the little churches scattered over the wide Empire, whereas in his time Zarathushtra's first ten years of labour had won barely a single disciple (cf. GZ 30 : 2).

He seems to have visited Khorassan once more, and here he probably wrote both the 'Living Gospel' and the 'Treasure of Life'; hence too no doubt he sent many of his Epistles, such as those to Babylon, Edessa (Urfa), Maisan and Ahwaz, and some of those sent to disciples whom he had to leave behind on going into exile. The Epistles to Menaq the Virgin and to Haṭa survived even as late as the 10th century, but now *all* have been lost. One addressed to Feroz and Rasin, No. 73, may be intended for the King's brother, the Governor of Khorassan, and his minister.

From Khorassan the little group will have moved on into Bokhara, and so into Western Turkestan. In a cave hereabouts Mani is said by Mirchand to have passed one year in solitary communion with Heaven; he came out of this with his 'Ertenk', a beautifully illustrated copy of a book covering the whole of his Religion. We are told that he completely covered the walls of this cave with his paintings, and even Ephrem speaks of his great talent in the painting art.

From the 'Ardavift' Müller gives us three little stories, which may refer to this sojourn of Mani in Central Asia.

The first tale is of a Messenger who came to Ardāv, the King of Turān, as a " doctor of Babylon . . . sent to him by the Gods " to cure a young girl. The name of this 'doctor' was 'Mar (*i.e.*, Saint) M——". After miraculously curing the little maid, the Saint raised the King into the air, and there proved his great wisdom by searching questions; after this, we are told, the nobles of Turan embraced the stranger's religion.

In the second story a certain "righteous man" presented himself to Khabara and his colleague Abursam, and there prayed, giving homage to the Word. When asked about his own faith, this man said that he adored and paid his vows to Jesus; his prayer had been heard, and he was given by Angels the "soul of Darāv" (is this 'Ardāv'?), and the (Spiritual) King's marvellous Robe. The two men fell at his feet and accepted him as their Master; he taught them to overcome the breast's twelve sins, the hands' nine, and the nine of the mouth—*i.e.*, Mani's three 'Seals' (cf. GPM 40:2). This seems to describe the conversion of Khabara (Gavriavi) and his friend, who may be the 'Abzakhyā' or Bahraya of Epistles 47, 49 and 67. The 'Righteous' is clearly Mani himself.

The third tells of a woman who violated the rule not to weep for her dead child. When she learned that the tears she was letting fall on his body were killing his Soul (a teaching of the Parsis also), she ceased. A "man of God", probably Mani himself, received her confession and promise of amendment, and prayed to God to pardon her and give her His grace.

After some years in Turkestan, Mani went on to 'China.'—by which is almost certainly meant Sinkiang, where his Faith ultimately became for some time predominant. Birūni tells us that he next visited Tibet, and if this is true it may be the earliest historical reference to that country—whose religion at the time was the darkest shamanism. Through one of the passes Mas'udi tells us, he came down thence into Kashmir, and so probably revisited his tiny churches in Sind.

During these eighteen years of travel Mani seems to have been nowhere molested or hindered in his religious work; this seems to show that the letters of Shapur still had power even in the distant marches of his Empire and beyond.

17. A Manichean King (A.D. 273-274)

News came to Mani that when Shapur, the King of Kings, had reached the town of Bih-Shapur he had fallen ill and died on 16th April, his son Hormizd (I), then Governor of Khorassan, succeeding him. Of this King we are told that he was definitely a disciple of Mani—which could hardly have made him popular with the Magians.

Hearing the news of the change of ruler, the Prophet at once hastened to Persia and met the new King, saying to him: " They call you a good King; *then it is for you to save men from* sin and to let everyone have the chance to live." He also offered, if the King so willed, to live with him from that day on and guide him, as he had formerly done with his father. He seems also to have suggested a visit to Assyria and that Hormizd should give him letters of protection for the purpose; this he at once agreed to do. Thus the mission, with the aid of Mani's books, naming here (MH. 43) ' The Gospel ' and ' The Mysteries ', was officially authorised. Unhappily for Mani, however, King Hormizd was dead within the year, not improbably poisoned by the orthodox; to the throne succeeded his son Bahram I, an irresponsible young man, cruel and vain, and a lover of pleasure. Mani's own comment reads: "The Satan was envious and swiftly snatched him away; his son placed the crown on his head in his place."

18. Mani's Last Journey (A.D. 274-277).

Mani seems to have realised his danger, for he at once travelled up the other side of the Tigris, meeting everywhere his little churches and giving great delight and courage to the disciples. He went as far as Na-(harwan?), where he knew his time in Mesopotamia would now be short. He crossed the ferry here, and was planning to retreat right across Persia to the comparative safety of Khorassan or Kushan. In this direction he got only as far as Hormizd-akhshahr (Ahwaz, still an important town of Khuzistan), where the King's peremptory order overtook him, forbidding him to proceed any further.

"Thereon," says the account in MH, on which we rely largely for the last scenes of Mani's devoted life, "he returned in vexation and sorrow; he came to Susiana". In the neighbouring province of Khuzistan the late King Hormizd had given him a small town to live in, and he may have thought for a while of retreating there. But he now knew his hour was come and returned to Babylonia itself, to meet his enemy and his fate face to face. After a brief halt in Maisan, his childhood home, he recrossed the Tigris and proceeded straight to Ctesiphon, then the winter capital. He may still have had some idea of persuading Bahram to let him withdraw quietly to Khorassan so as to leave him in peace to govern as he liked, but he evidently failed to meet the King here. Probably he had already moved with the Court to Belapat,[1] adjoining the fortress of Jund-i-Shapur.

In the fragment T. II. D. 163, Pattiq tells us: "At that time when the Righteous One (*i.e.*, Mani) left the city of Ctesiphon and together with King Baat *proceeded towards Pargalia*, that holy Mani *said* to me: 'Do not come again with his [2] *party at this* time, then tell *him that* he should leave us *and go to His* Majesty'." Of this King Baat nothing definite seems to be known, but the name, Henning points out, is Armenian, and the fallen Parthian dynasty to which Mani belonged still ruled in Armenia. His association with this Armenian kinglet was a serious grievance in Bahram's mind; could Baat have been a convert whom Mani was suspected of plotting to put on the throne? The narrator of MH adds that after the little party left Ctesiphon, "While he was on the way he hinted (to the disciples) about his crucifixion, saying to them: 'Gaze at me and sate yourselves with me, my

---

[1] Bēth Lāpāt, Belabad, or Vahi-andiok Shāpuhr, lay between Susa and Shushtar; it is now a total ruin and shows hardly a trace of the great royal city once standing there.

[2] *i.e.*, Baat's. Mani perhaps wished to dissociate his disciples from the dangerous company of this kinglet.

children, for I shall (soon) withdraw myself physically from you.'"

So they came to Pargalia. Here he went with King Baat to the lecture-hall (*hermēneia*) of the little church, where he met the local group of disciples, with an Elder or two. He gave them his last detailed instructions, two of which were "Take care of my books", and "Look after my widows and orphans" (*i.e.*, those of the Church). He told the Elect to be constant in teaching the Hearers, whose spiritual life depended so largely upon their efforts (MH. 35). At this place also came an urgent invitation: "All the brethren *begged the Lord to come to* Gaukhai.[1]"

Mani at once started off towards Gaukhai, to gratify the faithful of the Church there, and soon reached Kholassar[2] on the way. The much broken Turfān story of T. II. D. 163 takes up the tale here: "Then when *he was staying* in Gaukhai in Beth-Derāyē,[3] then the Elect *who were in* Gaukhai *gathered to meet us*. And I (*i.e.*, Pattiq) was *there*, and I announced the *news* in front of *several* disciples from among the twelve Teachers (*i.e.*, Apostles: cf. list in §15) and in the presence of Bahman" (? or the Divine

---

[1] Or 'Jōkhā', very near to Mani's birthplace at Baromia. This was a village on the swampy banks of the river of the same name between Khaniqin and Khuzistan, 30 miles east of the Tigris.

[2] Or Artemita, Deir Tadema, or Tīdemā, 11 farsangs from Baghdad, a small town through which runs the stream Silla or Kabir.

[3] Or Bādarāyā, now Badrai on the Persian frontier east of Ctesiphon and north of AnNukhailat in the Nahrawān province; the river of this name runs north and north-east of Qut.

Mind, *i.e.*, Mani himself)." Mani here seems to have told the news that he was on the way to Belapat to meet the King, though "he knew that if he left that place (*i.e.*, Gaukhai) he would not be allowed *to meet* his *disciples* again". We learn that King Baat was again present in the lecture-hall here also.

Pattiq seems to have had a vision, for the Turfan story goes on: " Furthermore, Pattiq saw another sign and said: ' I see that the Righteous One has risen, and for several days the Tigris *River is flooded with the Garment of Water*. . . . , that he majestically enters and leaves the Royal Gate. Thereon Kardel the Priest plotted with his friends who served before the King, and *inspired by* jealousy and cunning *worked evil against our* Lord." But Mani was ready to " fulfil his mystery through the Cross ", for he too must show the perfect love of God's Messengers by laying down his life for others (GPM 39: 2). So he set his face firmly, as Jesus to Jerusalem, to go up to Belapat to endure his destiny of pain and so to ascend to his eternal Rest in the Kingdom of the Father, whence he had come to work His will on earth.

19. Mani Accused before the King

The following story, though perhaps rather long, is of great interest because derived wholly from Manichean works, and I believe no attempt to weave these fragments together into a coherent whole has been made before; it throws light on a subject hitherto most obscure, though it is still in parts uncertain and obscure where the texts are badly broken.

Mani was now on his way, following the old road across Anatolia to the East through Susa and Persepolis. Meanwhile his enemies had been busy. The Parsi priests or Magi had already issued " lying screeds ", accusing him of various offences against Religion and of disturbing the whole Empire with false and pernicious doctrines (cf. Lk. 23 : 2).

" *So Mani* came to Belapat, the place of the crucifixion and the place where the chalice of the agony (?) had been mixed. When the Magi noticed him they asked: ' Who now is this who has come here ? ' and they were told, ' That is Mani ! ' When they heard this, then they became enraged and full of anger "; this was on the Sunday (MH. 60). " They went and accused him to Kardel; Kardel in his turn reported it to the Joint-Magistrate (?), and the Joint-Magistrate (?) went and forwarded the accusation to the Magistor (?City Magistrate), while the Magistor told the King (MH. 45)."

Filled with hate, a crowd of the Magi followed the City authorities before the King with their complaint: " They all cried out with one voice to the godless Judge, saying to him words in which there was no truth: ' Lo, in these days a man has appeared, fighting against us and bringing our affairs to nought. With one accord we implore thee, O King, do away with him, for he is a teacher who leads men astray ! ' When he heard these words the foolish man, King of these pitiless ones, was astonished, the evil-fated malefactor;

he sent, he called my Shepherd" (MP. 15), and thus "on Monday he was accused before the King (MH. 45)."

"*So my Lord* came *to the Palace* after he had *called* together me, Nūhzādāq the interpreter,[1] Kushtai, D— and Abzakhyā the Persian.[2] The King was at his dinner-table and had not yet finished his meal. The courtiers entered and said, 'Mani has come and is standing at the door!' The King sent the Lord this message, 'Wait awhile till I can myself come to you!' The Lord again sat down to one side of the guard, until the King should have finished his meal, when he was to go out hunting.

"The King rose from the table and, putting one arm round the Queen of the Sakas[3] and the other round Kerder (*i.e.*, Kardel), the son of Ardawān,[4] he came towards the Lord. His first words to the Lord were 'You are not welcome!' The Lord replied, 'What wrong have I done?' The King said, 'I have sworn not to let you come to this country' (M 3)!"

The Coptic story takes up the tale here: "Thereon did my Lord *greet the King respectfully, even* while his

[1] Note that Mani, whose own tongue was Syrian, did not care to risk misunderstanding in so vital an interview by speaking Persian, with which he was perhaps not very free.

[2] or: Baraias, one of Mani's Apostles.

[3] *i.e.*, of Seistan, then a dependent Kingdom usually ruled by the heir to the Persian crown; she may thus have been his sister-in-law.

[4] The name of Kardel's father suggests noble or royal blood; if Kardel were actually of the old Parthian house, it is natural he should be anxious to prove his loyalty by persecuting Mani. Some have identified him with Tansar (GZ p. lxxxi), who organised the Pehlevi scriptures and was a sort of Grand Vizier to the Royal house.

manner (?) *was unfriendly despite* the greeting. *Indeed, the King* answered, full of anger against him: ' I swore to you by my salvation and my soul, and the soul of my father *and of all who have entered Paradise* and live, that *if you came here* and walked on the Ba—, *I would put you to death* (?) ' (MH. 45). And in anger he spoke thus to the Lord: ' Eh, what are you good for, seeing you go neither fighting nor hunting? But perhaps you are needed for this doctoring and physicking—and you don't even do that ' (M 5) !

" The Lord thus replied: ' I have not done you any harm; I have always done good to you and your family. Many and numerous were your servants whom I have *freed* of demons and witches; many were those from whom I have averted the numerous kinds of ague; many were those who were at the point of death, and I have *restored* them ' (M 3)!

" *Then the King* called to *officers to lead my Lord into the Palace hall. There*, when he had gone into the King's presence he met *him* face to face. . . . As soon as the King saw him, he twisted his face into an angry laugh; he spoke to him the crowd of his words: ' See, for three full years you have been going with Badia (*i.e.*, Baat); which is the Law that you have taught him, that he has left ours and adopted yours when *you have led him* to the lecture-hall? Why have you not at least gone with him where I told you to go and come with him ' (MH. 46)?

" As soon as my Lord knew that the matter for some pretext against him had to be furnished (?), *so that the*

King might put him to death,' my Lord spoke *openly* in front of him, saying: ' Give to *me a chance some other day to talk of these things* before the kings and the nobles. I shall not explain (?) *anything today when sorrow is afflicting us* all ' (MH. 46).

" Then praise *came to my Lord from all the* nobles *who were there* in his presence, for on that day *the King was full of* grief over his sister, . . . the Mistress of the Robes, who had died at that time. The *King* spoke, saying: ' It is I who have *the choice of the time when you will answer me.* All the nobles *are now here with us, so you shall speak before me now* ' (MH. 46). Then in a mighty voice he wrathfully said to him: ' Who bade thee do these things, or who art thou? Thou doest deeds that harm (?) all men (MP. 15); who has sent thee? For whom are thy preachings (MH. 93) ? From whom hast thou learned thine assertion: Our affairs are more important than the world's? For since the beginning when the Parthians came to the mastery, these affairs of thine have never *prospered, nor shall they so* long as the mastery is in our hands ' (MH. 47)!" This definitely seems to show that in his mind Bahram identified Mani with the interests of the fallen Parthian dynasty.

" The glorious Mind answered and said to him direct (MP. 16): ' Know, O King, *that* I am the servant of the *God of Light,* who has sent me in order to choose the *Church out of a world which* has fallen into so many sins (MH. 93). It is God who has *sent me to call thee,* thou being a man, to the Law of Life, *and to teach thee* the perfect commandments of Christ' (MP. 16). Thereon spoke my Lord to him in the presence of all (the) nobles: 'Ask all the men about me. I have no human Master and Teacher from whom I have learned this wisdom whence I got these things; but when I received them I received them from God through His Angel (cf. §8). From God was sent to me a *message* that I should preach this in your Kingdom, for this whole world had wandered into error and got into a bye-path; it was *wilfully* fallen away from the Wisdom of God the Lord of All. But I have received it from Him and revealed the Way of the Truth in the midst of the whole world, so that the souls of this multitude might be saved and escape from the punishment (cf. GPM 88 : 1). For the proof of everything I bring is obvious; all that I *teach* existed *even* in the first generations;[1] but it is the custom that the Way of Truth is now and then revealed, and now and then conceals itself again' (MH. 47)."

This frank and unanswerable reply enraged King Bahram; "he parted his lips, he cried out in a *fury* (MP. 16): 'How comes it that God reveals this to you, while *the same* God has not *revealed* it also to us, even though we are still the lords of the whole land (MH. 47) ? Thou art a vile foreigner,[2] thou *art also a*

---

[1] Note how Mani, equally with Jesus and Muḥammed, claimed only to be restoring the primeval truths, purifying them from later accretions; he may here be referring to the revelations to Seth-el, son of Adam.

[2] Being of Parthian ancestry and actually born in a Mesopotamia at the time under Roman rule.

poor man lacking everything; thou art a man of *insignificance, unfit for God* to give this unutterable favour and gift' (MP. 16)!

"My Lord said (MH. 47): '*Those who are of* God do not seek after gold and the world's possessions (MP. 16); it is God who has the power *to reveal His Truth to the one He chooses* out of the *crowd of all* His *creatures* (MH. 47). It is God who commands, and there is no other commandment but His. It is God who teaches whom He will, and gives to him the Gift that surpasses all gifts, as a seal *that he is a* Prophet, the true Man of God in his deeds and his words (MP. 16)! *He may choose one who has no* might; *but who are we to* ask Him, saying: Strong *King, why dost Thou not reveal Truth to the mighty?* He reveals *it to me and not to* thee; *it is not fitting for thee to* ask Him angrily, saying: He has not appeared; let Him *appear to me*!' (MH. 47)" This dignified reply, so worthy of the Prophet confronted with an infidel tyrant, did not, of course, help Mani with the King.

"Then the King said to my Lord: 'Be silent!' (MH. 47). The lover of fighting, the peaceless one, roared in flaming anger, he bade them fetter the Righteous One, so that he might please the Magi, Persia's teachers, the servants of the Fire (MP. 16).

"But my Lord answered the *King*: 'What you will, that do to me, for I will speak the truth before you. King Shapur protected me, wrote letters about me to all persons of rank to this effect: Protect him and support him so that no one should offend and sin *against him*. But the proof that King Shapur gave me good support already lies before you, and the letters which he wrote for me to the nobles in every land that they should protect me. And also when King Hormizd *came* after King Shapur, then with him *also* I was *in favour*. It is you who *will dishonour* your own self; you have seen how Hormizd is greatly honoured ' (MH. 48).

"When the King saw that he persuaded *him by* every argument and each defence, *and that* there was no case at all against him, *then he passionately sentenced my Lord to* killing *after he had undergone* scourging (MH. 48). This is how judgment was given on the Victor, the Messenger, the Paraclete (MP. 19)! Lo, these are the deeds that are full of outrage of bitter-hearted men; this is the road they have made which will lead them to Hell! I have not seen a beast raging (?) like these, nor have I seen fire *so fiercely* consuming chaff; yet was there no merciful man standing up to snatch from them this sinless Righteous One (MP. 15)!

"He took the Shadow-maker *in the midst of heaven as his* witness; he said: 'Behold, O Sun, you are witness how in his shamelessness the King *sins* against me' (MH. 48)!

"Thereon the King ordered and he chained my Lord; he put three chains on his back (?), *locked heavy iron* fetters on his feet; a chain was fastened on his neck. A few young varlets slapped him (cf. Mk. 14 : 65), *they danced* (?) before him in insulting *him* (MH. 48). They shut him up in their prisons and loaded his limbs with iron; they took counsel against him in his evil counsels, that they might daily cast a slur on him (MP 23-24); the tyrant shut him in; at that time the whole world became dark" (MH. 91).

20. Mani in Captivity

"On the Tuesday . . . they went *and cast him into prison*; he confirmed his Church until Saturday. Afterwards *he was handed over to* all his haters; on the Saturday they sealed his fetters and brought him into the prison. They chained him on the 8th Emshir (*i.e.*, Jan.-Feb.) ; until the day when he went on high there were twenty-six days while he was chained with the iron fetters" (MH. 60).

The Lord Syrus now speaks: " How many days of fear, my Father, didst thou endure until thou hadst cut and severed the race of frightful men? Twenty-six days in all, and the nights of them, thou didst spend in chains in Belapat. O Renown of the Aeons of Light! O noble holy Image of God's Mysteries! O hands that gave freedom to a multitude of souls that are bound today in bonds of iron (MP. 15)! Bahram . . . did not believe in thy preaching, he listened to thine enemies, the deniers of thy Hope (MP. 48)! From the time thou didst refute their error, they loaded thee with iron and bound thee; they loaded thy hands and feet, and put neck-chains also on thy body. They threw thee into their prisons, thinking they could hold thee in; twenty-six days and the nights of them thou didst spend in irons (?) ' (MP 43)! "

Mani himself tells us: " They loaded me with irons as *is done* to sinners, they fettered me like thieves, they judged me like *criminals*, they all *insulted* me like sorcerers. From the day they bound me to the Day of the Cross there were counted (?) in all some twenty-six days, while they kept watch on me night and day, setting guards to keep watch on me. They put six neck-chains, they fettered me with *iron bars*, while all the Elect wept, and the Hearers, seeing the sufferings wherein I am. Those sinners, all of them, did not let me see my children and my disciples, my shepherds and my overseers, when they saw them coming to me. ... In the day they brought me before the Judge *to torture me* with the punishment (?) *of a scourge, they were* all of them firmly fixed *in evil*, ... *not one* of them aided me. All the lawless ones judged me; the impious, the creatures of sin, held me in their power amid the whole multitude, like a sheep that has no shepherd. They buzzed (?) at me like wasps, they roared at me like lions, saying to me in a loud voice, ' It does not please us that thou shouldst do these things! ' ... *Bahram* did evil to me in his wrath, he took counsel with his chieftains against me, he swore to me by his father's salvation, saying, ' I shall not leave thee in the world henceforth ' (MP. 19)!"

21. The Second Interview

The King apparently called Mani to him once again, having, it seems, forgotten he was a prisoner. " Thereon after this . . . *the King* remembered that fetters were on his feet, *so the officers* brought him hither. When he had entered in to the King (MH. 48) ", Bahram asked him about some girl who had gone to the King's capital, and demanded her return, failing which he said he would put Mani's head on the gate of the city of Belapat. " The King said to him: ' Show me the property . . . which she has *taken with her, and tell me in* which place *she is*; where has she gone? ' (MH. 49). But Mani was firm and would not betray the whereabouts of this girl, who was probably one of his royal disciples.

Then Bahram began to ask him about his doctrines: How many worlds are there, and how long will it be before evil is finally destroyed? Mani answered him briefly, and then " the King was silent (MH. 49) ". Evidently Mani next asked leave to talk with his disciples in the prison, and they too, looking lovingly at him, pleaded with the hard-hearted King for this privilege; it was granted, as was usual with those under sentence of death.

22. Mani Consoles His Disciples

The sadly mutilated story goes on: " He went to rest; then he sat (?) *on a bed*, and on those who belonged to him bestowed advice about each one of his affairs. Next he gave instruction about his children (*i.e.*, disciples) *who had faithfully clung to his* discipline while they accompanied him (MH. 50). He commanded the wise ones, that is, the Elect, to preach to the Hearers (MP. 35), saying to them: ' Preserve the

Righteousness before me,' because they *were grieving at being left as orphans* (MH. 50). *He said that Sisin* should be the Leader after him *until the day* wherein he should raise himself *to the Garden of the Light. Then he encouraged them, saying*: ' Be strong and firm of heart *so long as you live in the world,* and you shall do good deeds *in the Church and worship God through your fasting* and the psalms *which you sing* for the years of *earthly life.*' " Sisin himself he bade: " ' Govern the Church which I leave behind as the Leader after me ' (MH. 50)."

Indeed this arrangement was his response to a prayer from his disciples: " ' *Thou didst gather* thy children beside thee, thou didst embrace them all *as they cried to thee*: *Do not abandon* thy Church which is in the world; do not leave thy beloved, lest she lose the flavour of the salt that *thou* hast *won for her*! Thou didst appoint the twelve Teachers and the seventy-two Overseers; thou didst make Sisin Leader over thy children. When thou hadst set thine affairs in order, thou didst implore thy Father; He answered thee. (Then) thou didst leave them thy body and ascend *to thy* Kingdom ' (MP. 44)."

23. His Prayers to God

We have important pieces of the beautiful and instructive prayer he made thus at the hour of death. The Coptic texts read: " *Then it was time for him to come out from this world, and the disciples remained with him* while he escaped *from the body of this deceit.* He was sitting up *on the bed*, because *he saw in the heavens* the sign of the Angels who would *receive him on high. He asked* them to pray for graces for him and for the whole Church, while his body was *agonising from* stiffness of the joints of this house " (MH. 51).

" The Blessed One, our Lord Mani, he bent his knees, imploring mercy, crying out to God, saying: ' Open to me the door and give me release from my sufferings! The rulers of the earth have judged me in their wrath; *they believed* their lying words through the speeches of the *Magi, cruel* men who alter and change what is sweet and make it bitter. . . . They were stirred, they trembled, even the powers of the Evil One, they turned their sword against the Humble Man; they were unwilling indeed to see me in the streets of their cities (MP. 19-20). From the day of the great persecution to the Day of the Cross, there are six years;[1] I spent them walking in the midst of the world, like the captives among strangers (MP. 19). Each one pursued me *with eager cruelty* like a sheep that is followed everywhere by wolves '." He goes on, " ' *Hear, O God, the voice of the afflicted* while it weeps in the midst before his Father, that He should help him who is about to die ' (MH. 52)! "

" *Then* he spoke again, *calling on the Deities*: ' *Draw back* the curtain and the veil, *to admit* my petition and my prayer, . . . *and* to bring the Garment of *glory and receive* me out of this world (MH. 52). Also in my necessity *I have only to* look to You, for I have no power

---

[1] I do not know of any other reference to this ' great persecution ', which must have occurred, perhaps in Mani's absence, in A.D. 271,

to *move* or to lift up my head, or to move my hands and my feet, *because of* the iron (MH. 96). *I implore You to send the Angel who comes* to those who are confined *in the body and yet* stand firm *in the Faith*' (MH. 52)."

Mani continued his prayer: "'Lo, the sky and the earth and the two Luminaries, they bear witness of me on high that while I did good among them they in their cruelty have crucified me. I was gazing at my 'Twin' with my eyes of light, beholding my glorious Father, Him who ever waits for me, opening the Gate to the Height before me. I spread out my hands in prayer to Him, I bend my knees also in worship to Him, that I may divest myself of the image of flesh and put off the vesture of humanity' (MP. 19-20).

"'*Hear me, O Father*, while I roll myself before Thy mercy and before Thy lofty Bema (*i.e.*, mercy-seat). O Judge of all the worlds, hear the prayer of the Righteous. Do not be ignorant of *the children left* behind him, O true Father of the orphans and Husband of the mourning widow! O First of the Righteousness, hear the voice of the afflicted! *O my Father*, my Saviour—O Perfect Man, Virgin of the Light, draw my soul to Yourselves out of this abyss! Shame the hater through Your *mighty aid*! You have sent me to this place *to preach the message* of the Mind of the Greatness (*i.e.*, God); O Being of the *Light*, Thou hast sent and commissioned me; speedily *hear my* petition! Save the captive out of *the hands of* those who have robbed him, loose the fettered one from the iron! Draw up my spirit out of the statue (*i.e.*, body), my soul out of a *filthy place*! It has perished in the midst of this world *among the pains* that I have endured therein for the sake of Thy *Name* since my youth (MH. 53)!

"'Let Thy great Power *come speedily to rescue me*; *send* Thy mighty Angel *to save me from the hands of* malice, and that I may throw off my fetters *on the earth* and surrender the house (*i.e.*, body) to its lord (*i.e.*, Evil Matter); and he will shed blood and watch over his body. Clothe me *in the Robe of Glory that I find* in Thee; it is Thou who hast *chosen these my children;* they came on the earth with *Thy command to oppose* the Sects. For who asked Thee, whom dost Thou answer *when they question* before Thee, to whom givest Thou ear *when he complains and* calls to Thee *in misery?* Thou hast heard the men of Light orphaned before Thee (MH. 53)!

"'*I have clung to* Thy Hope . . . *and* preached *to mankind and renounced* the delights of the world *from my birth* until my old age. I found myself *rejoicing when I dared* to name myself with Thy great Name, saying: Thy Servant am I, the Messenger in the world! *I see the image of* Thy glory; *I depend upon Thy help;* it is Thou to whom I call *in my great need.* Do not shame me; answer me, O my Saviour! *Rescue* my soul out of the afflictions' (MH. 53-54)!

"His voice was heard before the King of Love (?) who had sent him. The Power came (MH. 54), a Messenger came from Paradise: 'Mani the Ruler wishes to depart' (BuBb 45-46)! *And then* was the reward given to the Messenger of the Light, *the great* Apostle of this generation, when he was to leave the world, the great Messenger of the land of the Great Babylon (MH. 54)!"

24. Mani Dies in Prison (Monday, 26th February A.D. 277).

" The signs were shown to him *that it was time to leave the world*. His body began to dissolve, his *chains* shook themselves and resounded. *Then* his beauty (?) began to change; his Image appeared *before his eyes, fashioned* from his face and his material-substance; his limbs *began to* quiver, the *lips* fell apart, *his body became* like a house that totters. . . . He began to crumple up *in pain*, while he *groaned* because of the *urgency* of his prayers, spreading out *his hands to Heaven while* his arms called upon *God*, . . . and *tears poured from his eyes* to dry *on the tortured cheeks* (MH. 54)."

Evidently some of the disciples now came to him secretly to remove the chains; they heard a voice coming from the body as the noble Soul tried to free itself, " when he was about to raise himself *out of the body of flesh*, the Righteous One lifting himself to the heaven of the great Kindly One, soaring away; the Messenger of the Light *returning home*, the Light-Pearl who shall *be brought* out of the restless Seas *of the world*. *They saw* his worth and his beauty, *they heard* the voice of the Honoured One, . . . the Messenger of the Light, while he *freed his* glorious *Soul* withdrawing from the body, . . . *and joining the* lofty Column of *Praise to ascend into the glorious Land of Light* (MH. 55)!

"The body of the Messenger *was reverently lifted* as (if) he would lay it in the *tomb*, . . . the *body* of Mani the Apostle *surrounded by* his host and his *angels*. . . . When *their* Lord and Master was about to go *from the world*, the disciples of Mani the Apostle were called the fatherless, the orphans. He took the time, he prayed; his prayer was granted, he left his children behind him —he left us knowingly. *The Angel came*, he smoothed for him his path on high. Oh, oh, *blessed are we, for* we have not sinned against him, and he has made us into a *garland and set it on* his head!

"He prayed piteously while his body *was in* the iron fetter. The tears flowed out *from his* eyes, his hands became loose (?), *his limbs trembled from the weight of the* iron chain, *his voice became feeble* while he prayed and implored God, *his Father in Heaven*, to listen to the voice of the *Righteous One and to receive his soul* in peace as he came forth from the world. . . . He implored grace from God *while things around him became as they usually are when a man is dying in the world* (MH. 56).[1]

". . . There came those who should draw near before his Soul: *the Angels came with the* trophy in their hand; *also* the *terrible* form *of the* demons appeared to him. She (*i.e.*, his soul) has strength *in remembering the labours* of the Messenger, *travelling everywhere in doing good* to the universe. It was the Angels *who prevailed*,

[1] Cf. GPM 75.

lxxiii

and they led him into the way of peace. Thereon he rested himself *in peace because* he had completed his work (MH. 57), and in great joy, together with Gods of Light who advance on his right and left at the sound of harps and joyous song—he flew in divine power (T. II. D. 72).

"They received him in *joy and led him into the Divine Hall.* When he had seated himself on the couch, *something* took his vision and it changed, it *began to fade* out. His children *uttered his* name, calling out *to their* Father. Thereon he asked for bread and salt; *it was brought* to him. He prayed over it; *the same* was done *in* the midst of his children. He kissed the . . . body. He spoke to them *very sweetly, saying*: 'Greeting from me to the Elect and the Hearers, my children!' *They came closer to* him; he laid his hand upon the *head of Sisin, saying: 'Use the place* that I have given *you for the help and strengthening of your* brethren . . . after me' (MH. 57-58). [1]

"Thereupon he stretched himself out *like a man sleeping* on his couch. They kissed him *lovingly when they saw that he was about to come* forth; they called aloud *on his name with tears,* weeping before him and *saying: O Father,* it is thou who art going *from us, leaving behind thee thy children to be* orphans after thee' (MH. 53)!

So Mani died; this was on the 26th February, A.D. 277, a Monday. The story of his death is told also by Amu and Oze'i (Ozeos), two of the Apostles, in Mir. Man. iii. p. 17.

[1] Cf. Lk. 22 : 32.

25. The Faithful Women

"From that day on until the *evening* (?), his body (was) lying there while his *Soul soared on high*, his eyes being calm and peaceful. Then went to him three women-Hearers of the Faith: Bānak, Dīnak and N—. They sat down before him and bewailed him; and they laid their hands on his eyes, they closed them lest they should overflow, for *so* it is *the custom to do* when someone's Soul has gone up hence, leaving the body.

"They kissed his mouth *in loving devotion*, while they mourned him, saying: ' O our Father, open thine eyes and look at us; stretch out thy right hand to thy Beloved (*i.e.*, the Church), who is full of gentleness and pity *towards thee*! Where are the thousands whom thou hast chosen out, and the ten thousands who have trusted in thee? For on account of the Truth and the Integrity which thou hast *given* to the earth, all lands must mourn for thee within thy Church, and publicly weep in thy congregations. For there are thousands to whom thou hast borne witness!' While their hands lay on his eyes they spoke this, weeping; but he did not answer, he lay there in silence. His speech had ceased, his mouth was still, he was at rest.

"O you children of the Righteousness, praise those women, thank them, and honour them *in your hearts* that they have closed our Father's eyes *after he had died* among the haters *of the Light* (MH. 59)!

"And then they departed, out of fear of the King that *he would punish them with cruel tortures when* the men had come forth. . . . The embodied one *withdrew from the holy body of our Lord, leaving it with the* Angel, and he led his Soul *on high, where his merit* was estimated. A voice resounded out *of Heaven:* 'Let him be henceforth without illness, without pain, having ceased *to suffer in the prison of the body!*' . . . He came forth and raised himself on high, together with the Power that had come in order to fetch him (MH. 59-60).

" On the second day of the week he *suffered*, on the fourth day of the month Phamenoth, at the eleventh hour of the day he gave himself up to death (MP. 18). At eleven hours of the day (*i.e.*, about 5 p.m.) he ascended hence out of the body to the dwellings of his greatness in the Height; he attained his form of the Divine and Perfect Image of the Light (MH. 60)."

26. Mani Enters Heaven

The story goes on: " He came forth and leapt on high with the Power that was come for him. See, this is how they *move* as the Divine Image *in a procession* appears out of the temple, *radiant as a* shining lamp! He was raised *up out of the darkness of this world* into the House; he lifted himself out of the world *into the heaven of* the Treasure, out of the realm(?) of *Evil into the Kingdom of* the great holy Righteous One, *leaving behind all sorrows*, namely, the world and all Sects *of error*: the haters and the scoundrels (MH. 60).

"The Righteous One who gives peace out of *strife* came forth between him and the demons and *bade His Angel* come down with the Messenger of *the Light in order to ascend on* high in triumph (?); *his descent* was out of his Racc,¹ he did *his work as* a good Interpreter; it is enduring (?). He leapt out of his *body, not caring for its fate or how the King would* bring down *ruin on it;* all his care was for the Soul; the *wicked* voice was silenced by the *music* of the Preaching. He raised himself out of the world *and its deceits;* he is the great Saviour, the *Teacher* of the Elect. The great Believer went to rest and ascended, *becom*ing the good Father of the orphans; he raised himself the Husband of the widows, the Teacher of the Scriptures, the *Singer* of the Psalmist's psalms! The Lord left (?) his servants, the Merchant his wares, the Master his pupils, the good(?) Planter his crops (MH. 60-01)!

" The Preacher of Life, the Interpreter of the land of the Great Babylon, departed like an arrow shot from a bow through this world, like a hero *spurning the delights of* the great habitable globe *of men, despising* the thirst (?) of this world *ond shining above it like the* eye of the moon *in its glory,* crowned like Seth-el *with brightness, leaving his children* down in the *world to mourn for him.* . . . So he ascended and went to the Rest, *and* the Gods and the Angels praised him, . . . the exalted Captive who has chosen them *out of the world now* withdraws himself . . . with the glorious Angel . . . into that Kingdom *of Light, the* realm of those who had gone to fetch him. *He who sees* his departure and this glory while he *goes up on high,*

---

¹ *i.e.,* from the Divine Kindred of Heaven; cf. GH. 44 : 2 and the Hymn of the Robe of Glory in GG.

and does not believe that it is his way *whereon he too must go*, he is a wanderer astray, for he has not let himself be convinced *by the example of* the Blessed One, the Messenger of the Light (MH. 61-62)."

27. Public Horror at the Tragedy

The Homilist proceeds: "*As for that holy thing*, the body, it was left lying on the bier, *still held in the* iron chains. Then the rumour about him *was spread* in the whole town; they heard in all *the city of Belapat* that he had ascended on high. Many men gathered together in groups and came. Thereon, *as the King was busy* worshipping (?), they drew him out and *brought him away from the* prison. They gathered *round him weeping, while some of the* Hearers *of the Faith* stood firm secretly *in the midst* of the heathen, *watching them* while they called to him, *the Messenger of the Light*, Mani, the doer of good, saying: 'Alas, and ruin *comes to us!* What a misfortune it is that is prepared *for our city*, that this good man should die in it through the *wickedness of his haters!* He has sinned against nobody, he has not *robbed any* of their property' (MH. 62)!"

It seems that someone carried to the King a report of Mani's death and the public distress on account thereof, for he ordered that the body be taken and laid on a sheet in the middle of the public street. This was the third Sunday, we are told, after he had fallen into the hand of his enemies; his fetter was removed, and the body was laid out in the presence of all the people amid their tears and expressions of grief.

28. The King Outrages the Body

Here a gap of three pages follows in our main text, but the story can be recovered from fragments of other sources. It is clear that the King doubted that Mani was really dead, and feared to leave the body for the people to venerate.

"In the madness of his wrath he wished by means of *many outrages* to destroy the beauty of thy limbs," cries the mourning psalmist. " Thou didst ascend in the *Column of Glory* on high without any hindrance, ... but thou didst cast down the dead body before *the face of* thine enemies (MP. 15). The lawless men were confounded, they brought their wrath upon the body (MP. 44) ; the murderous demon was enraged (?), he *gave out his* word, saying: ' Perhaps it is a drug of which thou hast *made use.*' He commanded the physicians and *the Magi* to examine the body, thy holy (?) body against which he mocked and plotted; he kindled fire in a great furnace (?) (MP. 15).

"He stripped off **Mani's** skin, filled it with grass (Alb. Chr. p. 191), dipped in certain medicaments and inflated; his flesh also he commanded to be given as a prey to the birds (H. 55). Lo, when his body was brought forth in the city of those sinners, when they had cut off his head and hung it up amid the whole multitude (MP. 19-20), they shed thy blood in the middle of the street of their city; they struck off thy head and set it on high upon their gate. They rejoiced in thy murder, not knowing that there is a judgment; for account shall be demanded of thy death and thy blood shall be avenged, their godless city shall receive the reward for the outrage it committed [1] (MP. 44).

"He was put to shame, the lawless Judge brought down his wrath upon his body; they hung his head upon the gate, not knowing what they were doing. The wise ones also who are among men (*i.e.*, the Elect) bore witness of his eminence (MP. 24). *His skin* they hung at the gate of Jund-i-Shapur, which is still known as the Mani Gate, saying; 'This man has come forward calling people to destroy the world; it will be necessary to begin by destroying him before anything of his plans be realised (Bir. Chr. p. 191).' *So they hung his skin on* the buildings of the city gates; he spilled his blood to no purpose—his murder even became a sign for all the men who pity him (MP. 15). Blessed are thy loved ones who shed their tears for thee, (O Mani); lo, the grief of thy body, the joy of thine ascended spirit (MP. 44)!

"Woe to them, the children of the Fire (*i.e.*, the Mazdeans), because they sinned against thy holy body —I mean the Magi who looked *upon* thy blood; they loved the evil genius of the Jews, God's murderers (MP. 43). They seized him and crucified him, . . . they scattered his congregations; . . . thereon, after they had crucified our Father, he completed the Mystery of his Apostolate (MH. 74-75)."

It is clear that Mani's death was the signal for a brutal persecution of his followers over wide areas of

---

[1] This imprecation was fulfilled; there is in fact today no actual trace of the city of Belapat.

the Empire, a persecution to be renewed from time to time until the Muslims overthrew the bloodstained dynasty; then the Religion which had stained itself with the blood of God's holy and gentle Prophet had to flee, shattered, from Persian soil to the refuge of India's all-embracing tolerance.

3. Mani, the Man and His Work

One who has read the foregoing pages on the life and death of Mani, fragmentary as the malice of men and the undiscriminating ravages of time have made it, one who reads the cries of passionate and adoring love which this Messenger awoke in the hearts of those who knew him best, and which are so inadequately represented in our GPM 35-39, 88, 91-92, will at once dismiss the cruel and lying slanders put out against him by polemists in the Christian and Parsi camps. The absurd fabricated life of Mani copied by so many out of Hegemonius's libellous pages, though it may conceivably be taken as a myth with deeper meaning, are so far from the truth found in these all-but contemporary accounts, that it were dishonest to defile our pages by further reference to them.

In Mani, then, we see a true religious reformer sincerely certain of the Divine source of his mission and inspired by a great ideal, as Jackson puts it in his *Zoroastrian Studies*, p. 188: " to bring the world, Orient and Occident, into closer union through a combined faith, based on the creeds known in his day". Was

lxxxi

that aim so utopian, then, an empty dream? The same great scholar writes (JRAS, 1926, p. 117): "Persia of the third century A.D. was capable, more than any other country, of producing a world religion, arising from an aggregate of the great religious systems of the world." To that mission Mani gave the whole of his mighty energy, the whole of his immense grasp of the tangled religious materials of the age, the whole of his boundless imagination and artist's skill in welding such fantasies into a single coherent plan, the whole of his rich philanthropy—which in its turn won the devotion of men and women who, for eleven centuries, were proud and happy to embrace exile and death for his name.

His extraordinary labours, wandering over vast areas of little-known lands, planting churches and teaching them by letters and books, and guiding them in a strong but simple organisation, show him to have been one of the very greatest men of the first millennium A.D. That he was fully aware of the ways in which his work surpassed even that of his great Predecessors is shown by several passages in the 'Kephalaia'. His very human pride in these achievements and in his five great and other minor books, which should for ever have kept intact the doctrine and life he had given, only draws him nearer to our human sympathies. The kindliness wherewith he defended the 'ugly Saint', his humour with the Nasorean and his own disciple Aurades, the ready wit with which he found texts for his sermons in the events of daily life, the personal

F

affection in which he loved to call his followers " my children, my brothers, my limbs, and my beloved ", the staunch courage shown to the persecuting King, the poetic talent so manifest in every fragment of his own writing and in the books of his followers, the skill in painting which made his very name a new word for a 'painter' in Persian, the love for music and fragrance so manifest in the teaching and practice of his Church—all mark him out as a real Saint to whom history has as yet failed to pay even a tithe of the due attention.

But amid these various qualities of greatness still shines out the brilliance of that one by which Mani himself chiefly willed to be known—the Messenger of the Light. Never for a moment does he himself claim to be divine; that doubtful and dangerous honour was, very naturally in his oriental environment, put on him by those who loved and revered him with such passionate devotion as their 'Luminary', their 'Life', their 'Father', and their 'God'. This last word should not shock the Western reader of today as it shocked the Westerner of earlier centuries; it conveys no hint of blasphemy at all. When the Indian calls his Guru 'God', he does not for a moment confuse him with the One Absolute beyond all forms and essences; he declares his voice the voice of God, just as the devout Catholic monk regards the Rule of his Order and his Superior as God's will. Mani's own frank admission of his humanity survived long enough even to be found in a Turfan fragment (M 49) referring to the 'Twin' or inspiring Angel sent to him by God: "And even now he himself accompanies me, he himself holds and protects me, and in his power do I fight with *the demons of* Greed and Satan (Lust), and teach men wisdom and knowledge, and save them from Greed and Satan." This Being he sometimes calls the Christ, sometimes the Comforter or Paraclete; it is only in so far as Mani becomes truly his mouthpiece that he himself becomes an '*alter Christus*', the promised Paraclete. St. Augustine and the rest were too much blinded by their own bigotry and resentment against a creed to which he had become apostate in an age of persecution, to view Mani's real claims with honesty or truth. In refuting Faustus the great Catholic doctor, besides an undergraduate ribaldry before the deeply mystical, and therefore very vulnerable, doctrines arising from the truth of God's omnipresence—relied mainly on the futile illogicality of the position: "I don't believe your claims because you are a heretic and a false apostle." The lawyer with a poor case abuses his opponent!

Mani's own statements show clearly to the student and lover of Truth, unclouded by passion or fanaticism, that he was a real Prophet of God, sent by Him to do a certain work in the world, and loyally devoted to that work until death took him home to God's bright Garden in the Paradise of the Light. It was this certain faith which gave him strength and courage, won for him the deep love of those admitted to his intimacy, and enabled him to plant a world religion which survived the most brutal persecutions in all the religious history of our still largely barbarous humanity.

Nor was Mani's a mere sect, a heretical offshoot from a preexistent religion. Jackson rightly says (p. 20): "It was a veritable religion and exercised an influence, for more than a thousand years, upon the lives of countless numbers of devoted followers, inspired by the ideals and high principles of its Founder, whom they accounted divine, and the example of whose martyr death they were led to emulate both at the time and in after ages." George Finlay the historian writes in '*Greece under the Romans*' (Dent's edition, p. 353): "The great success of Mani in propagating a new religion (for Manicheism cannot properly be called a heresy) is a strong testimony of this feeling. The fate, too, of the Manicheans, would probably have foreshadowed that of the Mohammedans, had the religion of Mahomet not presented to foreign nations a national cause as well as an universal creed. Had Mahomet himself met with the fate of Mani, it is not probable that his religion would have been more successful than that of his predecessor." While not identifying oneself with the unfriendly attitude here shown towards Islam, which is *not* in that sense 'the religion of Mahomet', we may also note that Islam arose in the religious vacuum of Arabia, and in a world weary of sectarian squabbles among the Christians, while in Mani's day Christianity was still kept pure by the fires of pagan persecution, and further east Mani had also to contend with an intensely jealous and a powerfully established State creed, linked with a young and vigorous dynasty and with the proud tradition of a former world-supremacy.

In a striking article in JAOS (1938, p. 240), Jackson writes: "Mani had the exalted fervor of a religious leader and founder of a faith that was once a rival of Christianity and Zoroastrianism, opposition from which latter led him to suffer a martyr's death as an adjudged heretic. Throughout in his make-up, especially if born with a physical weakness,[1] we can see a peculiar idealism and refinement, combined with rare vision. It has always been recognized that he had a poetic imagination, as shown in his cosmogonic fantasies, and also in a few hymnic stanzas that have been preserved. Tradition assigns to him exquisite skill as an artist, so that his name became in Persia a synonym for painter. His master hand as an adapter of a revised alphabet and a presumed pioneer in calligraphy—the latter art being especially cultivated by his followers—all bespeak a highly ideal and creative mind. He cared particularly for music and allowed to his followers the enjoyment of perfumes as something refined." Jackson speaks also of "his sensitive and spiritual nature, which was above all religiously so creative". Even at the risk of repetition, I feel these testimonies from one of our day's greatest Iranists are worth recording here.

[1] This is the old misunderstanding that he was lame in one or both of his feet, as reported even by AnNadim. We can now see that this really refers to the crippling effect of the fetters during his 'crucifixion'. The Parsis called him 'the crippled demon', much as Jesus was called 'the hanged felon'.

Mani's personal reverence and love for his acknowledged predecessors Zarathushtra, the Buddha, and still more for Jesus, whom he often called the "Son of God", betoken the width of his own religious view. It became natural for his Church to adapt itself to the special background of each environment it entered, and this may well have led others to view it as a 'heresy', clandestinely undermining the faith of the orthodox. Now, as Harnack says in his *Encyclopaedia Britannica* article (vol. xiv, p. 803): such "great adaptability is just as necessary for a universal religion as a divine founder in whom the highest revelation of God may be seen and reverenced". Unhappily, though the Manichean books are full of echoes and memories from the great Hebrew Prophets and Psalmists, a perhaps 'Aryan' anti-Jewish hatred led his followers, with their Marcionite forerunners, to a bitter scorn and rejection of the Old Testament, as inspired by the forces of Evil. This enabled their Catholic opponents, habituated to rely so largely on supposed prophecies in building up their theology, to arouse mass hatred against them among the ignorant.

There is no doubt that Mani himself laid great stress upon his 'cosmogonic fantasies', which were probably essential to winning the faith of Mesopotamian converts in his day. But they were certainly a grave handicap in competing with the comparatively simple cosmology of Catholic Christians and, perhaps understandably, awoke the ridicule of their polemic writers. The doctrine of an absolute Dualism might satisfy the superficial enquirer brought up in a Mazdean environment, but it cannot long content the truly philosophic mind. In trying to maintain it in the West, and at the same time to uphold the doctrine of Christ's universal immanence, the Manicheans became involved in absurdities which St. Augustine especially delighted in mercilessly exposing. But we may well doubt whether it was such subtle illogic which led to the final ruin of Mani's Church, so much as the pitiless violence and the vandal burning of its precious books, which it had everywhere and always to endure.

Spread, as it did, from Spain to Siam, and surviving in 'dangerous' form from the 3rd to the 17th centuries here or there, "it really became one of the great religions", as Harnack rightly says in his scholarly article already cited. For sensual cults it gave a spiritual, devotional and aesthetic worship, with a strict morality, and a simple if firm social organisation. Nor was that morality *too* strict; the extremer forms of its celibacy and non-violence were imposed only on the Elect, whose number was always very small, and they were voluntarily embraced by them; the lay masses were allowed a normal human life—as they are today among Catholics, when compared with that expected of a Trappist or Carmelite. And even so late as in its diluted form among the Cathari of Provence, none could ever impugn the saintly and noble lives lived by most of their 'Elect'.

Persecution, however, drove the Manicheans underground, and the need to hide their 'heresy' from the bigots around them must often have led to compromise and corruption of the Faith. In self-defence they became, as F. Legge says: "a perfectly efficient and capable secret society", and this intensified the suspicion, slander and suffering of all kinds to which they were always liable. The vilest calumnies pursued them through the centuries, and there are those even today who ignorantly use 'Manichean' as a term of abuse, to suggest incredible blasphemy and an enormity of hypocritical vice.

Yet, as Legge says in the same article (JRAS, 1913, p. 93): "A faith that held its own in the face of the hottest persecution for nine centuries is a rare enough phenomenon, and one which cannot be safely neglected by the student of Comparative Religion." In fact, Manicheism is every whit as important a world religion as Islam, Buddhism, or Christianity, and perhaps far more than Jainism, Sikhism and others usually allowed that title. Let us pay it what is due, at least now, after so many centuries of neglect.

4. Sisin and Innai, First Manichean 'Popes'

Mani entrusted his Church to the hierarchy of Apostles and Elders, at the head of whom stood, after a brief interregnum, Sisin in his own place as Leader. AnNadim (p. 334) reports the Manicheans of his own day as saying: "When Mani was taken up to the Gardens of the Light, Sis(in) arose after him as the 'Imam' before his taking up, and until he too was received (*i.e.*, died) God's Religion and His Revelation were standing firm." But for four years he could not exercise his authority, because no organisation could function during such a storm of persecution.

Flügel (Mani, p. 331) quotes a story which coheres well with the picture of the Persian King we have already seen. Bahram I buried two hundred Manicheans with their heads downwards in pits and their feet tied to stakes; "See," said he with ferocious irony, " the garden that Bahram the King has planted! " Many of the faithful died as martyrs, many fled to Khorassan, and there strengthened the Faith, many crossed the Oxus River and wandered as far as Turkestan. AnNadim (p. 337) tells us: " When Kosru (*i.e.*, the King) had killed and crucified [1] Mani and forbidden the people of his Kingdom to join together in the Religion, he turned to killing Mani's followers wheresoever he found them. They did not cease to flee from him till they crossed the River of Balkh and entered the Khan's realm (*i.e.*, Turkestan)." Others fled westwards, to Syria or Egypt, and Pattiq is said by Philaster of Brescia to have preached against the Old Testament in Rome itself by A.D. 280. The Faith was clearly already firmly established on the soil of Egypt, fertilised by centuries of Hermetic and Gnostic teaching; it had probably spread also to 'Africa', *i.e.*, Tunisia.

Sisin (A. D. 281-291). We draw most of his story from the 'Book of the Crucifixion' in MH, which tells

---

[1] Note how here the word 'killed' correctly precedes 'crucified'.

of his Master's sufferings too. After the year of massacre, we learn, " there came three further years *of peace*, without anyone sinning against his people *or being a cause of* trembling. Their anger was pacified, just as he (*i.e.*, Mani) had said while he was still *in the body*. Then but *a few years* after my Lord's crucifixion, *the dragon* began to creep, his anger gathered *on every side* from below; little by little *hatred* began to *break out* again *into violence* in every land, while the *King* heated up his anger until fifteen years *of his reign* (*i.e.*, A.D. 291) ".

It was during these years of uneasy quiet that the Faith spread rapidly east and west. In 282 Bahram II lost the twin cities of Ctesiphon and Seleucia to the Roman Aurelius Carus, and it was about that time that Amu, author of the beautiful account of the 'Light World' used in GPM 80, travelled in Central Asia, while Addai (?Adimantus) prepared in Africa his epitome of the Scriptures—drawing in turn from the 'Treasure', the 'Shapuraqan', the 'Mysteries' the 'Precepts', and the 'Two Roots'—which we may still have with us in its Chinese dress as 'CMT' (?).

By about A.D. 287 Julian, Proconsul of Africa, reported to Diocletian in alarm at the danger to Roman society implicit in the spread of this new Eastern religion, with its strange views on sex, war, agriculture and civic duties; Diocletian thought its propaganda was a sort of fifth column from Persia, to soften up her great rival in the West. By 290 Manicheism was prominent in the fertile Fayum district of Egypt, and the 'Psalms of Thōm' appeared in their original Syriac form, to be very soon translated into Coptic.

Next year, 291, the gathering storm broke in Persia. " Then came the wicked and the evildoors and pursued after him (*i.e.*, Sisin), for the Satan cherished envy *inwardly* and outwardly against his devotees. . . . The Kings *of the land* fell into anger, *and their hatred became* the raging fire. The wolves suddenly fell upon the flock of sheep to kill and to destroy; *wild beasts burst in* among the rams in order to ravage *the sheepfolds*; evil ones entered by force into the *Master's vineyard* and cut off the branches *with their fruits*; robbers broke into the treasure-chamber *and looted and* destroyed the treasures. The beast broke into the *flower-garden* and trampled it down while it was growing up, the *kite* burst into the dovecotes *and* scattered the timid birds (MH. 76).

" In every land *spread* the report of the crucifying of the chief(?) *leaders of the Church in* Persia, out of Maisan and Ctesiphon, in every town in the land of Susiana and Babylon. How many are *the* myriad *victims*, and the maidens and celibates yearly fell away from them (*i.e.*, decreased)! They captured and slew the *Teachers and Overseers* like sheep; they caught the Overseers *and looted* his treasures (*i.e.*, Mani's books?); they carried off *the Elect and the Hearers*, they slaughtered them like *lambs* (MH. 76).

" They appeared *in their midst like* small *children* before their teachers; *they were thrown* before lions, but the lions spared them *their lives*. A few they equipped

with weapons and forced to fight with bears (MH. 77)."
We are told that some were compelled to kill ants and
thus violate their Master's doctrine of non-violence.
"They sent horses *to fight* against them. They paid
heed *to every prisoner*, he was caught and mangled
cruelly with their teeth; they did not spare them, they
killed them. . . . A few of these they did not destroy (?),
so arrows were thrust in their sight, in order to see that
they were really killed. Like *papers* which have been torn
to shreds, they too were torn in pieces, *the King* watching them while they lay (?); then in their wickedness
they *urged and* asked them about everything (MH. 77).

"They crucified the youngsters, children, both
maidens and eunuchs. A few they sawed up in the
skins (?), *slaying* them, boasting that *they would destroy
the Church*. How numerous are the hateful deeds *they
did, telling* them that they were lying! They lowed (?)
piteously like a herd *of oxen dragged off in* chains yearly
by butchers. Like a head of cattle that has no master,
allotted to hundreds, to fifties, *they were slaughtered* in
land *after* land. . . . Their children were murdered
before their eyes (MH. 77).

"*Some of them* were *brutally* scourged; they crept
upon a few of them *to inflict tortures* on them; (on)
some of them again *iron* fetters were fastened, (and
they) were thrown into prisons (?) in hunger and thirst,
fasting *there in misery*, cold and affliction. They were
held up with their feet on the earth *pressing* thorns and
thistles and *brambles*, while they were hidden without
sunlight *by the wickedness of evil* men. They were envious

against the Righteous (?), ... they demolished their guardhouses, cut off *the fruit-bearing trees, broke down* the walls on all sides; they went *inside* his doors, they opened his gates. *Even he who* had no youngsters, they (?) too were violently *beaten*, his houses were torn down, the properties scattered. *Holes were made* in the ship in order to bring it to ruin, so that it might be sunk in the deep *of the ocean*, in order to cause the merchandise to be lost (MH. 78)."

In this crisis representatives of the churches went to beg Sisin for help in their agony, and he turned to vigil and to prayer. "'Look after my children,'" he cried; "'send to me thy Power to aid me in this peril! ... *The children of thy Church* perish *because they stand* fast in thy name; thy glory is in *them*, ever since the day when thou hast chosen *me and put a* great crown into my hand, *that I might oppose* the false Sects and all the societies *resistant to* thy Light. I have not lied about thy *Message*, I have not falsified thy Oath, I have protected *thy children* whom thou hast given me. Now *behold our* desolation and look upon my tears *of sorrow*. Thus have I strengthened myself while I was in the *hour of misery*; it is thine hour, do not make me despair *and fall into the* trap. Fill up *my heart* with the holy (?) *spirit*. Hear the voice of this 'widow' who *cries to* the Judge, for I have been judged in *that* my children have been killed in every land! *Of old we were* loaded with good things, and thy *kindnesses surrounded us*; *now* the sea has fallen into a tumult *everywhere*, wave *dashing against* wave (MH. 78-79).

xciv

"I am thy *garden*, thy gardeners are in me; I am thy *field* (?), I am thy corn, thy countrymen *are like a* slave while Thy children are *in danger* with me. Look after me, and have pity on mine; send to me *thy Power*, for I see the grief of my children; *the deniers* kill them, they slay *my little ones*, they burn up my households with fire!... I see my children overthrown *in the streets*, while the bodies of the *Elect* lie there *unburied* in every land, with the head of the foreigners and the *remains of* the flesh of the mourners and the widows (?) and the kinsfolk—the miserable ones who have *been torn to pieces by* the evil dragons. *Their bodies* have been rent asunder, their blood *freely* flowed upon the earth in every town. They scoff at me, their kinsmen, as the dupe (?) of our God (?): 'Thy God is the Light, this doctrine is His; thou, thou, why *are thy children driven* forth? Wherefore then are they massacred?' (MH. 79-80).

"I, now I turn to Thee, *crying for thy aid*. The kings have pursued me *day and night*, the rulers have not let me lack *a going* forth.... They have scattered the *congregations*, they have *barred* the doors of the temples (?) *against the faithful*; they have driven me out of my dwellings, settling down in my place; they have shown the *darkness of misery*, taken away my beauty, *silenced the voice* of my song. They have carried me into some dungeons (?) away from the sunlight, hidden *me away with* stealthy *cunning*. They have slain the prudent, *killed* the guileless, massacred my children, *tortured* my priests and devotees. They have *persecuted those* who stay resting *in the churches depending on* my *Wisdom and obedient to my* Discipline (?). Give heed to see how much they injure us, O my Father; *pitifully* send thy power to support the *courage* of those who are to be crucified (till they come) *to the* places of Rest, take to thee the souls of the Hearers who are to be destroyed by thy haters!' (MH. 80-81.) "

Though it is not quite certain whether this Prayer is directed to God Himself, or to Mani the Prophet, it seems clear from its terms that the fragment 'S 8' refers to the same general persecution: " For this cause are Teachers of the Light killed, and for this cause the Priests are mourning. He himself keeps all the kingdoms divided, and himself indeed shines over the Kingdom like (or: through) the Sun and Moon." There is no need to transfer it to the persecution under Anoshirwan in A.D. 528, as Jackson is inclined to do.

MH continues its story: "This took place in the years of King Bahram, the son of Bahram (I). Now (it was) he and the whole company of the Magi, and the denier *and hater* of the Giver of good things and of peace, *who had worked* the crucifixion of our Lord. When, then, after these great afflictions and perils *had increased* in this way, outwardly indeed *Sisin was silent*, but inwardly he consoled the 'man of *Light*', and his *prayers* aroused his Righteousness. They threatened (?) against him who had uttered that *Prayer that they were about* to crucify him (MH. 81).

" The world was filled with his glory; it reached the ears of the King of the *land, who had come* to that time in anger. They came *to plot against* the Righteousness; they went their *way to meet* with the deniers who had *risen up* again (?). They wrote lying pamphlets filled with wickedness, and showed them to the King; *they left them in the* keeping of the Magi *who were eager* to deny his Hope. *So they assembled,* all *of them,* the King and the nobles. . . . We came with the other *disciples, talking to* one another. Wickedness drew near *until at last* a great disaster happened; *the deniers showed* their anger, they expressed (?) *a desire to* condemn his devotees *before* the *King's* presence, namely the ' men of Light '. *The glory of* the Righteousness (being) behind them, they proclaimed *the Doctrine* (MH. 81-82).

"They brought him (*i.e.*, Sisin) before the King; he questioned him about all *the doctrines,* asked him about every separate *detail.* My Lord Sisin replied exhaustively, he persuaded him *to join him* in his place. But the King harassed him *with incitements to* lust, saying to him: '*Here is a girl!* ' He forced him: ' Have connections with her; obey me, fear *me* ! Now if you obey me, I shall *honour you.* You are a handsome man, why *ruin* yourself? Wherefore will you kill yourself? *It is you who would ruin* yourself, for I do not destroy you! Look after yourself; I *am ready* to kill you ! ' (MH. 82) "

It was only natural for the King who had overwhelmed the faithful in a reign of terror to hope now finally to destroy the Faith by thus corrupting its Leader with a public apostasy from the Messenger's essential laws. But Sisin was made of the stern stuff of the martyrs of chastity, like Thecla and St. Maria Goretti, he was ready, nay eager, to give his life as an offering of gratitude to his deified and beloved Master. The story goes on: "Then he *calmly* spoke to the King: 'Your words and deeds have well *agreed*!.' *He spoke plainly*, his heart was strong, he did not hesitate at all before him.

"*Then the King* brought swords, he set them in a row *before my Lord*. The King said to him: 'Look and see *these sharp swords; now fear and* accept my word!'.

"But my Lord Sisin said: 'I have One who is more to be feared than you, *to whom I look* up. I stand in awe of Him who *can altogether overthrow* your word!'

"Then the King was angry and said, 'Who is that before whom you fear more than before me?'

"*Sisin said, 'It is* before God my heart fears *greatly*!'

"Then *the King* once, twice, thrice *commanded*, but was unable to persuade him. He then picked up a sword *and* said to him, 'I shall kill you now with this sword (MH 82)!'

"*Sisin welcomed* the Cross, like his *Father the Messenger of the Light*, at the King's hands. He did not lose courage *before death at any time*. The crowd of the others *were watching him*; he was not afraid, but *he turned* to the other *devotees* (and) encouraged *them to enter on* the Rest above. *Then he laid down* the lordship which *he held*, he loosed his shoes, took off his *riband of* his own hair, he rejoiced (?) *at his destiny* (MH. 82-83).

"The King raised his hand and smote him with the sword *on his neck*; his blood flowed out like a *fountain*. They took three Elders *from among us*—

Apket and Abesira the brothers *of.* . . . With his crucifixion the riots (?) in the town took place; they crucified him *in public* at nine hours of the day (*i.e.*, 3 p.m.); . . . he went *up by the Column into the Land of Light.* The ten years that he had been Leader, his heart had never wavered; he drank the chalice of his Father's crucifixion, he went forth after him. He received the crown, he *walked* on the ways of his Saviour, *on the roads* of peace. He went to rest *in the Garden, and there* he found the recompense for his wrongs *and the pains of the world*, and the brothers also who were to be crucified *with him* (MH. 83)."

Innai (A.D. 291-303) The story goes on: "His word was laid upon Innai, *that he should* himself *be* the Leader of the Sect *in* his place." As Innai was born about the time of Mani's first proclamation and was now about fifty, he was old enough to take the troubled Church under his protection. He enjoyed the reputation, like his Master, of being skilled in medicine.

It is clear from our broken text that, soon after his murder of Sisin, the tyrant King became desperately ill and, when death drew near him, some of his courtiers ran to call Innai, a man gentle and kindly in nature. Innai willingly went to treat Bahram, in the belief that in this sudden opportunity God was bringing succour to the tortured Church. The writer says: "*The King received him with* oaths: 'I shall make *my cure* a remedy in the heart of you all, *I shall work for the* favour and the good of your Religion *if you save me. Do not imagine that* I have killed your sons, so that you *should fear me* and not heal me. I did not will *it, but* it was *these* evil *men* who accused them, *so they suffered.* Now express what is in your minds, do not be afraid! All this is past; from today on *you will be safe*!'

"So he then healed him *by praying to* God; he received honour, and Gods and *Angels* helped him. He received letters *of protection* from the King *to the nobles* in every land; he gave peace (?) *to the Church* before the face of the whole world. . . . *The King gave him his* hand when they were led to the banquet, *and permitted* that he should sit beside him *as they ate.* He gave him gold and silver; he did not accept it *lest it should tempt* him to acquire power *and wealth, for he wanted* only God and His Hope. He did *acts of respect and homage* before the King and the nobles; the courtiers (?) honoured him. Evermore did the *King prosper in his life,* he received victory and grace. *As for Innai, peace came on* his Religion, glory *came down from on high upon* the honoured and the disdained; *the Leader and the Overseers,* the Elect and the Hearers— *on them came grace* from God. The Righteousness (*i.e.,* the Church) *throve in all lands,* great glory came to it in the *whole world.* They built and organised *churches in every city* out of the places *where men live, and worshipped* in every place (MH. 84).

"Letters were written *to the* nobles on every river *in the Kingdom; they went* into the King's palace *in peace,* rest came down on *the ' sons of Heaven ',* on the Righteousness. They became friends *with the King,* with the great ones and the rulers *who held power* before the

Good. The three *last years of* Bahram this happened; *the Church was* in rest during that time, *peace came* to her, she was greatly honoured. Thereupon, after this he (*i.e.*, Bahram II) came up to Belapat and died; he went to rest at that time from the *troubles* of the world (?) (MH. 85)."

It seems clear from this wording that the story must have been written down very shortly after Bahram died, in A. D. 294, and before Diocletian persecuted the Manicheans so brutally two years later. There are several hints, as in MH. 81 where the first person is used, *we,* that it is the work of an eyewitness, at least in part. This may well have been Kushtai, Mani's secretary, or even Innai himself, who must end his work during his own lifetime. The story closes with recalling a prophecy of Mani that a brief persecution would give way to glorious triumph; and that could hardly have been referred to A. D. 291 by anyone writing after A. D. 296 when persecution began again.

In A. D. 295 Alexander of Lycopolis was opposing the work of Paapi and 'Thomas' in Egypt, dubbing Manicheism an arbitrary and irrational doctrine; several of its books had already appeared in an elegant African Latin, and probably also in Coptic. Next year Julian's complaint bore fruit; on 30th March 296 Diocletian extended the persecution of Christians to Manicheans, decreeing: "We order that their organisers and leaders be subject to the final penalties and condemned to the fire with their abominable scriptures. We prescribe that their adepts be to the last one beheaded, and decree that the goods of these people be confiscated to the State. If nobles and other officials, even the most highly placed, have joined this sect, . . . you will have their patrimony seized by the State and themselves sent to the mines (Cod. Greg. I. xiv, Tit. iv. 4-7)."

This edict let persecution loose in Egypt and North Africa; early martyrs in Egypt included Mary, Theona, Cleopatra, Plousiane, Apa Polydoxus, Eustaphius, Jemnoute, Psai, Apa Panai, and Apa Pshai. These mingled their blood with such Christian martyrs as Sts. Primus, Felician, Agnes, Beatrice, Susanna, Cyriacus and Sebastian in Rome; Lucia and Vitus in Sicily; Felix at Nola; George, Adrian and Gorgonius at Nicomedia; Mennas in Phrygia; Christina in Tuscany; Erasmus in Antioch; Chrysogonus at Aquileia; Alban in Britain; and Vincent at Saragossa. The Manicheans encouraged one another in martyrdom by relating the courage of the Christians suffering during three centuries beginning with Christ and Stephen.

Though King Narsi in that bloodstained year defeated Galerius; Persia again lost Mesopotamia and her western provinces to Rome; during his reign the Manicheans had rest in Persia (A. D. 296-303). One Abdial commented on the 'Mysteries', and Iannu (perhaps Innai himself) on the 'Treasure of Life'. The Faith grew strong in Lydia and even spread to the Balkans, for about 298 a "Manichean virgin of Lydia", named Bassa, was buried near to Salonika. Someone seems to have carried it to Malabar in India; here by A. D. 300, we are told, a village bore the name of 'Mani-grāma' (*i.e.*, Mani's town); people now think it was a mercantile colony of Persian 'Christians', I learn.

But in A. D. 303 the new King Hormizd II put Innaï to death on his accession, and in Iraq four more Leaders were murdered after one another in later years. The Religion was now deemed 'illicit' by the tyrant Emperors, both east and west; Persia and Rome, traditional foes of each other, united to persecute the ascetic and gentle Church of Mani.

5. Manicheism Down the Centuries

1. **The Fourth Century.** It is just possible that in founding the first Christian monastery in Egypt in A. D. 305 St. Antony was inspired by the fast-spreading asceticism of the Manicheans. By 312 the Faith was firmly established in Rome in the time of Pope Miltiades; 'Thomas' died in Egypt by 320, his 'Psalms' being already popular there; Hegemonius was now trying to kill Manicheism with ridicule through his absurd caricature of Mani's life and teachings in 'The Acts of Archelaus' (H.).

During the Nicene Council of 325, Constantine I got Musonian (or some say Strategius) to report to him on this doctrine, so as to choose between it and Christianity as a State Religion to replace the moribund Roman paganism. Next year he again brought its believers under the repressive laws and deprived them of the right to enjoy benefices. About

330 saw Herakleides' 'Psalms' appear in Coptic, the work of one whom Rufinus calls a disciple of St. Antony; so great was their immediate vogue that Antony had to forbid his monks all contact with Manicheans. At the same time Hierakas, learned in the Old Testament and in several languages, was writing Psalms of a new type at Leontopolis in Egypt (Epiphanius says in his book on the Heresies, 67 : 3). The scriptures were then being attacked by Aphraat in Mosul and Ephrem at Edessa and Nisibis, joined at Edessa more thoroughly by Eusebius (264-340).

Yet the Faith was spreading fast in the Western Empire on soil fertilised by many Gnostic sects now decaying; by 340 Coptic translations of the 'Kephalaia', the 'Psalm-book' and the 'Homilies' had been issued. Agapius about now published the seven books of his 'Heptalogue', in a winning if careless style, to hellenize his Master's teaching, and later on, this Commentary ranked as scripture. By 345 Serapion of Tmuis in Egypt, and Titus of Bostra in Iraq, were strenuously opposing the Faith (TB), and by 348 Victorinus wrote in Africa against Justin the Manichean. Aphtonius published his great Commentary at Alexandria in 350; it became so famous that Aetius came from Antioch to refute the Manichean scholar (H. E. 3 : 15), and despite Antony's warnings many of his Egyptian monks were being converted by the Manichean Psalms. Hierakas now wrote his Commentary, the 'Hexameron', near Arsinoe; he was a saintly and ascetic scholar, whose preaching made many converts. By the time St. Augustine was born in Africa, A.D. 354, Hilary of Poitiers reported that the Faith was already strong in Aquitaine, South France.

At this time Shapur II renewed persecution in Persia; in 358 he was visited by the Neoplatonist Eustathius of Sebaste, against whom St. Basil of Cesarea (329-379) and St. Gregory of Nyssa (351-395) took up the cudgels. Constantius (337-361) was so brutal to the Manicheans that many pretended to be Catholics, while others supported the Arians in Alexandria in the disorders of the period. Julian (361-363) granted them full tolerance, but he was soon killed by Shapur II, who recovered the lost provinces once more.

By 370 Eustathius was organising Manichean monasteries in Anatolia, where the Faith was spreading fast, while in Persia Atarpat the great High Priest issued in the 'Denkart' (3 : 200), a vile calumny against it which led to fresh persecutions. Gratian drove the faithful from the churches as 'heretics', while in 372 Valentinian I forbade all meetings of the Sect, and ordered presiding teachers to be fined, all present banished, and their buildings confiscated. Yet, despite all this, the young Augustine joined them as 'Hearer'; he tells us that he heard 'the Treasure' and one of the Epistles commented on by Addai, or Adimantus, read in Manichean assemblies. In 375 the Huns entered Europe, the signal for the fall of the Roman West. At Salamina Epiphanius in his book gave Manicheism a long chapter, which he based on Hegemonius and others; with characteristic stupidity he imagined that Thomas, Addas and Hermeias were still alive and preaching (66 : 12, 31).

Herakleides, by now very old, possibly wrote in 377 an account of the dualist monks in Egypt which was later used by Palladius in his ' Lausiac History '; he enjoyed high authority, and also commented on the Manichean scriptures. In Alexandria Didymus was now the chief opponent of the two Manichean sects there—the vegetarian ' Saddikini ' (i.e., the Elect), and the ' Sammakini ', who were said to be immune to poison. In far away Spain, Priscillian was in 380 accused by Ithacius and Hydatius of being a Manichean; in A.D. 385 he was the first martyr murdered by the ' Christians '—the first of a vast army through the ages. In Milan the Prefect Symmachus was influenced by the scriptures, then being studied by Augustine, who next year wrote his (naturally) lost defence of Mani's Faith, ' On Beauty and Finality '.

Persecution again flared up in the West. In 381, incited by the Catholics, Theodosius I again took away civil rights, and in 382 decreed that Manichean Elders, who lived in common for greater strictness in the Precepts, be put to death. Faustus, a learned Elder at Rome, fled back to Carthage, where he taught that " a man who prays to God has no need of a temple ", while in an Italian monastery Constantius was teaching one of Mani's Epistles on the aims of life. In 383 Theodosius I ordered that all Manicheans be sent into exile. It was during this mounting persecution of the Faith that Augustine deserted it in 382 and became its leading Christian opponent, the subconscious mind providing the necessary impulse for the change—a by no means unusual phenomenon.

Competing with the celibacy of the Elect, Christian priests in the East began to adopt celibacy in 385, while St. Ambrose in Milan, John Chrysostom, and Cyril of Jerusalem were opposing the 'heretics'. This was the year when Faustus, Manichean Bishop of Carthage, was accused before the Consul Bauto; on the kindly request of Catholics he was only exiled to an island, where he spent his time in writing. In Rome Constantius was now (384-388), disguised as a Christian, helping the Martari secretly to organise a Manichean monastery, and in the three following years Augustine, as a monk at Thagaste, wrote his books on Manichean Customs (AMM), on 'Genesis', and on 'True Religion'.

In about 385 Valentinian II (375-392) again decreed exile for all Manicheans, confiscated their property and annulled their wills; this was actually done in Rome in 389. At a very great age, well over a century, Herakleides died at Leontopolis in 390/1; in the latter year Theophilus made his savage attack on the great Alexandria Library—many priceless books of ancient wisdom being destroyed by his ignorant bigots. Augustine was now a Christian priest at Hippo in Africa; among several new books we note one trying to reconvert Honoratus whom he had himself once led to Mani's feet. Diodorus of Tarsus wrote twenty-five 'books' against the Faith, which had now by 395 spread strongly from Lydia into Paphlagonia.

Next year, 396, Augustine wrote his treatise to refute the one scripture he knew well—the Epistle called 'Fundamental' by him (AFE). He received a copy of Faustus's book, a sort of pastoral letter opposing Christianity, and refuted this in A.D. 400 in thirty-three books (AF), along with his rightly famous 'Confesions'. At this time there was a strong Church in Spain, Portugal and Galicia; under the guidance of Mark of Memphis they were studying the 'Treasure', in spite of the attacks of Bishop Evodius at Uzzala.

The last quarter-century was a time of fierce persecution in the Eastern Empire, while the Church was perhaps too small to attract much notice in Persia and was actually gaining ground in the West, aided by its use of the popular apocryphal Acts of Thomas and John, and the growing glory of virginity and the ascetic and monastic life. In spite of official interference, there were scholarly lectures in Rome, and some of the most intellectual embraced the Faith. In Central Asia, in an area largely held by Iranized Buddhists, it was perhaps slowly being orientalized to a form differing from the Christian form known in the West.

2. **The Fifth Century.** We know little of what happened in Central Asia during this age while the Huns were extending their conquests, and the history of the Faith in Persia is also dark, while the tiny Church in Malabar had probably been absorbed by the Christians, that in Sind by the Jains.

In A.D. 404 Julia of Antioch, a woman, came to convert the important city of Gaza to Mani's religion, and at the same time Philon was preaching it in the Sinai region, where the monk Nilus refers to the books, the 'Treasure' and the 'Mysteries', as known to him. In the same year Augustine wrote 'On the Nature of the Good' (NB), and against Felix, a Manichean priest who was in 405 captured with five scriptures. At first Felix was ready to be burned along with them if anything shocking were found in them, but considering the doctrine hinted at in GPM 8:2 and certain passages about Cain and Abel later quoted by AnNadim, he later recanted. Though Fortunatus fled from the new Honorian law outlawing all Manicheans as felons, Secundinus boldly wrote from Rome trying, without success, to win back Augustine to the Faith. By 407 the scriptures could circulate only secretly; any found were to be burned, and their owners tried for 'heresy'. At Carthage the Prefect Ursus severely 'questioned' many members of the Church.

Alaric the Goth took Rome in A.D. 410; ten years later Bahram V became King of Persia and throughout his Empire began to persecute the Christians, now suspect as 'Roman spies'; the persistent cruelty of the West to Manicheism seems to have convinced him that they at least were no enemies to his State. Quoting from the 'Epistle to Menaq the Virgin' (No. 60 or 61), Julian of Eclana in 425 accused Augustine of still holding Manichean views on chastity; similar doctrines were being taught by Ado of Adiabene (Kurdistan) at

Maisān near the Karun River of Iraq. Esnig of Golp, the Pakrevant Bishop, wrote of the 'Two Roots' derived from Zrwān as a doctrine held by the '*Zandiqs*', *i.e.*, Elect, then strong in Armenia. In 428 Theodosius II passed another decree of exile on Manicheans and other 'heretics', and under this law Nestorius, Patriarch of Constantinople, was sent into exile in Egypt in 431, for denying that Mary is mother of God. In 430 St Augustine died at his see in Hippo; Cassian warned his monks against the attraction of Manicheism—by which he must have meant its noble ethics and devotion, and not the fantastic cosmological myth.

In 439 Genseric's Vandal conquest ended the long Catholic rule near Carthage, but the many Manicheans still there found little relief, the Vandals within three years taking up the persecution. Rabboulas at Edessa (cir. 440) found their scriptures still widespread over Syria, Palestine and North Arabia. In 443, Pope Leo I (440-461) complained that there were still many Manicheans in Rome; he dragged many out of hiding, forcing them to betray their priest and teachers, exposing them to public ridicule, and burning masses of their beautifully copied and jewelled books before the church doors. On his incitement, many other bishops adopted the same barbarous conduct in Gaul, Sicily and North Africa—Turibius of Astorga in Galicia making himself notorious for his cruelty in 445.

The retribution fell in Persia; in 448 Yesdijerd II came to the throne and at once began a cruel persecution of the Christians, many of whom followed Nestorius.

Yet the Manicheans found no relief in the West, for in 445 Valentinian III had repeated the old Honorian law of 405. In mid-century the Faith was still strong at Edessa, while Proclus (412-485), the great Neoplatonist, was teaching in Egypt. Theodoret of Cyrrha wrote against the Manicheans between 451 and 458. In the following twenty-six years Feroz was King of Persia; during his reign Battai, a Kantean Gnostic east of the Tigris and south of Khaniqin, became a Manichean; he edited the scriptures and established a new sect in the Church.

Odoacer took Rome in 476, putting an end to the Roman Empire in the West; under his Arian successors the Manicheans enjoyed quiet for a while in outlying provinces. Under Zenon (464-490), Aristocritus published at Alexandria his 'Theosophy', an apology for Manicheism wherein 'Love' initiated 'Urania', the human soul; he showed that the doctrine was the same as was really taught by Jews, Christians and Heathen alike. Yet by 484 the Faith had been destroyed by the Vandals in 'Africa', and in 495 Pope Gelasius repeated Leo's cruelties in Rome. Nevertheless in Constantinople itself many from the highest classes in society, even at the court, were by the close of the century embracing Mani's creed.

3. **Sixth Century.** Kobad (488-531) was King in Persia when, about A.D. 500, Mazdak published his book, teaching much as Mani did in the 'Treasure' and the 'Two Roots'; he quickly converted many to his new sect, even from illustrious families. In 505 the

Romans under Anastasius I (491-518) regained Iraq, Mani's homeland. At this time Severus of Antioch was combatting the Faith, while Heracleon of Chalcedon condemned the three books: the 'Gospel', the 'Treasure' and the 'Book of Giants'. In 510 Pope Symmachus burned more of their books in Rome and, alarmed at the spread of their Church among Byzantine aristocrats, Anastasius decreed death to all who were loyal to the Faith. Pope Hormisdas burned more of the scriptures in Rome in 520.

About 521 Eustathius wrote to Timotheus, citing Epistles to Addas and to 'Scutian' (i.e., 'the Scythian', probably 'Khabarhat', or Gavriav). About four years later Justin I ordered that even those who failed to denounce or to boycott Manicheans should also be put to death. Compelled by this wickedness, Prosper in 526 became an apostate, and his 'Abjuration' became a model required from all who later turned from Mani to the Catholics. By 528 Mazdak had succeeded in converting King Kobad himself, preaching at Nishapur, and the Denawar sect of Manicheans carried their stricter life and doctrine to Western Persia, where members had in time become somewhat lax. That same year, while his father was still King, Prince Khusrau Anoshirwan, infuriated by the spread of the new Faith, treacherously massacred Mazdak and many of his followers at a banquet; after this crime he had eighty thousand Mazdakites and Manicheans killed, and the scriptures were severely proscribed throughout the Persian Empire.

Next year, while Simplicius was still fighting Manicheism in Athens, Justinian (Cod. Iust. I, 5: 11, 16) decreed that even apostates to Christianity who failed to denounce or persecute their former coreligionists, owned or saved from burning any Manichean scripture, should be put to death; the Emperor himself came out to prove by lectures that Mani's followers were pagans, and so beyond the law of a ' Christian' State.

By founding Cassino in 529, St. Benedict firmly established Western monasticism, while at the same time Eustathius was accusing Severus of being a crypto-Manichean. That year Olympiodorus, the last great Neoplatonist in Alexandria, passed away, and with him the world of the old Mediterranean Mysteries. In 533 the Empire overthrew Gelimer's Vandals in Africa and brought the desolated province back under ' Roman ' rule, but in 540 Khusrau I of Persia destroyed Antioch, and till 579 ruled from the Indus to part of East Europe and the Red Sea, with a good deal of Central Asia also.

Manicheans had secretly put copies of the 'Two Roots' in a Constantinople library and Zarachias wrote seven books against them, while Paul the Persian was opposing the Manichean orator Photinus. St. Benedict died in 543. By mid-century many books were being translated from Greek, Latin and Sanskrit into Persian, and by this time at least the Persian original of ' CMT ' existed, though it is probably far older. Between 563 and 567 the Turks took Soghdiana and other provinces where Manicheism was still strong, overthrowing the

Ephthalite Huns, and they soon showed themselves to be favourable to Mani's doctrine.

Manicheism by A.D. 570 could only exist in the West 'underground' or camouflaged in a Christian dress; it certainly greatly increased the importance of Satan in Western thought, and spread the idea that Hell is eternal—both ideas being dualistic and philosophically quite incoherent with the Christianity taught by Jesus and the Apostles. But the Faith was still strong in Antioch and other parts of the Near East, always susceptible to ideas of esotericism, asceticism and soterism. Muḥammed's birth in 571, though then unnoticed, opened a new era in the world's religious history.

Under Turkish rule in Central Asia, a candle miraculously lit itself, in 584, in some temple whose priest, probably a Manichean, was seeking leave to preach his own religion, and in fact the Faith was fully tolerated in that area for several centuries. There alone was it treated with wise humanity! In 590 the Turks conquered Tokharistan, Balkh, Herat and other provinces, and many of them became Manicheans. By this time King Hormizd IV had been severely defeated by Heraclius, and his throne became shaky. Syrian Nestorians had brought to Armenia copies of an 'Explanation of Mani's Gospel', with other apocryphal and 'heretical' books. Pope Gregory I (590-604) found many Manicheans had again appeared in Africa, Sicily and Calabria, and set to work to chase them out with their books.

H

4. **Seventh Century.** Early in this century Khusrau II tried heroically to restore the old days of Persian glory; in 614 his troops took Jerusalem, and in 616 overran Egypt. But the tide soon turned back; in 622 the Romans conquered Armenia and in 624 invaded Persia itself. To isolate them from the orthodox Christian enemy, all Persian Christians were in 625 compelled to embrace the Nestorian 'heresy', and many Manicheans seem to have found this a more acceptable apostasy than was the degenerate and ritualistic Mazdeism which then prevailed.

Already in 620 the Denawars were known as the T'i-na-pa in Chinese, having doubtless been met on the great 'silk route' over Asia. At Seville St. Isidore was fiercely opposing all 'heretics', most of them holding various kinds of Manicheism (601-636), and in 630 Theodore of Raithai, near Arabia, was resisting their Christology. Hiouen-tsang found them dominant round Merv in Western Turkestan.

The death of Muḥammed in 632 gave rein to a policy of aggressive military expansion; the simple fiery Arabs stormed over Iraq in 634, took Damascus in 635, Palestine in 637, Syria in 638, Egypt by 641; in 651 Khalīd, general of Abu Bakr, slew Yesdijerd III in battle and took the whole of Persia. Islām became the State religion there, and Mazdeism was for ever crushed, remnants of it fleeing to India.

By 645 Songtsen Gampo, Tibet's great ruler, had brought Buddhism to Lhasa, where it had long to struggle with the earlier shamanism of the Bön cult. Manicheism had already entered from the north and west, and certainly contributed its own elements to the complex now known as Tibetan Buddhism or Lamaism. The Manichean centre was more and more east and north of the Oxus, extending to the Pamir plateau. Called in to help the Persians, many Chinese embraced it, and by 650 it had reached China itself where, as Jackson points out, it held its footing for a thousand years. Having long been a victim of Mazdean hatred, Manicheism at first enjoyed Muslim sympathy; based on scriptures, it was a 'people of the Book' entitled to protection under Qur'anic law; its cult was extremely simple and in effect—despite the multiplicity of names —monotheistic; it claimed a single Prophet, condemned the use of idols, and rejected the worship of Saints, relics and the Virgin Mother.

But when Muʻawiya overthrew ʻAli's family and founded the Ummaiyad dynasty (661-750) at Damascus, everything from Iraq and Persia was suspect as pro-ʻAli, Shiite; the sect of the ʻZandīqs' (i.e., Tsaddiqīn, Elect) became a 'pernicious heresy', its books liable to destruction. The peace-loving followers of the gentle 'Kindly Light', Mani, again met persecution. Yet while the Muslims were unsuccessfully besieging Constantinople itself, the 'Doctrine of the Fathers on the Incarnation of the Word' was still able to quote two of Mani's Epistles—those said to be sent to Zebenas and to Kondaros the Saracen, which I cannot identify.

In about 650 Paul of Callinice and his brother John had founded in Armenia a semi-Manichean sect, known as the Paulicians, which was promptly attacked by Constans II. In 668, though some date this rather to 705, the Taoist book 'Hwa-hu-King', teaching the 'Three Times' and the 'Two Sources', was already banned in China for teaching later incarnations of Lao-tsü, one of which was as Mo-Moni (i.e., Mar Mani, the holy Mani). Between 670 and 692 Manicheism definitely entered Eastern Turkestan, where the Uighur Turks were mingling with Iranians and Scyths. Many of these were soon Manichean or Nestorian, but the majority were Buddhists—so the outer forms of the Faith slowly assumed a Buddhistic colour here, and in return undoubtedly influenced the Mahayana, specially in such sects as that of the 'Pure Land'. In spite of the insecurity of non-Muslims under Islamic rulers, the Denawars began after 690 to filter back in small numbers into Iraq.

An 'Aftadan' (*i.e.*, one of the *seventy* Overseers) or 'Fu-tuo-tan' in A.D. 694 carried through Kashgar, Kucho and Karashahr to the Chinese court his scripture, the 'Two Sources' (Per. *Do-bun-nāmag*; Turk. *Bu-iki-yiltiz*) which by A.D. 700 he had already translated into Chinese. By this time also in Maralbashi, east of Kashgar and half way to Aqsu, the Saka Kingdom had already a Manichean text in its own dialect; here the month of Buzadina (Bosanti) was a fast, two months had Soghdian names, and the State Religion was actually Manichean, though it viewed its rivals with a friendly tolerance it never itself received from others,[1] outside Central Asia.

At Constantinople in 695-698 Leontius said that the Manichean Canon included the Gospels of Thomas, Philip and the Infancy (all Gnostic in origin), and the 'Heptalogue' of Agapius, now about 350 years old. At some time during the latter half of this century, one called by the Muslims Abū Yahyā arRais was the Leader of the Faith (Arkhēgos, Imām).

5. **Eighth Century.** The Catholics still believed that Manicheism was strong in 'Africa', while it is doubtful if any openly professed the Faith as such there; yet it is true that dualistic modes of thought had deeply penetrated Christianity, and many who were not quite sure about God had no doubt at all about the Devil!

Islam was still rapidly expanding; already on the Atlantic shore by 700, it overran Spain in 711, having politically conquered Khiva and West Turkestan in 707. While Walīd I (705-715) was Caliph, one of the Manichean Elect, Zād-hormizd, founded at Ctesiphon a new sect, even stricter than the Denawars, and many in the hills of Media and Kurdistan joined him. His pupil Miqlāś, became the leader about in 722, of what was really a movement against the gradual secularisation of the Faith under its orthodox Leaders.

In 719 Ti-shö, King of Tokharistan, sent a great Manichean Teacher (*mozhag*) to China, recommending

[1] The friendly relations between Manicheism and its 'rival' religions in Kirghizia at this time are shown by the proximity of their Temples at AkBeshim in the Chu Valley, excavated in 1954-1955.

his vast learning to the Emperor and asking for him leave to build a temple there. Thus the Canon, perhaps nearly complete, came to China, and within two years there were in fact temples there for the ' Ming-kiao ', Religion of the Light, as it was called. By 729 the planetary week appeared in China, the days having Soghdian (i.e., Manichean) names, and Sunday also became a fast day (cf. GPM 57: 1); in 731 the document ' CMT ' was translated from Pehlevi by imperial order into Chinese. But things were going too fast; in 732 an edict refuted the Faith as a " perverse belief falsely styled Buddhistic "—Mani had here attained the rank of a Buddha!—and allowed its practice only to the foreign missionaries, called the ' Masters of the Hu of the West '. Yet the two favourite scriptures circulated freely in Chinese; these were the ' *Eul-tsong King* ' (probably Mani's Epistle, ' The Two Roots ') and the ' *San-tsi King* ' (or ' Three Times ', probably Mani's Epistle to Paṭṭiq, i.e., the ' Fundamental Epistle ' so well known to Augustine). These two gave the outlines of the myth in Mani's ' Wisdom ', and unhappily the same stress seem to have been laid on this element in the East as in the West.

Meanwhile the Emir Khalīd ibn 'Abdullāh alQasrī, under 'Umar II, let the Denawars settle freely in Baghdad, provided they kept clear of the extremist Miqlasis and were loyal to the famous Mihr (cir. 710-740), the orthodox Imam or Leader in Babylonia. This Muslim State support to the orthodox ' Mihriyand ' party led to a good deal of compromise in their way of living;

the adoption of Muslim names and customs became so frequent that after 724 Miqlāś led his followers into an open schism while Hisham (724-743) was Caliph in Damascus.

Their hatred for Ali's family had alienated the Ummayyad rulers from their Eastern subjects, and the loose character of several of the Caliphs combined with the definite check to Muslim advance at Tours in France, 732, to weaken their hold. Sedition rose and spread swiftly in Persia, especially in Khorassan, the Manichean stronghold, and in A.D. 750 Saffāh Abū'l 'Abbās overthrew the Caliph and founded his own Abbasid dynasty. Aided largely by them in the revolt, the early Abbasids showed great favour to the Manicheans, which led to further compromises and to an increase among the Miqlasi dissidents, while several Persian ascetic and Sufi sects arose in the East. At this time the Miqlasis recognised Buzurmihr as their Imam, while the Mihriyand followed Abu Sa'id Rahā, who came from Rai, the ancient Median capital and home of Zarathushtra's mother. Mansūr (754-775) continued the policy of toleration, and the orthodox Imam, Abū Hillāl adDehuri, an African Manichean, did all he could in his day to reconcile the Miqlasi schismatics, but in vain.

Meanwhile, fairly safe in their Armenian mountains, the Paulicians continued to increase, led by Constantine and Simeon about 730; a generation later their leader was Paul II, followed in turn by his sons Gegnasius and Theodore. The sect began to attract attention even in Constantinople. In Sicily Pope Gregory II (715-731) was still hunting for Manicheans to persecute, eager to extirpate what was now certainly well camouflaged under orthodox life and doctrine. The Faith had ceased to exist openly in the West and more and more tended to consolidate itself eastwards in Central Asia, though in 747 the work of Padmasambhava established Buddhism so firmly in Tibet as to leave no room there for Manicheism to spread.

At this time, 757, the Uighur Turks had an empire extending from the Tibetan border right across to the Yellow River, and in 760-780 Jouei-si and others were busy translating Manichean scriptures into their own Turkish dialect. With three other monks this scholar was sent to Turfan (Orkhon?), near Khocho, by the Qaghan of the Uighurs, Boghu Khan, or *toigän*, who had been converted at Honan-fu by some Manicheans in 762; in this eastern capital of the T'ang dynasty the 'Shapur-aqan', the 'Gospel', and the 'Epistle to Hata' (No. 65?) were then being read. That same year work began at Turfan on the Pehlevi Book of Prayers, the 'Mahrnāmag', we are told "on the order of the spiritual chiefs"; at this time the 'King of the Religion' (Ch. *Touan-Kong*), or Leader, resided (temporarily?) at Khocho, or Kao-'chang. The mission succeeded well; many thousands gave up Buddhism, burned its images, and became disciples of the 'Religion of the Light'. The Leader praised the zeal of Boghu Khan, and sent a Teacher (*mozhag*) and other monks to preach everywhere;

scriptures circulated in Pehlevi, Soghdian, Chinese and Uighur Turkish, and temples were rising in 768 at the capitals of Lo-yang and Tch'ang-ngan by a decree on 17th July. Three years later came the permission to build temples in four Tangtseu provinces—Hou-pei, Kiang-su, Kiang-si and Tchö-Kiang—for the "Light of the Great Clouds", whose monks wore white robes and coiffures. In May-June 799, the Manichean 'Masters' were ordered by the Chinese authorities to pray for rain.

Turning back to Iraq: by 764 Baghdad was founded, and within another eight years exact and literal translations of the Manichean works began to appear in Arabic; being anxious to gain something of Persian culture, the Arabs read these very eagerly. When many secretly embraced Mani's tenets, AlMahdi (775-785) ended the toleration with a savage persecution in which thousands lost their lives. The spirit of the time is well shown by AnNadim's laconic story; he writes (p. 338): "Now Muḥammed ibn 'Ubaidullāh, AlMahdi's secretary, was a dualist, and he confessed to that; then AlMahdi killed him." The Hermetists of Harran suffered at the same time. The prophet Hakem was then preaching in Khorassan. By 780 'Abdullāh ibn alMuqaffa was busy translating books from Pehlevi and Persian into Arabic, glossing them freely in a good style; this man, born at Huz, the capital of Fars, kept secret sympathies for the old Mazdean Faith in his heart; he even tried to write a book to equal the Qur'an. The famous Harūn arRashīd (785-809) actively persecuted the Barmecide house, said to be all Manicheans but one, and fond of pagan thought and the 'traditions of Mazdak'.

In about 765 Constantine V brought many Paulicians from Melitene to settle in Thrace, where they enjoyed full toleration and passed on their Manichean tendencies to the later sect of Bogomiles. Ten years or so later, we find Paul II's grandson Zacharias as their leader, and he was followed by Joseph and Baanes his disciple. With the blessings of Yazd-Mari-Aryānshā, the new 'Master' at Turfan, the priest Māri Yishū'-Aryāman and the deacon Māri Doshīst, one Nīshvarīg-Rōshan, son of the preacher Yazd-Āmad, in about 790 completed the 'Mahrnāmag', and by 795 appeared at Khocho a Turkish translation of the 'Travels of Amu (Ammōs)', the Apostle to Turkestan, and a Turkish life of the Buddha spread to the West, where strangely enough he was transformed into a Christian Saint!

At Kashgar in Iraq, Theodore bar Khoni issued his valuable 'Scholia' in 791 (K.), quoting the Syriac original of at least one of Mani's own books; we have used this extensively in our own GPM. At the same time Anastatius knew several of the scriptures personally at his Sinai home; it is clear that despite all the burnings copies still survived here and there in the West—and found people brave enough to read them. A very striking testimony to the reverence of the copyists dates from about 800 in Central Asia (cf. Müller: Handschriften, pp. 3, 5): "The Manicheans take the same care over adorning their Scriptures as the Christians over their churches. . . . I regret that these people insist on wasting precious silver to procure fine white paper and a brilliant black ink, that they give so much value to calligraphy and so encourage copyists, for in truth I have not yet seen any paper comparable to that of their books or any writing so beautiful." Even Augustine had paid like tribute in his day, four centuries earlier, referring to the gems and gold inlaid in their covers. Mani's last words to his Elect at Pargalia (§18), " Take care of my books ", were faithfully obeyed, even by the unknown villager who saved for us the three under the floor of his Fayum hut (MP., MH., and Keph.).

6. **Ninth Century.** By 806 we learn that the Uighur Manicheans drank only water and used no milk or other animal food, eating only in the evening. As an ' act of piety ', the Chinese built for them several temples.[1] About ten years later Tisong-detsen, King of Tibet, invited Indian Buddhists to his country to strengthen their religion. In 809 there was a rebellion at Samarqand, where the Manicheans now called themselves ' Sabaeans ' to secure toleration; Ma'mun (813-834), tolerant to sectaries, was even suspected by some of crypto-Manicheism; yet he threatened with death those who would not formally apostatise by spitting on a picture of Mani. During his time the Miqlasi leader was Iazdanbakht,[2] whose dreams were criticised by an

---

[1] On 22nd February 807, the Uighurs asked for temples to be built at Ho-nan-fu (Lo-yang) in Ho-nan, and at T'ai-yuan-fou in Shan-si; they were now treating with the Chinese on equal terms, one Qutlugh being the Imperial mason.

[2] The name means ' Grace of the Gods '.

orthodox writer, perhaps the Imam Abū Hilāl, in Epistle 59 addressed to the Hearers. When bidden to accept Islam, Iazdanbakht stoutly defended his right to freedom of religion. By about 830 he was succeeded at Ctesiphon by Abū 'Alī Sa'īd, under whom the books of the ' Zandīqs ' were again popular in Iraq; after him we find the name of his secretary Nasr ibn Hormizd, who continued to water down the tenets of the sect to resemble more closely the Mihriyand orthodox. In 843 there was, however, a wave of persecution in Baghdad, wherein seventy Manicheans died; as a disguise they began to wear the cap and sash of their Muslim neighbours.

Meanwhile, to the north, Nicephorus I gave all civil rights to the Paulicians in about 807, their leaders being now Sergius and Theodotus, who taught by letters a Christianized Manicheism. But in 812 Michael began a brutal persecution, killing ten thousand of those who would not curse Mani's holy name, and by 815 the Paulicians rebelled, crossing the frontier to Melitene under the rule of Ma'mun, who protected them; the persecution ceased again about 825.

In the East, after a banquet on 28th December 813, the Turkish Qaghan ' Pao-yi ' sent a message through Inanchu and his seven Manichean companions, with an escort of 3000 soldiers, to ask for the hand of Tai-ho, daughter of the Chinese Emperor Hsien-täng; this request was refused. When in 821 the new Qaghan was bold enough to send messengers to China to fetch the Princess to his court, the Manicheans were naturally suspected of political aims and fell from favour. Whereas in 820 Taher's Turks had established a dynasty in Khorassan favourable to the Manicheans,[1] and the pro-Buddhist kingdom of Tibet broke up in 839, at home disaster fell on the Manicheans. By 841 the Kirghiz took the Uighur capital, seized the Qaghan 'T'ai-houo' himself, and destroyed the State. There was a swift reaction in China; in 842 Manicheans were forbidden to live anywhere save in Kansu and the Uighur areas, and in 843 the Chinese princess was recovered from the Qaghan Ügä and taken home. Out of five temples in Yangtseu two were closed in 842, the monks being driven off to the north; in 843 an edict declared the 'Religion of the Light' illicit in all China, ordered the closing of all its shrines and the confiscation of all their goods, and the public burning by officials of their books and images. This naturally forced the Manicheans to meet at night and in disguise, the clandestine meetings producing vile calumnies and further persecution. During the next seven years, after several changes of fortune the Uighurs scattered to the south-east, the south and the southwest—to Turfan and Qarashar, and to the west towards Kutch'ar; they founded new Manichean States at Khocho, Kantcheou, Khotan and Turfan.

Around 830 Nicephorus of Constantinople was still able to use Mani's Epistles to Addas, Kondaros and

[1] Before 820 Ushrūsana, between Samarqand and the Jaxartes, opposed the Arabs and was taken by the Turks in 821, when they were called in by King Kāvus and his son Fadl, who later protected the Manicheans from Muslim persecution.

cxxvi

Zebenas—not identified in the list given by AnNadim. Photius (837-863), Patriarch under Michael III, denounced the 'Manichean' heretics who, fleeing from the cruelty of Theodore and Justinian continued to seek Muslim protection; about 850 some of the Paulicians rebelled and set up, under Karbeas and his son Chrysochir, the independent Republic of Tephrike allied to the Caliphs. In 862 Cyril and Methodius converted to Christianity Bulgaria, an area already saturated with Paulician ideas; but much of the old paganism survived underground for many centuries.

Round about 860-870, answering a querent in Ispahan, the Parsi scholar Martan-farrukh in his 'Shikand-Gumanig Vijar' refuted the Jews, Christians and Manicheans, giving a fair outline of the doctrinal scheme of the last. At the same time a valuable library was formed at Turfan—sermons, dogmas, rituals and scriptures, but unhappily no history—in Soghdian; parts of this are now in our hands. The Manichean books were still held a great danger at Constantinople. During the cruel persecution under Basil I (867-886) a new 'Abjuration' condemned by name the Epistles, Gospel, Treasure, Mysteries of Mani, the 'Apocrypha', Memorabilia, Commentaries, Heptalogue and Theosophy—though we need not suppose that all these were still extant there. This Anathema also named Mani's parents as 'Patekios' and 'Karossa', and his disciples Hierakas, Herakleides, Apthonius, Sisinnios, Thomas the 'Evangelist' (an obvious error), Boudas (? Addai), Herm(ei)as, Zakouas, Gabriabius, Hilarius, Olympius,

Zalmaios, Ianneus, Paapis and Baraias; many of these are already known to us. Four editions of a history of Manicheism appeared about this time—all lost now.

While Abū'lḤassan the Damascene was the Miqlasi Leader under Caliph Motammed (870-892), one AlYaʿqubi from Khorassan wrote a history of the 'Zandīqs' in 872, about the same time as a Persian dynasty, the Sofarids, took that eastern province. The actual scriptures of Manicheism now disappeared from the knowledge of the West altogether, after Peter of Sicily had visited the Paulicians and described their 'heresy' as simply Manicheism under another name.

7. **Tenth Century.** In 902 Ismaʿīl ibn Aḥmad the Samanid overthrew the Sofarids in Khorassan; Muktadir the Caliph (908-932) exiled all Manicheans from Iraq; many fled to the old refuge in Khorassan, others went with their Imam to Samarqand, where five hundred of them were soon arrested, to Soghdiana and Nukat in Ilak. Prior to this, AnNadim had known about three hundred of them still in Baghdad.

In 920 the Manichean Uighurs of Ch'en-cheou proclaimed Wou-yi as Emperor of China, being implicated in the Honan revolt against the 'Son of Heaven';[1] they were accused of celebrating vile nocturnal rites and again persecuted. By 950 those in Fukien were accused of using their books for sorcery, and on 4th April 951 a new embassy of Uighur Manichean Elect set out from Kansu with gifts to placate the

[1] Wou-yi was taken and beheaded along with Tong-yi and eighty others.

Chinese Government. In 961 their 'King of the Religion' sent more precious gifts from Khotan and West Tibet to the Emperor; by 971 they were busy in their white robes exorcising demons in China.

In 981-984 the Chinese envoy, Wang-yen-tö visited the Turkish areas and reported: " There are also Manichean temples there, and Persian monks who practise their own religions " (perhaps Nestorians?).

Meanwhile in 925 Persia had come under the rule of the Bouid dynasty, and by 930 the Manicheans had formed a powerful, civilised and prosperous State in Toghuzghuz; the ruler of the land, Nasr II (923-953), had become their convert. The Khorassan Government now resolved to extirpate Manicheans in their territory, but when the Toghuzghuz threatened reprisals on the more numerous Muslims there, satisfied themselves with the mere collection of the *jezia*—poll-tax. At this time Mas'udi of Baghdad knew four of Mani's books—'Giants', 'Treasure', 'Mysteries', and 'Shapur-aqan'. AnNadim in 940 found these four in the rich Baghdad library (?), together with the 'Pragmateia', the 'Precepts', and seventy-six Epistles. A little later, Mahbud, Bishop of Menbij, knew some of the books, and Gibrail ibn Nūh replied to Iazdanbakht's attack on Christianity.

In 940 the tottering Abbasids were overthrown by the Turks, while the Western Bouids, descended from the old Sassanids of Mani's day, controlled Baghdad; their love for science introduced a glorious age in Iran. In 977 the descendants of a Turkish slave formed at

Ghazni a dynasty that conquered Khorassan and, by 1050, much of North India.

Already by 910 the first Catharists, a Manichean sect of unusual purity, had heralded the second wave of Manicheism in the West. It was greatly reinforced about 960 by the preaching in Thrace and Bulgaria of one who called himself Bogo-mil, the 'friend of God', which had swift success there and soon spread into Bosnia, sending in a few years the neo-Manichean influences as far as Istria and round into Venetia.

A Chinese visitor noticed in 981-984 that Manichean temples were common in Khorassan, where about 987 Gardizi the Arab found the majority in the capital city still professed the Faith. He described how three or four hundred gathered daily in the house of the Prefect, probably a high church dignitary, to recite Mani's books, salute him, and then return home. All the Iranian and Turkish books in use there had been carefully copied. In 988 AnNadim published his wonderful 'Fihrist', a literary history of the Muslimized lands (N); he gave a most valuable account of Mani, his teachings and the history of his Faith—preserving many direct citations. He says that he at this time knew in Baghdad only five Manicheans, called the 'Achari', though many lived as 'Sabaeans' in the Iraqi villages, in Samarqand, and in other Eastern provinces.

In 996 the Turfan ruler was Arslan; he tried in vain to effect a marriage with the Liao dynasty. In 998 Mahmud of Ghazni drove Ilkan, King of

Turkestan, out of Khorassan, which now ceased to be a safe refuge for the dualists. Next year the Samanids in Mavaralnar fell, and in A.D. 1000 Biruni reported that it had taken him fourteen years to trace out in his Khiva home a copy of the 'Mysteries', called 'The Book of Books' by Rhazi the famous doctor, together with other parts of the Canon. Among the Western Uighurs most were still Manichean, so too many in Tibet and Turkestan, but few were any longer to be found further west outside Samarqand.

8. **Eleventh Century.** In about 1008 Emperor Lin-she-tch'ang slipped the two Manichean books already noted into the Taoist Canon, but this ruse did not succeed in winning toleration for the Faith. In 1019 this revised Canon was found secretly circulating in Fukien, and it was deposited in Lao-tsü's great temple in Honan, but this version made by Chang-kiun-fang was soon rejected by the Buddhists and Taoists, and in 1025 a new Taoist Canon was issued without the interpolated treatises.

By about 1035 Catharism was being openly taught near Turin in Italy, where many of the faithful were martyred at the stake as 'heretics'. Yet the neo-Manichean wave had spread strongly to France by 1050 and had swept over the Hungarian plains into Germany, and out from the Balkans to the Anatolian plateau. The corruption of many Catholic priests made great numbers of sincere Christians embrace it as a purer form of Christianity than their own. In 1061 many began to imagine Manicheism must have survived in

Africa under the Muslim rule, and several Popes vainly looked for it also in Sicily and South Italy.

To save them from some invasion, a well-preserved set of Manichean books, including the Hearers' ' Confession ' in Turkish, the long Chinese text derived from Addai's (?) Pehlevi, and a Code of the Elect in Chinese, were hidden away in a Kansu cave at Tün-huang, where they were found only in 1907 by European explorers. In 1092 Abū'lMa'ali found a copy of the ' Ertenk ' in the royal archives at Ghazni.

Under Mas'ud I the Seljuk Turks raided the Ghaznavid lands in 1037 and weakened their power; in 1097 they were able at Khiva to found a dynasty of their own under Atsiz. But they did not share the Uighur sympathy for Manicheism, which was by now fast dying out everywhere save in the Tarim Basin and in its Catharist form in the West. In 1056 the Bouids in West Persia and Baghdad fell; the last traces of Shapur's line vanished from history.

9. **Twelfth Century.** In Constantinople the orthodox burned Basil the Bogomile in 1118. By now Catharism had in Italy and France consolidated into a complete code of faith and ethics. So corrupt and vicious had many of the Catholic priests become, so worldly and greedy of money, that the people's revolt from them caused Catharism swiftly to become dominant in South France by 1150, and very strong also in Lombardy. In 1160 the Catharists celebrated the ' Bema '-rite at Köln in Germany, and in 1163 they were condemned by the Catholic Council of Tours; 1165 saw a public

debate between what now seemed like two rival Christian systems. Though the Catharists were condemned as 'heretics', naturally, they continued to grow in strength, and in 1167 they held a Church Council of their own near Toulouse, attended by their own five French Bishops and by two from Lombardy and Constantinople. In 1177 Raimond V of Toulouse invited a Roman mission to combat the growing Faith—the saintly life, devotion and kindliness of whose 'Elect' had won to them the peasants' hearts; and in 1180 a 'Crusade' against them was preached, which led to some persecution and devastation.

Further east, Shahrastani had a copy of the 'Shapuraqan' and the 'Book of Giants' in his Khorassan village, also a text written by the Manichean 'Imam' Abū Sa'id, and a 'Theology' by Abū 'Isā alWarrāk, who tells us that there were still followers of Mazdak in Samarqand, Tashkent, Ilak (Transoxiana) and Susiana. Some Manichean books were even known to Michael the Syrian in Antioch in 1166-1199. In 1183 the Ghaznavids fell, and Kharasmians overthrew the Seljuks in Iraq; the Ghori house in Afghanistan also came to an end about 1194.

In the Far East the Manicheans were involved about 1120 in Fang-la's revolt; their chiefs, we learn, wore a violet bonnet and black robes. About 1160 Hong-mai (1123-1202) called the 'Religion of the Light', started by Mo-moni the Fifth Buddha, a 'perverse sect', using his same two books in Fukien; in 1166 Louyeou (1125-1209) made a yet fiercer attack on it, petitioning the Emperor to stamp it out ruthlessly. He calls the Manicheans of his day magicians and demoniac deceivers, and complains that they hid under different names here and there in Western China, "deceiving the people who ran to them" because of their kindness. He tells us they were stubborn vegetarians, and thus tacitly condemned the meat-eating Confucius, and celebrated vile rituals by night; they taught of a 'Messenger of the Light' (Ch. *Ming-che*), used images and the books of sorcerers and impostors, which he had seen and condemned, though they used high official authorities for the printing and plate-engraving for them. Such books and plates must be burned at once, and anyone copying, painting, or engraving for them must be sent into exile for one year. He tells us the Manicheans wore white robes and black caps, and lived as batchelors; many of them were even soldiers or magistrates. Such should be given a month to surrender their pernicious books, images and vestments to the magistrates and so earn pardon, or a reward should be given any informer who brought them to suitable punishment.

10. **Thirteenth Century.** Papal legates vainly tried to convert the Catharists back to Catholicism in 1203-1204, and even St Dominic, living as a mendicant friar like their own 'Elect', had little better success in 1205-1217. In 1207 Innocent III let loose on them the so-called 'Crusade'; the men of North France invaded the South with brutal repression. At the capture of Béziers twenty thousand were massacred, of whom very

few in fact could have been Catharists, but war does not discriminate. When Carcasonne was taken, four hundred were burned alive and fifty hanged—all on the pretext of being 'heretics'; lynch law prevailed. So naturally the efforts of the friars, even the Pope's ' Poor Christians ' of 1209, could do little to win back the people to the ' Holy Mother '; as usual, repression only roused increased resistance. The ' Elect ' showed the utmost courage, visiting and consoling their people, just as the priests did in England in the later days of repression there; very very few of them fell away into apostasy. At Minerve, out of 140 of them 137 were content to be burned alive as martyrs, and at Casser all the sixty taken were burned at the stake (1210-1211). Simon de Montfort, leader of the invaders and archpersecutor, fell at the siege of Toulouse in 1217.

In 1229 Raimond VII surrendered, letting the Inquisition loose in his territories, and in 1232 the Dominicans undertook that wicked work. With the criminal zeal which brought an indelible stain on Catholic history, they allowed no defence whatever to the accused, and so thorough was their work that by 1240 there were only four thousand of the ' Elect ' alive in all Europe. The need for reform in Christendom had been stamped on, for a while, and the seed for the far more disastrous upheaval under Luther and his fellows had been sown in fertile soil. The murder of Peter, a Dominican and the son of Catharist parents in Verona, by unknown miscreants on the Como-Milan road, was made the pretext for a savage persecution in Italy also in 1252. So furious was the terror in Provence in 1268-1290 that by the end of the century Catharism was at its last gasp there, and the fairest province of the old Latin world was made a semi-desert.

Genghiz Khan (1178-1227) had broken the Seljuk rule in Khwarism in 1220, and their dynasty came to an end in 1231. In 1258 Hulagu's Tartars stormed Baghdad, ending the long-standing Caliphate there. About 1260 Kublai Khan's Mongols destroyed the Toghuzghuz Manichean State, and refused toleration to the Faith there; yet small communities still survived in Khotan and West Tibet. In 1280 Abū'lFaraq, known as 'bar Hebraeus', was able to refer to Manichean books still existing under the Seljuks in Mosul, where the Faith had been planted by Mani himself more than a millennium earlier. But by 1300 Arabic writers could speak of Manicheism only by hearsay; the Church had now vanished from their neighbourhood.

In the Far East about 1235 one Tsong-kien summarised and condemned the 'Two Roots' and six other Manichean books, named but still unidentified; he asked that the teaching and practice of this 'heresy' should be punished in China. The Taoist book '*Hwa-hu-King*' was again banned in 1258, and the Buddhist monk Che-p'an at that time referred to Manichean books—the last time they are spoken of as extant. However, in 1285 an enlarged '*Hwa-hu-King*' called Mani a reincarnation of Lao-tsü and also of the Buddha, son of Maya, (i.e., Gautama). This book was once again, and this time finally, banned; it was lost to us until a copy was found in the Tün-huang cave in 1907.

11. **The End of Manicheism.** From 1308 to 1323 Bernard Guy carried on the persecution of Catharist remnants, and by the time he had finished his work the most cultured part of France and Europe was a ruin and its beautiful language, Provençal, was destroyed. About a century later, in 1420, Catharism still existed in Bosnia and Bulgaria; indeed there are traces of it even now in the folk-lore and legends of the people here and there—even as far afield as in pre-revolution Russia.

In 1345 Baghdad became the Persian capital; 1387-1405 was the wild reign of Timurlang; in 1468 the Turkomans came to brief power in Persia until 1500, when Mirchond wrote the story of how Mani the 'Zandīq' painted his Gospel in an Eastern cave, and the Sufids came to the throne in that historic land.

The last but one important edict against Manicheism was that of 1368 in China; it condemned the Faith as a cult of sorcerers and forbade the making of Manichean paintings; at the same time it condemned the semi-political Societies of the White Lotus, and of the Black and White Clouds (*Payun-tsong*). In 1374 the Ming Emperor issued the following Code of Repression, which is the last important historical reference to the Faith: " Every Master or sorcerer who pretends to invoke heretical deities, writes out charms, pronounces spells over water, . . . evokes Saints, and gives himself the titles of ' King of the Doctrine ', ' Great Protector ', or 'Mother Instructress'—as well as the Societies which lyingly call themselves 'The Cult of Maitreya Buddha', 'The Association of the White Lotus', 'The Religion of the Venerable of the Light', 'The Sect of the White Cloud', etc., which all give themselves to the practice of heretical teachings that trouble good (order)—when they secretly keep images (of their Gods), burn incense to them, and hold assemblies where they gather by night and disperse by dawn, pretend to practise good works and (so) deceive the people—for the chiefs it (i.e., the penalty) is strangling, for those who follow them, to each one a hundred blows with a heavy club and deportation for life to (the distance of) 3000 *li* (i.e., 1000 miles)." East, as West, had found no way of competing with this unwanted fellow-religion save the brutal and infantile illogic of violence. I have no idea how many Manicheans perished under this Edict of 1374, but in 1390 it was repeated—and the 'Religion of the Light' disappeared.

Yet in 1646 we still hear in China of the 'Sects of the White Lotus and of the Black Cloud', wherein faint echoes of the perished Faith may have lingered; in 1813 members of the 'White Lotus' stormed the Imperial Palace in Peking, and in 1860 a Chinese book actually appeared, attacking Christianity and Manicheism as if they were equally live issues. Last of all, even up to 1911 a law was still in force in Vietnam (Indochina), proscribing the 'Religion of the Venerable of the Light', which could hardly have been existing there in actual fact.

12. **Recovering the Traces.** For centuries the absurdities of Hegemonius were our only source for knowing Mani the man, and the angry polemic of Western bigots, with St. Augustine's gentler and painstaking immaturities, our only source for his doctrine. The word 'Manichean' became a mere term of contempt for the ignorant to fling at one another, and the very existence of a world religion as great as Buddhism or Islam became the shadow of a memory; men thought it a wild and unimportant Christian heresy in the West instead.

With Flügel's fine work in Germany in 1861 the tide began to turn, and when in 1872 he published the Arabic 'Fihrist' even encyclopaedias began to do justice to Mani. In 1902-1904 the original Manichean documents found at Turfan began to be published by Müller (M) and Salemann (S) in Germany and Russia respectively; these taught us how far we could rely on the Christian opponents, and we found that their outline was in fact remarkably fair, all things considered—far better than their treatment of Gnosticism. In 1907 came the great discovery of the Tün-huang library, with its many priceless treasures. Using the new materials, Alfaric in 1918 brought out his masterly study on the nature and history of Manichean scriptures. Already in 1889 Kessler had laid the foundation for a true estimate of the Faith, and Pognon in 1898 had given us the valuable publication of bar Khoni's materials. In 1931 Jackson published his scholarly collection of 'Studies', many of them previously issued as papers in various journals. In 1933 came the richest haul to date; 3500 pages of original Manichean scriptures, largely intact, were recovered in Egypt—comprising the ' Psalms ', the ' Homilies ' and the priceless ' Kephalaia '. Much of this was published with exemplary speed and efficiency by Alberry and Polotsky, together with translations in English or German, in 1938-1940, the rest still, in 1955, awaits publication.

We have now adequate material for a total reassessment of the importance of Mani and his ' Religion of the Light ' to the history of human thought. Alberry himself in England, Widengren in Sweden, Henning and Nyberg in Germany, with Polotsky in Israel, have worked and are working on this material, which may yet be further reinforced by new discoveries, whether in Egypt or in the sands and caves of Central Asia. Mani's love for his own books, and the reverent care his disciples bestowed on them, must have saved many in places where they await our discovery and delight in this age of restless search for knowledge.

6. Why Was Manicheism So Hated?

After reading its history, even so sketchy as here outlined, one naturally asks Why. Eleven hundred years this Faith existed in the open somewhere, yet hardly ever was it free from persecution. Men and women gave their lives gladly for Mani's name from England (two were burned at York) and Spain to the eastern provinces of China. As Mani would have said, the world could endure countless worldly tyrants but was enraged at his very name and rejected his gentle yoke. What really caused this bitter insensate hatred?

Christians. Manicheism was long the strongest rival of their Faith, for it could parallel or excel all its assets. As a personal Redeemer, the deified Mani was not notably less attractive than Jesus; and by honourably incorporating Jesus in its own scheme it robbed Christendom of most of this its greatest advantage. The noble ethical code of the Gospels and Epistles was equalled or exceeded; the organisation was equally simple, centralised and charitable; the claims of its priests to superior wisdom and divine guidance were excelled by those of the Elect; the barely intelligible Jewish psalms were replaced by psalms and hymns of great literary beauty, more easily spiritualised and with the gentle lure of countless allusions to the 'mysteries' of the Doctrine; they were reinforced by the free use of congregational refrains which made the ordinary believer a sharer in actual public worship, and by a very wide extension of education which opened the Scriptures of Mani to countless believers everywhere. Calligraphy and accuracy and beauty in translation-work were further attractions to the Manichean books. The great reliance of Christians on fancied Jewish prophecies to bolster up their doctrines was undermined by the total rejection of the Old Testament by Manichean writers, if not by Mani himself; at the same time their free use of Jewish and Christian apocrypha (Alfaric gives a long list) naturally led to their being taken as Christian Gnostics and so accused of being merely 'heretics'.

Legitimate complaints against their teaching include the untenable idea of a 'corruptible God' implicit therein, repulsive to every philosophic mind of the age; the difficulty of the Trinitarian dogma was intensified by what looks like crude polytheism; their greatly exaggerated dualism—Evil or Matter being all but equal to God, as among many ignorant Christians even today —with its consequent hate of the body, led to the exaltation of virginity—already the mood of that age—and of asceticism in food, etc.; this was, of course, suited and practicable only for world-renouncers and monks. All religions have a substratum of myth, carried over from the childhood of the race, when "Where did it come from?" "Who made it?" are natural questions. The Bible stories of Adam and Eve, Noah and Jonah are adapted to the mental age of about six, but the Manichean myths were, in elaborating the grand Gnostic concept of Sophia and the Prodigal Son, even more childish and incoherent than these; and they were rightly rejected by an age which could produce an Augustine, an Origen, and the great Neoplatonists and Stoics.

The grand truth of God's omnipresence immanent in every speck of what we call 'Matter', though almost instinctive in lands permeated by Upanishadic thought, seemed merely funny to the less philosophic, less mature, West. To its spokesmen it seemed a fitting butt for sarcasm and for undergraduate humour—which sometimes transgressed the ordinary canons of decency.

But we must remember that Manichean vegetarianism was *imposed on*, and voluntarily adopted by, only the Elect—as it is equally imposed on the Carmelites today; it is no funnier in the one case than in the other, nor is it in either case sprung from hypocritical claims to purity. Ignorance of the real reason for its adoption—too subtle for superficial thinkers—does not justify ridicule.

Persecution started as soon as the Christians had power in their own hands under Constantine, and it drove Manicheism largely underground. The inevitable secrecy of their rites and the hiding of their scriptures from bigoted pyromaniacs gave the Christians the same excuse for inventing scandal against them as, under similar circumstances, the pagans had used against themselves. The known Manichean contempt for marriage, as entangling the Spirit still deeper in Matter, thus naturally led to charges of immorality and of sex-aberration—to which the little we know of the Manicheans in fact most emphatically do not point.

Lastly, the ignorance of the original languages of Manichean Scriptures among Christian priests and writers forced them to rely almost wholly on what had been translated and could circulate freely in their own Latin or Greek. Unhappily, the translators seem to have attached far too much importance to their Myth, whose absurdities were obvious to all but the pious believers; where they presented the devotional side, as in the books of the Psalms, the appeal was direct, and its effect was great and immediate.

But beyond all other reasons for the Christian hatred of Mani and his Church stood the simple fact that it alone—after the failure of the antifeminist Mithraism—could meet it as a rival on equal terms in nearly every phase of religious life and teaching, and far excelled it on the life after death.

Mazdean Parsis. Underlying all outer causes for their hatred for Mani was certainly the dark suspicion that he had secret political motives. A scion of the overthrown Parthian house, he could and did receive help and support nowhere in the Empire more than in the old Parthian homeland around Khorassan, and in Armenia where the fallen dynasty still survived. Loyalty to the Mazdean State of the Sassanids inevitably depended on loyalty to the Sassanid faith of Zarathushtra —in the face of which Manicheism could, in a warlike age, only seem a foreign innovation corrupted with Chaldean myths and contemptible 'Christian' effeminacies, like gentleness and humanity. Nietszche and Bahram I might well have become good friends!

Dr. Dhall, in his *Zoroastrian Theology*, lists specific oppositions between the rival faiths: (i) while Manicheism sought to draw the good Soul out of an evil world, Mazdeism taught the Soul to fight under God to banish evil from the world. (ii) While Mani said the flesh is evil and the Soul should flee from the body, Mazdeism says that only the passions are evil, and that the Soul must strengthen its body as an ally in the spiritual war. (iii) Mani held marriage impure, a hindrance to union with God, and child-bearing a sin that imprisons 'God' (i.e., the Soul) in flesh; Zarathushtra had taught that celibacy is a vice, and man's duty is to rear up children to be God's warriors. (iv) While Mani said that property tempts the Soul away from reliance on God and increases worldliness, Mazdeism holds that honestly earned and wisely expended wealth is meritorious and mendicancy is a hateful thing. (v) Mani believed in subduing the body through fasting and penitential prayer, while the Parsis hold that fasting, which weakens the body to be used in God's war with evil, is a great sin. The unbiased student can certainly see the truth in both points of view.

But the two great Faiths had much in common; their concepts of the origin of Evil, the ages of struggle and the eventual triumph of Good; the idea that God is manifest in great Forms, like the Ameshaspentas and the 'Emanations'; their ideas of the Saviour's descent to rescue the Light on which Darkness has aggressed, of the 'Maiden-Image' embodying the merits of the righteous in the hour of death, and of the ascent of the liberated Soul to Behisht, the Land of Light—and many many others, were almost identical. The enmity between them may well base partly on the envy of the Magi, intolerant of any possible rival system; but it seems equally due to blind patriotism and xenophobia as to any philosophic divergence from the people's norm at the time.

Muslims. At first they were attracted by the simplicity of its organisation, so like their own, its freedom from a ritualistic and idolatrous priesthood, as that of the Christians seemed to them, its reverence for Scripture so like their own for the Holy Qur'ān. It was only when, being identified with Iraq and Persia, it began to incur suspicion of alliance with 'Ali's fallen family, that it fell from the favour of the Ummayyads. The 'Abbasids came to power through a revolt in Khorassan, no doubt aided by the large Manichean elements there; so the early Sultans favoured it again, until they found that the lure of Persian learning to which Manichean studies led was slowly drawing important Muslims away from their own God-given Faith. Then intolerance became the rule; the Manicheans were henceforth safe only where as in Toghuzghuz, they were physically strong enough to threaten reprisals. Most fled from Islamic lands to the peaceful Tarim basin and the outlying plains of Khiva and Samarqand. Here they showed in their day of power that tolerance to be expected of them, and it was probably the ravages of Tartar and Mongol which at last blotted out the Faith. But on the whole the Muslims seem to have been the least cruel of all the enemies of Manicheism.

Confucians. Here too the causes for hatred were somewhat involved. First, the foreign origin, always enough to prejudice the somewhat complacent Chinese mind; then, the dark suspicion of hidden political scheming, for which the Manicheans in A.D. 821 certainly gave some grounds. As in the West, persecution forced them to meet in secret under the cover of night, and here too this led to charges of vile rites, sorcery by means of the names of foreign Gods, necromancy, and the like. The adaptability, necessary if a religion is to spread beyond its homeland, led to their adoption of Buddhist and Taoist legends, names and doctrines—and this led to Manicheism being regarded as a deceitful heresy. The strict vegetarianism of the Elect, and their ascetic life, seemed a standing reproach against the principles of their own great Prophet and Sage, Confucius; their very kindness and countless charities to the people seemed an underhand ruse to entice them away from the sound rules of life held by their ancestors from time immemorial—just as in our own times in the case of foreign Christian missionaries. China has always been suspicious of and hostile to innovations, particularly those coming from abroad.

7. Can a Religion Die?

In combating German militarism mankind has twice in our days been taught that violent resistance does not achieve its end; it merely spreads the evil into new fields of activity—the vanquished infect their victors with their own disease. Apparently 'the free world' has yet to learn that the same is true in fighting Communism—atom bombs and a 'sanitary cordon' only spread the unwanted system further and convert those most bitterly opposed to it.

"The blood of the martyrs is the seed of the Church," said Tertullian. Persecution may drive out from a body its weaker members, but it strengthens the strong and draws in brave and sturdy souls from outside. Thus the persecuted Faith grows stronger, the more its foes try to strangle it with their violence. Yet, in the story of Manicheism, history does show that a Faith *can* be destroyed by persistent and widespread brutality. The outer form of it at least vanishes from the earth, its name is no longer feared or hated by its rivals—it goes underground.

Where is Manicheism today? A superficial glance would answer, ". Nowhere; it is dead." Look again. The physical body of this great religion, once spread over the known portions of three continents, has indeed vanished. All physical forms and bodies are perishable, fleeting, even our own; all external churches and creeds, founded by infinite Wisdom, mediated through the goodness and labours of great Saints, to help, inspire and guide mankind on the road to God, they serve their time and later centuries—but at last they fade and disappear. Some still lingering on the earth are visibly doing that even now. Yet as the body of each one of us will vanish in its turn, dissolved back into the inchoate elements of earth, to be reused, modified, by our children's children, while the Soul lives on its timeless life under its own conditions; so too, while the names and forms of a Religion vanish, return to the vast ocean of the subconscious mind—thence to arise again and again, as Jung has shown us, in modified forms of human thought and faith—the soul of that Religion lives on unshaken in the dreams, aspirations and ideals of mankind.

It was so with Manicheism. Built upon the noble life, the love and devotion of the Founder and his early followers, formalised by the Scriptures which they left behind, encouraged to heroic self-abnegation and vigorous evangelism by the cruelty they always had to face, lit and rejoiced by the glory promised to the faithful after death's brief pains—the 'Religion of the Light' served its time and disappeared from our eyes. Yet the light of Religion still shines upon us and, being the inevitable product of the human mind, illumines even the humanist side of materialistic Communism as well, though it be the greatest seeming enemy of Religion in our present-day world.

Manichean thought survived—in the ascetic life of countless monks and nuns striving for sainthood against the restless clamour of the world, the flesh and the devil; in the passionate personal love for God as the Spouse of the human spirit so typical of Catholic, Sufi and Sikh devotion; in the fierce defence of God as being *all* Good, totally opposed to the very existence of any kind of Evil, which characterises many sects today; even in the childish love of fairy stories so typical of the seven-year-old, which produced the Myth of Man out of the rags and tatters of a hundred earlier forms, and which in our present world still fashions myths of other kinds.

cxlix

"The proper study of mankind is Man," said Pope; all that the human mind has produced is of interest to the truly catholic, i.e., the cultured, human mind. Whether that product of human thought still lingers visibly among us in the present, or has faded into the mists of a forgotten past, it is still our concern, still gives delight in its sympathetic study. The 'dead' religion is as vital as those still deemed to be 'alive'; "there is no death, what seems so is transition," the poet declared of the human soul, and it is equally true of every human thought. Like the wave from a stone dropped in the water, it goes on and on through all space and eternal time.

8. On the Rationale of Dualism

The way Dualists reason is well shown by the following epitome drawn from *Zoroastrian Theology*, by Dr. M. N. Dhalla, the eminent Parsi scholar, with which the Manichean would be in full agreement: " Evil is as complete and independent as Good, sharing with it the pairs of opposites. God cannot be the source of both, or He would be a contradiction and a chaos. If Evil comes from Him He cannot be all-Good or deserve our worship; if He is all-Good, Good only should exist; but Evil too exists, so it must be independent of His will. If He, for some purpose, wills both Good and Evil, then His will, He Himself, is imperfect; if He wills only Good, then someone else wills Evil, the Devil.

"To say God created Evil that man might choose and value Good, is to say He poisons men that they may seek the cure. The all-wise God would not will to create His own opponent; if He did not foresee the consequences of such a creation He is not omniscient; if He created Evil as a test or means of training, then He is cruel and not Good. The wise could not knowingly produce an enemy to afflict and even destroy men; the wise always act for the good and happiness of all. As the Devil is always for the hurt of all beings, God must have been unwise to create him. If God cannot uproot Evil, then He is imperfect, ignorant; but He is perfect and does know how to uproot Evil. Being both merciful, all-knowing *and* omnipotent, He both can and will ultimately destroy Evil.

"Quoting from Sg. 51 : 95-97 : ' If it be said that the Adversary was created originally good by Ormazd (i.e., God), from whom he afterwards revolted and became evil, [1] then it shows that the Adversary possesses a more powerful will than that of the sacred Being, since in that even the power of Evil is thus able to break His commandment and diffuse more harm in the world than the good of the sacred Being.' God should not then have created a rival thus to defy and to triumph over Him, and God is to blame for creating in the Devil so strong a will, tending to all evil. If it is to be compensated later on, this shows God's inefficiency, being unable to give happiness in Heaven without first giving misery in the world.

[1] The normal Christian explanation; cf. App. III. 17.

"God cannot be both Good and Evil, blessing and cursing, helping and injuring, nor could He harm His creatures and still be their Friend. All Evil comes from the evil spirit trying to take this world to be his own. God cannot create Evil and then punish men for falling into it, and still be just; no justice could inflict a boundless punishment for a limited sin, or give endless pain to His creatures for yielding to the Evil He has Himself produced. But as God *is* infinitely just, Evil cannot be produced by Him.

"If He is merciful He cannot let demons loose among His children to afflict and ruin them; if He can destroy Evil and does not, yet punishes the wicked, He is neither just nor merciful. He created the world for a wise purpose, for happiness, so He cannot will ruin and slaughter; this must be the will of a hurtful Evil spirit. If it be said Evil arises from man's perverted will and man is set up to frustrate his Creator's will to Good, this too is injustice, for when God has to punish the wicked He could not have created in them a will that leads to sin and penalty. Man falls into sin because his goodness is imperfect, corrupted by the Evil spirit. Evil is primeval and does not arise from the will of man, but is rather associated with the dominance of flesh over spirit "—or, as the Manichean would add, is inherent in the very nature of flesh, of Matter itself.

Answers to all this have been framed by those opposed to the dualistic view, but this is not the place for considering their validity or otherwise. It is a tremendous problem, the crux of all human philosophy, how to reconcile the omnipotence and omnipresence of Good, whereon faith must ever rely, with the obvious existence of its active opposite; and the last word thereon will probably never be spoken while man is only man.

9. The Organism of the Church

The Manicheans were organised in a five-rank hierarchy symbolised by the five-stepped 'Bema', and relating to the five stages of spiritual unfoldment in the human and Divine mind. On the pinnacle of this pyramid, like the Messenger on his Bema, sat the personal successor of the Prophet.

The **Leader** (Copt. *Arkhēgos*; Per. *Aēthrapaiti, Erpad*, High Prelate; Ar. *Imām*; Ch. *Fa-tchou*, the 'King of the Religion') was, like all the senior Manicheans, at first a wanderer among the churches. His diocese was the world from Spain to China, where the Faith had penetrated; his work was to encourage amid persecution, to prevent corruption of the Teaching, to guard against any falling away from the Founder's lofty ideal of life. The first seven Leaders died as martyrs, and then some fixed place where the supreme authority could be found was needed, so their successors came to reside at the capital Ctesiphon, and then at Baghdad—until they were forced by prudence to withdraw to the safer Samarqand, and finally, so it seems, to the Chinese borderlands.

1. Under this 'Father' were the twelve **Masters** or *Teachers* (Per. *āfūrēnṣar*; Ch. *afu-yin-sa*, or *mou-shö*; Pehl. *ḥrebatagān*; Sogh. *mwck'*; Turk: *mōzhag*). Like the Christian Apostles, each of these took one country for his scene of labour. There they organised the churches and, touring constantly from place to place, held the faithful loyal to their ideals. They were known as 'the Sons of Gentleness (or Patience)', and Chinese texts tell us they were in charge of the 'blessings', presumably of mankind.

2. Next, their sphere perhaps limited to provinces, came the seventy or seventy-two **Illuminates** or *Overseers* (Ar. *muṣammasîn*, the sunlit ones; Turk: *'ēspasag*; Per. *Khurōkhwān*; Ch. *hu-lu-hwan*). These were sometimes called 'Bishops' and were known as 'the Sons of Knowledge'; they were, we are told, in special charge of doctrine.

3. The third rank was that of the **Elders** or *Priests* (Pehl. *Atarwanān*; Per. *arghwāngān sāhpāsak*; Ch. *ngo-hwan-kien sai-po-sai*; Turk. *maghīstag*; Ar. *qissīs*, clergymen). They were called the 'Sons of Reason (or Intelligence)'; each was in charge of a single local church and responsible for reciting the scriptures, prayers, hymns and confessions of public ritual and worship.

4. We now come to the **Elect** (Per. *dēnāwar*; Pehl. *vicīdagān*; Turk. *dintar*; Ch. *ts'iuan-kien*; Ar. *ṣaddīqīn*, the true—a word which later corrupted into '*zandīq*' became a contemptuous term for dualistic heretics). These were called 'the Sons of Discretion (or Secrecy)',

doubtless because the esoteric teachings and explanations were entrusted to them. Unable to enter their Order, St. Augustine wrote against them with all the bitterness of frustration. Their other names in Persian—the Celibates, and the Righteous Pure Ones—bespeak the lofty character of their life, and down to the later Middle Ages among the Cathari their history belies the unworthy slanders of the Christian polemist, who saw his own boyhood vices reflected outward on the lives of others. They were easily picked out for persecution by their paleness and ascetic looks, and even by their enemies no word could be uttered against their gentleness, courage and nobility. They are compared in GPM 40-41 and in Keph. 83 to the Perfect Pearl sought out by the Divine Fisherman.

Like their superiors, the Elect too had to live lives of ceaseless wandering. The temples (Turk. *cāidān*; Ch. *tchai-t'an*, or *fa-t'an*) had a library, a lecture-hall, (*hermēneia*), a hospital, a place of worship, and a refectory, being five-fold like everything else Manichean. But they had no dwelling-rooms; the Elect took monastic vows to regard no place as their home on this material plane, but moved here and there preaching the Faith to all, and sleeping as guests of Hearers, or under the trees. Their only property might be a single black robe, to be replaced each year when worn out. They might not labour with their hands or earn a living, but must depend wholly on pious offerings, and when Hearers did not bring them any food on a certain day they might beg that evening. They must always deal humbly and gently with the outer world, and carefully avoid giving even the slightest pain or offence to animals or plants—so they naturally forswore meat, eggs, strong drink and agriculture, which includes weeding, pruning and the killing of insect pests. Their food was limited to a single meal a day, to be taken in the evening, with a light collation in the morning. They fasted very often and observed the great 'Chakhshapat-Fast' during the month when the Sun moves through Aquarius and Pisces, ended by the great Bema-Festival. They might not build or own a house, nor ever be alone by day or night lest the breath of slander blow upon them; nor might they even touch a member of the other sex, even while accepting food at her hands. A Manichean made no other distinction between men and women, it is pleasing to learn; and it is certain that the higher ranks were open to all alike. Apparently membership of this Order accrued to those able to control their passions and to live up to the very high demands the rank required of them.

5. Those who could not embrace these lofty ways of life formed the masses of the Manichean Church, the **Hearers** or *Catechumens*, of whom St. Augustine once was one, (Pehl. *niyōṣagān*; Turk. *nighoshak*; Ch. *t'ing-tchö*; Copt. *katēkhoumenoi*). They were known as 'the Sons of Inquiry (or Understanding)', and were bound by the simple code of the Manichean 'Ten Precepts', or Chakhshapat, and observed the Four Daily Prayers, adding the three optional 'hours' when they could. They undertook to protect and support the Religion, to

train for its service a child of their own, an orphan or a slave, to accept the onerous duties of the higher Orders. They were allowed to marry one wife only, and might labour in the fields, but were totally forbidden to take any part in war. Every Sunday was a fast to them till a common meal at sunset, and they spent most of the day at prayer or hearing the Scriptures read and explained; there was also a partial (?) fast on seven days in every month, Mondays also being days of prayer in honour of Mani's death that day. Kneeling, they offered to the Elect of their own local church a sacramental alms (*miyazdā*), consisting of wafers, with fruits and vegetables like melons, grapes and cucumbers, together with fruit-juices and sherbets, but of course no wine. The violence involved in producing these was no sin because dedicated to the purifying of the Light-Sparks through contact with the Saints (GPM 59: 2).

The fragment M 135 tells Hearers to "strive for the salvation of your souls so long as there is strength in your bodies", and to give one part of every day to social duties, another to their worldly business so as to keep the family above want, and the third part to their spiritual needs. A very noble picture of the dignity of the common Hearer is outlined in GPM 42-44 and 47. We can have no doubt whatever that great numbers of the men and women drawn to Mani's feet did much to live up to that high ideal and then, dying with their inner eyes fixed on their beloved Lord, went straight to dwell with him for ever in the lovely Land of Light.

10. The Books of Mani

Of most of these books we possess only a very few tiny fragments, so efficient was the work of the destroyers, and we are left for the most part to speculate on what they may have contained.

1. *Shāpur-āqān*, written first of all, and in Persian to honour King Shapur I and perhaps to assure him that Mani had no hostile political aim. It was probably written in A.D. 242, soon after he went to India; AnNadim, Biruni and Ya'qubi name it, but the Western and Coptic writers do not seem to have known it, at least under that name. Possibly it was largely replaced by later books, in the better-known Syriac. There is likelihood however that the Syriac ' *Apocrypha* ' (i.e., Hidden Things), noted by Photius and the 9th century Greek ' Anathema ' as Mani's fourth book, may have been a translation of this, for Manicheans were swift and efficient in translation work. It was, in fact, a Revelation, derived from Mani's ' Angel-Twin ', and must have contained a generally Gnostic type of cosmogenesis and eschatology.

Biruni gives us the opening passage (used in our GPM 30: 1), which evidently narrated the origin of the following revelation, with an account of Mani's own birth and his call to Prophethood. It probably included the long passage about death in our Appendix I preserved by AnNadim, and the striking story of the Last Judgment given in M 470-482; Ya'qubi tells us that it also described the Soul and the Universe. It seems to have been one of AnNadim's chief sources, including the long and unsavoury story of how evil took root in Adam's family. A fragment was found in a Turfan manuscript, probably part of the whole text.

2. *The Great, or Living, Gospel*, said by Mirchond to have been written and illustrated in a Turkestan cave during a one year's retreat, for an illustrated copy of it is probably the same as the ' Ertenk ' or ' Erjeng ' also called by Hadju Chalfa the ' Destūr-Mānī ' (Mani's Law), and in Coptic the ' Eikōn ', or ' Image '. It is generally given first place among Mani's books, and the Psalmist (MP. 46) says of it: " He has the antidote that is good for every disease; there are twenty-two compounds in his remedy, his Great Gospel, the good tidings of all those who belong to the Light." To this is added (MP. 139) that it is " the King of the Writings, . . . his New Testament, the Manna of the Skies, the Inheritance of the Earth (?) ". Yet neither Faustus nor Augustine shows sign of having heard of it.

Biruni tells us that it contained twenty-two chapters, each beginning with one of the letters in the Syriac alphabet; he complains that while it refutes all Christian beliefs, the Manicheans claim that it alone contains all truth. A Turfan list of books refers to the *Alaf* and *Tau* (first and last letters of the alphabet) Gospels and the ' Gospel of the Twenty-Two ', which included the story of Jesus. Another fragment gives us its opening words: " I Mani, the Messenger of Jesus the Friend, in the love of the Father, of the Glorious One " (cf. the opening words of the Epistle quoted by Augustine), followed by the extract from M 17 we have used in GPM 33: 2. To it also seem to have belonged several surviving fragments on the Crucifixion and Resurrection of Jesus.

But in fact we know *very* little of its nature or contents. Photius tells us that it distorted Christ's life in a docetic sense; Diodorus of Tarsus and Heraclion refuted this. A commentary on it was carried by certain Syrians to Armenia, says Samuel of Ani. It was well known later in the West, at least by name; an illustrated copy was in the royal archives of Ghazni as late as A.D. 1092. It is just possible, as Alfaric evidently thinks, that it was a sort of explanation of the lost ' Gospel of the Twelve ', as implied by Theodore Abu Kurra of Harran (Alf. 2: 36). Ibn'ulMurtadā shows that it began with an account of the almost omnipresent ' King of Light ' who " dwells in the navel of His world ". Ya'qubi adds that it treated " of Prayer and the means to be used to free the Spirit ", while Biruni puts in that it proclaimed Mani as " the Comforter foretold by Christ " and the " seal (i.e., standard) of the Prophets ".

3. *The Treasure of Life*, called in MP. 139 " his second great book, the *remedy* and the cures, . . . the shame of the Sons of Error "; on this MP. 46 has the interesting comment: " His waterpot is the ' Treasure ', the

'Treasure of Life'. In it there is hot water; with it there is also some cold water mixed." An Nadim calls it 'The Book of Vivification'. The work is referred to by most writers, from Hegemonius and the 'Kephalaia' down to the 13th century, and it evidently enjoyed popularity. The main theme seems to have been a detailed account of the Myth of Man; Ya'qubi says it taught "what parts of the Soul came from the pure Light, and what parts proceed from the vicious Darkness". From Mas'udi we learn that one chapter refuted the Marcionite dogma of a third, intermediary, Principle. Named quotations by Augustine, Euodius and Biruni deal with various incidents briefly told in our GPM 8: 2, 7, and 87; one of these is cited as from 'Book 2' and another from 'Book 7'. It is probable that the long extracts in Severus of Antioch and in S 9 derive from this book, and a long section of the Chinese 'CMT' is probably epitomised therefrom.

Evidently the need for a shorter version of the story was soon felt, and Epiphanius speaks also of a 'Little Treasure', while Cyril, Nilus and Heraclion mention 'The Treasures'. It is quite possible that the famous 'Fundamental Epistle' was in fact that epitome, or it may have been the even more enduring book, 'The Two Roots'. Ianou (? Innai) wrote a Commentary on the original longer version (Syr. *Sīmethā*), which acquired canonicity among later Manicheans.

4. *The Book of Mysteries*, whereof MP. 46 says: "His knife for cutting is the 'Book of the Mysteries'"—

which implies that it was largely a polemic or refutatory work, to prune away ulcerous doctrines from the world. AnNadim gives us a list of its eighteen chapters, which supports this idea; it evidently dealt with the esoteric life of Jesus (? from a Gnostic angle), refuted the special teachings of both Bardaisan and the Hebrew Prophets (as several later writers also aver), and clarified Mani's own relationship to his Gnostic predecessors. The nature of Soul and Body was defined and, according to Biruni who quotes from chapters 12, 13 and (?) 18, clearly it taught reincarnation as a purgatorial misery till the world's end; Biruni adds that Mani adopted this doctrine while in India. At least a part of the book was in the form of a dialogue between Jesus and his apostles, as often in Gnostic and later apocryphal literature. Alfaric deems it probably an answer to the 'Book of Mysteries' used by Bardaisan's followers.

Commented on by Abdial in the apostolic age, it was known to most authorities down to the time of Rhazi (A.D. 1000), who quoted from it with enthusiastic praise, as Biruni tells us. From AlIranshari the latter cites the passage we have used in GPM 25, from a context denying that Manicheans idolatrously worshipped the Sun and the Moon, which must have been a very early charge against them.

5. *The Pragmateia*, i.e., "What ought to be done ". AnNadim, not understanding this Greek word, simply transliterated it into 'Faragmaṭiya' and referred elsewhere to a Book of ' The Precepts of the Hearers ' with a chapter appended on those of the Elect. The book

is named by MP. 46 and called "his soft sponge that wipes away bruises", i.e., removes the injury done to Soul by the corrupt flesh. It probably covered in greater detail the ground of our GMP 54-66 and much of that dealt with in the closing chapters of the 'Kephalaia'. Augustine (AMM. 74), when speaking of "a rule of life drawn from an Epistle of Mani", is probably referring to one of the Epistles 2, 13, 14, 19, 21 or 11; but these in their turn probably summarised or expatiated on parts of this lost book. In his refutation of Faustus, Augustine often seems to be citing this book, which must have spoken of the fasts and feasts, the offerings to the Elect, the liturgy of hymns and psalms to be sung at home and in the churches, the rules for entry into Religion, the 'Ten Commandments' and the 'Seven Alms', the Precepts of the Elect governing their clothing, diet, non-possession and ceaseless homelessness. In the 'Preface' to the 'Kephalaia' it ranks third after the 'Gospel' and the 'Treasure'.

6. *The Book of the Giants*, which MP. 46 calls "his excellent swabs", i.e., perhaps, 'purifier'. It is said to have been written in Syriac and then translated to Middle Persian, thence to Soghdian, and so to Old Turkish and Arabic; and also from Syriac direct to Greek. It was known to the later Byzantine and Muslim authors and, as AlGhadanfar says, was full of stories of the great 'Giants' or 'Heroes', Sahm and Nariman, and of the fallen 'Watchers' of primeval times (cf. GY 2a), drawn from Semitic and Iranian folklore.

W. Henning, in his ' Neue Materialen zur Geschichter des Manichäismus ', in the Bulletin of the School of Oriental and African Studies (1943), vol. ii (cf. ZDMG 1936), collected many fragments of this book which had been found at Turfan and elsewhere, but it is hard to trace in these any coherent story. But there was evidently a close connection with the story told in 1 *Enoch*, Shahmīzād and Hōbābīsh being clearly the ' Semiazas ' and ' Khobabiel ' of the earlier Jewish apocryphon. In the ' Kephalaia ' (24, 27 ff, and 92-93) there are allusions to this book, the name of which in Middle Persian seems to have been ' Kawān '. The fragments we have are mostly in Uighur Turkish, Soghdian and Middle Persian. Apparently one section (M 363) told how Jesus brought ' the Religion ' to Shitīl (i.e., Seth-el), Mani's prehistoric predecessor, and Enoch himself is, in TM iii. 23 and M 101, 911, called " the Messenger "—' Khunoch Burkhan ' (cf. 1 Enoch 10, 17).

7. *The Book of the Letters*, called by MP. 46 " the narthex (vestibule) of every cure ", and by MP. 139 " the zeal of the Elect, the joy (?) of the Hearers, ... the Robe (?) of the . . . ., the judgment of the Righteousness ". It was known to AnNadim in the 10th century, and contained seventy-six ' Epistles ', mostly addressed to (or in some cases perhaps written by) individual disciples, or to churches—among which we may note India, Kashkar in Iraq, Armenia, Ctesiphon, Babylon and Ahwāz; while others are named by their subjects. These last are very numerous, and

seem to have covered the whole field of Manichean theology, ethics, liturgy and social customs. Nothing could better restore our knowledge of this vanished religion than the much-to-be-desired discovery of this lost book. We have in fact considerable portions of 'Epistle 7', 'the Great Letter to Patteq', thanks to Augustine's refutation of it; and 'Epistle 1', the famous book on 'The Two Principles, or Roots', must be largely on the lines of the first chapter in our present 'Gospel of the Prophet Mani'.

a. The Two Principles. This seems to have been the main source used by bar Khoni, Alexander of Lycopolis, Titus of Bostra, Theodoret of Cyrrha, and to have been used also by Severus of Antioch, AnNadim, and the compiler of the Chinese text 'CMT'. The Turkish Hearer calls it "this holy book of the Two Roots", and Tsong-kien says (13th century) that in it men and women are taught not to marry or converse together, not to rely on human medicines, and to be buried quite without possessions, even nude (JA 1913, pp. 354 ff). It seems to have covered much the same ground as 'The Treasure of Life', but without its copious details.

b. The Fundamental Epistle seems to have been the one Manichean work with which Augustine—as an African Hearer of the 4th century—was really familiar, and of which he possessed a copy. He gives us long verbatim quotations, including the first words, which definitely recall the opening of the 'Great Gospel': "Mani, an Apostle of Jesus Christ, by the providence of God the Father". This form seems to be modelled on that of St. Paul, but it was quite a usual mode of address in the formal Epistles of the age. The style shows the usual oriental overloading with metaphor, and the rather longwinded sentences usual with Mani —in whichever language he is translated. There is not the slightest doubt that Augustine has kept exactly to his text, so far as he goes. Unhappily, he breaks it off in the middle, and isolated citations elsewhere do not help us to restore with certainty the argument of the latter half of the book. But they do suggest a fairly close parallel with ' The Two Roots ', and seem to have covered the whole story of Satan's revolt, the creation of Man around a Spirit caught in Matter, the Mission of Jesus, and how Evil was deceived by his ruse and his disguise, and so on to the Last Day, with its Heaven or Hell as the fruit earned by every soul.

This book was known to Ephrem as the essence of Manichean faith, and it seems to have been the main source of Mardan-farrukh in his ' Shikand-Gumanik Vijar '. It is probably the book that was known in China as ' The Three Moments (i.e., Ages) ' and laid down by the Tün-huang Code and the ' Khuastuanift ' as vital for converts.

c. There are fragmentary references and citations from the Epistles to Hatā (M 733), and to Menaq (Menoch) the Virgin, Mēsōn (M 731) and perhaps a few others also.

8. *The Two Psalms*, called by MP. 139 " the Citadel of the Angels, the Life of the Living, ... the Day of

. . . . , the Salvation of the Hearers (?) ". In MP. 46 this book is coupled with 'The Words', and in the Preface to the 'Kephalaia' with 'The Prayers' of Mani—both of these being probably the same; it was probably bound along therewith. The 'Kephalaia' tells us that " these three Words are the expression of the whole Doctrine; all that has been, all that shall be, is written in them " (p. 5, line 28). It is just possible that from them are derived several passages we have used in GPM 36-37, 88, and they may well be reflected also in many passages of the 'Manichean Psalmbook', as also in S 502.

9. *The Prayers of our Lord.* This, noted in our Coptic texts along with the foregoing, was evidently unknown in the West. It may well be the source for the long prayers recorded by MP and the 'Kephalaia' as having been uttered by Mani in his last moments. I do not think it probable that AnNadim's daily ritual of prayer is drawn from this book—it seems in its tone late or definitely secondary.

11. The Sources of our " Gospel "

A. Coptic

Inevitably, the first and main source is the wonderful group of original Manichean books found in early Coptic translation in Egypt, so far as it has been available to me in published form.

clxvii

One day in 1930, a Cairo antiquity dealer offered Mr. A. Chester Beatty a bundle of inscribed papyrus, evidently very ancient and taken from bound volumes. His story was that it came from a wooden box in the cellar of a ruined house at Medīnat Mādī, in swampy land to the south of the Fayum. The damp, the crystallised salt in the desert water, the action of worms or 'white ants', did great damage to the manuscript, sticking the pages so fast together that some could be parted only in fragments. The costly wooden cover, probably once inlaid with jewels, had been anciently torn off, and the dealer himself had roughly broken the mass into smaller pieces, so as to find easier sales; indeed, it is a happy chance we have as much as we do have of this most tremendously important and unique find. Mr. Beatty at once bought it on the spot, entire, and handed it over for study to competent scholars.

The whole mass was neatly written, by several scribes, in the 'sub-Akhmimic dialect', on stout papyrus of very superior quality and buff-white in colour, slightly glossy in surface; it was bound together but not as a roll, in the form of a codex, as was already known to have existed even in the second century. It proved to fall into three natural groups of texts, most of which have now been published.

1. The long-lost '*Kephalaia* (Keph.)' (Copt. *ṅkephalaion ṁpsah*; i.e., 'Headings (of the doctrine) of the Teacher'). This book had been translated from Syriac, and was in the 5th century regarded as a part

of the Manichean Canon. It contains the record of conversations between Mani and his disciples, not included in his own books, and may well have been written by about A.D. 275-280; the Coptic manuscript has been dated to about A.D. 340. It, or the published part of it, contains 95 chapters on varied topics on 244 pages—some of these went to Vienna, while the bulk was printed with a German translation in 1935-1937 by Dr Carl Schmidt, H. F. Polotsky and Böhlig, in Berlin.

2. *The Manichean Psalmbook* (MP.), written clearly and mostly in one fine handwriting on pages in size 27 by 17.5 cms, the writing covering on an average a space of 17 by 10.5 cms. It is believed to derive from an earlier Greek translation, save for the ' Psalms of Thōm ', which seem to have come straight from Syriac and may well have been written by A.D. 290 and translated by A.D. 325, or earlier. The other Psalms, written by Herakleides and others, may have been translated by about A.D. 340. Our actual manuscript is dated by Schmidt at about 350-400; it may therefore even be a first copy of the original translation into Coptic. Many of the Psalms have metrical form and great literary beauty, while the parallelism of older poetry is also found; the majority use refrains and end with a victory-wish for certain saints or martyrs, among whom ' Mary ' is the most popular (possibly she was a relative of the copyist). The metres are simple and have analogy with those of ancient Egypt and the Syriac texts of early Mandean scriptures, to which the ' Psalms of Thōm ' are specially close. C.R.C. Alberry

published the Second Part of this book with an English translation in 1938; this has been available to me. Part One was then under study, and is said to have included liturgical psalms for Sunday fasts, for Vigils, and for the Paschal season—45 pages in all, while Part II contains 234 pages, including a fragmentary index. A few additions stand in another hand, and the index covers only part of the extant texts, which now include seven distinct collections with fragments of two others. This book is four centuries older than other known poetry in Coptic.

3. *The Manichean Homilies* (MH.), consisting of four very early books, of the utmost value to a portrait of Mani as man and as teacher. *The Threnody of Salmai* (Copt. *pthrēnos ṅsalmaios*) was written between A.D. 277 and 300, by a personal disciple; it bewails his cruel death and expresses eternal love for Mani. *The Story of the Great War* (Copt. *plogos ṁpnac ṁpolemos*) was written by Kushtai, Mani's personal secretary; it purports to trace the history of the Church through an age of persecution to the age of peace and righteousness, with an apocalyptic story of the return of Jesus and the Last Judgment. Based ultimately on the 'Little Apocalypse' of Mt. 24-25, etc., and directly perhaps on parts of Mani's lost 'Shāpur-āqān', it has close parallels with the apocryphal Jewish Apocalypses of Elijah, etc. *The Limb of the Crucifixion* (Copt. *pmeros ṁptewo ha-tstaurōsis*), apparently an all-but eyewitness account of events around Mani and his first two successors, from the death of

Shapur I in A.D. 273 to the death of Bahram II, who granted tolerance, in A.D. 294; it was certainly written within nine years of this event, before Innai's martyrdom in A.D. 303. At the end comes a short but fervent *Epilogue* on the greatness of Mani who, ascended to the Light-World, yet dwells with his Church on earth. The whole collection may have been put together by Amu (Ammos), who is named, and a collaborator; the Epilogue seems to have been added not much after A.D. 330 by the later editor, who translated the Syriac text into Coptic for the use of Egyptian Manicheans.

B. Chinese

4. *Moni-chiao Hsia-pu-Tsan* (British Museum Or. 8210/2659: cited as BM.). This is a long roll, 750 cms. in length, well preserved. On the back are an account of Amitabha's Light-Realm, and other Buddhist works, this bespeaks the friendly relations of the two Faiths at Tün-huang. Translated from ' Parthian ', which the translator calls ' Sanskrit ', into Chinese, it includes twenty-seven hymns out of an original three thousand. As Tao-ming converted couplets into quatrains, he much enlarged his source and preserved for us a complete collection of hymns of his selection, including several of apostolic age, by Sisin, Amu and others. Some have even a phonetic transliteration of the original to facilitate their recitation by those ignorant of the meaning of the ' Parthian '; most have rubrics guiding their use. W. B. Henning published an English translation in the

clxxi

BSOAS 1943 and JRAS 1926, pp. 116-122. There are in all 423 stanzas.

5. *Moni Kuang-fo-Chiao Fa-yi-lio* (i.e., Epitome of the Religion of Mani, the Buddha of Light), usually cited as ' Chinese Manichean Text (CMT.) '. This too was found at Tün-huang, by d'Ollone in 1908, and it was published with French translation and valuable notes by Chavannes and Pelliot in JA 1911, pp. 499-621, and JA 1913, pp. 99-383. This translation I have been content to use. Translated by Imperial order in A.D. 731, the manuscript we have dates from about A.D. 1000; it contains portions derived from Mani's own books, probably mainly verbatim.

6. *Rules for Entering the Religion* (CRER.), probably dating from the 8th century, were published by the same two scholars with a French translation in JA 1913.

C. Syriac

7. *Theodore bar Khoni's Scholia* (K.), written to refute Mani and other ' heretics ', contains long passages which are almost certainly direct citations. The relevant portion was published by Pognon in 1898 (*Inscriptions mandaites des Coupes de Khouabir*), and again in Corpus Scriptorum Christianorum Orientalium (Script. Syr. II, vol. 66)—which St. Mary's College at Kurseong, Bengal, very kindly made available to me.

8. *Ephrem Syrus*: Prose Refutations of Mani, Marcion and Bardaisan, in C. W. Mitchell's two volumes

(London, 1912); of this only extracts cited by other authors have been available to me here (Eph.).

9. *Titus of Bostra*; his refutation (cited as TB.), written in Syriac, has been available to me only in the Greek of Migne PG vol. 18, cols 1069-1264, kindly lent by St. Mary's College also, with many other sources.

10. *Severus of Antioch*, published in Cumont's Recherches sur le Manicheisme, vol. I (Paris 1908), for the most part available in translations only.

D. Arabic

11. *AnNadim's 'Fihrist al'Ulūm'* (N.), a study of the pre-Muslim literatures of the Islamic world, including a most valuable account of Manicheism from books and oral traditions extant in Baghdad late in the 10th century. There are ten large pages in the Arabic text, which was published by Flügel at Leipzig in 1872; his translation of 1862 was not traced out here. This work contains many verbatim and epitomised citations from the Scriptures, lists of the Epistles and of chapters in two books, and incidents from the history of the Church. AnNadim's attitude is very fair and factual.

12. *AlBiruni's India*, and the *Chronology of Ancient Nations*, both translated by C. E. Sachau, 1879; I could not find a copy of the Arabic text. There are several direct quotations from the Scriptures.

E. Iranian

13. *Shikand-Gumanik Vijar* (SGV.), in Pazend; Mardan-farrukh, the Parsi scholar about A.D. 860, reports

the Myth of Man. Jackson publishes the text, along with West's translation from SBE. vol. 24: 'Pehlevi Texts, V'. For a polemic writer, this author seems to have been very fair.

14. *Turfan Fragments*, found in Central Asia after 1902 and published in various books, of which I have had only citations to use, made by Jackson, Alfaric, Reitzenstein, etc.: Müller's 'Handschriften-Reste in Estrangelo Schrift aus Turfan', 2 vols., 1904, and C. Salemann: 'Manicheische Studien I, St. Petersburg, 1911, etc. Many of these fragments, being in Mani's original tongue, are probably his own words.

15. *W. Henning*: Ein manichäisches Bet-und Beichtbuch, Berlin, 1937, cited as BuBb.

16. *Andreas-Henning*: 'Mittel-iranische Manichaica aus Chinesisch-Turkestan', in 1932-1934—not available here in India.

17. *Mahrnāmag*, sadly broken fragments of a Liturgy, translated in the book of Alfaric.

18. *Injunctions of Mani*, in Pehlevi, a caricature issued by Atarpat in the 'Denkart', (III, 200: 1-13), and published with translation by Jackson. The author was minister of Shapur II, unable to look at Mani without hostile bias.

F. Turkish

19. *The Khuastuanift* (i.e., 'Own Confession'), found by Stein in 1907 in the cave temple known as the 'Hall of a Thousand Pillars' at Tün-huang. This is a roll

14 ft. 8 ins. long and 4 ins. broad, supported on a stick of hard wood. Tough paper of the T'ang period is covered in fine Manichean script, the leaves of paper being carefully pasted together to form the roll. It contains in all 338 short lines, and falls into 22 sections, each dealing with a particular group of sins. Another fragment is in Leningrad; this continues from line 28 but has no vowels written; it was published by Radloff in 1909. The whole text, with English translation, appeared in JRAS, 1911, pp. 277-314; in Le Coq's original publication it bears the number T. II. D. 178: 1-3. See our Appendix II.

20. *Türkische Manichaica*, by A. von le Coq (cited as T. II. D. etc.,), comprises fragments from Turkestan, many of them translated from Mani's original books. Here also I have had to rely on citations, with fragments only of the Turkish text.

G. Greek

21. *Hegemonius: Acta Archelai*, cited as 'H.', published in Migne's PG 10: 1405-1528. Here we have a reliable account of Mani's teaching as seen from a hostile angle, yet remarkably fair; Hegemonius adds a wholly fictitious story of Mani's life, which was unintelligently copied by later writers and has prevailed in encyclopedias even to our own days.

22. *Alexander of Lycopolis: contra Manichei Opiniones*, cited as 'AL.', a briefer but valuable outline found in Migne's PG 18: 414 ff.

23. *Theodoretus: de Fabulis Haereticorum,* cited as ' T.', an angry but accurate comment on the Myth Story, found in PG 83: 377-381.

24. *Epiphanius: Panarion,* ch. 66, found in PG 42: 29-172, and cited occasionally as ' E.'; this is a long-winded and almost wholly secondary account of very little value.

25. *Serapion of Tmuis: contra Manichaeos,* a writing of very little importance and found in PG 40: 90-924.

26. *The Greek ' Abjuration '* of the 9th century is found in PG 1: 1461-1472; it gives a fair account for its late date.

27. *Euodius: de Fide contra Manichaeos;* a few passages from his extracts from Mani's own books have been cited here.

H. Latin

28. *St. Augustine of Hippo* (388-405 A.D.), one of our chief hostile authorities. His facts prove correct, but his arguments are worthless and often childish. His chief books on Manicheism are: On the Manners of the Manicheans, (' AMM ') (Migne's PL 32: 1345-1378); against Faustus (' AF.') (PL 42: 207-518); against the Fundamental Epistle (' FE ') (PL 42: 173-206); on the Nature of the Good (' NB.') (PL 42: 551-572); and against Fortunatus (PL 42: 11-130).

29. *The Commonitorium,* an ' abjuration ' found in PL 42: 1154-1155, and translated in our Appendix III.

30. *Prosper's Conversion* from Manicheism, dating from A.D. 526 at Lyons, an important refutation or

anathema found in PL 65: 23-30, and in part translated in our Appendix III.

Through the courtesy of St. Mary's College, the rare and valuable set of Migne's Patrologies, Greek and Latin, was put at my disposal, and I was able to copy the texts of most relevant passages. Other important sources from which I had to draw materials will be found noted in the Bibliography. My work on gathering these materials was spread out over the years 1943 to 1954.

THE FRONTISPIECE

The speculative portrait of Mani here used is derived from a contemporary coin of Characene (near Maisān), whose ruler seems to have been a convert, combined with the Chinese portrait found in the cave frescos at Tün-huang, probably dating about A.D. 800, and another source. No claim for its absolute accuracy can be put forward, though it may not differ greatly from the actual appearance of the Prophet at about A.D. 255.

A BRIEF MANICHEAN CATECHISM

1. *How did this Universe come into existence?*
It has always existed on the subtler planes: Two Realms, one of Light ruled by God, and one of Darkness ruled by the Evil Spirit. When Evil irrupted into the Light-Realm, the physical universe was designed for their gradual separation.

2. *What are the ' Two Sources '?*
All existing things derive from one of these two: the infinite Light of spiritual Goodness, the bottomless Darkness of evil Matter, coexistent and totally opposed to one another.

3. *What is God?*
The infinite and ineffable beneficent King of the Light, manifesting Himself in vast cosmic Powers or Emanations to overthrow the aggression of evil Darkness on His spiritual Realm, and also immanent throughout the universe.

4. *Has the physical world any real existence?*
Certainly it is real, but it exists only until its purpose is achieved by the separation of the Light and Darkness. Compared with the Light-World's eternity, it is only a fleeting shadow dissipated by the dawn.

5. *Is it Good or Evil?*

It is a mixture of Good and Evil, Spirit and Matter, Light and Darkness. So it will be dissolved when these eternal opposites are separated from each other, the Light having been cleansed of all contaminating shadows.

6. *Why was it created, and by whom?*

The Divine Mind, or 'Living Spirit' fashioned it as a means of liberating Soul from Matter, the Light-Sparks of God from the enslaving Darkness—through the practice of the twelve virtues and the loving labours of the Luminaries or Saviours.

7. *What is Man?*

Man is a divine Spirit imprisoned in a body of flesh created by the demons to ensnare his divinity in their world of darkness.

8. *What is the Individual Soul?*

The Soul is a Spark of God's Light, a part of His very Being, separated off from Him to be absorbed into the darkness of Matter and gradually to refine and purify as much of it as possible. Divine in source and end, its powers are limited while held captive in the body.

9. *What brought the body into being?*

Charmed by the spiritual beauty of the Light, the demons of the Darkness tried to capture it for themselves; so they made the body, to draw the Soul's attention away from God, its full perfection, to the lower pleasures of the flesh.

10. *What is Sin?*

clxxix

Sin is the Soul's disloyal turning from God to Matter, accepting the sensual delights in place of spiritual ecstasy. Certain acts which tend to this have been listed as sins—such as violence, sex-lust, and possessiveness.

11. *How did Sin come into existence?*

Intoxicated by the Light of God, the Evil Spirit rebelled against Him and sought it for himself. This egoistic act of pride was the fountain-head of all Sin.

12. *Is Matter eternal?*

Yes, it has existed from before time, and will survive time itself. But it is only now that it is in revolt; it will at last be vanquished by the Spirit, bound for ever in the Abyss, its Powers totally destroyed.

13. *What are the ' Three Moments '?*

The Past, wherein Evil and Good were wholly separate from each other; the Present, wherein the former's aggression has caused a mingling and confusion of the two; the Future, wherein they shall again be separated—the Light in eternal peace and bliss, the Darkness in the ruin of perpetual captivity.

14. *Why did God create the Individual Soul?*

To cooperate with Him in freeing all Light or Spirit from its slavery to Matter, herself the first, by warring ceaselessly with spiritual weapons on Evil everywhere, and by helping to refine and uplift all beings—human, animal, plant and even mineral—through intimacy with the holiness of Saints. This, then, is our duty on earth.

15. *How was Soul imprisoned in the flesh?*

Sent forth by God to enter and subdue rebellious Matter from within, the Soul is caught and swallowed up by the evil powers of its Darkness and forgets its real nature and its mission. Thus it becomes a miserable and helpless slave.

16. *How can it become free?*

By uprooting the desires those evil powers personify, and by gradually refining and spiritualising itself from all that is gross, material, it will at last be freed.

17. *Can it do this unaided?*

Possibly, but in fact the Soul is helped at every stage by God's grace and the assistance of His Saints.

18. *How does God help it to be free?*

Manifesting as Intuition in the Soul, as the light of Conscience and of Grace, He works from within, eliminating the vices and dark desires, and planting the fragrant flowers of every virtue in the heart.

19. *What disciplines should the Soul follow?*

The mortifying of the flesh by chastity and prayer and fasting, the observance of total harmlessness, and a life of humility and loving kindness, with purity of thought and diet.

20. *How does the Evil Spirit gain control of a man?*

When his mind is off its guard, evil thoughts and desires enter in through some weak point in his nature, opened by some sense-impression; then they encroach step by step until the whole has been corrupted.

21. *How does the Divine Mind free him from that control?*

Entering the heart through the spoken word of God's Messenger, it replaces all downward with upward tendencies, all vices with the opposite virtues, until the whole nature henceforward is a pure throne for the Christ to reign upon over his life.

22. *Has Man the power to choose aright?*

His power is limited only by the effects of his own past choices, which set up a habit only the utmost effort can break. This effort is made possible by the awakening call of God's Messenger—Mani, Jesus, or another.

23. *Is there such a thing as 'Fate'?*

Fate or Destiny results from the Individual Soul's past choices of action, and it binds until those actions have been undone by other actions. It is therefore ultimately under our own control.

24. *What causes the instability of moods?*

The Soul is sometimes nearer to Spirit, at times to Matter, according to the prevailing planetary aspects in its horoscope, and to the purity or coarseness of the foods it allows the body to consume.

25. *What is the reward of righteousness?*

The purifying of the Individual Soul from all defilement, and its victorious entry upon eternal life in the blissful Land of Light with God and all the Angels and happy Souls.

26. *What happens to the wicked?*

Those who deliberately prefer Evil to Good make the freeing of the Soul from Matter impossible for themselves. Then they take birth after wretched birth in Matter, till they become so grossly material that there can be no escape. And that is Hell.

27. *So Manicheism teaches Reincarnation?*

Yes, as a Hell, or as a purgatorial suffering involved in being attached to the fleshly body and its delights. Love for the body necessarily causes its reproduction age after age.

28. *How do Rebirths come to an end?*

When the Soul turns from bodily desires to a full yearning after the Spirit, from worldly pleasures to devotion for God, His Messengers and His Church, it can no longer be born on a material plane, nor can it even wish to be.

29. *What is Death?*

Death is the temporary or final release of the Spirit from its material prison. When the Light-Spark is purified, death is its entry on eternal bliss and glory in God's Realm of Light.

30. *What happens to the Soul at death?*

The good, pure, righteous Soul is adorned by the Angels in its robes, crowns and garlands of light, and led into the Light-Kingdom; ordinary Souls are driven back on the paths to rebirth in the physical world; evil Souls are dragged by the demons into their hells of darkness, fire and misery.

31. *How does God check the victory of Evil?*

He Himself comes forth in some Divine Emanation to war upon and overthrow the Evil, or He sends a Messenger of the Light to encourage and strengthen men in resisting it.

32. *Can true Knowledge be given by another?*

The Saint or Messenger of God comes to enlighten men with the Teaching and the Ethics, the 'Wisdom' and the 'Righteousness', which lead to freedom. But only those in whom the Intuition, or 'Light-Mind', is awake will welcome or benefit from his Message.

33. *What, then, is the Teacher's part?*

To awaken the Soul to its own latent divinity, to guide it on the purifying path, to carry it through the liberating door of death into the endless glory of the Spirit.

34. *What are the Qualifications for this Path?*

The knowledge that one is the Soul and not the Body, a firm resolve to live only for the spiritual aim, devotion to God and His Church which keeps that resolve a living power in the life, loving humility and gentleness to all, and persevering effort for self-purification.

35. *Is it necessary to renounce the world?*

Yes, for its attractions must be overcome and ultimately its standards and ways of living be abandoned; no, in the sense that it is here and in the world that the Church, and each component Soul, must labour for God's plan of liberation until its purity has set it free for ever.

36. *Is there only one code of life for all Manicheans?*

The ordinary moral and religious law is binding on all alike, but the 'Elect', who resolve on swift treading of the Path, have voluntarily embraced for themselves a code of higher standards.

37. *How does man find God?*

Roused by God's Messenger from the drunken sleep of fleshly ignorance, he realises his identity with Spirit and his temporary bondage to the body; then he resolves to be free and patiently works at his own liberation—refining his thoughts and practising all spiritual virtues till he is pure enough to see God in the hour of death.

38. *Where then is God?*

As eternal King of the spiritual Light-Realm, He dwells transcendent over all that is; as manifest in the Powers of the Light, He wars for its total liberation from the aggressing Darkness; as immanent in every atom of Matter everywhere, He awaits that liberation which He alone can bring about.

39. *Has He any real Temple?*

He is immanent in everything and manifested there to the seeing eye; therefore God's Temple is the universe and every particle within it, sacramentally, but more especially is it the heart of the Saint who longs for Him.

40. *What are the Gods and Angels?*

They are Emanations or Expressions of the nature of the One God, the King of Light and Father of all, come forth from Him to bring about His final victory over Evil.

41. *What is our relationship with them?*
They aid our struggle to escape the darkness of Matter, and we must not fail to reverence, love and worship them as our Champions, Protectors, Friends.

42. *Who are the ' Messengers of the Light '?*
Saints and Prophets sent by God from age to age to teach men the truths of life and how they can attain to Him in whom alone all happiness is found.

43. *What is the Church?*
It is the organised assembly of the faithful Souls called by God and His Messenger to choose the Light, and to labour for its freedom everywhere from the Darkness. It is a wonderful Unity in Him, based on Love and Wisdom fully shared.

44. *What happens when Soul is wholly freed?*
The physical worlds created for its freeing cease to exist, the Light becomes supreme, while the Darkness and all Evil, together with those who choose to merge therein, are forever subdued or sunk into oblivion.

45. *What is the Final Goal of all life?*
The freeing of the Soul from all defilement, so that it shines with God's pure glory and can live eternally in the bliss of His realised Presence and a sort of mystical unity with Him.

46. *Is this a Dualist Religion?*
Most certainly it is, in the fullest possible sense, for Good and Evil, Spirit and Matter, Light and Darkness are eternally independent and opposite Forces, between which every Individual Soul must choose.

47. Can you sum up this Religion in a few words?

It is the teaching of God's Prophets which awakens the Soul to a knowledge of its spiritual nature, so that it strives under its guidance to purify and free itself from the defilements of material darkness and ignorance.

LIST OF ABBREVIATIONS

A and M	Ancient and Modern
AF	Augustini contra Faustum
A. Fort.	Augustini contra Fortunatum
Akkad.	Akkadian
AL	Alexander of Lycopolis
Alf.	Alfaric
AMM	Augustini de Moribus Manicheorum
App.	Appendix
Ar.	Arabic
Av.	Avesta
Bab.	Babylonian
Bir. Chr.	Biruni: Chronologies
Bir. Ind.	Biruni: India
BM	British Museum Chinese Hymns
BSOAS	Bulletin of the School of Oriental and African Studies
BuBb.	Bet- und Beichtbuch (Henning)
CE	Catholic Encyclopedia
Ch.	Chinese
CMT	Chinese Manichean Text
Cod. Greg.	Gregorian Code
Cod. Iust.	Justinian Code.
Copt.	Coptic

Cor.	Epistles to Corinthians
CRER	Chinese Rules for Entering Religion
E	Epiphanius
Eccl.	Ecclesiastes
Eno.	Books of Enoch
Eph.	Epistle to Ephesians
Eph.	Ephrem
Eth.	Ethiopic
Ezek.	Ezekiel
FE	Fundamental Epistle
Gal.	Epistle to Galatians
Gen.	Genesis
GG	Gospel of the Gnostics
GGS	Gospel of the Guru-Granth Saheb
GH	Gospel of Hermes
GI	Gospel of Islam
GJ	Gospel of Jesus
Gk.	Greek
Gk. Abj.	Greek Abjuration
GMC	Gospel of the Mystic Christ
GP	Gospel of the Pyramids
GPM	Gospel of the Prophet Mani
GY	Gospel of Israel
GZ	Gospel of Zarathushtra
H	Hegemonius: Acta Archelai
Haer.	Augustini de Haeresibus
Handsch.	Müller's Handschrift-Resten
H.E.	Eusebian Histories of the Church
Heb.	Epistle to Hebrews
Hip. Ref.	Refutations by Hippolytus

Ign. Eph.	Epistle of Ignatius to Ephesians
Isa.	Isaiah
JA	Journal Asiatique
JAOS	Journal of the American Oriental Society
Jn.	John
1. Jn.	First Epistle of John
JRAS	Journal of the Royal Asiatic Society
K	Scholia of bar Khoni
2 K.	Second Book of Kings
Keph.	Kephalaia of the Sage
Lat.	Latin
Lk.	Luke
LXX	Septuagint Version
M	Müller's fragments
Mahr.	Mahrnāmag
MH	Manichean Homilies
Mir. Man.	Mitteliranische Manichaica
Mit.	Mitchell
Mk.	Mark
MP	Manichean Psalms
Mt.	Matthew
Müll.	Müller's book
Mus.	Muséon
N	AnNadim's Fihrist
NB	Augustini de Natura Boni
N. T.	New Testament
O. T.	Old Testament
Parth.	Parthian
Per.	Persian
PG	Migne's Patres Graecorum

Phl.	Pehlevi
PL	Migne's Patres Latinorum
Ps.	Psalms
q.	quoted by
Rev.	Revelations
Rom.	Epistle to Romans
S	Salemann's fragments
SBE	Sacred Books of the East
Sg.	a Parsi work quoted
SGV	Shikand-Gumanik Vijar
Shahr.	Shahrastani
Skt.	Sanskrit
Sogh.	Soghdian
Sol.	Solomon
Syr.	Syriac
T	Theodoretus
T. II. D. etc.	Turkish fragments from Turfan, etc.
TB	Titus of Bostra
Thes.	Epistles to Thessalonians
TM	Türkische Manichaica
Turk.	Turkish
ZDMG	Zeitschrift für die Morgenlandische Gesellschaft

Ordinary abbreviations, common in all books, are omitted from this list: e.g., lit., i.e., A.D., etc.

SYNOPSIS

Chapter One: THE MYTH OF THE SOUL. 1. There are two eternal Opposites: Good and Evil, Light and Dark; 2. The evil Darkness having irrupted into the sphere of radiant Goodness, 3. God brought about a mingling of the Soul—a Spark of the Light—in dark Matter in order finally to overcome the Evil. 4. In great agony the Soul cried out for aid, and the Christ came down and, showing its divine origin, woke it from the sleep of illusion. 5. As the theatre for its gradual release, the physical world was brought into being from the blend of Spirit and Matter, 6. the human virtues being designed as the means of liberation, 7. drawing the Soul up to God by way of the Luminaries (human teacher and divine Enlightener) and the Ideal of humanity. 8. The very beauties of creation are used to awaken its aspiration and so to tend towards release; 9. to check this trend the Dark Powers invent the counter-attraction of sex-desire and the host of fleshly delights. 10. Incarnate Man, imprisoned in the body's dark desires, is enlightened by the Messenger of the Light, 11. who plans and builds the horoscopic sphere as the field for his gradual escape from its planetary bonds, 12. until when all Souls who so desire are freed the balance is destroyed, together with the whole root and source of Evil, and Righteousness is restored to sole unchallenged power at last.

Chapter Two: POWERS OF HEAVEN AND HELL. 13. The one true God is the eternally blissful Father of the Light, 14. who manifests Himself in threefold Aspects running through the whole of life and form, 15. and in many Emanations, the first of whom is maternal pity and understanding, 16. and the second a comradely fellowship that rewards the efforts of the Soul, 17. the third constructs the details of the life which the final victory of Righteousness will crown. 18. Then comes the Demiurge, who fashions the environment of that life, ths *kṣetrajña* wherein the Soul must fight till victory, 19. followed in turn by the Soul's five Qualities or Aspects—the clear Intuition, 20. the penetrating power of Thought, 21. the mighty heroism of Reason overwhelming dark illusion, 22. the kindly Consideration, 23. and the steadiness of Decision or Will, based on the commonsense of worldly experience. 24. To aid their work comes forth Enlightenment, personified by the radiance of the Sun and in the twelve Virtues of the godly life, 25. taught by the glorious Messengers divine and human, 26. and so led from the darkness of ignorance to the glorious light of Holy Church, the communion of the Saints, 27. over which preside the perfect chastity of a beauty that captivates even demons from their evil schemes, 28. and the immaculate incarnate Word of God, Jesus the beloved Light and Friend of all, first Rose in the Father's Garden, the life that shines in every form. 29. Against these glorious Beings the Evil Spirit dares to rise, helped by the corrupting demons of Greed and Wrath and all their host.

Chapter Three: MESSENGERS OF THE LIGHT. 30. To rouse men to spiritual life, God sends an unbroken line of Messengers of whom Mani himself is one, 31. and they can be recognised by their perfection in virtues and by five glorious attributes. 32. Their work is to purify the heart of every evil, and to enlist the Souls in the mystical unity of the Church, 33. but those who understand and who yearn for freedom will alone benefit by their labours. 34. Great among these Messengers was Jesus, who liberated countless thousands, gave his life as a sacrifice for perfect Love, and founded a living Church; 35. now has Mani shone forth, the new Enlightener, who comes to renew and complete the work of his predecessors, to the joy of all suffering Souls. 36. Greatly indeed has Mani laboured, more than all before him, to enlighten, comfort and bless all beings with the Truth. 37. What can be compared with the glory of the Spiritual Teacher who frees the Soul from the misery of its darkness, 28. and dwells evermore among his children as their Guide, their Friend, and King, helping them by absolution to new efforts on the spiritual Path and to the joyful confidence of a certain final victory? 39. His love for us is a perfect reflection of God's infinite Love for all, a sacrificing ecstasy of Love.

Chapter Four: THE CHURCH OF THE LIGHT. 40. The Elect are those who take on themselves the higher laws of a life of strict asceticism and total harmlessness, sharing lovingly with others the spirituality they gain; 41. they are a link between heaven and earth, so we should not worry about any human frailties that they may show. 42. The Hearers are those who try to live noble and abstemious lives of devotion to God and to His Church; 43. those who are really sincere are the glory and strength of the Religion, 44. while those who live in the world with the perfect detachment of the Elect share their glory and are liberated in this very life. 45. To share what we have with others is the greatest joy, and thereby also we gain a fuller possession of our graces and build up the spiritual oneness of the whole, 46. the happiness of which is our one real aim. 47. Enriched and served by such worthy members, the Church will tread the path to a future glory that can know no limit.

Chapter Five: THE WAY OF RIGHTEOUSNESS. 48. The Soul in bondage recalls her heavenly origin and remembers why she came down to mingle in the world, 49. whereby she has now become entangled in the toils of flesh and kept away from God, the Source of all bliss, in constant chains of birth and death. 50. To the Soul thus imprisoned comes the loud summons of the spiritual Enlightener or Guru, calling her to return to her Father's Land of Light on high, 51. and reminding her of the transitory worthlessness of embodied life. 52. The Soul at once arises and determines to renounce the futility of flesh, and to carry out the liberating work for which she came. 53. But as only the Free can liberate another, the Soul cries to God for aid in this agelong struggle against the gloominess of Evil, 54. and the Messenger from God tells her how to carry on the fight until success, 55. encouraging her to face all the difficulties and oppositions which her efforts will arouse—for only struggle can prepare for rest, and suffering for joy. 56. Nor should she be anxious at the ebb and flow of her changing enthusiasms, which are due to the planetary aspects and the varying purity of her food and outer contacts. 57. Fasting can give great help in subduing the cravings of the flesh, 58. and so can constant joyful prayer and aspiration, 59. and generous kindness with the giving up of properties which fetter the Soul to earth; 60. the highest road is a total harmlessness which carefully protects even the humblest spark of life from ruthless clumsiness. 61. Gentleness and integrity of heart are the twin attributes of all the Saints, 62. and of those who are wholly devoted and will certainly attain the goal. 63. In them the Divine Mind works to transmute their human qualities into the Divine, to establish in them the Image of the Father of the Light, 64. in any one of His five great Forms, manifesting the primal Faculties of Mind in helpful wisdom for the uplift of our whole creation. 65. It is a long hard fight to be free of all that would drag us down, but if we struggle steadily and bravely from today the final victory is sure, 66. and the Soul finds herself liberated from the world and lifted into unison with God.

Chapter Six: LIBERATION OF THE LIGHT. 67. The final battle is when the body makes its last attempt to hold back the escaping Soul from the joy of death. 68. The hour for that fight is very near, and the Soul eagerly looks forward to its entry on the higher life, 69. bidding its earthly friends rejoice in its dawning bliss rather than mourn for the form about to disappear. 70. But this last struggle demands all her strength and more, so the Soul calls for help to her beloved Lord, who is bound to help His devotee in the hour of need, 71. for she has given her whole life in His service, crucifying the clamours of the flesh. 72. So close has always been the union of their wills that the Soul feels she goes to her beloved Spouse to become wholly one with Him;

73. the Lord indeed assures her that He will be ever with her and guide her into every bliss. 74. Thus inspired, she breaks the chain that holds her down, 75. and while the demons of the Darkness flee in dismay receives the tokens of her victory, 76. when every deed and motive stands revealed to the pitiless gaze of the awakened conscience in the light of the eternal Law of Righteousness. 77. Joyfully the released Soul goes on her bright way to Heaven, and the ecstasy of spiritual Marriage, 78. carrying with her the blessed memories of all that her love for God has helped her to achieve, the reward for which is now the eternal Presence of the Lord and all whom she has loved. 79. The Lord Himself leads her into that blessed Land, 80. where she shares the infinite blessedness of the redeemed, 81. sending back to those left behind a cry of joy that stirs them to like efforts, that they too may come to that which she has won.

Chapter Seven: THE END OF THE WORLD. 82. At last the Light-Sparks will all be freed and the Darkness overthrown; 83. then will be revealed the perfection of our Humanity which reflects God's loveliness, 84. and incorporates every Soul capable of forming part of that great beauty. 85. This world is growing old and hastens towards decay, from which we can easily see how near the Consummation must have come, 86. when the Souls will face that final tribunal which puts apart for evermore the Darkness and the Light, and frees Righteousness from the contaminating cruelty of Vice and Ignorance. 87. Those who prefer to join the powers of the Darkness have their will; they are made one with it and share its gloomy fate. 88. Mani implores the millions of humanity to hear his call, to choose the Light and so avoid the misery of the Darkness; he does all he can to win them round, but the decision rests in their own hands. 89. Not one of those who seek for God, who yearn to be of His, can ever fall away, for the petty merits of his own life are infinitely enriched by those of the Church's Saints to whom he has attached himself; 90. the faithful therefore speed happily on the tide which runs to the feet of God and the realm of endless peace and joy.

Chapter Eight: EPILOGUE. 91. How can we adequately thank the God-inspired Teacher who has opened these infinite glories to our hearts, and who constantly guides and strengthens us till we can enter on our joy? 92. It is only by a full surrender of all we have and are to that divine Master and the Church that he has formed on earth that we can give a token of our love and gratitude. 93. But more than all else our adoration pours forth to God, the Source of every Good, the loving Father of our Souls, the King of Paradise, 94. whose loveliness is too sweet for us even to comprehend, whose power and omnipresent love and wisdom draw our hearts continually to Him. 95. Let us then aspire ceaselessly to return to Him along the path of Righteousness laid down by His Messenger to us, and so shall we attain the endless joy and peace of His radiant Presence and merge our very beings in His love!

CONTENTS

	PAGE
The Gospel of the Prophet Mani . . .	vii
Preface	xi
Introduction: The Third Century—Mani, the Messenger of the Light—Mani, the Man and His Work—Sisin and Innai, First Manichean 'Popes'—Manicheism down the Centuries—Why Was Manicheism so Hated?—Can a Religion Die?—On the Rationale of Dualism—The Organism of the Church—The Books of Mani—The Sources of our "Gospel"	xvii
A Brief Manichean Catechism . .	clxxvii
List of Abbreviations . . .	clxxxvii
Synopsis	cxci
Contents	cxcvii

CHAPTER ONE: THE MYTH OF THE SOUL

1. The Two Sources, 2. Darkness Invades the Light Realm, 3. Soul Enters Matter, 4. The Rescue of the Soul, 5. Creation of the Sky and Luminaries, 6. The Role of the Virtues, 7. The Work of Moon and Sun, 8. The Maiden of the Light, 9. Man Comes from the Demons, 10. The Coming of Jesus, 11. The Great Builder's Work, 12. Last Things 1

	PAGE
CHAPTER TWO: POWERS OF HEAVEN AND HELL	

13. God, Supreme Father of the Light, 14. The Holy Trinity, 15. The Mother of Life, 16. The Friend of Lights, 17. The Great Builder, 18. The Living Spirit, 19. The Custody of Splendour, 20. The King of Honour, 21. The Light-Adamas, 22. The Glorious King, 23. Atlas the Supporter, 24. The Third Envoy, 25. The Sun and the Moon, 26. The Column of Glory, 27. The Light-Maiden, 28. Jesus, 29. The King of Darkness 45

CHAPTER THREE: MESSENGERS OF THE LIGHT

30. Earlier Messengers, 31. Signs of a True Messenger, 32. The Work of a Messenger, 33. Is Acceptable to Some, 34. The Mission of Jesus, 35. Mani's Birth Brings Joy, 36. Mani's Mission, 37. The Glory of Mani, 38. The Bema-Festival, 39. Love Divine 88

CHAPTER FOUR: THE CHURCH OF THE LIGHT

40. Who are the Elect? 41. The Glory of the Elect, 42. Hearers of the Wisdom, 43. The Greatness of the Hearer, 44. The Perfect Hearer, 45. Mystical Unity of the Church, 46. Prayer for the Religion, 47. The Religion's Glorious Future. 130

cxcix

PAGE

CHAPTER FIVE: THE WAY OF RIGHTEOUSNESS

48. The Fall of the Soul, 49. The Body is a Prison for the Soul, 50. The Awakener's Call, 51. Death is Inevitable, 52. The Soul Resolves, 53. And Appeals for Aid, 54. The Way to Life, 55. Courage under Suffering, 56. Fluctuating Moods, 57. Fasting, 58. Prayer, 59. Holy Poverty and Almsgiving, 60. True Harmlessness, 61. A Sure Path, 62. Sincerity of Heart, 63. The Work of the Light-Mind, 64. Five Kinds of Masters, 65. Exhortation to Spiritual Effort, 66. The Soul is Righteous Now . 156

CHAPTER SIX: LIBERATION OF THE LIGHT

67. The Agony of Death, 68. The Righteous is Called, 69. He Comforts His Friends, 70. And Prays to Jesus for Help, 71. Having Always Preferred Him to the World, 72. The Bride to her Spouse, 73. The Lord's Reply, 74. The Soul Breaks Free, 75. Deathbed Scenes, 76. Individual Judgment, 77. Joy of the Freed Soul, 78. Depart, O Manichean Soul! 79. Jesus Takes her Home, 80. The Land of Light, 81. The Triumph of a Holy Death 207

CHAPTER SEVEN: THE END OF THE WORLD

82. The End is Near, 83. The Last Statue, 84. Perfect Justice will Prevail, 85. Signs of the

	PAGE
End, 86. The Universal Judgment, 87. The Fate of the Wicked, 88. The Messenger's Appeal, 89. None of the Faithful Perish, 90. The Path of the Redeemed	254

CHAPTER EIGHT: EPILOGUE

91. Thanksgiving to Mani, 92. Total Surrender, 93. The Eternal Infinite, 94. Is Endless Love and Sweetness, 95. Mani's Last Message	276

Appendices: I. *Fragments of the Scriptures*: The Coptic Summary of the Myth, From " The Fundamental Epistle ", Severus on the " Two Sources ", AnNadim on the " Two Realms ", The Soul is Aroused, From " The Treasure of Life, Bk. VII ", The Work of the Great Builder, The Vivification, AnNadim on the Religion, AnNadim on the Three Kinds of Death 295

II. *Khuastuanift, the Hearers' Confession* 326

III. *Anathema against Manicheism* . 336

IV. *Fading Footsteps of Manicheism*: The Bogomile Book of John, Extracts from a Catharist Gospel, Extracts from the Yazidi Books . 340

Index 363
Bibliography 369
The World Gospel Series 373

CHAPTER ONE

THE MYTH OF THE SOUL

This great parable, like those of the Prodigal Son in the Bible and the fallen Sophia and the sleeping Prince in the Gnostic books, tells how the human Soul, a 'spark' of divinity, came into the exile of flesh, of ignorance and helplessness. The story begins by stressing the total contrast between Spirit and Matter, Good and Evil, Light and Darkness; then it tells how the condescension of the one and the arrogance of the other led to the two being mixed in a real 'bondage'. Then we learn how, to separate the fallen pure Spirit, God devised the machinery of the universe and the virtues, which gradually refine and free the Soul from its chains, with the aid of His 'avatars' and Messengers. At last, when its work is ended, the 'world' ceases to be, Good triumphs, and Evil is for ever made harmless or destroyed.

1. The Two Sources

1. There are two Sources[1] (K. 313 : 13-14) unborn and everlasting (T. 1 : 26), God and Matter, Light and Darkness, Good and Evil

---

[1] Syr: *tryn hww kynyn*; the Gk. word used is *phusis*, nature. These two are the fountains out of which all comes, both good and bad, respectively.

—in all ways quite opposite, for the one shares nothing with the other [1] (E. 14), God being good and having nothing in common with Evil [2] (H. 24). For while the Light is a good Tree full of good fruits, Matter is an evil Tree bearing fruits consistent with the root [3] (T. 1 : 26). Now the fruits of that evil root are fornications, adulteries, murders, avarice and all evil deeds, . . . which God has not planned (H. 17). (It is) as when two Kings are fighting against each other, being enemies from the first, and having each his own property (H. 7).

2. Now the Good Source dwelt in the Region of Light, and He was named the 'Father of Greatness',[4] and His Five Glories [5]

---

[1] Gk. *hōs kata mēden epikoinōnein thateran thaterōi*; Theodoret has: "God is remote from Matter and knows it not at all, nor Matter Him". The Chinese version reads: "In the Former Time there are yet no heavens and earths: solely Light and Dark exist, one apart from the other. The nature of the Light is Wisdom, the nature of the Dark is Folly; in all their movement and in all their rest there is no case where these two Principles are not opposed" (CRER. 2a). Cf. also App. I. 3. They are, in Chinese, the *Eul-Tsong*.

[2] "God excels more in Good than Matter in Evil" (AL 2).

[3] Cf. the Good and Bad Trees of Jesus in Mt. 7:17-20.

[4] Syr: *Abhā de Rabbūthā*; Phl: *Pīd 'ī vazurgīi*; Ar. *Abū'lKabīr*; Gk. *Patēr tou megethous*; Copt. *piōt n̄te tmn̄tnac*.

[5] Syr: *şekīnāth*. These 'Five Tabernacles' of God are parallel to the five aspects of the human mind or soul, variously named (cf. GPM 3:1 etc.). They are also directly related to the five

THE MYTH OF THE SOUL

were dwelling with Him: Mind, Knowledge, Reason, Memory, Will (K. 318 : 15-17); and there is no limit to the Light from above, nor to the right or left (N. 329 : 9-10). And lined up with God there are other Powers, just like handmaids, all good: the Bright and the Light and the Above—all these are with God (AL. 2).

3. But the Evil Source, named the 'King of Darkness', he was dwelling in his Dark Earth, in its five worlds[1] (K. 313 : 18-19): Smoke and Fire and Hot Wind and Danger-Water and Gloom; . . . nor is there limit to the Darkness from below, either to right or to left (N. 329 : 8-10). And with Matter are the Dim and the Dark and the Below . . . and others like them, all evil (AL. 2).

Mani begins by proclaiming the eternal co-existence of the two opposing Forces of Good and Evil, each with its own set of five manifestations to express its own nature. Though limited by the very existence of its antithesis, Light is the greater and more powerful in all ways save those tainted with the evil nature.

"Sons of the Living Spirit" (GPM 19-23), *i.e.*, of the Demiurge—the Mind being in fact the actual creator of the universe, as in GA 6. The Syr. names are *haunā, madde'ā, re'yānā, maḥṣabhthā* and *tar'ithā*; the Gk. names are *Nous, Ennoia, Phronēsis, Enthumēsis, Logismos*; the Copt. names are *Nous, Meeu, Sbō, Sajne, Makmek*.

[1] The dark equivalent of God's Five Glories; the various languages name these phases of Evil variously. See also the account in GPM 29.

2. Darkness Invades the Light-Realm

1. Now after many ages Matter was divided against itself,[1] and its fruits against each other (T. 1 : 26); Matter became disorderly, and it produced and increased and kept emanating many Powers.[2] So then, having increased, it pushed on, not knowing the existence of the Good (TB. 1 : 12); and when the War had begun, and some were chasing while others were being chased (T. 1 : 26), as it rose up more and more, it saw both the earth and the light of the Good (TB. 1 : 12); in the course of conflict the Darkness passed beyond its own boundaries (H. 7).

2. So after each of them had come to know the other, and the Darkness had begun to contemplate [3] the Light, having as it were acquired a passion for the better thing,[4] it

---

[1] Gk. *diastasiasai pros heautēn tēn hulēn*, disharmony being an essential quality of Evil, and so too of Matter.

[2] *Cf.* the picture given in GH 2 : 2. There was a close parallelism between the various soteristic doctrines of the age.

[3] *Or*: gaze at.

[4] The aggression was actually prompted by a desire for self-betterment natural after a sight of God. So too the ambition to be "like Gods" led to the fall of Adam in Gen. 3:5, and the demon "conceives in his heart a desire for Enlil-ship" in the Babylonian Genesis (Heidel: KB. 6:1, p. 46). "They were induced to invade God's Region because of the beauty they saw" (AF. 21:10).

pressed on to mingle with it (H. 55), in order to attain to what was not its own [1] (TB. 1 : 12), and even desired to occupy this Source, dispossessing God.[2] . . . Moving irregularly, for such is according to its nature, Matter came to God's own place, or to Light and Brightness and all such things (AL. 3, 8), and resolved to proceed, as it were, to a certain haste, taking this as a proof of familiarity with the Light (TB. 1 : 20).

3. Therefore Matter rushed on, with the demons and the phantoms,[3] and the fire and the water, against the Light that had appeared. . . . Then having gazed at the Light, they (began) to enjoy it and to wonder at it, and to resolve on warring against and seizing it without delay, and on blending their own darkness with the Light (T. 1 : 26).

4. When the King of Darkness had decided to go up to the Region of Light, then the Five

---

[1] "The Race of Darkness coveted the Realm of Light bordering on their territory, and from a desire to possess it formed a plan to invade it . . . wishing to take by force the good they desired for its beautiful and attractive appearance" (AF. 19 : 24).

[2] So too in GY 1 A, Satan's pride led to his fall and ruin.

[3] *or*: mental images, Gk: *meta . . . tōn eidōlōn*; there may be here some hint of the word 'idol,', false religions and idolatry being one of Evil's strongest lures.

Glories trembled (K. 31 3 : 21-23), and God was alarmed at the mass charge;[1] for He had no fire to strike with bolts and lightnings, nor water to cause a flood,[2] nor iron, nor any other weapon that can be devised (T. 1 : 26). So then He determined to avenge Himself upon this (Matter)[3] although lacking evil to punish it with, for there is no evil in God's House (AL. 3).

Aggressive violence is of the very nature of Evil, so on its first view of the beauty of its Enemy it naturally tried to attack and secure for itself what seemed so attractive. As in many other faiths, Pride led to the first rebellion against the Divine Order. And the absence from God's nature of all such evils as the mind or the means for violence gave the Aggressor an initial advantage in the fight for supremacy, so that God had to plan some other way to restore the menaced peace and happiness of the universe.

[1] Augustine taunts Faustus: "The repose of your God (is) shaken by the revolt of the Race of Darkness and suddenly disturbed by the attack of enemies." *Cf.* the Coptic: "The Great (?) Father therefore took the first step. He strengthened all His Angels, saying, 'Assemble, all of you, and guard yourselves from the eye of the Evil One which has looked up!' One of the Sons of Light looked from on high and saw him; he said to his rich brethren: 'O my brethren, the Sons of Light in whom there is no waning or diminution, I looked down to the Abyss, I saw the. . . . Evil One, the Son of Evil, desiring to wage war. . . . I saw their cruel armour which is ready to make the war, I saw snares set and nets cast and spread, that the Bird which should (come) might (be) caught (and that) it might not escape from them'" (MP. 204 : 4-21).

[2] *i.e.*, the fire that burns, the liquids which drown and poison, instruments of evil.

[3] "God too has desires, but they are all good; and Matter likewise, which are all evil" (AL. 2).

3. Soul Enters Matter

1. Then the Father of Greatness considered and said: "From these five worlds of Mine I will not send the Five Glories [1] (even one) of them to the War, because they were created by [2] Me for rest and peace, but I Myself will go out and see to this revolt" (K. 313 : 23-27). He devised the plan against Matter just because it had desired the Good,[3] ... to send on that account towards Matter a certain Power which is called the Soul, which should wholly permeate it [4] (AL. 10, 3). Now the Soul in men is a part of the Light, while the Body is of Darkness and Matter's handiwork; ... and there are these names

[1] In Chinese *wou-pen-ming-shen*; the Greek Abjuration calls them "the five Splendours gifted with intelligence", and the Syriac, "the five bright gods" (*hamṣā alāhē zīwānē*), the Turkish, "the Light gods" (*yaruq tängrilär*). The Gk. list is also found in the Gk. Acts of Thomas.

[2] *lit* : to, for.

[3] Even Evil merited upliftment by its aspiration to attain the Good; God used the Soul, a part of His own Being, to pervade and refine at least most of Matter.

[4] "The member of God has been mixed with the substance of Evil, to repress it and to keep it from excessive ferocity" (AMM. 36), and " before the establishing of the world, Souls were sent in this way against the Hostile Nature in order that, subduing it by their suffering, the victory might be given to God " (A. Fort. 2 : 22). Augustine, though hostile, seems usually a fair summariser of Manichean dogma.

of the Soul: Mind, Thought, Intention, Consideration, Reason (H. 7, 9).

2. So that there might be no more evil for it but all things good (AL. 12), having taken a certain portion of the Light, He sent it out as a sort of bait and fishhook for Matter [1] (T. 1 : 26)—a Power of the Good, not yet sensible Light but an emanation of God [2] (TB. 1 : 20). (First), the Father of Greatness called forth the Mother of Life,[3] and (then) the Mother of Life evoked the First Man;[4] then the First Man called forth his five Sons, like a man who puts on armour for war.[5]

---

[1] Surely, if matter had been wholly evil, it could not have been attracted by the Light it saw ! Nor could a totally evil Matter hold the perfect Soul. Gk. : *hoion ti delear kai ankistron tēi hulēi prosepempse.*

[2] The inherent radiance could only shine forth vividly when the Soul had attained to maturity.

[3] Syr. *Emmā de Hayyē*; *cf.* GPM 15.

[4] This 'First Man' is the Cosmic Christ, the 'Word', the Divine Man of the Gnosis; Syr. *enāṣā qadmāyā*; Ch. *Sien-yi*. He is the 'Perfect Man' or the ideal of all humanity, manifesting God before the beginning of the worlds. " Our Father the First Man, the Lord of Richness, (owner of the) armour of Light (MP. 137 : 17-19), whose victory and garland are blessed " (MP. 1 : 26-27).

[5] " The First Man, who came down from the Race of Light to war with the Race of Darkness, armed with his Waters against the Enemy's waters, and with his Fire against their fire, and with his Winds against their winds, . . . was armed against smoke with Air, and against darkness with Light " (AF. 2 : 3). The Coptic writer says: " Since the time when he stirred himself and rose up against

Before him went out an Angel called Nahash-bet,[1] holding a crown of victory in his hand —so the First Man spread the Light in front of him. Then when the King of Darkness saw it, he considered and said, " What I was seeking from afar I have found near by "[2] (K. 313 : 27—314 : 6)! For Matter, having gazed at the Power sent forth, longed (for it) like a sweet-heart, . . . was infatuated with the Power seen as if altogether forgetful of its own nature. . . . (Meanwhile) Evil was still advancing and straining itself and coming nearer to the Light (TB. 1 : 21, 36), and that was laid open and spread out beyond it (T. 1 : 26).

3. The First Man gave himself and his five Sons (K. 314 : 6-7) in the five Elements [3]

the Light (that) he might come and reign over the Land o the Living, then the First Man came forth against him; he *emerged* out of the House of the Living and hindered him " (Keph. 67).

[1] Possibly *Nahaṣ-ṣebet* (snake-staff, *i.e.*, lightning), or *Nehṣā-bed* (lord of augury); in Gk. he is called *Stephanēphoros*, the wreath-bearer. The concept appears again in the Angel who approaches the dying with the three Gifts (GPM 75 : 2).

[2] The same sentiment is used by Augustine, who was, after all, a Manichean for nine years and never wholly threw off the old influence.

[3] These are the purest forms of subtle matter, used by the descending Redeemer as protection from the coarser vibrations of the lowest planes of gross Matter. " The Primal Man . . . mixed up with the Race of Darkness his members or vesture or weapons—that is the

(N. 329 : 21) as food for **the**[1] five Sons of Darkness, just as a man who has an enemy mixes deadly poison in a cake and gives it to him [2] (K. 314 : 3-10). Then, warring on him in return, the Rulers of Darkness (H. 7) charged up, . . . snatched from the Light (TB. 1 : 36), swallowed what had been sent (T. 1 : 26), devoured from his panoply what was the Soul (H. 7) and distributed it to their own Powers (TB. 1 : 20). When they had eaten these, the intelligence of the five Bright Gods [3] was taken from them, and they were

Five Elements—which are also a part of God's substance, so that they were subjected to confinement and pollution " (AF. 11 : 3). Tammuz too, in Chaldean myth, was stripped of his " shining adornment ", and Ephrem (IV 629 : 2) has: " My beautiful garments were (swallowed up) and do not exist."

[1] *lit*: his, an obvious error.

[2] Such vivid similes, characteristic of Mani's own style where we have it, vindicate the authenticity of bar Khoni's sources.

[3] "He waylaid (them) with his net, which is the Living Soul. . . . (They found no) possibility to escape (his net), . . . he shut them in like fishes " (Keph. 58). " After that he drew the Good Soul out of the Five Elements, the armour of the Lord First Man, and bound it in the pollution. He made it like one blind and deaf, senseless and debauched, so that it knew not its first Origin and its own Source. He made his pollution and bound the mute Soul in prison; demons . . . tormented that prisoner . . . and mocked it; he made it hateful and wicked, hostile and malicious " (S 9). The Chinese has: "When these five Bright Bodies had endured such sufferings day and night, and were imprisoned by the demon and chained in the body of flesh, they forgot their first feelings as does a madman or a drunkard " (CMT. 14). " The substance and nature of God was in danger of being wholly corrupted by the Race of Darkness; to save the rest a part was actually corrupted"

like the man bitten by a mad dog or a snake,[1] because of the venom of the Sons of Darkness (K. 314 : 10-13).

4. So in this way ... was the Soul mixed with Matter,[2] one unlike thing with an (other) unlike, and in the mixing the Soul has come to feel with[3] Matter (AL. 3), and has been fettered and, as it were, snared in a sort of trap[4] (T. 1 : 26).

To combat this danger, God sent out a part of Himself, sacrifice being of His very nature, and so the

(AF. 11:3); "He covered Himself with a veil that He might not see His own members taken and plundered by the assaults of the enemy" (AF. 18:7). This 'veil' was the darkening of the 'Five Bright Gods', the five aspects of the Mind, the ' Five-God ' (*biş-tängri*) of Turkish documents, each corresponding to one of God's ' Glories ' and to one of the ' Elements '; Manicheism delighted in the detailed working out of such correspondences, on the principle " As above, so below ".

[1] In Ephrem (II, p. 166 stanza 86) also, the confusion is caused by the bite of a snake. There are many signs of the familiarity of Syrian writers with Manichean and earlier ' heretical ' writings.

[2] " The whole Rulership was fastened, . . . being mixed with one another, the Light with the Darkness, and the Darkness with the Light " (Keph. 131). " A member . . . of the Divine substance itself must be sacrificed to the whole host of demons by being introduced into the nature of the Hostile Race" (AF. 32 : 22).

[3] *or*: assimilated; Gk. *sumpathein*. The Coptic gives a brighter picture: " fighting (?) for my holy Robe, for my shining Light that it might lighten their darkness, for my sweet fragrance that it might sweeten their foulness. . . . A part therefore went forth from my Robe; it went and lightened their darkness; my sweet Fragrance went and sweetened their stench" (MP. 205 : 15-23).

[4] " The five kinds of demons clung to the five Bright Gods just as the fly attaches itself to the honey, as the bird is caught by the lime, like the fish that has swallowed the hook " (CMT. 3).

human Soul (and that pervading everywhere) came into being to subdue the enemy from within, to overthrow its evil tendencies by its own sufferings and its yearnings to return to the blissful Light above. Soul manifests in the five mental qualities, which have to tame the lower nature's savage desires. Stage by stage, through spiritual realm after realm personified by Divine emanations, Soul came down into the dim borderland where the Light blended with the Dark, and so prepared for the War which ends with the final elimination of gloom and the restoration of every divine 'Spark' to its primal home of bliss.

Seeing in the Soul a flash of the so desirable and coveted Light, the evil spirit of Matter rushed on it impetuously and absorbed it in the prison of his own darkness. Hidden by this mass of gloom from the glory of its own nature, the Soul forgets its inherent godliness and loses the sweetness of reason and of piety, being fettered fast in the bondage of its body and deceived by the false flickers of its adopted separativeness and aggressive pride.

4. The Rescue of the Soul

1. Then the First Man was cruelly afflicted down there by the Darkness (H. 7). When the First Man came to his senses,[1] he put up seven times[2] a prayer to the Father of Greatness (K. 314 : 13-14), and the Father heard when he prayed (E. 46). God therefore pitied

[1] lit: mind (*haunā*).

[2] So the Elect had seven daily prayers, of which the Hearers observed at least four (cf. GPM 58, and the prayers in 'Pistis Sophia').

him (AL. 3) and called for the Second Evocation, the Friend of Lights; and the Friend of Lights evoked the Great Builder; and the Great Builder called forth the Living Spirit [1] (K. 314 : 15-17)—another Power emanated from Himself (E. 46).

2. Then the Living Spirit called his five Sons:[2] the Holder of Splendour from his Intelligence, the Great King of Honour from his Knowledge, the Diamond of Light [3] from his Reason, the King of Glory from his Thought, and the Supporter [4] from his Deliberation;[5] these came to the Region [6] of Darkness and found the First Man absorbed by the Darkness, he and his Sons (K. 314 : 17-22).

[1] The Manichean Demiurge, Cosmic Mind planning the 'all'.
[2] Their names in Syr. are *Saphath-Ziwā, Malkā Rabbā de Iqārā, Adāmōs Nūhrā, Melekh Sūbhhā and Sabbāla* (?), and in Ch. *Siang* (Thought), *Sin* (Feeling), *Nien* (Reflection) *Sseu* (Intellect) and *Ti* (Reasoning)—parallel to the five 'Bright Gods' of GPM 3 : 1. It is a further elaboration of the concept of personified aspects of Mind, Cosmic as well as individual.
[3] The word 'Adamas' means what is hard, unbreakable, clear and invincible; this Being parallels Mithra, the 'Sol Invictus' who overthrows evil in open conflict, like St George and the Archangel Michael.
[4] Atlas, from Gk. *tlao*, suffer, endure; also called Omophoros, with similar meaning of bearing a load. The old Greek myth of Atlas is used here.
[5] The equation between the aspects, sons, of Mind and the personifications of Cosmic Mind, is here worked out; see also GPM 19-23.
[6] *or* : earth, world; these words interchange freely.

8. Thereupon the Living Spirit called with a (loud) voice,[1] and the Living Spirit's voice resembled a sharp sword (K. 314 : 22-24) swift as the lightning; and it became another God [2] (N. 329: 31-32) and revealed the form of the First Man. Then it said to him: "Peace to thee, O good one among the wicked, light amidst the darkness, god dwelling among wild beasts who know not their honour!"[3] Then the First Man answered him, saying, "Come in peace, bringing the merchandise[4] of calm and peace!" He also said to him, "How are our Fathers, the Sons of Light, faring in their City?" The Caller said to him, "They are

---

[1] This is the mysterious 'Call' (*Khroshtag*), paralleled by the awakening cry of the Saviour in GPM 73, answered by the Soul in its 'Reply' (*Padvakhtag*) or the 'Resolve' of GPM 70-72. These Turkish names correspond to the Syr. *Qaryā* and '*Anyā*, the Ch. *Chouo-t'ing* and *Houan-ying*; they resemble in one way the Mazdean pair Haurvatat and Ameretat, and join the Five Sons to make up the list of the Seven Mahraspands.

[2] A striking phrase: Ar. *wa kāna ilāhān ākhira*. The Soul itself in GPM 66:1 is said to become God, though the usual concept is rather that it is to live for ever *with* God in light and bliss, cf. GPM 66 : 2, 72 : 2, 75:1, App. I. 10 : 1.

[3] *or*: wild beasts ravening in hell.

[4] The word is generally used to refer to 'merits' or good deeds brought home with it by the soul, but is here evidently the grace or merits brought to the soul by its Redeemer while rousing it from the 'sleep' of (spiritual) death with the cry: "Awake, you who slumber and sleep in the cavern (?), that you may be told the news" (MP. 197 : 16-17)!

THE MYTH OF THE SOUL

prospering"[1] (K. 314 : 24—315 : 3); and coming down he gave him a right hand[2] and led (him) up out of the Darkness (H. 7).

4. Then the Caller and the Answerer[3] united and went up towards the Mother of Life and the Living Spirit;[4] and the Living Spirit put on[5] the Caller, while the Mother of Life put on the Answerer, her beloved Son;[6] and they went down to the Earth of Darkness, to the place of the First Man and his Sons (K. 315 : 3-7).

Afflicted by this bondage, the Soul knows enough to cry to God for help, and the merciful Father at

---

[1] The Psalms of Thōm give a full version of this conversation; cf. our Appendix I 5.

[2] Hegemonius (7) tells us, "For that reason if the Manicheans meet each other they give the right hand as a sign of having been saved from the Darkness"; there is much in the Kephalaia about this Right Hand, and the Kiss of Peace, and the Salutation which accompany it.

[3] They represent the cooperation between the one to be saved and his saviour; the former must respond to the latter's invitation.

[4] "As the Call and the Reply went up from the hell into the height, then came Living Spirit and the Mother of the Living hither speedily. They make the God First Man ascend out of hell and come forth, and they send him to the heaven of the Gods. And the Mother of the Living, and the God Living Spirit, these separate (?) the 'Five-God' from the God First Man, and (then) they prepare themselves to create and make the earth and the heaven (T. II. D. 173 b)"—a Turkish translation evidently from an original Scripture.

[5] The technical term for a mystical at-oning with.

[6] She is the 'feminine' aspect of God, the 'Mother' who intercedes for fallen man, as in GPM 6

once puts forth certain of His own Powers to create a means to save the Soul from its self-sought suffering. Those who were to create, to rule, to teach the worlds came into manifestation, and so we have the Divine Persons and Names whereby Mani seemed to give free rein to the old polytheistic trends which had already begun to mould Christian theology. Especially came the Living Spirit, the 'Autoeides' of another school, the 'letter' that came to the Prince in Bardaisan's (?) lovely poem (see GG), to awaken the Soul to a realisation of its own inherent divinity—the Guru, like the lion that led a cub brought up by goats till its roaring became a feeble bleat, and then showed it its reflection in a pool. So is the Soul reminded of its royal destiny and helped by the spiritual Voice to invoke more potently the help of the redeeming aspects of God the Light.

5. Creation of the Sky and Luminaries

1. Next the Living Spirit ordered three of his Sons,[1] the one to kill and the other to flay the Rulers, Sons of the Darkness, and to deliver them to the Mother of the Living.[2] The Mother of the Living spread out the heavens with their skins and made ten

---

[1] Only two are noted specifically here. "The Rulers rebelled and lifted themselves against the Living Spirit... because they knew and felt he would bind and fetter them with a strong chain" (Keph. 58).

[2] "The great mighty God Living Spirit (proceeds to) tuck up his robe in the tenfold heaven and to don the Water-god as his shield" (T. II. D. 121).

heavens,[1] while their bodies were flung to the Region of Darkness and made eight earths [2] (K. 315 : 7-12). Then this Living Spirit created the universe and, having brought the three other Powers [3] and gone down, he led up the Rulers and fastened (them) in the firmament, which is their sphere [4] (E. 48).

[1] A very ancient element from mythology—the skies being formed out of the skin of a gigantic demon. The text here has 'eleven', an obvious error for the usual 'ten'. "There are eight worlds and ten heavens" (AF. 32:19).

[2] As made of the grosser portions of flesh, the 'bodies' form the material for the eight earths. The fragment S 9 gives a full account of these creations, with which *cf.* our App. I. 6. "For this reason the Messenger of the Light named Pure Spirit, out of the five kinds of demons and the five Bright Gods, by combining the two forces, constituted the ten heavens and the eight earths of the universe" (CMT. 3).

[3] "Having put three other Powers on himself, he came down and brought away the Rulers and fastened them in the firmament which is their body, the Sphere" (H. 7). Ephrem is in error when he says this was done by the First Man, going on: "he flayed them and made this sky from their skins, and out of their refuse he compacted the earth, and some of their bones he melted also and piled up the hills". SGV. says: "The sky is from the skin, the earth from the flesh, the mountains from the bones, and the plants from the hair of the Demon Kuni: the rain is the seed of the demons who are bound on the Sphere" (10-14). We learn that 'Adamas' kills the Rulers, the 'King of Glory' flays them, the 'King of Honour' delivers them to the Mother of Life; these are the 'Three Servants' (*telāthā 'abhdīn*) of GPM 8:2.

[4] So we have the demon referred to as "the prince of the power of the air" in the somewhat Gnostic Eph. 2:2. "He fettered them in the heaven and the earth; he placed every one of them on the place suited for him; he measured each one of them by his pride and his humility. A few of them he confined (in a prison), others of them he hung up head downwards, a few (were) crucified, others sat down always, a few of them were tied under their

18 THE GOSPEL OF THE PROPHET MANI

2. Then the five Sons of the Living Spirit were each one inducted into his work: the Holder of Splendour, who holds the five Bright Gods by their waists while the heavens are spread out below their waists; the Supporter, who kneels on one knee and bears the earths; and after the heavens and earths were made, the Great King of Honour sits in heaven's centre and keeps watch over all of them[1] (K. 315 : 12-18).

3. After having crucified[2] the Rulers in the Sphere (E. 49), the Living Spirit then showed his forms to the Sons of Darkness, and from the Light which had been swallowed by

comrades, tortured by means of a hard fetter. Under himself he has given others authority over one another to work his will on those who are under them" (Keph. 51-52). "Their root is fastened to it, so that they may not escape from the bonds of their chain " . . . " so that not one of (them escapes) his hand " (Keph. 88, 55). " He bound 1800 Rulers in every Aeon and set 360 over them, and he set five other great Rulers as lords over the 360, and over all the bound Rulers who are called in the whole world of mankind these names: Saturn, Mars, Mercury, Venus, Jupiter " (*Pistis Sophia*, p. 360).

[1] It is noteworthy that here too, as in para 1, only a few of the Sons are actually referred to in detail.

[2] As in the story of Mani's own death, and perhaps in Christian books of the same age—the apocryphal Acts, etc.—the word is often used for fastened, tied up, tortured—in any way. So too, Widengren tells us, Marduk, in the Chaldean myth, put 300 conquered deities in the heavens, forming the universe from the slain Tiamat, demon of the deep, and man from her consort Kingu.

them out of these five Bright Gods he refined the light and made the Sun and Moon.[1] (K. 315 : 18-21). From Matter he withdrew as much of the Power as had suffered nothing much from the mingling, . . . which in spite of the mixing retained its own virtue; so the Sun and the Moon came into being (AL. 3), the Luminaries that are remnants of the Soul [2] (H. 7). But what had come to appreciable harm (became) Stars (AL. 3) more than a thousand [3] (K. 315 : 21-22) and the all-embracing heaven (AL. 3). Of the Matter, then, whereof Sun and Moon were created, the part was thrown out of the universe and is that Fire which burns indeed but darkly and dim quite like Night [4] (AL. 3).

[1] "Now they so distinguish those Ships, namely the two Luminaries of heaven, as they say the Moon is made of good Water, and the Sun of good Fire" (Aug. de Haer. 16). This is confirmed by passages in the Kephalaia.

[2] Because the Sun and Moon are from the purest of the Light first recovered from contamination, they fittingly become the gateway, path, and means of refinement for other Souls, leading them up to the Source of Light (cf. GPM 25).

[3] Syr: *nuhrā yathīr men alpā*. Reading *elpē* Cumont takes this as "the stars beyond the vessels" (*i.e.* Luminaries), but Jackson rejects this. The originating light is less pure, and this is why the stars are not so bright as the Sun and Moon!

[4] Dark Fire, derived from the dregs after removing the light of the Sun and Moon from the contamination.

4. Then again Matter of itself created the plants (H. 7); and in the other elements, both plant and animal, in these the Divine Power is unequally mixed [1] (AL. 3). Now the Evil Spirit by foresight knew that the Light, being attracted by Sun and Moon, would soon be purified and freed, ... so he planned this microcosm, such as humanity, cattle and other creatures, as an exact copy of the Macrocosm,[2] together with the rest of embodied creation. ... The world is a bodily formation of the Evil Spirit, formed of the bodily elements of the Evil Spirit (SGV. 16 : 23-24, 8-9); from the mixture of both Natures, that is, of Good and Evil, the world has been made [3] (AMM. 36).

. To rescue Soul bound up in Matter, this very Matter itself had to be fashioned into a universe subject to law; this very obedience imposed upon its

[1] Gk. *anōmelōs ... memigmenēn.* Some have the Light in them purer and more plentiful than others; among the brightest were said to be fruits, melons and cucumbers—the butt of Augustine's humour.

[2] The Kephalaia works out this correspondence in some detail. "When these were carried off by some of the Rulers as spoil, they took power from all of them individually and made up the man who is the image of that First Man and united the Soul in him" (H. 7)—but this anticipates GPM 9 : 2.

[3] A basic doctrine preserved, it is clear, in exact quotation by Augustine: *de commixta utraque natura, id est boni et mali, mundus est fabricatus.* Man feels in himself the duality of his own nature, the spirit warring with the flesh, as St. Paul puts it.

evil qualities of disorder—"crucifying the demons" and binding them to a form moulded of their own very nature—enabled God to overcome the rebelliousness inherent in every form of Evil. So the Divine Manifestations of Mind each took over the control of a part of this vast universe, and the luminaries—Sun and Moon and Stars being themselves formed from Light—were devised as means to attract the Light-Spark held in dark Matter, to draw it up to its eternal Source, and so to free it from the entangling impurity.

6. The Role of the Virtues

Now when the Living Father saw the Soul afflicted in the Body (H. 8), then the Mother of Life and the First Man and the Living Spirit stood up in prayer and implored the Father of Greatness.[1] So the Father of Greatness heard them and called forth the Third Evocation, the Messenger [2] (K. 315:27—316:2). Having come, then, he prepared for himself the work for the saving of the Souls; he put together a machine with twelve Buckets [3]

[1] "Then the God First Man prayed to his Mother, and his Mother prayed to the Righteous God: 'Send a Helper to my son, for he has fulfilled your wish and (so) has come to distress'" (M 21).

[2] "The prototype of all God's 'Prophets' and 'Saviours' who come down to help man to Liberation.

[3] The water-wheel, or *sakiyah*, still used in countries of the Middle and Near East. The twelve 'buckets' which descend into the ocean of *samsāra* to lift up the 'living water', the Soul, are the twelve virtues to be cultivated—each of them the gift of the higher side of one of the Signs of the Zodiac, expressing consecutive stages

(H. 8), the twelve 'Virgins'[1] with their robes and crowns and characteristics. The first is Royalty, the second Wisdom and the third Victory;[2] the fourth is Contentment,[3] the fifth Purity[4] and the sixth Truth; the seventh is Faith, the eighth Patience[5] and the ninth Sincerity;[6] the tenth is Kindness,[7] and the eleventh is Justice,[8] while the twelfth is Light (K. 316:2-8). On being turned round by the Sphere this (wheel) draws up the Souls of the dying. (H. 8).

Matter then formed itself into a counter-attraction, a physical universe to draw the Soul's desire back from the glory of the spiritual and to fasten its attention upon this visible, so that it might again forget the

in spiritual growth. Astrologers will easily identify the Signs from the lists of the Virtues here and in GPM 31:2; *e.g.* Royalty, Aries; Justice, Aquarius, esoterically viewed.

[1] These are the "twelve Daughters of Time (*Zrwān*)" of T. II D. 171, and the "twelve Light-Sovereigns" of the Chinese texts. Le Coq III p. 16 speaks of "the twelve Majesties which emanate from the God of the Majesty of Law and resemble the bright Sun-god with his twelve divine Virgins" (cf. GPM 13:2).

[2] *i.e.* that bringing final liberation (*bōxtagēft*).

[3] *or*: Joy, Persuasion, Reconciliation (*peyāsā*).

[4] Another reading is Modesty; Phl. Splendour, Majesty; Ch. Religious Zeal.

[5] Ch. Endurance of Wrongs (Skt. *titikṣa*).

[6] *or*: Integrity, Justice, Righteousness.

[7] *or*: Grace, Goodness (*taybūthā*).

[8] Ch. Uniformity of Heart; *i.e.*, Impartiality, the brotherly feeling with another conferred specially by the eleventh Sign.

beauty of the yet unseen. So God replied by sending out to the human Soul a divinely illumined Teacher, the Messenger of the Light, who revealed the first steps up by the Path of Righteousness, the twelve great virtues symbolised and conferred by the zodiacal signs after conquest of the opposite evils innate in them. While the rotating universe pursues its ceaseless course, the practice of these virtues gradually refines and elevates the Soul towards the endless Light of perfection.

7. The Work of Moon and Sun

1. The Sun and the Moon . . . are Ships conveying the Souls of the dying[1] from Matter to the Light[2] (T. 1 : 26), always separating the Divine Power from Matter and escorting it to God. . . . For in waxing the Moon receives the Power . . . and becomes filled therewith in the due time (AL. 3-4); then it brings about (its own) waning by discharging the freight (H. 8) to send (it) on to the Sun, and that returns (it) to God.[3] And having done this, it receives again a migration

[1] Gk. *thnēskontōn*.

[2] This is the doctrine forcibly condemned in our App. III 13. The Ch. text puts it thus: "Further Pure Spirit had made two Luminous Ships, which he sent on the Sea of *Samsāra* (constant life and death), to let them carry good across to men and to bring them back into their first world, so that their Bright Nature (Soul) might at last be calm and happy " (CMT 15).

[3] A curious explanation for the waxing and waning of the Moon! Mani had to convey spiritual teaching through such materialistic fantasies because his audience were mostly at that mental stage. " And the base of the Moon had the type of a Ship, while a male

to itself of the Soul from the next full Moon and ... . lets it pass on automatically to God (AL. 4). And so the Ferry fills and again disembarks the Souls drawn up by the 'buckets', until it has saved its own share of Soul (H. 8).

2. When the Moon, then, has handed over the freight of Souls to the Aeons [1] of the Father, they remain there in the Column of Glory which is called the 'Perfect Man'; ... it is a pillar of light because loaded with the Souls that are being purified [2] (H. 8). Now the Moon ... first receives the radiant Souls from Matter, and then deposits (them) in the Light (T. 1 : 26), and it does this continuously (AL. 4); this is the way in which the Souls are saved (H. 8). So the Sun began to purify the Light which was mixed with the demons

and female dragon steered. ... The figure of a Babe was on the Moon's stern, who guided the dragons that robbed the Light from the Rulers" (*Pistis Sophia* p. 359).

[1] The 'Aeons' play a prominent part in Gnostic thought also. They seem almost to correspond with the Jewish and Christian Archangels and to the 'Glories' of GPM 1:2, Ameshaspentas of Mazdeism.

[2] Cf. GPM 26 This concept goes back perhaps as far as the Divine Ladder of GP 33 or beyond, together with the washing and clothing of the Soul in a lovely Robe. It corresponds with the Church of elect souls, with the 'Perfect Man' or Christ, whose mystical body these are. To join this, or the equivalent 'Last Statue' of GPM 83 and 87, is the purport of religion, the aim of all effort at spiritual self-purifying.

of Heat, and the Moon began to purify the Light mixed with the demons of Cold;[1] that (Light) rises up in the 'Column of Praise' with the hymns and worships, the good deeds and kind works which are sent up[2] (N. 330 : 23-25)

Luminaries always draw the heart of man towards the Infinite Light, the Source of all their beautiful brightness. This truth was mythically expressed by the Soul being drawn Godwards by the changing and lesser light of the waxing Moon and then passed on to the steady and changeless greater brilliance of the Sun. Purified by the twelve virtues, countless Souls are thus continually raised from the dark ignorance of a wicked world into the glorious Ray of Light which leads straight to God—the mystical unity of liberated Souls which forms the hierarchy of the Church, the glorious Ladder which Jacob saw raising souls to heaven, whereon God's angel messengers come and go. This Ladder is built of prayer and praise and kindly deeds.

8. The Maiden of the Light

1. (The Living Spirit) made the Wheels[3] —the Wind, the Water and the Fire;[4] and

---

[1] Demons of Heat and Cold come also in App. I 5:4.

[2] The Souls are uplifted by all the prayers and praises, and the meritorious deeds of the faithful who compose the true Church and share its 'treasury of merits'.

[3] Syr. *aggānē*; Turk. *üc tilgän*; Ch. *san-luen*; Copt. *psamet ṅtrokhos*. The exact significance of the Wheels escapes me, unless they represent the three *guṇas*, the triplicities of Astrology; they are 'of use to' the five aspects of mind or soul, and protect them from the poisoning by evil. See note to GPM 18:2.

[4] Perhaps the Fixed, Mutable and Cardinal of Astrology.

he went down and formed[1] them below near the Supporter. Then the King of Glory evoked and raised over them a covering, so that they might ascend over these Rulers confined in the earths and be of use to the five Bright Gods, lest they be burned by the Rulers' venom (K. 315 : 22-26).

2. Now when the Envoy came towards these Ships,[2] he ordered the Three Servants[3] of Manbed[4] to make the Ships move; he bade the Great Builder construct the New Earth,[5] and the Three Wheels to go up. Now when the Ships rose and came to the centre of the sky, when the Envoy[6] showed his male and female forms and was seen by the Rulers, Sons of Darkness, male and female (K. 316 : 8-14), who were in the firmament. . . . A certain Virgin, fair, bedecked and very alluring, . . .

[1] Jackson understood this as: 'he made them glide'.

[2] *i.e.*, the Moon and the Sun, which probably represent, in one sense, the Personality and Individuality through which the Soul gradually evolves towards perfection in the 'Church' or 'Column of Glory'.

[3] Apparently corresponding to the 'Three Wheels', or can it be, as suggested by others, the Three Servants of the Living Spirit in GPM 5 : 1-2?

[4] The Persian name for the Supporter, Atlas or Omophoros.

[5] Syr. *ar'a hedathā*. Cf. the work done in App. I. 6.

[6] Here, clearly, the 'Third Envoy' of GPM 24; also the 'Messenger' of GPM 6.

appeared to the males as a comely female, and to the females as a handsome and attractive youth (H. 8), and in the Sun was seen an Image somewhat in the likeness of a Man (AL. 4). Now at the sight of the Envoy, who was lovely in his forms, all the Rulers were filled with desire for him—the males for the shape of the female and the females for the masculine shape.[1] In their desire they began to emit that Light which they had swallowed from the five Bright Gods[2] (K. 316 : 14-17).

[1] "An Image of Light was revealed (in) the home of the beasts, ... in the land of the foul stench, ... They came to see his Image, they grovelled, they became mad because of its brightness, they arose that they might mark his likeness, they fell, ... they arose that they might mark his beauty, they were sweetened with his fragrance. ... They bent their knees, (they) worshipped him, ... they sang to him: ... 'Thou hast come in peace, O Son of the Brightnesses that shall be the illuminer of our worlds. Come and rule over our land and set peace in our city!' The demons were saying this with their mouth, yet planning evil nevertheless in their heart" (MP. 214 : 1-17).

[2] This Myth, in all likelihood pre-Manichean, was fully narrated in 'The Treasure of Life'; *cf.* App. I. 5. The Christian polemists scathingly condemned it, but it is no more unsavoury than some stories related almost with relish in the Old Testament. Beauty, and the desire for it, is in fact used as a means of rescuing the Soul's higher nature from enslavement to the gross, the ugly and unspiritual. A similar story is that in the Hindu Puranas, where Mohini, an *avatar* of Vishnu, so charms the demons' senses that she wins away from them the immortality (*amritam*) destined for the Gods. Augustine taunts Faustus with believing such a story: "Remember thy beautiful gods and goddesses exhibiting themselves to excite desire in the male and female Rulers of Darkness, so that the gratifying of this passion might effect the liberation of this God who is in confinement everywhere, and who needs the help of such self-degradation" (AF. 15 : 7).

3. Thereupon that Sin which, like the hair in the dough,[1] was shut up in them mingled with the Light which came out of the Rulers. . . . Then the Envoy hid his forms; he parted the Light of the five Bright Gods from the Sin which was with them, and it fell upon the Rulers from whom it had dropped;[2] but just like a man disgusted at his own vomit[1] they did not accept it (K. 316 : 18-24).

4. Then it fell on the earth, half of it on the Wet and half of it on the Dry[3] (K. 316 : 24-25); now that which fell on the Dry sprang up in five Trees (K. 317: 2-3)—from that are grown plants, trees and grain[4] (SGV. 16 : 35), while that (on the Wet) became a horrible

---

[1] Two more typically vivid Manichean similes; we speak of a 'fly in the ointment' with a similar purport.

[2] So evil falls back on the head of him who works it: the 'Law of Karma'!

[3] "(The Sin) entangled itself with the Light; it got out and came down from the Dry and the Moist; (out of) the Dry it formed the trees, but in the Sea it immediately formed itself and made a great rebellion in the Sea" (Keph. 92). Cf. the 'beast from the Sea' in Rev. 13:1. The 'Sea' is as usual a symbol of the emotional nature wherein Lust arises.

[4] "Among those used in forming the heavenly bodies were some pregnant females. When the sky began to rotate (*cf.* GPM 6), the rapid circular motion made those females give birth to abortions which, being of both sexes, fell on the earth and lived and grew and came together and produced offspring. Hence sprang all animal life in earth, air and sea" (AF. 6:8).

monster [1] in the likeness of the King of Darkness. The Diamond of Light was sent against her; he fought with her, defeated her, turned her on her back, struck her in her heart with a Spear,[2] thrust his Shield on her mouth, and placed one of his feet on her thighs and the other on her breast [3] (K. 316 : 25—817 : 2).

Here is the myth which, in the crude form taken over bodily by Mani from an earlier Chaldean paganism, aroused the understandable ire and ridicule of Christian polemists. Let us, in trying to follow its strange symbolism, remember the painfully intimate relationship of spirituality and sensuality—the one being but the reverse of the other; the fallen priest flies from his God-devoted chastity to the poor consolation of a sexual entanglement; the artist drowns his genius in women's arms and drink; the demon of Lust lurks in the very heart of the spiritual Light and Fire. We may not like this, but the whole universe was designed to trap Evil in its own snare, and desire can be conquered—only by another desire! So the story tells how the 'Maiden of the Light's' beauty snared the demons by the very force of their own unholy lusts for what is eternally immaculate, beyond the reach of all their coveting. In the very act of their aspiring after the unattainable loveliness, which attracts each

---

[1] *lit*: hateful beast—the female demon, Lust.

[2] Syr: *dōrṭiyā*, the Syr. word *ōrṭiyā*, being confused with the Gk. *doration*.

[3] A symbol of the 'Three Seals' of Manicheism. The Redeemer controls the evil one in thought (heart), word (mouth) and deed (body), trampling on the lower instincts (thighs) and the higher passions (breast). This is the ancient theme of Marduk and Tiamat, God and Chaos, St. George and the Dragon, a favourite among myths. Cf. the similar story in GPM 21:3.

according to his own tendencies, the higher life
hidden and held in the darkness of sensuality escapes
into the brightness of the spiritual life and knowledge,
while the dross left behind sinks into a deeper gloom
and vileness. So were born the lower creatures, void
of sense—the plants and stones, and the ancient mighty
Dragon, personifying Evil and Darkness in his very
form, strives in vain against the Hero-Warrior known
to other myths as Perseus, Michael or St. George.

9. Man's Body Comes from the Demons

1. These Daughters of the Darkness [1] were
already pregnant from their own Nature, and
at sight of the beauty of the Envoy's forms
their foetuses dropped,[2] fell on the earth, and
ate the buds of the trees. Then the Abortions [3] consulted together; they remembered
the Envoy's form they had seen, and asked,
" Where is that Form we saw (K. 317:3-8)?"

2. Then said Ashaqlun,[4] the son of the
King of Darkness, to the Abortions: "Bring

---

[1] *i.e.*, the female Rulers suspended in the air: "They have been
hung to the revolving Wheel on account of their hardheartedness;
so that because of the Wind and the movement by which they
turn they may not know the place whereon they stand . . . on the
revolving Wheel of the Stars " (Keph. 119).

[2] Syr: *neḥeth* here, probably, should read *iḥēt*, aborted, we are told.

[3] The idea of the Abortion was also common in Gnosticism; cf.
1 Cor. 15 : 8.

[4] Gk. *Saklas*; note that he is not the original Demon Ahrimēn,
but his ' son '. *Cf.* the story as in App. I. 2 : 9-14.

me your sons and daughters (K. 317 : 9-10); come, give me some of the Light we have taken (H. 10); it is I who will make for you a form like what you have seen (K. 317 : 10-11), which is the first man [1] (H. 10)." Then they brought it and gave it to him [2] (K. 317 : 11), and, moved by jealousy, Matter made Man out of itself by mixing with the whole of the Power, having also something of the Soul (in him).[3] However, the form did much to let Man gain somewhat more of the Divine Power than other mortal living things, for he is an image of the Divine Power [4] (AL. 4).

[1] *i.e.*, the human 'Adam', not to be confused with the heavenly 'First Man' of GPM 3-4, though he is a sort of reflection thereof on a lower plane.

[2] "He said to his companions: 'Give me your light, and I will set up a form like the Form of the Lofty One.' As he had said, (so) they did and gave (it) to him, and he on his part established (the copy)" (Keph. 138)—an example of how close the Greek and Syriac refutators kept to their sources.

[3] "The good things drew him to Life because of their image and their form which was laid on him, while the evil things drew him to Death in order to rule by means of him and to take the Kingdom and through him to swallow the whole universe" (Keph. 157). The Mandean Book of John (52: 3) says: "Out of fire (evil) and water (good) was the body of Adam created." Hermes also recognises this dualism in man's nature (GH 40 : 5).

[4] Syr. *dēvā taqīfā*. Man's dignity is somewhat preserved by this assertion that he is not wholly the child of demons: Gk. *huparkhein gar auton theias dunameōs eikona*. Man is indeed the 'image' or reflection of God (*cf*. Gen. 1:26, in GY 1:8), to be eventually built into the Shining Image which is the 'Last Statue'; the 'Column of Glory'.

3. So Man was fashioned, not by God ... but by the Ruler of Matter [1] (T. 1 : 26); he consumed the males, and the females, he gave to Nebroel [2] his mate. Then Nebroel and Ashaqlun united together,[3] and she conceived from him and bore a son whom she called [4] 'Adam'; she conceived again, and bore a daughter whom she called 'Eve' [5] (K. 317 : 11-15), (both) giving her some of their lust to seduce Adam [6] (H. 10).

[1] A teaching forcibly refuted in App. III. 4. "When the Demon of Greed had seen these things, he conceived anew a wicked plan in his poisoned heart; then he ordered Saklas and Nebroel to imitate Pure Spirit and Excellent Mother. . . . They formed the body of Man, and there imprisoned the Light Natures to imitate the Macrocosm. So then the flesh body, with its corrupt and evil Greed and Lust, was the faithful image point by point, though smaller, of the heavens and the earths; . . . there was not a single formation of the universe they did not reproduce" (CMT. 7). This idea is elaborately traced out in the Kephalaia.

[2] The name also appears as Nemrael, both forms suggesting a Semitic origin like those of Michael, Gabriel. Perhaps the earlier form is N'apla'an.

[3] In Ch. they were known as Lou-yi and Yelo-yang.

[4] *lit*: and she called his name.

[5] Syr. *Hawā*. AnNadim gives us the very unpleasant continuation of this barbarous mythical story down to the third generation, to show how Lust and Greed established power over humanity.

[6] The usual unfair suggestion that female lust is stronger than male, that, in fact, it is woman who is the tempter! "When the Demon of Hatred, the master of Greed, had seen that, he therefore conceived feelings of annoyance and jealousy; then he made the forms of the two sexes, male and female, to imitate the two great Luminaries which are the Sun and Moon, and to deceive and harass the Bright Nature till it embarked on the Boats of Darkness and, led by them, entered hell, passed through the five states of existence and underwent all sufferings, and so that finally it might be hard for it to be delivered" (CMT. 16).

Out of the fallen Matter from which spirituality has fled, lured by the dream of loveliness glimpsed in its brightness as the 'Maiden of the Sun' (*Sun* is a feminine word in Semitic languages)—the Demon King, son of Satan, Ahrimēn, the Enemy, fashioned from Matter's darkness forms in human shape. In these he imprisoned the sparks of Light which had not yet escaped. Because man, even in his fallen state, has a consciousness of the Light which we call his 'conscience', he is the highest of all mortal things. His outer form, the 'man' we see, is constantly renewed by the union of the twin demons Wrath or Pride, and Greed or Lust. These two rule his life until God's Messenger awakes in him the yearning for the lost Light; then he struggles through to freedom by conquering all desires that lead to slavery.

10. The Coming of Jesus

1. Now whereas Adam was created beast-like, Eve was lifeless [1] and motionless; but the male Virgin [2] whom they call Daughter of the Light and name Ioel, gave Eve [3] a share of Life and Light. Next Eve freed Adam from bestiality,[4] then was she thereupon stripped naked of the Light (T. 1 : 26).

[1] Gk. *apsukhon*, soulless.

[2] Spiritual beings like this Ioel, who appears also in the Gnostic Book of Baruch, had for the Manichean no separative sex. Ioel seems to be perhaps the 'Maiden of the Light' of GPM 27.

[3] The Greek Abjuration (3) says: "Eve forsooth received her life when a male Virgin was invoked, while Adam was freed from savagery through Eve".

[4] Note that it is Woman who takes the first steps towards civilisation, inventing pottery, basketwork, cooking and agriculture; as

2. So they (both) asked for the Redeemer,[1] and the Mother of Life and the First Man and the Spirit of Life[2] (decided) to send to that 'first child',[3] one who should free him and save him, show him the Knowledge and the Righteousness,[4] and rescue him from the demons (N. 331 : 7-9). Being kindly and pitiful, . . . the Good Father sent from the bosom . . . His beloved Son . . . into the heart of the earth and into its lowest parts . . . for the saving of the Soul. . . . Now while coming the Son changed himself into

the reward, she becomes subordinate to man and loses the chance to develop and liberate the Light in her mind as easily as man can do. She is 'stripped'.

[1] *Lit*: the Messenger of Good Tidings, the Evangelist (Ar. *alBaśiru*). This awkward phrase refers to the 'Gospel' of GG, the Awakening Call, or the King's Letter which rouses the sleeping Prodigal. The part was played by Jesus, as by all other true Men of God who have striven to rouse their brethren "lost in earth's dark night". "Now every Five-Light (*i.e.* Soul) (being involved) in the struggle implored the God First Man : 'Leave us not in the body of the Darkness, but send us strength and the Helper!' And the God First Man replied to each one praising (him): 'I shall not leave you in the power of the Darkness!' . . . "If they have not prayed, then they will not be helped by the God First Man; but their glory is in every prayer" (M 2).

[2] Note here the same three who interceded with God to send the help for the heavenly prototype 'First Man' in GPM 6.

[3] *i.e.*, the first one to be born or generated (Ar. *alMolūdi'lqadīmi*).

[4] *i.e.*, the Doctrine and the Ethics, essential parts of all religion: How man was parted from God, and what practices draw him back to Him again.

the form of a Man¹ and appeared to men as a man, being no man, and men fancied him to have been born (H. 8).

3. Jesus the Radiant² approached Adam the Innocent,³ and awoke him from the sleep of death,⁴ so that he might be rescued from the Great Spirit;⁵ and like a righteous man who meets a man possessed by a mighty demon⁶ and quietens him by his art,⁷ so too was Adam when that Beloved had found him sunk in the deep sleep.⁸ So he woke him,

[1] The power to change his form in plane after plane was essential to the true Messenger (cf. GPM 31:1, GMC 8:4 and in the Gnostic Ascension of Isaiah). Forcibly refuted in App. III 8, this doctrine seems yet to have been hinted at in the remarkable passage in Phil. 2:7-8. Western Manicheans found much in St. John and St. Paul to support their teachings.

[2] *i.e.*, the glorious Jesus, before descent and after resurrection: Syr: *Yeso'a zīvanā*; Copt. *Iēsous perrie*, the dawn, the splendid one.

[3] Syr. *tammīmā*, simple, harmless; evil does not originate in man, who is only the 'child' of evil forces.

[4] A favourite metaphor in all mystical literature; cf. the Tamil woman-saint, Āndāl, in her '*Tiruppāvai*' (vv. 9, 11, 15): "Is it a light slumber, or does she lie through some enchantment in deepest sleep?... O favourite of His, why do you sleep and neither stir nor speak?... Are you still asleep?" It is the 'sleep' which overcame the Prince in Egypt, in Bardaisan's poem.

[5] Syr: *rūhā saggīthā*, actually dual: Lust (Ch. *T'an-mo*) and Greed (Ch. *Yuan-mo-t'an-tchou*; Turk. *Soq-yāk*) together make up the Great Demon, Shumnu or Ahrimēn (Aṅrimainyu).

[6] A 'righteous man', like Jesus or Mani himself, naturally had power to drive out evil spirits.

[7] Ephrem says in a hymn: "He too healed the wound with commands and not with drugs."

[8] Syr: *be ṣentā saggīthā*; *lit*: in a great sleep.

took hold of him, and shook him (K. 317 : 15-21). Then Jesus... spoke to the 'child' who was Adam, and made clear to him the Gardens and the Gods, and Hell and the demons, and the earth and sky, and the Sun and Moon. Then he warned him against Eve, showed him her reproach,[1] and forbade him (to touch) her (N. 331 : 10-11); he drove away from him the Seducer,[2] and bound the Great Queen[3] far from him. Thereupon Adam examined himself and realised whence (he came);[4] and **Jesus** showed him the Fathers on high and his own Self in everything,[5] thrown into the teeth of leopards and ... elephants, swallowed by the greedy and chewed by the gluttonous, eaten by dogs—

[1] The constant tendency, even unawares, to awaken lust—which results in drawing Spirit down into Matter, a new birth of fallen spirituality. Thus Mani condemned all sexual intercourse as demoniacal: "It is not proper to arrange for posterity, because that is to co-operate with the Evil Spirit in maintaining mankind and cattle, and forcing Life and Light back into bodies—nor even to cultivate plants and grain" (SGV. 16 : 39-41).

[2] *i.e.*, Lust.

[3] *i.e.*, Greed. *Lit*: female Ruler (*le Arkōnttā saggīthā*).

[4] *or*: what he was. It is like the old Indian fable of the lion-cub brought up among goats, who realised his nature and assumed the qualities of a lion when showed his own image in a pool.

[5] This is of course the "Jesus hanging on every tree", in Augustine, the immanent pantheistic universal Soul crucified in Matter, the 'Cross of Light' in Coptic texts (*e.g.*, GPM 60). To ununderstanding Christians the idea seemed a wilful blasphemy.

mixed and imprisoned in all that is, and bound in the stench of Darkness (K. 317: 21-27).

4. Then (Jesus) raised him[1] and made him taste of the Tree of Life;[2] and thereupon Adam looked and wept, he mightily lifted up his voice like a raging lion, saying: "Woe, woe to the maker of my body, and to the binder of my Soul,[3] and to the Rebels[4] who have enslaved me! (K. 317 : 28—318 : 4)".

The extremity to which the 'Spark' has now been reduced leads then to an appeal to God for help, and immediately that help descends—in a human form, but in reality a total Divinity without dilution with human nature. This anointed one, known to Mani also as 'Jesus the Son of God', came down to fallen man, roused him from the drunken sleep of ignorance, showed him his royal destiny on high as a

[1] The word could also mean 'baptized', as Widengren shows. Exorcism, baptism and a sacramental eating of the Tree of Life (Syr. *īlān ḥayyē*) was normal to Mesopotamian ritual—even as in the Catholic Church today. This 'Tree' is in the West Jesus, in the East Srōsh—the Living Wine; or it is the Cross (Ephrem, Hymns IV 769:2). In Hymns II 521:11, Ephrem says, "The Tree of Life which was hidden in Paradise grew up in Mary".

[2] This 'tree' is, in one sense, the Living Vine of Jn. 15:1. Note that it is Jesus here who rouses the Soul to its inner divinity and gives it to eat of the Tree, while in Gen. 3 it is the demon who has lulled it into apathy and complacency—reversing the roles.

[3] Syr. *'al gābhōl paghrī we'al asōrēh de naphṣī*; the last word may well be 'Self'.

[4] The same Rebels, of course, who revolted against God's supremacy in the Land of Light and succeeded in capturing the Soul during the subsequent War (GPM 3:3).

part of God's eternal Glory, warned him against the sexuality and degradation which corrupt his sensual nature, let him glimpse the immanent Deity, the 'spark of Light' hidden and suffering in all that is, and helped him to resolve to strive for freedom.

11. The Great Builder's Work

Now for every sky he made twelve Gates with their Porches high and wide, every one of the Gates opposite its pair, and over every one of the Porches wrestlers in front of it. Then in those Porches in every one of its Gates he made six Lintels, and in every one of the Lintels thirty Corners, and twelve Stones in every Corner. Then he erected the Lintels and Corners and Stones with (?) their tops in the height of the heavens; and he connected the air at the bottom of the earths with the skies. Next round this universe he put a Moat,[1] to throw into it the darknesses that are distilled from the Light,[2] and behind that Moat he set a Wall,[3] so that of that

---

[1] "The Moat which is full of terror (and dread of) the shackling of the attacking demons", says the passage in *die Stellung Jesu*, p. 112.

[2] "But the dregs and the darkness were gathered together and thrown down into the Abyss" (Keph. 133). Cf. Rev. 20:3.

[3] Cf. GPM 35:3. The whole passage may usefully be compared with those in M 98-99 and in our App. I 7.

Darkness separated from the Light nothing should escape (N. 330:16-22).

This section is hard to place. It relates equally to the first creation told of in GPM 5 and to the second creation of the perfect universe in GPM 12. The symbolism is largely astrological, based on the twelve zodiacal signs, the six aspects, the 360 degrees, and the guardian Wall with the Pit wherein corrupting Evil finally perishes at the end of time. This is the 'field' wherein Man's fight for liberation must proceed, the '*kurukṣetra*' of his own nature, which is an exact reflection of the Macrocosm that exists 'without'.

12. Last Things

1. Now all the Emanations—Jesus, who is in the Small Ship,[1] and the Mother of Life, and the Twelve Pilots,[2] and the Maiden of the Light,[3] and the Third Envoy[4] who is in the Large Ship,[5] and the Living Spirit, and the Wall of the Great Fire, and the Wall of the Wind and the Air and the Water and of

[1] *i.e.*, the Moon, which comes down into the lower planes to gather up the 'load of Souls' out of Matter—which is the work specially of the Masters in the world.

[2] *or*: Shipmasters. Apparently nearly the same as the Twelve Maidens, Hours, Virtues, Sovereigns, etc.

[3] Seemingly the bisexual (*i.e.*, asexual) pure Being that manifests the Divine beauty to captivate the demons and so to draw the best aspiration out of them.

[4] *i.e.*, the 'Elder': Gk. *presbutes*, or *presbeutes*, often confused.

[5] *i.e.*, the Sun, which shines out the full glory of God's beauty on the world, awakens it from sleep, saves it from fear, and guides it on the Path.

40 THE GOSPEL OF THE PROPHET MANI

the inner Living Fire—wait near the Small Luminary[1] until the Fire consumes the whole universe (H. 11).

2. At the end of time (E. 58), as soon as all the Nature of Light has been separated from Matter (T. 1 : 26) entirely (AL. 5), when the Elder [2] has shone forth his Image . . . when the Statue [3] has come (H. 11), then the Supporter [4] on seeing his face lets the earth slip (E. 58). So the Height collapses upon the Depth, and Fire blazes up (N. 330 : 28-29), and thus the agelong Fire ignites the earth (E. 58), the outer Fire falls and consumes both itself and all the rest of the Matter which remains intact [5] (AL. 5). Then will God hand it over to Fire and make (of it) a single 'Lump' [6] (T. 1 : 26), the tangle which the

---

[1] *i.e.*, the Moon.

[2] The Third Envoy appears again at the end to reveal God's perfect Image, which is the Mystical Body composed of all good beings united in Him: Gk. *ho presbutēs hotan prophanēi autou tēn eikona . . . hotan ho andrias elthēi.*

[3] Copt. *andreias*, the 'Last Statue' of GPM 83.

[4] "Omophoros then throws off the earth, and so the mighty Fire is set free and consumes the whole world" (H. 11). This 'Supporter' is, of course, Atlas, the fifth Son of the Living Spirit; cf. GPM 23.

[5] Gk. *kai to allo sumpan ho ti d'an leipētai tēs hulēs sunkataphlexein.*

[6] Syr. and Gk. *bōlos*, a heavy unintelligent mass or clod of mud.

Sun and Moon could not unravel [1] (N. 330 : 27), and with it also the Souls (T. 1 : 26) who have sinned much and been guilty of great unbelief,[2] who seem like dregs in the midst of the 'Lump' when the Fire has melted all (Eph. Mit. 2: 87). Then again he lets the 'Lump' slip after the New Aeon,[3] so that all the souls of the sinners are bound to the Aeon[4] (H. 11). In it has been collected all the Light that was mixed and mingled in created things (Eph. Mit. 2-87), and these things catch fire (N. 330: 29). Now this Fire outside the universe . . . is Matter itself,

[1] "God immersed Himself in the pollution of Darkness and ... will never wholly emerge, but the part which cannot be purified will be condemned to eternal punishment" (AF. 32 : 22). "Some extreme particles of this good and divine nature which have been so defiled that they cannot be cleansed are condemned to stay for ever in the 'Lump' of Darkness" (AF. 2 : 5). "But the Gods were not grieved because of every little Light which mingled with the Darkness and could not be separated, because grief is not natural to them. But through the gladness and joy which are natural to them, through that they are of cheerful mood" (M 2).

[2] All our sources rank persistent disbelief as equal to the worst of active sins; it amounts to calling God the Truth, a lie, and so aligning oneself with Evil through the appalling blasphemy.

[3] Another technical term of, to me, uncertain significance; it may be simply 'the new age', the 'new heavens and new earth' of Rev. 21 : 1, the 'Restoration' of GZ 49-51 and GH 35. How *false* the allegation of Atārpāt in the Denkart 3 : 200 : 12 : "There will never be a perfecting of the world"! So near the truth and so utterly untrue!

[4] *or*: for ever, *or*: to the (old) age.

altogether unmixed with the Divine Power[1] (AL. 26), and the burning does not cease until what was in it of the Light disappears— and the duration of that burning is 1468 years[2] (N. 330 : 29-30).

3. Now when this affair is ended and Ambition,[3] the Spirit of Darkness, sees the freeing of the Light and the ascent of the Angels, the Hosts and Guardians, she is humbled. She watches the fight; then the Hosts press on her all around, and she flees to the Grave already promised her (N. 330 : 31-32). The architect and builder of that Grave . . . is the one named the (Great) Builder, who in the days of his trouble became fashioner of the Grave of the Darkness (Eph.). So he imprisons her in it (N. 331 : 1), thereupon he closes up that Grave with a stone which is the size of the earth [4]

---

[1] Gk. *kath heautēn, to akrikōs amikton pros tēn theian dunamin.* Thus it is undiluted evil. Note that it is *evil* which is flung into the Fire, and even that, according to AnNadim, is burned until *all* of it has been purged and all the Light is freed. Here we find the same purgatorial nature of hell fire deduced by the early Christian Fathers from such passages as Mt. 18 : 34.

[2] *cf.* M 470 *cahār sad bast ūd ṣast sār.* Why this number?

[3] Humāmah, who appears also in several Mandean texts, probably the same as the greedy and rapacious Envy-Demon (*Āz*) of the Turkish fragments, and 'Self-Willed' of the Pistis Sophia.

[4] Because evil had spread all over the earth.

(N. 330 : 32—331 : 1), the Macrocosm whence the Builder cut whole stones for the Grave of the Darkness (Eph.). And the Light at last finds rest from the Darkness and its mischief (N. 331 : 1-2).

4. Now after this will be a restoration of the Two Natures [1] (H. 11) to the(ir) same original state [2] (E. 58); the Rulers will dwell in their own lower regions, while the Father (enjoys) the higher, having regained His own (H. 11). So all the Race of Souls will be saved, and what once perished will be restored to its own Flock [3] (H. 25).

The whole redemptive machinery of the universe, all the Great Ones who have manifested to rescue the

---

[1] On this Restoration, when evil is finally overthrown, all religions delight to fix our hopeful gaze.

[2] "It is not possible that the image of the (Living) Man should come to the homes of the beasts. The Light (shall) go to the Light, the Fragrance shall go to (the Fragrance), the image of the Living Man shall go to the Living Land from which it came. The Light shall return to its place, the Darkness shall fall and not rise again" (MP. 215 : 1-6). "In the Latter Moment instruction and conversion are achieved; the True and the False are each returned to its Root; the light is returned to the Great Light, while the darkness is returned to the Massed Darkness (*bōlos*)" (CRER. 2 c).

[3] Lat. *et salvabitur omne animarum genus, ac restitetur quod perierat proprio suo gregi*. So overpowering was the universalist belief in the early centuries that even the Manichean dualists could not escape from the teaching of St. Paul in 1 Cor. 15 : 28. It was only later that an exaggeration of the demonic power led to a belief that he could cheat God of some of His eternal Souls and so defeat His omnipotent will. What childish foolishness is this unconscious blasphemy!

Soul from its bonds in Matter, eagerly await the consummation when the 'sons of God' appear, when Evil is destroyed together with those Souls which have by their own choice fully identified themselves with it, spurning the soft callings of the Spirit, and when Greed and Desire—joined in the demon of 'Ambition', which is aggressive egoism—are finally shut away in the eternal Tomb, so that they can never again come out to disturb God's Realm, Light's blissful Garden-Kingdom. Then the balance will be restored, then will God again be 'all in all', and the rebel spirit of the Darkness—which is egoistic pride—be for ever confined in that darkness where alone it is at home. Then will the Soul be gathered in by the loving Shepherd to its eternal abode in Light and Happiness among the Angels and the Gods.

CHAPTER TWO

POWERS OF HEAVEN AND HELL

We turn now to the direct Manichean sources for a clearer and more detailed study of Mani's teaching and the practices inculcated by the Messenger of the Light. First we have a brief resumé of what we are told of the various Emanations of God's Power and Wisdom—where we shall surely be struck by the fervent love and adoration devoted to Jesus, the beloved Predecessor of Mani himself, who exhausts language in trying to sing his glory through lovely epithets. Then we are shown how vital to us men is the work of the Living Spirit and his five great Sons, while we must try to realise how Mani tried, with partial success, to avoid the twin dangers of Polytheism and of an actual dualism between *equal* Forces.

13. God, Supreme Father of the Light

1. He is the Father of the Greatness, the Glorious One who is adored, for whose greatness there is no measure, who is the First

Aloneborn,[1] the First Eternal, who was . . . before everything which has been and which shall be, . . . the Root of all the Lights [2] (Keph. 34-35), the King in the wisdom of the incomparable Sweet Dew.[3] . . . His delicate and wonderful Radiance shines in and out [4] . . . and is ignorant of nothing; He gathers and collects the embodiment of good deeds,[5] . . . can make us equal to the many Saints (BM. 47, 225, 230).

2. His twelve 'Hours', His twelve Maidens who surround Him, the garland-laden 'Victories' who give adoration to their

---

[1] Copt: *pṣarp m̂monogenēs*; not that He is the 'only-begotten Son' of any, which were absurd, but that He is 'His own Son'—*i.e.*, self-existent, truly independent.

[2] Whence all manifestations emerge or emanate. "My God, Thou art the ever-living Tree . . . Thou art the ever radiant Life" (Man. III. 28.). "The eternal Zrwān is the Life-Light, and He is more radiant than all Powers and Kings " (Man. III. 6.).

[3] In Ch. this phrase nearly always seems to stand for 'immortality'.

[4] His Light is everywhere, all-pervading, within and without the Soul and every speck of Matter—for all are but 'sparks' of Him. A truly Hindu sort of phrasing. Yet *He* is invisible, in Himself: "The Father dwells in a secret Light . . . which Paul calls Inaccessible" (AF. 20:6, 2). He is in Babylonian myth the eternal Ea; in Persian Zrwān of Infinite Time; in the Turkish Āzrua, while the Latins called him *Beatus Pater Magnitudinis*—the Blessed Father of Greatness.

[5] *i.e.*, the 'Column of Glory', the 'Last Statue', the 'Perfect Man'—which is the holy 'Church' appearing as God's true Image and thus welcoming the righteous Soul at death.

King,[1] their harps in their hands, the lutes in their palms, ... while they sing to the Hidden Father [2] (MP. 133 : 16-21)—the Messengers who have finished their course running in joy glorify Thee as they go to the Light for their garlands (MP. 145: 9-11)! There is no other God at all [3] (MP. 66: 14).

3. The fruits of the Good Tree [4] are Jesus the great Dawn of Glory,[5] the father of all the Messengers; ... its Reflection is the holy Church; *its Intellect* the Column of Glory, the Perfect Man; *its Insight is the* First Man, who dwells in the Ship of the *Living* Water;[6] its Thought the Third Envoy, *who dwells in* the

---

[1] Sarcastically Augustine says: "The God of thy song is a real King, bearing a sceptre and crowned with flowers, ... twelve Seasons, clothed in flowers and filled with songs, throwing their flowers at their Father's face, ... three in each of the four regions around the Great Deity. ... Hast thou then seen face to face the King with the sceptre and the flower-Crown (AF. 15:5-6)? And did Augustine see the Holy Spirit like a Dove?

[2] *i.e.*, the Unmanifest—Copt. *piōt ethēp*.

[3] He alone is *real*; all other Gods derive from Him and are but expressions of His qualities.

[4] *Cf.* GPM 1:1 and App. I 3.

[5] Because the hope of glory for all lies in him, as he shines with the pure Light of his Father, God.

[6] *i.e.*, the Moon, often associated with Water, because of its obvious tidal effects, and its influence on the psychic and emotional self.

Ship of the Living Fire[1] that shines in *the Sun;* while the Mind is the Father[2] who dwells in the *Greatness that is perfected* in the Aeons of the Light[3] (Keph. 20: 3-5, 14-20).

4. See, the 'Four Days'[4] *are* these: God, the Light, the Power, and the Wisdom—God, who is in the Aeons, and the Light that is over them, the Power which upholds the 'All', the holy Wisdom that is in the Church (MP. 134 : 6-10).

First, we are shown the infinite King of the Light, wise, eternal, benevolent, known to us, as to Hermes, as the Mind, and revealed in all the glorious Powers of His creation, who all adore Him as their ineffable Source. In Himself truly absolute, He shines forth like the fabled Triangular Window whereof Augustine tells us—through the three Aspects of His Light (Knowledge), His Power (creative Omnipotence) and His Wisdom (the grace of redeeming Goodness). To

---

[1] *i.e.*, the Sun, symbolising the inner sight of a mind cleared from all the mists of feeling, and so able to raise the Soul into the clarity of Divine Mind.

[2] Of course, this is the Cosmic Mind, out of which all *this* has come.

[3] Here God's 'five Glories' are correlated with the great factors in spiritual life—rising from the power of meditation or reflection, to the pure Mind, which is the only God. Elsewhere the mental faculties are named in slightly different terms.

[4] *i.e.*, the perfect Lights. AnNadim gives the same list. The Unmanifest, of invisible Light, reveals Himself as a Trinity of Goodness, Power and Love—the Infinite Point becoming a Triangle. So bright is the Light of the Point that its glory is hidden from our eyes; He is the One Invisible.

Him through these three Aspects must ascend all prayers and hymns that the Soul may be saved from its bondage.

14. The Holy Trinity

1. Glory (and) victory to the Father, the God of Truth, and **His**[1] beloved Son the Christ, and the Holy Spirit the Advocate[2] (MP. 49 : 29-30)! Jesus the Tree of Life is the Father,[3] ... the blessed Light-Mind is the Son, the Maiden of the Light, ... this sweet one is the Holy Spirit (MP. 116 : 7-11).

2. Pious[4] love for the sign of the Father, *know*ledge of the Wisdom for the sign of the Son, the keeping of the Commandments for the sign of the Holy Spirit (MP. 116 : 1-3)!

---

[1] The text has 'Thy'.

[2] Mani understood the word to mean the inspiration of the faithful; to him, that was God's Spirit, the inspiring Angel; to his followers it was Mani himself, whose teachings inspired them to a nobler life. Naturally, then, the deifying process soon set in.

[3] *Cf.* Jn. 10:30. No Christian could have revered Jesus or glorified him more than the Manicheans did—even though their reverence forbade them to accept a *literal* birth from a woman's womb as impossible for the all-pure God. For a like reason Catholics have had to insist on the immaculate conception of Mary herself. "His Power dwells in the Sun and His Wisdom in the Moon.... The Holy Spirit, the Third Majesty, has his seat and his home in the whole circle of the atmosphere. By his influence and spiritual infusion the earth conceives and brings forth the mortal Jesus, who as hanging from every tree is the life and salvation of men" (AF. 20:2).

[4] *lit*: God-loving.

May we gain for ourselves love towards the Father, the faith that is in us towards the Son, the fear of our heart towards the Holy Spirit! The seal of the mouth for the Father's sign, the calm of the hands for the sign of the Son, the purity of virginity for the Holy Spirit's sign [1] (MP. 115 : 28-33)! So let us pray, my brothers, that we may find the Father, and fast daily that we may find the Son, and discipline our life that we may find the Holy Spirit (MP. 116 : 13-15).

3. Glory to our Lord Mani through the Father, honour to his Elect through the Son, blessing to his Hearers through the Holy Spirit [2] (MP. 116 : 19-21)!

We have spoken of the One King, sole God, revealed in His three Aspects, and now like Faustus may try to assimilate this vision to the Trinity as taught to Christians. But here we may note some startling differences which seem far greater than the obvious likeness, and in fact Mani's speech is not of the Christian Trinity at all. The repeated trilogy of life's factors associated with the Three Aspects will repay deep study and prolonged contemplation.

[1] Here we have the three Seals taught by Mani—control of speech, and action, and thought or feeling, expressed through vegetarian harmlessness and truth, self-control, and chastity. The four *Spiritual* Seals are given elsewhere as Love, Faith, Devotion and Wisdom (*cf.* GPM 13:4).

[2] From the correspondences in this section we may gain a bright view of Manichean spirituality: arrange them in three columns, then.

15. The Mother of Life

1. The Fount[1] of every blessing and all the prayers is the Mother of Life,[2] the First Holy Spirit (Keph. 43 : 28-29), the First Mother who has come forth from the Father and first appeared[3] (Keph. 34 : 27-29), the Glorious One who is the beginning[4] of all Emanations that have come to this world[5] (Keph. 82 : 1-3).

2. Know that the grains of the dust (?) of the earth can be measured, *with the whole* universe, one can count the dust (?) of the earth year after year *and number* the sand-grains of the whole world; but the length of

[1] *or*: source. Remember it was her prayer which won aid for ' First Man ' from the Father of Greatness.

[2] Syr. *Emmā de Ḥayyā*, a name also known to the Quqites; Per. *Rām-ratukh* (giver of joy); Ar. *alBahīyah* (the Radiant); Turk. *Ögütmis ög* (the Excellent Mother); Ch. *Shan-mou* (the Excellent Mother); Gk. *Dunamis tou Agathou* (Power of Good); she is also called in Per. *Ordovàn màdh* (Mother of Pity). In 2 Eno. 62, 70 we hear of a 'Mother of the Living', which name is given by Melito to Eve, as does also Gen. 3:20 (LXX). In the Naassene Document this ' *Mētēr Zōntōn* ' is 'Jerusalem Above', *i.e.*, Paradise. The name is often given also to Mary.

[3] God necessarily first manifested in the tender love of a Mother, even before His ' children ' could come forth from Him.

[4] *or*: source; she is the 'fount of graces' through whom all God's blessings come to man.

[5] " The Good Father, then, perceiving that the Darkness had come to dwell on His earth, put forth from Himself a Power which is called the Mother of Life, and this Power then put forth from itself the First Man " (H. 7).

time the Great Spirit passed in the Father, *the* First Standing,[1] that one cannot count. He first formed her thus, He kept her in His inner Chambers in quiet and in silence;[2] but when she was needed, (then) was she called and came forth from the Father *of Greatness*; she looked after all her Aeons of the Light (Keph. 70 : 24-32).

Necessarily, the first manifestation of God is His Activity, known in Skt. as the *śakti*. The maternal side of Deity cannot be long shut away from any form of human religion; Mary naturally sits beside the enthroned victorious Jesus. To the Divine Mother are specially assigned chastity, virginity, sweetness and faithfulness; her tenderness goes out chiefly to beginners in the spiritual life, for her wisdom springs from the sympathy of God's own 'intuition'. Ages and ages before the world arose, she was there awaiting the destined moment when she should help creation through the aspiration of true prayer to the blessedness of peace.

16. The Friend of Lights

The Second Emanation (MP. 137:55) is the Beloved of the Lights,[3] the great and glorious

---

[1] *i.e.*, the First Being that ever *was*.

[2] She seems to occupy a place between that of the preexistent Messiah (*cf.* GY 99) and the all-but eternal Wisdom (*cf.* GY 55A) in Jewish thought.

[3] Copt. *pmerit ñnouaine*, the Syr. *Ḥabbībh nahīrē*. Who does not love the Giver of the Reward—which is God's blissful company?

POWERS OF HEAVEN AND HELL   53

Beloved, the Honoured one (Keph. 34 : 29-30), the Lovable of the Angels, the giver of a garland to the *victors* (MP. 137 : 56-57), the one of the garlands (MP. 144 : 20), the ordainer of everything (MP. 137 : 59) who has come forth from the Father (Keph. 34 : 30-31).

This mysterious 'Beloved of the Angels', born from the Father's Thought and bearer of rewards to the victorious Soul, comes next in the line of Emanations. For the certainty of a glad welcome to the overcomer is already there when the Mother's sympathy and love have roused the Soul to effort towards the God of perfect Light.

17. The Great Builder

His Son whom He produced, who is (MP. 137 : 60-61) the great glorious Builder, the Great Architect[1] who has built the New Aeon[2] (Keph. 82 : 9-10) of Joy (Keph. 79-34) as a delight (?) and a *home* for the Fathers of the Light, but as a dungeon and a prison for the Enemy and his Powers[3] (Keph. 82 : 10-12).

---

[1] A title for one Aspect of God handed down to our own days by a certain widely spread Society. In Latin, the *Opifex*, he is not so much the actual craftsman as the architect who plans and supervises.

[2] His work is also touched on in GPM 11 and App. I 7.

[3] Note the duality of his work—it is the Law of Righteousness we call 'Karma': good for the good and bad for the evil ones; he builds hell and heaven equally. " So then the universe is the

He of the incorruptible works, the indestructible buildings (MP. 137 : 63-64) has *judged by a righteous law* the Chambers of the *Enemy* that they should no more vomit[1] death; he has established a prison for the Enemy on the very summit of the Building, *but* has set up a throne for the First Man and all the Fathers of the Light who have waged war on the Evil and have vanquished it (Keph. 79 : 34-80 : 4).

Having rightly resolved to follow this aspiration, the Soul then imitates the 'Great Architect' who planned this universe and lays wide plans for the rejoicing of the Gods and the conquest and subdual of all evil powers. The Path is trodden, not by the lazy dreamer but by the active warrior and worker in God's war on rebel forces.

18. The Living Spirit

1. *The beginning of* all Warriors is (Keph. 43 : 35) the Living Spirit,[2] our first Right

dispensary where the Bright Bodies are healed, but it is at the same time the prison where the demons are chained " (CMT 4).

[1] *or:* erupt, emit. These 'chambers' are the five divisions in the Realm of Darkness, named in GPM 1:3.

[2] Per. *Vāxṣ-zīndkar*; *Vād-zīvantag*; Turk. *Küclüg-tängri*; Ch. *Tsing-Fong* (Pure Wind) or *Tsing-fa-fong* (The Wind of Pure Law), called also the Kindly Light (*houei-ming*); Syr. *Rūhā de Ḥayyā*. Augustine (AF. 20:9) speaks of the " Mighty Spirit who constructs the world from the captive bodies of the Race of Darkness, or rather from the members of your God in subjection and bondage ". This is the Demiurge of Manicheans, equivalent to the Bab. deity Ramman.

Hand (MP. 2 : 5) which the Mother of Life laid on the head of the First Man; she armed him, strengthened him, put a hand on [1] him, sent him to the war.[2] ... The second Right Hand again is what the Living Spirit gave the First Man when he had led him up out of the conflict. Corresponding to *the* mystery *of* that Right Hand has been the right hand which is *among* men when they give it courteously to one another [3] (Keph. 39:3-5, 19-24).

2. In his might the Living Spirit did seven things: (*i*) He brought up the First Man out of the conflict as a pearl is *brought* up out of the sea;[4] ... (*ii*) he spread out those who had rebelled (and) crucified them in every body;[5] ... (*iii*) he trampled and subdued (?) and fastened the beings of death; ... (*iv*) he established the Ships of the Light; ... (*v*) he called his five Sons and assigned them (to

---

[1] *i.e.*, touched, *or*: helped.

[2] *Cf.* GPM 3:2.

[3] *Cf.* the note to GPM 4:3, Note 15.

[4] Copt. *the ñoumargaritēs euñtef ahrēi abal ñthalassa*; it is the spiritual Pearl to gain which the prodigal Prince went down to Egypt in the poem of Bardaisan.

[5] *Cf.* GPM 5:1. As Jesus is crucified in all, so too are the powers of evil.

duties); they took over the Zone[1] and took up all the burdens of the universe. He also called three Living Words and set them *over* the Three Vehicles,[2] another over the Giant (Keph. 85 : 22-33); he secured the root of the Wheel in the Sea-Giant[3] (Keph. 122 : 23-24): *he also summoned the* ' Call ' *that it might mix with the five Bright Ones;*[4] (*vi*) when he had established the Zone, he arose and sent out of himself many Powers and Angels to place themselves round the Zone on every side until he had fully settled the works: . . . then he took a few of them into his Chambers and put others on watch [5] (Keph. 85 : 34-86 : 6).

3. (Lastly), (*vii*) at the time when the Envoy *revealed* his glorious Image,[6] then the *Living* Spirit appointed Gods and many

---

[1] *i.e.*, the area between earth and heaven, wherein the battle rages on the ' border '.

[2] *i.e.*, the ' Three Wheels ' of GPM 8:1, lifting Soul from the deeps on high; can they be the three types of spiritual *sādhana*?

[3] This is the monstrous being conquered by the ' Light-Adamas ' in GPM 8:4 and 21:3, which emerged " from the Sea and began doing evil " (T. III 260).

[4] *i.e.*, the subtler elements, corresponding to the mental aspects.

[5] *lit*: waking-places.

[6] Cosmically, this is still in the future, though individually it is timelessly continuous, and has already taken place in the past when the demons saw the beauty of that Image and fabricated man in order to imitate it (cf. App. I 2:9-14).

Angels, ... they occupied it, so that the whole Building might not *fall* (?). ... Another great glorious work again *which* he will carry out at the End is the Last *Statue* [1] which he will bring up to the Aeons of the Light and *enter* in and take power and reign (?) (Keph. 86 : 7-14).

From the vast power of Active God aid at once comes to the struggling Soul, for He is the Spirit of Vitality who planned the cosmos and brought it into being for the fulfilling of God's Will. The same immensity of activity then wells up in, pours down upon, man's heart and organises his inner cosmos as it has already moulded the macrocosm of which it is so perfect a reproduction. At both levels, all is done to enable the release of the imprisoned Light and the overthrow of the rebels arisen from the darkness of the lower nature.

19. The Custody of Splendour

The Holder of Splendour[2] (Keph. 170:24), Pity, the Messenger of Light who maintains the world (CMT. 37), who is over the tenth heaven,[3] who controls the chain of the ' All ',

---

[1] *Cf.* GPM 83.

[2] *i.e.*, the guardian of God's glory who himself shines therewith. "The Holder of Splendour with six faces and flashing with light, ... who has in his hand the remains of those members and who bewails the rest as captured, bound and defiled " (AF. 15:6; 20:9) " holds the heads of the elements and suspends the world ... in his hand " (AF. 15:5; 20:10). In Chinese he is known as *Tch'e-she-ming-she*, the *Pāhragbed* (Av. *Pathrapaiti*) of Iran.

[3] The highest; so he governs the head and senses of Man, representing his highest faculty, Intelligence or Mind.

in whose hands is the Dawn,¹ (with) his Light-faced Disc, his Gods and his Angels (MP. 138: 29-34) in the summit of all things. His authority is over the three heavens (Keph. 170:25-26), in **his** watch *Sin* tried to bubble up to the Envoy's Image,² but it was restrained far from that place and again withdrew downwards in disgrace (Keph. 171 : 12-15).

This glorious personage, the Phengokatokhos and Splenditenens of the Western writers, is King of the radiant heights of Heaven, the Lord of furthest Space. He controls the mighty movements of the stars and the countless worlds revolving round them; it was in the remote epoch of his special 'reign' when Evil first arose and made the great revolt which tried to displace God from His throne.

20. The King of Honour

1. The Great King of Honour³ who is Thought⁴ (Keph. 92 : 24-25) (is) *the* second

---

¹ *or*: Radiance, Glory, *i.e.*, of God; *cf.* Ps. 19:1.

² *Cf.* the myth of the Rebels in GPM 2, etc.

³ This is " the King of Honour surrounded by armies of Angels " (AF. 15:6), known in Iran as *Dahībed* (Az. *Daiṅhupaiti*) and in China as *She-t'ien ta-wang*, the Great King of the ten heavens, typifying Integrity or Good Faith, and personifying Strength and Joy.

⁴ *i.e.*, Concrete Thought, arising from factual Knowledge (*cf.* GPM 4:2); this rules over the lower 'heavens' or mental planes, while the 'Splenditenens'. of Abstract Thought rules three higher planes. This also keeps the lower, demonic, instincts under control and has his seat in the *heart* of man.

POWERS OF HEAVEN AND HELL 59

Son of Light . . . who looks after the root of *Light* (MP. 138 : 35, 38), the strong God who is *in* the seventh heaven [1] (MP. 2:9)—he is the Judge of all the firmaments who gives a law of truth . . . to all the Powers and all the Richnesses *of the* firmaments (Keph. 80 : 6-9) while he judges the demons, the creatures *of the* Abyss (?) (MP. 2:10-11), **and** rules over **man's** heart (Keph. 172 : 8-9).

2. In his watch [2] a malice and an anger arose, namely the Watchers of the sky, who came down on earth during his watch.[3] They did everything of malice, they revealed the arts in the world, showed Heaven's mysteries to men (until) a ruinous rebellion [4] broke out in the earth (Keph. 92 : 26-31), and those who were sent came down until they subdued them (Keph. 171 : 18-19). The task was allotted to the Four Angels;[5] they chained the Watchers

---

[1] Counting from below upwards; he controls the lower seven out of the totality of ten.

[2] *or*: camp, beat (as of sentry) (Gk. *parembolē*).

[3] Copt. *manrais* (*lit*: waking-place). This is an allusion to the old Semitic (?) or Iranian myth found in GY 2 a and fully narrated in the lost 'Book of the Giants', in Enoch, and in the Book of Adam and Eve.

[4] *lit*: a rebellion and a corruption, evidently hendiadys.

[5] Angels of the four Cardinal Points, who in another ancient story shut out the erring Adam and Eve from Paradise. Their names are given as Michael, Uriel, Raphael and Gabriel.

with a chain for ever in the prison of the Darkness (?)[1] and annihilated their sons [2] on the earth (Keph. 93:25-28).

3. Before ever the Watchers had rebelled and come down from heaven, a jail was built for them and established in the depth of the earth under the mountains. Before the sons of the Giants were born, who have not known righteousness and divinity in themselves, thirty-six towns were arranged and founded (?) for them, so that the sons of the Giants might dwell in them ... who pass a thousand years alive [3] (Keph. 117:1-9).

The Second of the Five likewise dwells on high and controls the lower skies, where are bound the Powers of the Air, the Dominations and Rulerships who lead Souls into evil. It was during his period the Angels fell away, as narrated by 'Enoch', and through pride became demons troubling earth until the time had come for them to be bound and burned. Their fate was already prepared even before their rebellion, when they with evil motives taught the secrets of Heaven's might prematurely to unworthy men. Are they not at work today, with sub-atomic powers?

[1] *lit*: Blackness (*kemkamt*). Their leader was Azazel, according to 1 Enoch. St. Cloud thinks these were the disobedient Stars whose migrations compelled a new calendar in oldest Egypt.

[2] The 'sons' of the Watchers were the 'Giants' of GY 2 and countless other versions of the same very old Titanic myth.

[3] An allusion to the great age attained by the first Patriarchs—Adam 930 years, Methuselah 969 years, Jared 962 years; *cf.* also the contrast with our present shortlived generations in GPM 85:1.

21. The Light-Adamas

1. The third Guardian (is) the Diamond [1] of (MP. 138 : 40) the unsubdued Light [2] (MP. 2:12), who is the Insight [3] (Keph. 91 : 25) that treads upon the trembling *foundation* of the earth ... which is laid (?) in the midst of the worlds (MP. 2 : 13-14), that Visbed-god who stands upon this earth (M 472), who controls Matter (MP. 138 : 42) and *his authority reigns from the firmament down even to the earth; and he has* impregnated by his authority the Sphere and the worlds of the Air, together with the four other worlds that are placed

---

[1] The word means what cannot be crushed, extremely hard, invincible. So there seems a certain correspondence between this victorious Light and the 'Sol Invictus' of Mithraism, a religion dominant in the same age.

[2] "The great Warrior, the Weapon of those of the Light, (the defender) of his land" (MP. 137 : 14-16); "the Warrior, the strong one of manifold activities, who subdued the Rebels by his power" (MP. 1 : 25-26).

[3] *or*: Perception. This Power governs the thorax of the human body and the higher astral planes, wherein the sense-perceptions are interpreted in subtler feeling and enjoyment. This is a realm of emotional conflict, wherein the 'Censor' of the psychologist tries to repress the 'evil urges' ever rising from the lower strata of the self. So while he himself is happy in his invincible might, his spear has to be always active on the lower planes of material energy. In Chinese he was known as *Kiang-mo sheng-she*, "the Unconquerable Warrior with a spear in his right hand and a shield in his left" of Augustine (AF. 15-6); cf. GPM 8:4. In Iran he was *Visbed* (Av. *Vispaiti*), and in Latin '*Adamas Heroa*', symbolising Light and Perfection.

upon this earth (Keph. 170 : 31—171 : 4). (He is) Contentment, the victorious Messenger who subdues the demons (CMT. 37), (together with) his Gods and his Angels (MP. 138 : 44), the forty herculean Messengers and the seven Columns, . . . each of whom supports and individually upholds the heavenly world and . . . wholly represents the form of the Conqueror of Demons (BM. 134).

2. Now when the Sin which sprang forth from the Rulers, which is Matter, . . . had come down to the earth, it fashioned the tree and placed itself within the wood thereof and fashioned the fruits[1] (Keph. 137 : 23-29), (then) the Abortions came down and moulded the formation[2] of the flesh also in the watch of the Diamond[3] (Keph. 171 : 19-21). The Rulers formed Adam and Eve by means of the energy of the Sin which had entered them in the fruits, they designed him according to

---

[1] So evil penetrated even into vegetarian food, working out the vices of greed and gluttony further to corrupt the Soul.

[2] *or* : material, substance.

[3] The purely sensual side of man's nature thrusts itself up into the 'watch' of this higher emotional ruler; thus it is that the emotions of art and religion and pure beauty are so often shot through with vibrations of a lower, grossly physical or even sexual, type.

the Image of the Lofty One[1] (Keph. 138: 17-19) so that by means of them they might reign in the world.[2] They performed all the works of desire upon the earth, the whole world was filled with their desires; this is how also they persecuted the churches and slew the Messengers and Righteous ... at times from generation to generation (Keph. 93:3:8).

8. One of them was the Sea-Giant,[3] the one swept out of the Sphere,[4] ... which caused the Sea to accept her; her own desire was her shaper and formed her alone into a nature which is the root of death. But when she came up in the Sea ... that she might spoil the works of *the glorious Source* of Life, the Diamond of the Light was at once sent against her,[5]

---

[1] God had not to make Man in His own image, but the Dark Powers so delighted in His once-seen beauty that they must try to copy it with a creation of their own (cf. GPM 24:3 and GH 2:3-5).

[2] The same motive is given in App. I 2:10.

[3] This Sea-Giant, to whom the whole machinery of physical nature was linked, has already been introduced in GPM 18:2.

[4] She was composed of the refuse left when the Maiden's beauty charmed the Light out of the demon Rulers and some of the devitalised 'matter' fell into the 'wet parts' of the earth (cf. GPM 8:4).

[5] 'Hades has been stirred up and rebelled, and those of the Abyss have put their arms upon them, ... the stinking and foul demons have prepared to make away with me!' When the Mighty One heard, ... He called an Envoy, the Adamas of Light, ...

64 THE GOSPEL OF THE PROPHET MANI

the great Teacher [1] of Strength; he overthrew her [2] in the regions of the North [3] (Keph. 136 : 28—137 : 3) between two mountains in the place which he had prepared for her (Keph. 115 : 20-21), he trod on her, he set his foot on her until the end of the world [4] (Keph. 137 : 3-4); (and now) he holds the massive Dragon inside a mountain, vanquished and overthrown [5] (M 472).

the pitiless, the subduer of the Rebels, (saying): 'Go down, go, O Adamas, succour the Youth . . . who is below the pit at the bottom of Hades. Put fetters on the demons' feet, put iron on the goddesses' hands, . . . the false gods who have rebelled, bind them beneath the dark mountain . . . and come up before thy Father.' The Adamas armed himself and sped down; he helped the Youth, . . . he put fetters on the demons' feet, he put iron on the goddesses' hands, . . . he also bound beneath the dark mountain the false gods who rebelled, . . . and came up before his Father. His Father said: 'All hail to thee!' " (MP. 209:15—210:14).

[1] or : Insight.

[2] The perception of their real nature lets man conquer the lower urges rising from the body. So too, after an initial check like the First Man's, Marduk overthrows Tiamat, the dragon of the Deep in Babylonia, and treads on her with uplifted scimetar (Bab. Epic of Creation). In Mandean texts, also, the Rebels are associated with the Sea.

[3] In the dark and sunless North the demon races of Mazandaran lived, according to Iranian ideas; but here it may be repelling an invasion into the zone of the Divine quarters, according to Babylonian ideas.

[4] After which she comes to her final judgment (cf. GPM 87: 3 and 12 : 3).

[5] The story is paralleled also in Rev. 20: 1-3; The 'mountain' is Ch. *Wei-lao Kiu-fou*, Ar. *kōf*. The Shapur-aqan tells us that the world rests on a mountain; so the demoness is imprisoned in the world.

POWERS OF HEAVEN AND HELL

Next comes the Divine Hero, the Warrior-God who fights and overcomes the evil Dragon and thus protects, maintains the world against its ancient foe. Standing on the earth itself, his head above the firmament, he watches and guards the whole sphere of human activities, ready at any moment to rush to the aid of man so sorely pressed by the darkness of the lower nature in forms varying from a vegetative apathy (*tamas*) to a persecuting cruelty (*rajas*). It is he who, manifesting the Power-Aspect of the Supreme, finally conquers the demon of Greed and Wrath and restores peace to the troubled Light-Spark that is the Soul.

22. The Glorious King

1. The fourth Son of Light, who is the King of Glory[1] (MP. 138 : 45-46), (is) the holy Counsel,[2] who turns (?) in the Abyss (?) the Three Wheels—**those** of the Wind, the Water and the living Fire [3]—the armour of

---

[1] This 'Glorious King' was known in Iran as *Zandbed* (Av. *Zantupaiti*) and the *Vad-ahrām Yazd*; in China as *Ts'ouei-kouang ming-she*. The Latin name '*Rex Gloriosus*' is less liable to be confused with the King of GPM 20.

[2] Confusion is often caused by the variation in names given to the five aspects of the mind.

[3] He is specially associated with these Wheels for uplifting the Soul represented by the 'living water'. His sphere is the 'lower astral' plane, the passionate nature of the lower emotions through which must run the path to spiritual upliftment. The wheels are the 'noria', or waterwheels with twelve 'buckets', of GPM 6. "The Glorious King setting in motion the Three Wheels of Fire, Water and Wind" (AF. 15 : 6); "another turns the Wheels of the Fires and Winds and Waters in the depth" (AF. 20 : 20).

our Father the First Man [1] (MP. 2 : 15-17), that Wind-raising God (M 472), Wisdom, the Messenger of the Light who awakes the Splendour (CMT. 37), who subdues the stomach [2] and rules the fire in it [3] (Keph. 172 : 13-14); for it is the King of Glory who controls the Three Wheels, and his authority is imposed on the three earths that are over the Supporter's head (Keph. 171 : 5-7).

2. Again, then, in the watch of the Great King of Glory who is the great Perception [4] (Keph. 93 : 9-10), a movement came into these three earths (Keph. 171-21-22). When the Envoy showed his Image, . . . because of the earthquake (Keph. 93 : 12-13, 20) the way for the passage and ascent of the Three Wheels . . . was blocked (Keph. 171 : 23-25) and the fountains of the Wind, the Water and the

---

[1] *i.e.*, they represent the Three Vestments (Ch. *san-yi*), as in Müller: Handsch. p. 39 : "Then by the same purifying he clothed the Sun-god (*Mihr-yazd*) with three garments (*pēmōg seh*), namely the Wind, Water and Fire". So too do the three types of religious *sādhana* act as armour for man in the war with evil.

[2] *i.e.*, the digestive fires, appetites, and sensual desires, seated in the lower abdomen.

[3] *cf.* GPM 57 : 2.

[4] This is the sense-perception of mind, disturbances in which are liable to block the upward way until the Redeemer himself comes down to open it up again. When the senses are confused, how can truth be known, or practised?

Fire were held back. Jesus descended, he put on Eve,[1] and straightened the paths of the Wind, the Water and the Fire; he opened the springs for them and arranged for them the way of their ascent (Keph. 94 : 2-6).

The glorious Ruler of the Atmosphere where the three upper Elements work to uplift the Soul on its Godward way is inspired by Wisdom and labours ceaselessly to keep the redemptive plan continually at work. When the evil powers expressed in human wickedness tried to obstruct that work, when wicked men warred upon the earlier Churches, Jesus came forth from God under his patronage to re-start the activity of salvation, and he enabled the Religions once again to help men upward on their road to God.

23. Atlas the Supporter

His Brother also, who is near him, the fifth Son of Light, (is) the stout-hearted Hero (MP. 138 : 51-53), that Manbed-god who stands on the lowest earth and keeps the earths in order (M 472). Patience, the Messenger of the Light who is in the bowels of the

---

[1] Note that while it was Eve who seduced Adam into sensuality, it is also Eve who raises him to the higher state wherein progress again becomes possible (*cf.* GPM 10 : 1). The first Eve ruined man, the second (*i.e.*, Mary, as Catholics declare) opened for him the path to Paradise again: " *Sumens illud Ave, Gabrielis ore, funda nos in pace, mutans Hevae nomen* "—reversing the letters of the name Eva to the auspicious ' *Ave* ', Hail.

earth[1] (CMT. 37), *the* Supporter, the great Burdenbearer who treads upon the *depth with the soles of* his feet, holding up the earths with his hands, lifting up the load of the creations [2] (MP. 2 : 18-20). The Supporter has authority ... over this great earth on which he stands and *over* the four Supports that are at his feet (Keph. 171 : 8-11), (together with) his three glorious Columns, his five holy Vaults,[3] his Gods and his Angels

---

[1] Ch. *Ti-tsang ming-she*, Tibetan: *Sahi-sñin-po* (the earth embryo), Turk. *Yir-aghlïqï* (earth-bowels), *i.e.*, the Skt. *Kṣiti-garbha*; in Iran he was called *Mānbed* (Av. *Nmānōpaiti*); he symbolised Fragrance and Wisdom.

[2] This figure, familiar to classical scholars as the Giant Atlas, really goes back in prehistoric Egypt to the great deity Shōw who, kneeling on earth on one knee, upholds the sky with two hands in the posture of prayer. He is called Patience because of the arduous nature of his work. Resting in the lowest spheres of materiality, he represents the physical senses and rules the humble feet of the human body. "With knee fixed he bears up the great mass on his strong shoulderblades ... and with bent knee propping it with arms on either side" (AF. 15 : 5-6). "The greatest Atlas supporting the Holder of Splendour on his shoulders lest he become wearied and throw away his burden and so prevent the completion of the final limiting of the 'Lump' of Darkness" (AF. 20 : 9). "Another holds it up from below" (AF. 20 : 10) ; "when he is wearied with bearing it he trembles and thus becomes the cause of an earthquake" (H. 7).

[3] I do not think we can certainly explain these 4 Supports, 3 Columns and 5 Vaults, but they are probably connected with the account in M 98-99, well illustrated by Jackson. It may be no accident that the figures 3, 4, 5 are those of the sides of the Pythagorean right-angle triangle—a natural symbol of the geometry underlying our physical earth—which is not all evil or gross matter but includes the beauty and goodness of the Divine Light pervading every speck of it.

(MP. 138 : 56-58) that are spread over the earth¹ (MP. 145 : 5). In the watch of the Supporter, again, the lower columns were exposed and revolted against (?) their bondage²; a great earthquake happened in that place³ (Keph. 171 : 25-27).

Standing among us, his feet steady on the lowest planes of human existence, the incarnation of Patience calmly bears the weight of all upon his shoulders. It is his endurance of this suffering which lets the Soul persevere through all the trials of its long pilgrimage, until it is ready to enter once again its lost Kingdom of the Light. It is this glorious Power, previsioned in the ' Atlas ' of classical myth, who when he trembles under the appalling burden is the unwilling cause of earthquakes; when the depths of man's life are shaken, the convulsion spreads even to the highest places of the Soul.

24. The Third Envoy

1. The Third Envoy⁴ (is) the King of the Zone (Keph. 82 : 18), the God Mithra from

---

¹ Even physical matter itself has been corrupted by Sin, and so occurs the ' earthquake ' which is one cause of death. Hegemonius goes into much detail on this topic.

² *or*: fetter.

³ *or*: on that occasion.

⁴ *or*: Messenger: Syr. *izgaddā*; mid-Per.'*izgand*; Sogh. *azgand*; Akkad. *asgandu*; from the Sumerian *ashganda*. The Phl. is *aṣtak* or *paighāmbar* (prophet). In Gk. he is called *presbeutes*, in Per. *freṣtagh rōṣan* (Av. *fraēṣta*). He is a Messenger of the Light, and regarded as an emanation from Cosmic Mind. The Gnostic

the Chariot of the Sun (Müll. p. 18), the picture [1] of the King of the Lights [2] (Keph. 35:18), the very Lord of all the Counsels [3] (Keph. 82 : 18-19), the Second Greatness, the King who is in these worlds, the God in God's place, the Form of the God of Truth [4] (MP. 138 : 61-64). *His Greatness* is the Light-Ship of the Living Fire *wherein he dwells*, being established in it (Keph. 63:35—64:2), his twelve Maidens, his twelve Steps, the *Maidens* who sing to him [5] (MP. 138 : 65-67).

2. *He drew out the* beauty from all the Powers and drew *it up* on high, he purged the

---

Baruch-book (Hip. Ref. 5:21) speaks of "His third Angel (Messenger) Baruch", who came "to the help of the Spirit that is in all men." The word 'Angel' or 'Apostle' is used of Shammash in the Sumerian hymns, and of Christ in the Syr. Acts of Thomas. This is the *Third* Envoy, counting the First Man and the Living Spirit as his predecessors.

[1] *or*: bust.

[2] He is not really different from the Unmanifested Lord of All.

[3] As manifested Light, he is the clarity of pure Intelligence shining in the mind and showing the right answer to each problem.

[4] He manifests the Hidden Father through the Sun's glorious radiance—both the physical disk visible to our eyes, and the spiritual Being behind it. The correspondence is with the 'Aten' worshipped by Akhenaton the Egyptian King.

[5] Being the perfect Image of the Infinite Father of Greatness, he too has His glory of the twelve virtues (*cf.* GPM 13 : 2) "The Twelve Majesties that emanate from the God of the Majesty of Law and resemble the bright Sun-god with his twelve Divine Maidens"—so we see the 'Judge' too has his bevy.

dregs into the Abyss. . . . The Envoy showed his Image and refined the Light; for this reason the Sin [1] ran up, and he hid his Image. The Sin . . . fashioned the trees, the Abortions fell down, and finally Adam and Eve were formed in the flesh (Keph. 56 : 17-24).

3. The Envoy . . . did not come there to show his Image to the Rulers in the world . . . so that all the Rulers and Authorities might fashion a Form *on* his Image, but he came . . . for *the sake of* his Soul and his Son . . . crucified in the 'All', . . to give him [2] life . . . *and to* work for him [2] an escape, to free him [2] from every fetter and all the bonds in which he [2] was chained and bound, and to save him [2] from the affliction.[3] But as soon as the Rulers saw him they lusted after his Image;

---

[1] The 'Sin' is the arrogance of the dark nature trying to displace the Light, whose loveliness necessarily generated admiration and desire in all who saw it. From this vain attempt of Matter to imitate Spirit arose the whole lustfulness and passion of our life, which prevent us from any more seeing God's beauty as it really is.

[2] Copt. she, her—*i.e.*, the Soul's, *psukhē* being feminine.

[3] Even before human bodies and natures yet existed, the Soul was already imprisoned in Matter—*i.e.*, in its lower kingdoms. God showed His beauty to win the Soul for its upward struggle, but it led to the Dark Powers holding it even closer in the more immediately attractive human form. The metaphor is given that a modest girl who goes into the street goes veiled; if by chance the wind blows aside her veil and ruffians see her beauty, that was not her desire—yet the evil arises from their evil thoughts of her.

they reflected in themselves that they had nothing like it in their creation; they sealed his Image in their heart, ... they moulded Adam and Eve upon his Image without (the) approval of the Greatness. ... But they have copied (it only) in seeming, but have not *copied* (it) in the truth [1] (Keph. 133-135).

The Manifest God, a perfect Reflection of the ever-Invisible, the spoken 'Word' of Truth and Wisdom, rules under Him as King of all the universe. Seated, as it were, in the glorious Sun, emblem of perfect Light, source of all our life and joy, he is ceaselessly adored by the twelve virtues that represent him in our individual life. It is his Light which attracts the Soul, awakes it from the poisoned sleep of spiritual drunkenness, repels the noxious reptiles that lurk in darkness, and comforts the eye with sight of all the beauties of the living world. He it is who comes to save the Soul from its bonds, to lead it up to the Source of his own infinite Light, the all-glorious King of all. Glimpsing for a moment the beauty of the spiritual, the powers of Matter devise the poor copy that is known to fallen man as 'love', the sexual hunger that leads to procreation and prolonged imprisonment of the ever-radiant Soul in the dark and clinging toils of flesh, the drugged sleep of its ignorance.

25. The Sun and the Moon

Now the Life and Joy, the Faith and Truth wherein the man lives, correspond to the two

---

[1] Human love is a sham, a forgery, as it were, of real love: Copt. *autanten de henoutanten alla mpoutanten hen tmntmēe.*

Light-Ships,[1] for the Living Soul [2] goes up in them and by their means vanishes [3] (away), comes up from the Abysses below and attains to the Height above (Keph. 172 : 24-29). (So) the Sun and the Moon are our Path, the Door by which we advance into the world of our (true) being [4] (Bir. Ind. 2 : 169)—the Moon-god that gathers the dead (TM. 3) (and) tastes not sleep; the Sun-god that raises up what has been refined,[5] the seal and likeness of the Father's Image, the sign of Joy, the exalted Victory (MP. 2 : 21-23). It is the Gate of Life and the Chariot of Peace (carrying) to this great Aeon of the *Light*, . . . it is the Gate of the ascent of Souls (Keph. 158 : 31-159 : 2). See how many are the loving

[1] *i.e.*, his good qualities depend upon their help. These are the divine qualities which redeem the Soul from darkness, so they correspond to the saving Luminaries, Moon and Sun.

[2] Per. *girēv-zīwanag*; Ch:.*yi-lieu-eul-yun-ni*; Skt. *jīvātma*.

[3] The phrase *erbal abal* almost means 'ceases to exist', 'dissolves', but here we need not press its meaning so far, even if a Hindu might urge that in fact the 'living soul' (*jīvātma*) does dissolve when it meets God (*Paramātma*). May be—but Mani was not a Hindu!

[4] Christians and Muslims sometimes accused Mani's followers of rank paganism in adoring the Luminaries, not realising that they held them as a sort of metaphor for the saving Powers. "They very specially honour the Sun and the Moon, not as Gods but as the Way by which it is possible to attain to God" (AL. 5).

[5] *i.e.*, the *spiritually* dead, those lost in the drugged sleep of materiality. "Another (Power) going round the heavens gathers with his beams the members of your God from sewers" (AF. 20:10).

deeds it does for men: ... at the time when it come to this world and dawns (Keph. 159: 12-14), there are five characteristics in the Sun which it shows:[1] ... its light, ... its beauty, ... its peace, ... the life of the Living Soul, ... for it gives a power to the Elements [2] (Keph. 161-162).

Manicheans hotly denied that they *worshipped* the Luminaries, which to them represented God's saving power and the gracious aid of the Redeemer-Christ. They were but emblems of the Divine salvation, and as such were fervently revered, because it was mythically through them, through the Powers they in fact revealed, that the Soul is freed from flesh and matter and drawn to the Height where God, the infinite Light, appears to her.

26. The Column of Glory

Also the Envoy's Son (MP. 139 : 18), the Great Mind [3] which is the Column of Glory, the Perfect Man (Keph. 92 : 5-6) to whom

---

[1] Ephrem says: "It is the Sun which because of its purity goes and comes every day to the House of Life." "His light shines on the earth through a triangular window in heaven" (AF. 20:6); cf. Notes to GPM 14.

[2] The original gives long and vivid details of the services of even the physical Sun to living beings.

[3] This is the 'Vohumanāh' of Mazdeism, the *Vahman* of the Asiatic texts of Manicheism, as Widengren shows; it is the same in effect as the 'Light-Mind' of GPM 63 and reflects Cosmic Mind (the Logos) in the redeeming life of the 'Christ' or Saviour.

all the churches gather,[1] and to whom all the *Light* that has been refined out of the world returns (Keph. 82 : 22-24). The Baptism of Life, the Washing-place of the Souls,[2] the Harbour of those who are in the open sea[3] (MP. 139 : 22-24) (is) the diamond-like[4] Column supporting and upholding the world (BM. 365). the stout-hearted one (MP. 139:25) spreading (and) filling all things with his own wonderful body and his own great strength' voluntarily promising graces to the favourite son who lives alone[5] (BM. 365).

Formed by God, the Church which is the mystical unity of the Perfect Man, One Christ formed together out of all the Souls of "just men made perfect", this Pillar of Radiance leads the upward-trending Souls

[1] In its wide catholicity this sounds almost Indian. Copt: *pete sare nekklēsia tērou sōuh araf*; the tense shows that it is a continuous process.

[2] This entry into the Mystical Body of the Righteousness is the real 'baptism', not of course any merely external rite which publicly proclaims that entry.

[3] *i.e.*, worldly life—Skt., *samsāra-sāgara*. Even in the Coptic books we often find such Indian touches, reminding us of Mani's early visits to Sind and Kashmir—and of the common Indo-Iranian background.

[4] *or*: adamant, invincible. "Upon this Rock will I build my Church, and the gates of hell shall not prevail against it" (Mt. 16:18).

[5] A curious phrase, suggesting the hermit-life, if our translation is correct; I do not have the Chinese text of these hymns. The underlying idea is clearly the 'treasury of merit' shared by all in the Church who live righteous lives.

from earth to Heaven. Those admitted to the common treasury of merit shared by this Mystical Body of the Lord, washed in the true baptismal flow of repentant tears, of prayer and fasting and generous alms to enrich the Church, both inward and mystical, outer and visible—these form the Path of Light that leads straight to God Himself.

27. The Light-Maiden

The beginning of all the wisdoms of the Truth is the (Keph. 44 : 8-9) splendid and beautiful (M 74) Maiden of the Light (Keph. 44 : 9), the Soul of the Father [1] (Keph. 84 : 20), her Father's beloved Daughter, the blessed (MP. 2 : 27) Light-Maiden, the glorious Wisdom (Keph. 35 : 15) who by *her* ineffable beauty puts to shame the Powers that are full of *lust* [2] (MP. 2 : 27-29), who takes away the heart of the Rulers and the Powers by means of her Image, while she carries out the purpose of the Greatness (Keph. 35 : 16-17) and executes justice on the Ruler of the Wet and the Ruler of the Dry [3] (Keph. 80 : 27-29).

[1] In that she carries out His will.

[2] An allusion to the bisexual appearance of the Light to the demons, which made them release much of their own stolen splendour in love and admiration; *cf.* GPM 8 : 2 and App. I 6.

[3] This seems to refer to the female and male demons respectively, infatuated by the sight of so much beauty variously adapted to each of them.

Due honour is also paid to that pure Flame of Beauty who showed herself to the heart's dark forces, so that at least by her loveliness she might confound their wickedness and draw from them the captive Soul towards the Light in a wild leap of aspiration. As the Gopi bound to the pillar by the jealous physical husband spiritually burst her bonds and fled unhindered to the eternal Husband of all Souls, the universal Krishna, so do the Souls escape from the foul bondage of the flesh when they see the attractiveness of Divine Light and flee to God for refuge. That same power of love which once bound them in the degrading slavery of lust and passion is now transmuted to the liberating flame of Love that burns all bonds away.

28. Jesus

1. The pure and wonderful Wisdom is Jesus the Radiant, the self-revealing angelic Maiden [1] (BM. 369), the glorious Dawn through whom eternal life is given (Keph. 35 : 13-14), who is the Releaser and the Saviour *of* all the Souls [2] (Keph. 82 : 20-21). The Physician of the wounded (MP. 2 : 24) is the King of Medicine for the sick, he brings the afflicted joy and happiness (BM. 369). The Light-Mind, the Sun of hearts, the Maiden, Mother of all the lives (MP. 145 : 7-8), the Path that the wanderers seek, the Door of the

---
[1] Manichean theology knows no sex-difference in spiritual beings.
[2] Note, here also, the universality of Jesus's work.

treasury of lives (MP. 2 : 25-26), the Straight Way which leads into Life (MP. 193 : 18), Jesus the Dawn is equally called 'Father'; his Great*ness* is the Ship of the Living Waters wherein he dwells *and is established* [1] (Keph. 64 : 2-4).

2. Jesus, the true Hope (MP. 88 : 23), the true Guardian (MP. 151 : 4), the Saviour of the Spirits and the Helper of the Souls (MP. 166 : 20-21), the King of Saints (MP. 159 : 19), is the First Gift that was given; Jesus is the Father's holy Flower; Jesus is the First to sit upon the Luminaries; Jesus is the Perfect Man in the Column; Jesus is the Resurrection of those who have died in the Church (MP. 59 : 15-18), the Tower of the Kingdom which protects [2] the Father's Treasure, . . . the Perfect Day of Light, (that) of the unsetting Sun, the holy Bread of Life come from the skies, the sweet Spring of water that wells up into Life, the true Vine of the Living Wine, [3]

---

[1] *i.e.*, the Moon, because it actually rescues the sleeping Souls and so comes to its own glory. As the Moon follows and serves the Sun, so Jesus his eternal Father.

[2] *lit*: is over.

[3] *Cf.* Rev. 2: 7 and Syr. liturgies; Qurilyona writes (*quoted*, Widengren, p. 135): "The Vine is Christ. who came to us, in love he stretched out to us the cluster" (*cf.* Jn. 15 : 1). Mandeans also freely use this figure.

the joyous Branch of the fruitbearing Tree, God's new Plant of the fruits of Life, the joyful Bridegroom of his Church, the Shepherd of the sheep wandering in the desert of this world [1] (MP. 193 : 17-26)!

3. Jesus is a mighty Light, ... the Lamp of all the Aeons, the Flower of the Mother of the Lights, ... the Light of the Beloved One, ... the Beauty of the Fair One, the Twin of the Perfect One, the Pair of the Wise One; [2] (he is) the Father of the Light-Mind, the Safety (?) of the Church, the Merchandise of the traders [3] (?); the collective [4] Mind, our enlightening Knowledge, our perfect Reason,[5] our good Memory,[6] our blessed Will;[7] (he is) the Love of the beloved, Faith of the faithful, Perfection of the perfected, Endurance of the

---

[1] Enjoy and contemplate the wealth of these loving and adoring epithets lavished on Jesus by the Mani-taught poet; many of them derive from St. John's lovely Gospel.

[2] Jesus is the better self of all our five mental faculties, as of all else that we know and love.

[3] *i.e.*, the merits gathered by souls on earth, the gain added to the 'talents' given them for trading; woe to those who leave these idle! (*Cf.* GPM 76: 2 and Mt. 25 : 14-30).

[4] *lit*: collected.

[5] *or*: Intuition or even Thought (Copt. *sbō*).

[6] *or*: Counsel (Copt. *sajne*).

[7] *or*: Intention (Copt. *makmek*).

enduring, Wisdom of the wise, **and** Knowledge of the enlighteners; our Stairway which goes to the Light, our Ladder that leads on high; the Chest of the Good, the Ark of Salvation; the Comfort of the weepers, the Joy of those who grieve, the Gladness of those who rejoice, the Compassion of the compassionate (MP. 166 : 23—167 : 17), the Kindly Light and the Awakening Sun (BM. 135).

4. (Jesus is) the King of perfect Wisdom, ... the wonderful and precious Flower of the Light (BM. 160), the Comrade [1] who comes to the Messenger and appears to him, being an intimate of his, accompanying him everywhere and helping him always out of all the troubles and the dangers [2] (Keph. 36 : 6-9). (He is) the First of the Messengers, *Guide* of those who are in the flesh, the blessed Comrade, [3] the *Virtue* [4] of the Father of the Lights, the Robe of the Aeons, the Armour

---

[1] *or*: Twin, Pair, Equal (Copt. *saiṣ*).

[2] It is Jesus, therefore, who was the actual 'inspiring' Paraclete who taught Mani even in his childhood vision. This is a very striking fact, possibly hinting at a time in his life when he was drawn to (Gnostic) Christianity.

[3] Copt. *saiṣ*; it means more than simply a companion; almost a 'double', like Thomas, the Twin of Christ.

[4] A five lettered word ends with . . . *tē*; I have restored *aretē*.

of the Gods, he who is in the Battle with the fighters,[1] who rejoices with those who rejoice, the beloved Comrade, the Walls that are not breached [2] and control [3] the boundary of the 'All', the blessed Fruitage (MP. 139 : 25-30).

5. *Thy* holy Womb is the Luminaries that conceive thee; [4] the trees and the fruits, in them is thy holy Body, my Lord Jesus (MP. 121 : 31-33) hanging on the Tree [5]—Child, Son of the Dew, Sap [6] of all the trees, Sweetness of the fruits, the Eye of the skies, Guardian of all treasures, the Watcher (?) who bears the 'All', the Joy of all created things, the Repose of the worlds ! My God, thou art a wonder to tell; thou art within, thou art without, thou art above, thou art below, . . . near, . . . far, . . . hidden, . . .

[1] *Cf. Light on the Path*, 2: 2, 4: " Look for the Warrior, and let him fight in thee. . . . When once he has entered thee and become the Warrior, he will never utterly desert thee; and at the day of the Great Peace he will become one with thee." The student of the *Gīta* will understand.

[2] *or*: parted.

[3] *or*: hold, possess.

[4] *i.e.*, no body of a woman—an idea the Manichean felt to be horrible and even blasphemous.

[5] The pantheistic Jesus, who is immanent in all and shares in every suffering of the human (and other) Soul (*cf.* GPM 10: 3).

[6] *lit.* milk, juice. He is the hidden Life flowing through all.

revealed, . . . silent and yet speaking (too) [1] —thine is all the glory (MP. 155 : 24-39)! (Thou sayest, O Lord:) " I am in the ' All ', I bear the skies, I am the foundation, I support the earths! I am the Light that shines and gives joy to the Souls! I am the Life of the world, I am the Sap which is in all the trees, I am the sweet Water that underlies the sons of Matter [2] (MP 54 : 25-30)!

How can we restrain the adoring love that pours out at the feet of Jesus, the Radiant One, the Bread of Heaven that contains all sweetness, the gracious Shepherd of all souls, the Lamp and Beauty of the Way, the infinite Reward! Words fail Mani and his disciples to express their fervour at the thought of this perfect Son of God, who graciously offers himself to be " crucified on every tree "—the eternal Sacrifice whereby we and all beings are in being. They pour forth a stream of poetic fancy, a lovely litany of Names, on each of which the mind and heart would gladly ponder. Knowing Jesus as man's beloved Friend and Guide, eternally present as comforter and warrior at his side— but more than this—the Manichean found Jesus present in every atom of the world wherein he lived, sacramentally there in all the fullness of his loveliness, as surely as the Christian could find him in every crumb of the consecrated Wafer, every drop of the consecrated

---

[1] An outburst of ecstatic realisation of the actual omnipresence of the all-beloved personal Lord, which almost recalls the bliss of Swami Ramatirtha in his *In Woods of God-Realisation*.

[2] "Jesus Christ . . . is the son of this First Man . . . bound up in all the stars" (AF. 2 : 4-5). In Z. 131 we have, "Jesus the Compassion, the Thought, the Truth, the Judge, the King of Righteousness".

Wine. A kind of pantheistic ecstasy arising from this real vision gave him strength to endure the cruel torments of a persecuting world for twelve centuries and more, and most certainly the Manichean yielded nothing to his Christian brother in devoted love and worship for the blessed Jesus, the Father's holy Flower, in whom he found the perfection of all that was good in himself and in the Church.

29. The King of Darkness

1. Now the Evil Tree is Matter, . . . which exists in its evil land *that is filled with darkness* and death [1] (Keph. 22 : 32-35); that is the King of those of the Darkness who lay in wait for the Living Soul with his net at the beginning of the worlds. (Now) his net is his Fire and his Desire [2] which he has thrown over the Living Soul . . . the law of Sin and Death that reigns in all the Sects,[3] (Keph. 29 : 18-21, 35) snaring them through the teaching of an error . . . which is full of craft and malice and evil tricks (Keph. 30 : 1-2, 5). It is the Sects that carried on the evil persecutions of God's Enemy (MP. 4 : 30-31), (but even) before the error and the scandal of the

[1] *Cf.* GPM 1 : 1 and App. I 3.
[2] *or*: lust; perhaps hendiadys: 'fiery desire', an apt phrasing.
[3] A word used specially for the 'false' religions of the time.

Sects appeared in the world the blessed Christ was appointed and born against them, so that he might extirpate their error [1] (Keph. 117 : 28-31).

2. (Now) there are five shapes in the King of Darkness: his head *has a lion's face*, *his* hands (and) feet have a shape of demons and devils, *his* shoulders have an eagle-form, while *his* belly (?) *has a dragon-shape*, (and) his tail is formed like a fish's.[2] . . . There are in him five other qualities: the first is his darkness, the second is his stench, the third his ugliness, the fourth is his bitterness, his very soul, (while) the fifth is his heat which burns like a *lump* of iron that is smelted in the fire. . . . His body is hard and very strong, just as

---

[1] *Cf.* the preparations before the coming of the Giants, in GPM 20 : 3.

[2] Several apocryphal books of the age essayed such descriptions of the Evil One—which survived among the superstitious almost to our own day. This one clearly combines the qualities of the five kinds of living being: two-footed, four-footed, flying, swimming and creeping—with each of which corresponds one of the five realms of darkness, one of the senses, and one of the evil Sects (of para. 1). Parallel descriptions may be found in the Mandean *Ginza, e.g.*, 278 : 19-21; *cf.* also the Bab. winged dragon, and the Serpent, Lion and Dragon to be trampled on by the Righteous in Ps. 91 : 13. 'The animals born in each of those elements— serpents in the gloom, swimmers in the waters, fliers in the winds, quadrupeds in the fire, bipeds in the smoke " (AMM. 14)—is this why so many find charm in nicotine? These five types correspond with the dragon, fish, eagle, lion and demon of the Chinese list also.

Matter, which is the desire of death,[1] has built it in toughness;[2] ... there is no ... iron tool ... could cut it up. ... He strikes and kills by the word of his magic; ... when he speaks it is like the thunder in the clouds; ... he is terrible in his voice ... and inspires his Powers with dread, ... and they fall down on the earth. ... He grasps all that he hears from their mouth, ... he even knows the wink they give as a sign among themselves; .. but their heart is not clear to him; ... he knows and marks only what is before his eyes, ... he does not see what is afar, not does he hear it [3] (Keph. 30-32).

One glance at the monstrous Demon of the Darkness that dares oppose these glorious Beings of the Light, and we have done. Drawing his imagery from the religions of the past, Mani like the Jewish apocalyptists of his age painted a terrible portrait of this figure of all essential Evil and his five horrid realms that oppose and parody the five Glories of the Light. Capturing the Soul that descends to war with, and so to transmute and purify and redeem, the filthy Matter which veils his evil nature, the demoniac Dragon controls by violence

---

[1] *i.e.*, the desire that leads to death, the fatal desire.

[2] *lit*: hardheartedness.

[3] Like the Evil Spirit in GZ 45 : 2 (*cf*. GPM 2 : 1), his powers are limited and he has little knowledge; *knowledge* is God's gift, and the key to spiritual freedom.

Five Dark Rulers

Realm	Part of Demon	Shape	Metal of Body	Flavour	Spirit in the World
Smoke	Hands, Feet	Demon	Gold	Salt	Tyranny of Rulers
Fire	Head	Lion	Brass	Sour	Arrogance of Officials
Wind	Shoulders	Eagle	Iron	Pungent	Idolatrous Error
Water	Tail	Fish	Silver	Sweet	Superstitious Rites
Gloom	Belly	Dragon	Lead, Tin	Bitter	Prophecy, Sorcery

and fear the Powers of his realm and holds the Soul prisoner in the five-walled castle of the body. But we may note for our comfort how his powers are limited and so the door to sedition and disunion in his evil realm are opened wide; when Satan is against Satan, the righteous comes near to freedom from his chains!

· CHAPTER THREE

MESSENGERS OF THE LIGHT

Mani now gives us an outline of the Spiritual Path to God—beginning naturally enough with some account of the great spiritual Teachers who have shown it to men. Their teachings benefit those who are ready to follow them, and so Seth, Zarathushtra, the Buddha, Jesus and Mani himself in turn were able to found Churches in the world and to liberate the souls of men from the ancient error. Great is the glory of such a Messenger, and great is naturally the gratitude we feel for him who has done so much for us; but the best way we can show that gratitude is by availing ourselves fully of the means he brought for us to sanctify our lives and to find God through the one true path of sacrificing Love.

30. Earlier Messengers

1. From time to time Wisdom and Good Deeds [1] have always been brought to mankind by Messengers of God (Bir. Chr. p. 209); in

---

[1] *i.e.*, Doctrine and Ethics, Gnosis and Righteousness, the theory and practice of religion.

age after age have Messengers been sent by Zrwān [1]—Shitīl,[2] Zarathustra,[3] the Buddha [4] and the Christ [5] (M. 101. H).

2. *The Messenger of the* Light, the shining Luminary, *came to* Persia to Gushtasp the King;[6] *he chose out* righteous and truthful disciples *and preached* his Hope [7] in Persia. But Zarathushtra (Keph. 7 : 27-31), the famous Master and Leader of Mazdean religion (M 543), wrote *no* books; his *disciples who came after* him remembered and wrote *the teachings of the books* which they read today [8] (Keph.

[1] One of the old Iranian (or Armenian?) names of Infinite Time; *i.e.*, the Eternal King of Light (*cf.* GZ p. lxxxii).

[2] *or*: Sēth-ēl, son of Adam, and according to many apocrypha the first of God's Prophets. The Mandeans ascribed to him the birth of their religion, and Mani was probably brought up as a Mandean.

[3] *i.e.*, Zaradusht, Zarādēs, or Zruṣc, *i.e.*, Zoroaster, *cf.* GZ 26-27.

[4] Here spelt *Būt* in M 101 and *Bouddas* in Keph. Perhaps the ' Buddus ' referred to by bar Khoni as pupil of Secundinus may be the same. In a sense Mani was the Buddha's pupil.

[5] In M 101 *Masīhā*, the 'Messiah', anointed one; *cf.* GJ and GMC. This list is not exhaustive: other names included Aurentes (? Mahavira), Plato, Hermes and, in effect, Paul—whom all Christian Gnostics hailed as the greatest of Apostles.

[6] This is the Vishtāspa met by Zarathushtra in GZ 30, who became the Mazdean ' Constantine '.

[7] A technical term for the 'Hope of Salvation', *i.e.*, gospel, religion.

[8] According to Parsi tradition, the Avesta was actually dictated by the Prophet to Jāmāspa (see GZ p. lxxi); but probably the many scriptures did actually assume their present form later—much as the Kephalaia reproduced parts of Mani's own books.

7 : 31-33); *he revealed* . . . the Two Natures which fight with one another. . . . They honoured *him* more than all (other) Messengers; . . . Zarathushtra was even buried in the tombs of the Kings,[1] . . . they made *a royal garment* and honourably laid him *in a tomb* in the land of the Hindus [2] (MH. 70 : 9-18).

3. When the Buddha came in his turn (Keph. 7:34) to India (Bir. Chr. p. 209), and Aurentes [3] and the others . . . who have been sent to the East (Keph. 12 : 15-16), the *disciples* have *reported* of him that he too preached *his Hope and taught* much wisdom. He chose out **and** completed his churches and revealed to them *his Message*. But there is only this (fact) that *he* did not write his wisdom *in* books; his disciples who came after him, it was they who *recalled* something of the wisdom they had heard from the Buddha.

---

[1] This agrees with Parsi tradition. Slain by Turanians at Balkh, the Prophet was given a royal funeral by the heartbroken King.

[2] *i.e.*, the land then under Indian cultural influences. Seistan, near Afghanistan, was in Mani's day almost wholly Buddhist, and this is anachronistically reflected back on the age of Zarathushtra (cir. B.C. 600).

[3] I do not know to whom this name refers. Mahavira is possible because Mani seems to have been in friendly contact with Jains in Sind.

and *recorded it in the* Scriptures¹ (Keph. 7 : 34—8 : 7).

4. In another (age they² were taught) by Jesus to the West (Bir. Chr. p. 209); (and) the earlier religions *were true* so long as pure Leaders were in them³ (T. II. D. 126). After which the present Revelation, this Prophecy in this latest age, has come down to Babylonia through me, Mani the Messenger of the True God⁴ (Bir. Chr. p. 209) *to* the other Sects and the other Heresies. . . . To each one of them I have made known that his (own) wisdom and his scripture is the truth which I have unveiled and shown to the world⁵ (Keph. 7 : 3-6). I have

---

[1] It is universally admitted that we have no writings direct from the Buddha's hand; what is regarded as the Canon can hardly date back to within a century of the Buddha's death.

[2] *i.e.*, the Doctrine and the Ethics, Wisdom and Good Deeds.

[3] A frank admission that religions are usually corrupted after the Founder and his immediate followers pass away. Manicheism cannot have been wholly exempt, though the precaution of writing his own books may have helped Mani to postpone the evil day.

[4] *or*: the God of Truth.

[5] *i.e.*, I am revealing the real, if esoteric, teaching of every religion. This claim was openly ridiculed, of course, by the orthodox of each original faith; Gk. Abj. 6 condemns "all those who say that Zarathushtra, the Buddha, the Christ, Mani and the Sun are one and the same". Mani does not seem to have said quite this, but that they all came from the same One God—a very different matter!

written them *in my* Light-books;[1] ... **but** what I have not written ... remember it according to your ability and so far as you know it, and (then) write a fragment of the plentiful wisdom you have heard from me, ... so that it may not be corrupted [2] (Keph. 5-9). If you write it and admire [3] it, *then shall you* be very greatly enlightened, and gain profit, and be freed *through the power of the Truth* [4] (Keph. 9 : 7-10).

Mani taught clearly the Theosophical idea that whenever needed great Masters of the One Wisdom come forth with a message, a Gospel, from the Light —to warn and comfort, to guide and inspire, men on the homeward way. Besides the predecessors here named, we have references to Hermes and Plato as two others of equal rank, true Messengers to the pagans of Egypt and of Greece (cf. Ephrem, apud Mitchell II p. 98). Mani makes much of the fact that while all his predecessors limited their preaching tours to their own native lands, he first travelled far and wide in foreign countries, and he first with his own hand wrote books to preserve his teaching intact and pure.

[1] His own seven books: the Gospel, the Mysteries, the Letters, the Giants, the Pragmateia, the Shahpuraqan, and the Treasure of Life.

[2] This was the request which led Kushtai or another to write the book 'Headings of the Master' (Kephalaia).

[3] Perhaps an allusion to the old gnomon that *wondering* precedes the full attainment of knowledge and so of rest.

[4] Jesus said: "The Truth shall set you free" (Jn. 8 : 32). Copt: *ṅse-er remhe hen pcam ṅte tmē.*

31. Signs of a True Messenger

1. If Mani and other Prophets come to this body, then they can be known in five ways: (i) by Gentleness such as characterises the Divine First Man[1], (ii) by Austerity like the Divine Living Spirit, (iii) also by outward Beauty just like the bright Sun-god, (iv) by Wisdom like the God who gathers the dead,[2] the Moon-god, (v) by Changes of Form just like the flaming Light-Goddess,[3] the beloved Daughter of the God Zrwān,[4] the great King and Ruler of Heaven, the most beloved Light-Mind,[3] (Man. I. 24.)

2. If the Elect (?)[5] fully possess the twelve Bright Hours: ... Great Royalty, Wisdom, Victoriousness, Joy, Zeal, Truth, Faith, Patience, Sincerity, Good Deeds, Uniformity of

---

[1] Turk. *Xormuzta-täñri*.

[2] Turk. *ölügüg tiriglügli-bäg ai-täñricā*.

[3] The Maiden of the Light who assumed various forms simultaneously to infatuate the various kinds of demons. Like Paul, God's real Messenger has to "be all things to all men" (1 Cor. 9 : 22), in order to save some at least of them.

[4] This is the Mazdean *Vohumanāh*, Divine Mind teaching and guarding the Prophet, as Mind the 'Shepherd' does for Hermes (GH 1-8; GZ p. 40).

[5] *i.e.*, possessor of true Religion (*denāwar*).

heart,[1] Total Light within and without [2] . . . —they always produce wonderful knowledges in their body and mind, also they are kind and amiable, calm and harmonious. Such signs [3] show that the Trees of the Twelve *Light*-Forms are putting forth their first buds; on those Trees the precious unequalled Flowers continually blossom in plenty; when they are open, their brilliance illumines everything. Within each of these Flowers countless evolved Illuminates [4] in turn and ceaselessly evolve their numberless persons (CMT. 78), who are the armour of kindness, the strongwalled courts,[5] the wonder-forms of the essence and flower of the world; [6] they are the bodies and lives of all sentient beings [7] **and** always

---

[1] This may be the Skt. *sthitiprajñatā*, calm in all things.

[2] The last two Virtues, associated with Aquarius and Pisces, will interest Astrologers; they well symbolise the brotherliness and sensitivity of the last phases of spiritual growth.

[3] *Cf.* the signs of various kinds of Masters or Saints in GPM 64.

[4] *lit*: Buddhas of transformation. The Buddha arises from the heart of a lotus-flower, for Illumination springs from the heart of each individual Soul, and the Soul is pictured as an opening lotus. The Illuminate can always adapt himself to changing circumstances and needs. Ch. *houa-fu*, the Turk. *burxan* or *yalavaci*, Masters.

[5] *i.e.*, protection of their devotees.

[6] *i.e.*, the flower of humanity.

[7] *i.e.*, they enjoy complete unity with all that lives.

add strength to those who enjoy Nature (BM. 236-237, 202).

Muhammed (GI 19, etc.) usually calls himself 'God's Messenger' and gives the sign that a true Prophet preaches the oneness of God and righteousness of life; the Sikh Guru gives signs like those usual in Indian thought. The Manicheans include one sign common to the docetic schools of Gnosis—the ability to disguise the self by changes of form—along with sweetness, simplicity of life, brightness and understanding, like those of the Gods. Even ordinary men, adorned with the twelve Virtues, saints, shine with only a lesser light.

32. The Work of a Messenger

1. When any Messenger of the Light appears in the world to teach and convert the host of living beings in order to save them from their sufferings,[1] he begins by bringing the sound of the wonderful Law down through the gate of their ears.[2] Then he enters the Ancient Dwelling[3] and, using the great magic prayers, imprisons the swarm of venomous serpents and all the wild beasts, no longer leaving them free. Next, armed with the Axe

[1] The usual motive for the 'Buddhas of Compassion'.

[2] The doors of the soul are the ears, its windows are the eyes; so the Message enters the heart through the *ears*, for no written word can avail so powerfully as the living voice, Ch. *ts'ong eul-men*.

[3] *i.e.*, the Soul, corrupted by evil thoughts, feelings and deeds, which are here, as in St. Teresa's *Interior Castle*, aptly called snakes and vermin. We saw that in GPM 3 : 3, the drugged sleep was caused by the bite of a 'snake'.

of Wisdom,[1] he cuts and fells the poison-trees and uproots their stumps, as well as all the other impure plants.[2] At the same time he has the Palace Hall[3] cleansed and splendidly adorned, and a seat placed there for (the throne of) the Law;[4] afterwards he sits down in it. . . . When he has entered the Old Town and destroyed the hateful foes, he must quickly separate the two Forces, the Light and the Darkness, and no longer let them mingle[5] (CMT. 18-19).

[1] In the Indian tradition, the sword of *Viveka* (discernment) and its correlative *Vairāgya* (disillusionment). "Thereupon the God First Man, making the Fire-god into an Axe, split the devil's head; and then, making the Fire-god into a Spear seventy myriad miles in length, he (pierced) the devil's head with the point of the Spear" (T. I a).

[2] "He that is small among those who are on high stepped forth, the Son of the Brightnesses and the Richnesses armed himself and girt his loins, he leapt and sped down into the abyss, . . . he came into their midst that he might make war on them. He humbled the Son of Evil and his seven companions and his twelve ministers, he uprooted their tent and threw it down, he put out their burning fire" (MP. 204: 23-31). . . . He seized their cruel armour, . . . he broke their snares that were set, burst also their nets that were spread. He let out the fish to their sea, he let the birds fly in the air, . . . he let the sheep (go) into their fold, he rolled up his wealth, he took it . . . up to the Land of Rest" (MP. 205: 1-8)—an exact parallel to the "Harrying of Hell" described in the 'Gospel of Nicodemus'; cf. GMC 63.

[3] *i.e.*, the mind, or heart.

[4] So that the divine Light-Mind, Christ, may reign over the heart and life of the Hearer.

[5] There must be immediate *action*, putting away the bad 'Old Man' and putting on the good of the 'New Man' that is Christ (cf. Rom. 6: 6, 12).

2. (O) Messengers, since you are Shepherds of the Light-Flocks, . . . always zealously gather the soft and timid (?) Lamb-Sons,[1] and personally defend and cover the pure Race of Light![2] . . . You must be like that able Shepherd-Lord who catches and saves the Lamb-Sons from wolves and tigers![3] . . . Be each of you the brave, strong and wise Pilot,[4] and ferry these wandering Sons into the strange Land;[5] they are the adored and precious treasures of the Venerable of the Light;[6] remove them all from the Sea[7] by means of your bodily Ships, . . . and return them quickly, as they are, to the Lord; . . . send them back swiftly to their Native Land, the place of peace and happiness (BM. 211-212, 217, 249-251)!

[1] *i.e.*, the childlike trusting members of God's Flock, the Church.

[2] A common phrase among Gnostics also; we sometimes hear of the 'Race of Darkness' as well. This means the Souls, who are all sparks of the One Light.

[3] Demons, or evil thoughts, feelings, words and deeds.

[4] Steering the Light-Ships, Moon and Sun, with their cargoes of Souls.

[5] It is 'strange' only to their lower mind, for that heaven is our true 'Native Land', to which we always, if only unconsciously, yearn to go, the Paradise of all our hearts.

[6] *i.e.*, the King of Light, God, who alone is to be really adored (cf. GPM 93 : 1).

[7] *i.e.*, of worldliness, *samsāra-sāgara*—whence come the pure Pearls of spiritual perfection.

Thus is the work of the Teacher or the Guru described; it is almost wholly interior, and consists in the replacement of the passions, down to their very roots, with all the highest virtues which can adorn the inner nature, so that the pupil may make his heart a throne for the Perfect One, who will henceforth speak and work through his purified soul.

The devotee then appeals to the great Masters thus to come and to purify the souls of all the faithful, to free them from their bonds, and to lead them rejoicing to their eternal Home, where they have always belonged.

33. Is Acceptable to Some

1. The man in whom the Mind[1] is, his is the Wisdom; as soon as he hears it he welcomes it to himself; but he in whom there is no Mind, who is alien to it, does not take it to himself, nor does he listen to it[2] (Keph. 208 : 4-7). (And) every weak Soul which has not accepted the Truth belonging to her perishes without any rest or happiness[3] (Bir. Ind. 1 : 55). God's Word is sweet when it finds ears to hear it; it does not lodge in a

---

[1] *i.e.*, specially the 'Light-Mind', the spirit of the Christ.

[2] Those who are of God hear His voice (cf. Jn. 10: 3; those to whom things spiritual are a meaningless void remain deaf to all the charm of His sweet words.

[3] For in religion, in God, alone is happiness; one who cannot know Him can never hope to experience real or lasting joy.

closed mind, makes not its way (in)to a
polluted shrine.¹ It lodges with virgins and
dwells in the heart of celibates; its grace
overshadows those it lodges with, (so) they
gird up their loins and arm themselves to
fight with the Dragon² (MP. 151 : 17-21).

2. The Blessed will accept this Offering,
. . . the Wise will know, the Strong will
again seek the goodness of the Learned³
(M 17). Blessed indeed is he to be deemed
who has been initiated in this Divine Gnosis,
freed by means of which he shall continue in
eternal life⁴ (FE. 2).

But there are many who will reject this gracious
aid, who prefer the crude excitements of passion to the
sweetly subtle delights of the spirit. Only he with a

[1] The shutters must open to the sunlight, prejudice be put aside to see the brightness of the truth. Nor can purity be to the impure —it is "to the pure all things are pure", and the foul polluted mind can know nothing of the bliss of purity or truth—it corrupts all that touches it.

[2] Truth entering the heart is immediately active. The hearer cannot rest inactive in the world, but at once rises to fight for Good against the powers of Evil (cf. GPM 45:4). "Be strong in war and fight with the ancient Serpent, and you will receive an eternal Kingdom" (Agraphon 192).

[3] This passage comes from near the beginning of the 'Gospel'. "To him who has shall be given"; wisdom and love continually feed upon themselves and grow great.

[4] Eternal life is not to be earned in the vague future; the acceptance of it *now* at once puts the Soul in that timelessness, and being free from the drugged sleep of ignorance he *is* already, timelessly, eternally, in that state of blissful Liberation.

mind to receive the Truth, in whom the Divine Mind has found a home, can give it shelter in himself; it is only when the heart is clean it can be the dwelling of the Word of God 'incarnate' as the Master. And then its faith naturally becomes active, labouring with unflagging courage to spread the Empire of the Light and to overthrow the hosts of Darkness. Only those who thus, inspired by the Light within, labour for Righteousness without can know true happiness—here and hereafter.

34. The Mission of Jesus

1. This name Jesus, there is a grace surrounding it (MP. 151 : 22) (for) it is Jesus who gives repentance to the penitent. He stands in our midst, ... he is not far from us, my brothers, even as he said in his preaching: " I am as close to you as the raiment of your body "[1] (MP. 39 : 19-24)! Jesus (MP. 91 : 20), thy burden is light for him who can carry it [2] (MP. 151 : 23); thou hast made the Cross a Bema for thyself and hast given law [3] thereon; [4] ... thou hast made the Cross a Ship for thyself [5] and hast sailed upon it (MP. 123:29, 34).

[1] Probably quoted from some lost apocryphal gospel, this is like the known fragments of those of Thomas, and the Egyptians, both certainly approved in Manichean circles in Egypt.

[2] *Cf.* Mt. 11 : 30, here quaintly modified. It is easy for his lover.

[3] *or*: judgment.

[4] *Cf.* the agraphon: " Christ reigns from the Tree."

[5] The Ship that carries the Soul from dark realms like this world to the bright Kingdom of the Light.

MESSENGERS OF THE LIGHT

Many are the marvels of thy nativity, the wonders of thy Cross; yet when I say " thy nativity "—who created thee, my Lord (MP. 120 : 19-21) Jesus eternally, Life from Life (T. II. D. 116)?

2. They came to the Son of God, he was thrown into a filthy womb—he who is in the 'All', in whom the ' All ' exists[1] (MP. 120 : 25-27)! For he was led from world to world, from age to age[2] (MH. 86 : 30-31); he passed by the Sources[3] (?) by taking on their likeness, he mocked the Authorities by imitating them,[4] the Powers and Dominions he darkened all of them! These things he did on high, floating (?) in the heavens (MP. 193 : 27-30) and (then) he came down to the substance of the flesh (Keph. 61 : 23), the vesture of *humanity*.[5] God

---

[1] This looks like a passionate protest against the idea of the human birth through Mary, but it shows that the usual view that to a Manichean the idea of Jesus being *born* from the womb was always unmentionable blasphemy is only partly correct. Copt: *aupōh apṣēre ṁpnoute, aunajef auate eslame—pei etṣoop hemptēref ete ptēref ṅhētef.*

[2] *or*: from Aeon to Aeon.

[3] Copt. *arkhēu*; could it be for *arkhōn*, Rulers?

[4] The common Gnostic concept: *cf.* GMC 8 : etc.

[5] Christians could hardly demand a more positive statement of the humanity of Christ: Copt. *nefei apitne aplasma ṅtsarx, . . . pskhema ṅtmentrōme.*

became Man; he went about in all the land, he took a man's likeness, the raiment[1] of a slave[2] (MP. 194 : 1-3). He came for all the sheep *of His flock*, because he knew there was no other *to rescue them* (MH. 95 : 16-17). He had come without a body,[3] yet his apostles declared of him that He took a boy's form,[4] an aspect like us men;[5] he came down and manifested in the world in the Sect of the Jews (Keph. 12 : 24-27).

3. Jesus dug a river in the world,[6] he dug a river, even he of the sweet Name; he dug it with the spade of Truth, dredged it with the bucket (?)[7] of Wisdom. The stones (?) he dredged from it are like pellets (?) of incense,[8] all the waters that are in it are roots *of* Light (MP. 217 : 19-24). He also

---

[1] *or*: vesture, form, aspect (Copt. *skhēma*).

[2] This again could be a Christian speaking: Copt. *apnoute erōme, afkote henpto tēref, afji oueine ṅrōme ouskhēma ṅcaouan*; *cf*. Phil. 2 : 7-8, an all but exact paraphrase.

[3] Startling, to the orthodox Christian! Copt. *ṅtafei khōris sōma*.

[4] This idea is frequent in the Acts of Thomas and of John, both of them familiar in Manichean and Gnostic circles.

[5] *lit*: these men.

[6] As it were, a canal to carry the waters of life to needy souls.

[7] *or*: well, basket (Copt: *beer*), an unknown word.

[8] *i.e.*, the Souls recovered from the world were like fragrant jewels.

freed ... the inconceivable Light in the whole Building ¹ (Keph. 61: 24-25), vitalised, saved and gave the victory to those who are his own, while he slew, chained and annihilated those who are alien to him (Keph. 37 : 22-24). So then at the very time when he had cut down the *last* of the evil Trees with his Axe, he uprooted them *and burned them* and their body with his Fire,² so that thence*forth* they should not grow (again) or produce fruit that is bad to eat.³ ... Afterwards *he* on his part planted his *good* plants, *the* Tree of Life ⁴ that will make good fruits (Keph. 53 : 21-27).

4. He gave *the* Call and the Hearing to the Elements,⁵ he formed Jesus the Child ⁶ (Keph. 61:25-27); he chose his disciples, the beginning of his sheepfold; he traversed Judea looking for stones; ⁷ daily he went to

---

¹ *i.e.*, that of the Great Builder, the heart, or the world.

² The fire that Jesus came to bring (Lk. 3 : 9 and 12 : 49).

³ *Cf.* GPM 32 : 1.

⁴ *Cf.* GPM 1 : 1 also Rev. 22 : 2.

⁵ *i.e.*, he roused even nature itself from its spiritual sleep and elicited response from it.

⁶ In the heart of mankind; *cf.* Gal. 4 : 19.

⁷ Presumably precious stones, *i.e.*, lovers of God, redeemed souls.

the seashores seeking after pearls.¹ ... He planted his shoots in the field of his Elect, he sowed the seed in the soil of his Knowers.² The sound of his shout went out to the whole (inhabited) world,³ his sheepfold filled the corners of the universe.⁴ The Kings who heard laid down their crowns, the firstborn of the land flung away from them their garlands,⁵ ... for his sake the rich ones of the earth became poor⁶ (MP. 194:4-6, 27-32; 195 : 1).

5. Satan entered into Judas the Iscariot,⁷ one among the twelve of Jesus; he betrayed

---

[1] Several of the Apostles were called on the beach of the Sea of Galilee (*cf.* Lk. 5 : 1-11).

[2] Alluding to the Parable of the Sower. The word need not mean ' Gnostics ', simply those who personally knew Jesus.

[3] Copt. *oikoumenē*.

[4] Copt. *kosmos*—the whole organised ' world '.

[5] This may refer to the "Wise Men', often assumed to have been Kings or may anticipate the later royal triumph of the Church; I do not think up to Mani's time any Kings had become converts (Abgarus of Edessa?); certainly by the date of this Psalm none had abdicated on that account.

[6] This must certainly often have been true enough in days when to be a Christian meant sure ostracism and often enough torture and death.

[7] Surely a direct allusion to Jn. 13 : 27. In these Psalms we have interesting characterisations of all the chief early disciples, such as: *Bartholomew*—the rose of love, . . . the sign of freedom from care, for he does not take with him the day's bread"; *Peter*, "the unshakable foundation . . . of his Church, who was crucified upside down";

him before the Sect of *the* Jews with his kiss, he handed *him* over into the power of the Jews and the band of soldiers. Then *the Jews* seized the Son of God, judged him lawlessly in an Assembly and unrighteously condemned him, although he had no sin. They raised him upon the wood of the Cross, they crucified him on the Cross together with robbers;[1] they took him down from the Cross and laid him in the tomb; *but* after three days he rose from the dead. He came to his disciples and appeared to them, he clothed them with power and breathed his holy Spirit into them, *he sent* them out into all the world to preach *the* Great*ness,* while he in his part raised

Thomas, "a merchant that finds gain in the land of India, . . . the sweet smell that went to India; . . . four soldiers at one time pierced him with the point of the lance; they surrounded him on all sides and made his blood flow. How many mysteries he did!" *Andrew,* "the first holy statue, . . . a mind strong (?) in how much! They set fire to the house beneath him, he and his disciples were crucified"; *James,* the "spring of the new Wisdom. He was stoned and killed; they all threw their stone at him that he might die under the storm"; *Mariam* (*i.e.,* Mary), "a netcaster hunting for the eleven others who were wandering, the spirit of wisdom" (*cf.* Mk. 16 : 9-11, Jn. 20 : 17-18); *Martha,* "the breath of discretion, a joyous servant"; *John,* "the flower of virginity; he too was made to drink the cup, "fourteen days imprisoned that he might die of hunger"; *Salome,* "the grace of peace, an obedient sheep"; and *Thecla,* "a despiser of the body, the lover of God". Some of these reflect the 'Leucian' Acts.

[1] "We believe the whole, especially the mystic nailing to the Cross, emblematic of the wounds of the Soul in its passion" (AF. 32 : 7).

himself up to the Height¹ (Keph. 11 : 30—12 : 10).

6. The dozen of Apostles became a garland to this Amen; the Amen answered them, he explained to them his wonders:

> "Amen, I was seized; Amen again I was not seized!
>
> Amen, I was judged; Amen again I was not judged!
>
> Amen, I was crucified; Amen again I was not crucified!
>
> Amen, I was pierced; Amen again I was not pierced!
>
> Amen, I suffered; Amen again I did not suffer!"[2]
>
> Amen, I am in my Father; Amen again my Father is in me!—
>
> But thou wishest the fulfilment of my Amen:

---

[1] It is hard to find anything unorthodox in all this; it shows no trace of docetism—yet Faustus hints in the passage in the previous note that they understood the whole story in an esoteric sense, consistent with the Hymn following.

[2] This passage adheres closely to the Hymn of Jesus and the story of the Crucifixion in the Acts of John (*cf.* G.R.S. Mead's two little books in *Echoes from the Gnosis*). To the ignorant it seems a paradox; those with any kind of spiritual experience will understand the Truth can be expressed in no other way—the most dreadful pain is at times exquisite bliss.

MESSENGERS OF THE LIGHT

> I mocked the world, they could not mock at me!"
>
> Amen, Amen, Amen, Amen again, the four-faced God;[1]
>
> Glory and honour to the Amen, the Father of the Greatness!
>
> Blessing and holiness to Jesus, the Son of the Amen!
>
> Victory to the Holy Spirit who has guided [2] us to this Amen [3] and his holy Elect (MP. 191:1-16)!"

7. At the time when *Jesus* appeared (?) *in the land of the West*,[4] then he *chose out a Church and pro*claimed his Hope *and his Revelation* [5] to his disciples (Keph. 7 : 18-21): (then)

---

[1] The 'Tetraprosōpon', symbolised by the four letters in the Holy Name in Hebrew—YHWH, יהוה, and referring to the Unmanifested manifesting as a Trinity (*cf.* GPM 13 : 4); we have a Trinitarian theology here too.

[2] *or:* taught.

[3] This name is often spelt here with a preceding 'H'. Long before this time it was used at the end of prayers in Jewish, Christian and Gnostic circles, and I think it futile to try to guess any meanings other than the obvious affirmation of belief and self-association with the prayer. *Here* it symbolises the 'Real'.

[4] From the view of Persia and Mesopotamia where Mani lived, Palestine is, of course, to the *west*; yet it lies north-east of Egypt where these Psalms were translated. Here we seem to have a hint at the lost Syriac original. In those days Christianity was not spread more in the West than in the East; it had taken root far and wide in Iran and beyond.

[5] *or:* Righteousness, *i.e.,* code of ethics.

he went up and rested in the *Land of* Light (Keph. 61 : 27-28). After him they wrote the *teaching he gave to them and* his parables,[1] *his precepts of righteousness*, and the signs and wonders *which he showed to them*; they wrote a book describing his *life*[2] (Keph. 7 : 23-26).

The story of Jesus, Mani's immediate forerunner, is then briefly told. We note here many thoughts derived from early Gnosticism, such as the gradual descent with intensifying disguise in para. 2, already taught in the Jewish Gnostic 'Ascension of Isaiah', and the constant stress on the (physically) unreal nature of his body and its sufferings (cf. Acts of John). His liberating work in the world is beautifully described with rich and swiftly changing metaphors, while the story of the Crucifixion could have been written by any Christian. The hymn here given is a very close copy of the 'Hymn of Jesus', so grandly set to music by Gustav Holst; inset in the Acts of John, it seems to have been used by the Manichean (?) Priscillianists of Spain around A. D. 385. The exact meaning of ' Amen ' here escapes me; it may be only " in truth "—but is clearly used as a mystic name for the Supreme Lord, as by many Gnostics.

[1] "The writings are not the production of Christ or of his Apostles, but a compilation of rumours and beliefs made long after their departure by some obscure semi-Jews—not even in harmony with one another—and published by them under the names of the Apostles, or of those considered the Apostles' followers, so as to give the appearance of apostolic authority to all these blunders and falsehoods" (AF. 33 : 3). These harsh words of Faustus are just what Christians say about the so-called N.T. Apocrypha; modernist critics might have agreed with the opponent of St. Augustine here.

[2] The restoration of this paragraph is largely speculative, but I have built it on other fragmentary references, and the Coptic words would just fit in the broken spaces.

35. Mani's Birth Brings Joy

1. Out of Paradise[1] has come an Envoy, a Herald from the Kingdom (M 4), a Messenger with a dear name, the Chosen God, the holy Mani (M 99), the gracious Word (M 64)! This is in his own Song: "I am the First Stranger, the Son of the divine Zrwān, the Son of Sovereigns (S 29)! Out of the Light and (from) the Gods am I, and have become a foreigner to them[2] (S 108), I have become alien to the Most Excellence! The enemies have assailed me, I have been led by them down to the dead (M 7)!"

2. O loving Comrade,[3] thou art illumined by the signs of the Sun,[4] thou Ruler of Good, the likeness of the divine Zrwān (M 801)! Thou art the new Teacher of the East[5] and Promoter[6] of those of the Good

---

[1] The word is Iranian, *Bahisht*, not Christian.

[2] This verse has a typically Gnostic sound: *az rōṣan ū yezdān hēm, ūd ʿzdyh bwd ḥēm az ḥwyn*; cf. GPM 50: 2.

[3] or: Twin; *'ispēxt ayē pramēn pahīqērb*.

[4] *i.e.*, by bringing light, safety, joy, etc. to men, as the Sun does.

[5] or: the province Khorassan, where Manicheism early flourished.

[6] or: Leader,—the Head of the Religion.

Faith,[1] for thou wast born under a brilliant Star in the family of rulers[2] (M. 543)!

3. A new light-bringing Sun has come, a new Messenger, a Teacher in[3] the East[4] (BuBb. 32)! Lo, the Morning has come, lo, the Sun shines on *us*—the 'Morning' is the Truth, (and) the 'Truth' is the Commandments (MP. 146: 17-20), the 'Truth' is the Son of God[5] (M 18)! To the afflicted has come the Teaching; . . . the News has come from the God[6] of Gods (Mahr. 364-365)! Mani, the King of[7] Righteousness,[8] to whom the Adorable of the Light[9] promised wisdom and the Saints promised kindness, has come to the world[10] from beyond the Three Realms—to revive our natures, to become the great King

---

[1] The phrase *Vahī dēnān* was commonly used for Mazdeism also.

[2] *zhē zād hay pad parōzh axtar andar tōhm 'ig saḥreyārān.*

[3] *or*: from.

[4] *or*: the Province Khorassan, where Manicheism early flourished.

[5] Derived apparently from Mani's 'Gospel' as the answer of Jesus to Pilate's half-mocking question: "What is truth?" Read: *rāstēft bāg-pūhar ast.*

[6] *i.e.*, the divinest God.

[7] *i.e.*, the Head of the Religion (Sogh. *dēnsār dhār*: Parth. *dēnsārdhār*) a term used in Denkart 9: 42: 7 for Zarathushtra.

[8] *i.e.*, the sum of all the Elect, the perfect Church; (Syr. *zaddīqūtā*, Sogh. *ardāvya*, Parth. *ardāvēft*, Gk. Copt. *dikaiosunē*).

[9] Ch. *Ming-tsouen*; *i.e.*, the Supreme God.

[10] *i.e.*, Skt. *samsāra*, the sphere of recurring births and deaths.

of Medicine,[1] the just Judge, to open the fountain of immortality,[2] plant the life-giving Tree, deliver the hosts of his Native Land, gather the Sons of Light, to become the Shepherd of the tender and gentle flocks, put wall[3] and moat around the fields of blessings, to nourish and beautify the seedlings and fruits of the clean and pure Law, to become the Guardian and Protector[4] (BM. 374-376)!

4. Let us bless our Lord Jesus who has sent to us the Spirit of Truth![5] He came and separated us from the error of the world, he brought us a mirror in **which** we looked and saw the universe[6] (MP. 9:4-7); (he led us up) to Paradise, where the breeze brings lovely fragrance[7] (M 64)!

5. Gladly and joyfully were the highly blessed Light-beings led on when thou wast

---

[1] *i.e.*, the (spiritual) Healer.

[2] *lit*: sweet dew, *i.e.*, *amritam*, ambrosia.

[3] *or*: embankment; *cf.* GPM 11.

[4] Here we have a complete outline of the work of every true Messenger from God.

[5] Here Mani is declared to be the 'Paraclete' promised by Jesus in Jn. 14: 16-17, 26; so he was, to the Manicheans.

[6] *Cf.* the thought in Agraphon 93, probably from the lost Gospel of the Egyptians: *ita me in vobis videte quomodo quis vestrum se videt in aquam aut in speculum*; also *cf.* 1 Cor. 13: 12.

[7] *Cf.* GPM 80: 3.

born in royalty![1] The twelve (Signs) and the world's atmosphere were in a happy mood; all Gods (and) those like (them) were made to become full of joy.[2] O friend, through thee is secured (?) the house of the mountain-plant and stream-fed soil, the palace and the open hut![3] When the beautiful maids and youths from the Light-Mind[4] saw thee, they blessed thee through praises in unison, O faultless Youth! From all sides small drums, harps, flutes, gave again and again the sound of poetic melodies! The Gods all stand facing the Son of the Ruler of the Race;[5] a voice from the air[6] sings the melody of a lyric of the World of Light, speaking thus to the *Messenger* of the Light: "The Judge is born, happiness created! O Crowned One, best and highest of all the Gods,[7] three things have

[1] This certainly seems to confirm that Mani was of royal birth; it reads: *tō zād aiy bd ṣahrāyeft*.

[2] *Cf.* the joy of nature when Zarathushtra was born (GZ 26 : 3), Jesus (GMC 7-9), Sri Krishna (Srīmadbhāgavatam 10 : 3), and the Divine King (GP 46).

[3] *i.e.*, both rich and poor were blessed.

[4] Text: *Manūhmed*, the Cosmic Mind expressed through the incarnate Teacher.

[5] Mani too is here called 'the Son of God', who is the King of all Light-'Sparks', the souls of men, etc.

[6] *i.e.*, an *ākāśa-vāṇī*, such as Hindu Puranas often bring in.

[7] And here Mani seems identified with God Himself.

been assigned for thee to do: to abolish death, strike down the Foe, exalt [1] the whole Garden of the Light (M 10)!"

6. O Saviour of Souls (M 74), thou art a Son of God (M 785)! Thou hast received adoration, hast soared up to the *Height* and drawn up the whole Light-Paradise; the terrible (?) Ruler is for ever bound and the abode of the Dark ones is abolished![2] O Friend of the Light,[3] First of Humanity,[4] thou wast present when the Father (expressed) the desire![5] ... Thou hast come with well-being,[6] thou Spirit of the Light; let His well-being be on thee who art the Father's own! O true outleading God,[7] the higher Gods whose glorious diadem[8] ever *shines on thy brow* praise thee, O Living Spirit, holy holy God, my Lord Mani (M 10)!

---

[1] *or*: draw up.

[2] This can only happen when the body, dwelling of the demons, has been finally discarded by the saints in the hour of death.

[3] *Cf.* GPM 16; *Friyānāg Rōṣān*.

[4] *i.e.*, mortals.

[5] *i.e.*, that a Messenger should visit the earth (*cf.* GZ 52, Heb. 10 : 9).

[6] Primarily spiritual, but worldly prosperity also.

[7] *i.e.*, who leads souls out of the darkness into Light.

[8] *lit*: diadem and glory—probably a hendiadys.

Christians being perplexed by a swarm of warring sects and theories, harassed by recurring persecutions, the hour had come for a new revelation. Mani appeared in the world at a time of crisis. Handicapped by its association with the rigidity of ancient Israel and its rites, the faith of Jesus had lost the adaptability which could have won the immemorial East, and must henceforth labour among the wild and unsophisticated peoples of the West and North. The hope of the new spiritual light illumining the vast lands of Asia rested now with the new Messenger, whose birth was naturally a "tidings of great joy" to those who sought for light. He too, like those who went before him, laboured for the freedom of all God's sons, 'sparks' of His Light exiled in the prisons of the gloomy Darkness.

36 Mani's Mission

1. Then the Luminary [1] said (Keph. 42 : 32): " I Mani, the Apostle of Jesus [2] (M 17), I have gone out of the land of Babel, whence I was to call a Call in the world (M 4); I shall cause living streams to well up for the thirsty, that they may drink and *live* " [3] (Keph. 90 : 18-19).

2. The Luminary said again (Keph. 43 : 25): " Without weapons, without *armour I have subdued* distant towns and far-off lands through

---

[1] One of Mani's favourite titles in the Kephalaia, because like the Sun he brought redeeming light to mankind.

[2] See also the note 5 to GPM 35: 4.

[3] So too said Jesus, in Jn. 4: 14.

the Word of God, while they bless my name and it receives glory in all the lands. . . . The Kings, nobles and officials have striven *with (all) their power* [1] with me to break me away from this Truth; they could do nothing against me! If now I had been alone, why could not all those who have contended with me succeed against me? . . . As no single man has known how to conquer me in all the world, so is it also (to be) with my sons, no one shall be able to conquer them. . . . I have strengthened my Church, have made it my own, have placed in it all good things that are in any way of use to it; in all lands far and near *I have* planted the Good (and) sowed the Truth (Keph. 100 : 32—101 : 8, 15-17, 22-25); by me has a Palace [2] been built and a throne having goodly rest for the Soul and Spirit (M 5)! Apostles and Envoys have I sent out to all the lands, so that the earlier Apostles who preceded them have not done as I have done in this hard generation, save only Jesus, the Son of the Greatness, who is

[1] *or*: with all their powers, *i.e.*, military and governmental forces.
[2] *Cf.* the Palace Thomas built in the heavens for King Gondaphernes, in the Acts of Thomas.

116 THE GOSPEL OF THE PROPHET MANI

the Father of all the Apostles.¹ . . . For this great Door which I have opened lies open to the Gods and Angels, and Men and all the Spirits and the living Souls who are ready for Life and everlasting Rest (Keph. 101 : 25-29, 34—102 : 3)!"

3. The Messenger (Keph. 9 : 21) himself subdued the great Sea, he also subdued the Rebels in it,² . . . he set guards over them to watch them. He lifted up the fallen, healed the wounded, woke those who slept, reminded those who had forgotten, enlightened the eyes of the Righteous that they might go up and see the Land of the Light,³ gathered those who were scattered, made the poor ones of darkness shine, laid down and levelled the course his Living Father enjoined on him, (and) smoothed the royal road from here to the Land of Peace, . . . so that the Righteous might walk on it⁴ . . . and see the Land of

---

[1] A remarkable testimony to Mani's direct predecessor.

[2] *i.e.*, the demons of passion, greed, lust, etc., which infest the emotional nature in this world.

[3] Mere virtue alone does not give this spiritual vision; that is a special gift of God at His pleasure to the righteous. We know that Amu (Ammōs), was one of Mani's apostles who had this vision (*cf.* GPM 80, mostly from his hymn).

[4] *Cf.* Isa. 35: 8 in GY 83 : 3.

Light. A radiance is put on them, a diadem [1]
is tied upon their head, and they are added
to the number of the Angels (MP. 213 : 6-21).
(And finally) he perfected his mystery through
the Cross (MH. 11 : 15).

4. Our Lord (Keph. 16 : 26), we worship
thy sufferings which thou didst endure for thy
children's sake, for thou didst leave thy great
glory, and come and give thyself for Souls.
Thou didst put on [2] shape after shape until
thou hadst visited every race,[3] for the sake of
thy loved ones, until thou hadst chosen them
in their midst! *Thou didst cross* the earth,
the seas, and the *deserts* also; thou didst
seek out thy Beloved, thy Church, until thou
hadst found her (MP. 42 : 28—43 : 4)! The
beloved Son, Christ Jesus, sets a garland on
thee in great joy, for thou hast built
(again) his building that was destroyed,
illumined his path that *was* hidden, set in
order once more his Scriptures which were

---

[1] *or*: turban.

[2] *or*: take, "being all things to all men".

[3] *Cf.* GPM 34 : 2, but it also refers to the way Mani adapted his teaching to the backgrounds of the various lands he visited, so that it could take root everywhere.

118 THE GOSPEL OF THE PROPHET MANI

confused,[1] explained his secret Wisdom [2] (MP. 12 : 28-32)!

Here we let Mani himself speak of his untiring labours (cf. also GPM 88:1) for mankind in fulfilling the pledge taken before his birth, and we note his very human pride in having done more than all his predecessors save only Jesus, the "beloved one of the sweet name". Then the devotee takes up the tale, closing with words of gratitude for the wonderful things his Teacher has done.

37. The Glory of Mani

1. Our Lord Mani, the Messenger of the Light, the Tongue that speaks no lie, our glorious Father, the Gentle One who loves (his) children [3] (MP. 139 : 47-52), the Tree of Life full of gay fruit [4] (MP. 80 : 24)—he gives life to the dead and illumines those in darkness [5]

[1] The Qur'an puts the same charge that Christian Scriptures have been corrupted in the interest of certain doctrines preferred by the Church. But so far as I myself have read, proof of this is still inadequate.

[2] Mani here claims to be a true Gnostic, revealing the mysteries, the Esoteric Knowledge that lies within the words of earlier Scriptures.

[3] A touching tribute to the personal manner of the Prophet: peniōt naglaos phelcēt mmaiṣēre: Cf. "a bruised reed he shall not break".

[4] This of course identifies him with God, as in App. I 3:1; the 'fruit' are of course the disciples' virtues, as in Jn. 15:4-5 (GMC 52).

[5] Clearly, the spiritually dead are referred to; Mani nowhere claims to have worked 'miracles' of the more vulgar type: zīvēnēd ō mūrdagānā, ūd rōcēnēd ō tārīgān.

(M 311). Mani (is) the Sovereign Light, . . . the Spirit of the Light, . . . Father of the blessing, . . . compassionate and incorruptible . . . Place of Repose (Mahr. 233, 415, 271, 274, 283), (also) the Mind and the Wisdom that dwell in his Scriptures, his Five holy Books [1] (MP. 139 : 52-54) !

2. Thou art the supreme Self,[2] thou art the First and Last [3] (M 83), the immortal Wind of Life (M 47), for thou art the proclaimer of Truth in the Beginning, the Middle and the End [4] (MP. 7:8-9). Fortunate for us that through thee we learned and accepted thy teaching (M 233)!

3. When I think of thee, my Lord, great is the fear that surrounds me; when I desire

---

[1] Five is the specially holy number. The list is usually given as: the Living Gospel, the Treasury of Life, the Mysteries, the Pragmateia, and either the Shahpuraqan or the Book of Letters. In these books abides the very spirit of Mani himself, as the Guru dwells in the Guru Granth Saheb (GGS 54:7) and Yahweh in the Law.

[2] A strikingly Indian-sounding sentence: *tō tō ēē grēv vazurg.*

[3] *Naxvēn ēē ūd 'ustōmēn.* Cf. Rev. 22:13 and GPM 93:3; in both places this declares eternity and is a divine epithet.

[4] *i.e.*, in the Three Times—before creation, this present age of mingled good and evil, the final Restoration.

to give thee glory, I do not find to whom I should liken thee (MP. 151 : 26-27)! To what shall I compare thee, my Lord? I shall compare thee with the Sun that shines forth, that comes daily with his rays and gives delight to all created things (MP. 145:21-24)! Who will not rejoice when the Sun is about to shine on him (MP. 151 : 11)? To what shall I compare thee, O Beloved? I shall compare thee with a great River that gives gladness to the worlds *and the waters of life* to the parched fields! I shall compare thee to a good Farmer who cares for his trees and daily gathers their fruits (MP. 145 : 25-31)! When I seek thee I find thee within, shining upon me;[1] perhaps I too am worthy to *hear* the divine Call! *When I* myself come to thee, fair is thy glory in my mouth, my Lord (MP. 151 : 28-30)!

The devotee pours out fervently a passionate expression of his love and adoration for the Enlightener, the tender Guardian, who is ever with him, strengthening him and giving him joy and peace even in the hour of agony.

[1] As the Messenger of Light, Mani is also the 'Light-Mind' that enters, shines within, awakes and guides the willing Soul (cf. GPM 63).

38. The Bema Festival

1. The great High King is seated on his Bema,[1] he looks at the deeds of every one of us (MP. 21 : 27-28)! This is the Bema of Jesus and the Maiden of the Light and the Judge of the Church (MP. 20:31—21:1); this (is the) Day whereon his dawning and his light appear (MP. 30:28-29). The whole air gives light, the Sphere *shines* today; even the earth also puts forth blossom, the waves of the sea are still, for the gloomy winter that was full of trouble has passed away—let us too escape from the iniquity of evil! . . . See, today (?) every tree has been renewed once more! See, the rose-flowers have spread abroad their beauty, for the worm [2] (?) that harmed their leaves has been taken away[3] (MP. 8-18-21, 14-16). Cut thou also the chains and the

---

[1] The rostrum for Athenian orators, the dais whereon the most important persons sat at a feast. It was approached by five steps, corresponding to the five Glories of Mind, to the stages of spiritual enlightenment, and the grades of the Manichean hierarchy culminating in the Leader himself. Its presence in the Prayer-Hall, richly adorned, ensured the sacramental presence of the glorified Lord to judge, pardon, teach and divinise the faithful. This was specially done at the anniversary of Mani's ascent to heaven after death—with rejoicings much like the Christian Easter.

[2] An unknown word *snah*; it may be parasite, bond, rot, blight.

[3] *or*: cut, severed. Nature shares the joy of the faithful.

worms (?) of our sins! (MP. 8 : 16-17) Now then we make festival observing[1] thy holy day, and passing the night keeping vigil in thy joy, O Glorious One; . . . so wash us now in the dewdrops of thy happiness (MP. 41 : 16-17, 20)!

2. For this is the Day which thou hast given us as a present[2] that we may beseech thee, our Lord, and thou (mayest) forgive us our sins (MP. 20:28-30); he who despises today shall be despised on the day of laying aside the body (MP. 21:11-12). We worship thee, O Advocate,[3] and we implore in the presence of thy Bema that thou mayest forgive us our sins that we have committed in the whole year! For there is no one in this flesh who is free from sin in his heart;[4] it is thou alone who art the searcher of hearts—forgive us what we have done (MP. 25:18-23)! Look upon thy beloved ones, O Blessed; pity thy children, . . . give us the grace of absolution (MP. 29 : 20-22)!

[1] *or*: perfecting.
[2] *Cf.* Ps. 118 : 24. Prayer *is* rejoicing, as we find in GPM 58.
[3] *i.e.*, the 'Twin', who always accompanied Mani; and now in the same way Mani will always accompany us, ready to help in need.
[4] *cf.* GY 37 : 1-2.

3. O Soul, . . . this visible Bema, the Word, has been set before thee that it may sow in thee through what is visible[1] the memory of the hidden Law[2] which thou hast forgotten since the day thou didst drink the water of madness. O Soul, see, to thee has come the grace of the Day of Rejoicing; do thou reveal without fear all thy sins today[3] and remember thy end and prepare thyself in thy works, for the Bema of Wisdom moves thee thereto (MP. 7 : 14-21). This is the Way of Truth, this is the Stairway that leads on high,[4] which shall take us up to the Light (MP. 22:6-7); come then, and walk on these holy steps[5] (MP. 7:32)! From the beginning he is this Way, namely the First Man, and Jesus the Radiant, and the Spiritual Advocate; they have summoned thee, O Soul,

---

[1] Thus the 'Bema' was a true sacrament—"an outward and visible sign of an inward and spiritual grace". It *may* have originated in the vision (?) of Mani at his death, narrated in his 'Life', §24, when he distributed bread and salt. The Manicheans certainly had some kind of Eucharist like the Catharist 'Consolamentum' (see article in CE).

[2] *or*: judgment—*hep*.

[3] Doubtless in some such form as the 'Khuastuanift', our App. II.

[4] The figure popular even in Ancient Egypt of B.C. 3000 (GP 33).

[5] *i.e.*, the five steps of the Church, leading to the Lord on the throne upon the Bema.

that thou shouldst go up on high thereby (MP. 22 : 7-10)!

4. Let the Bema become for thee a landing-place of thy lifetime,[1] a cleansing-place of thy life, a chest filled with teaching, a ladder to the Height,[2] a measuring-balance of thy deeds (MP. 8 : 1-4). Receive the holy Seal from the Mind of the Church and fulfil the Precepts (MP. 22 : 11-12), to accept most actively every injunction, command and seal of perfect peacefulness (S 32): that we lie not, . . . kill not, . . . eat no flesh, . . . purify ourselves (MP. 33 : 19-22). The Judge who is in the Air will himself give thee his three graces;[3] thou shalt receive the Baptism of the Gods in the Perfect Man; the Luminaries will perfect thee and take thee to thy Kingdom; thy Father, the First Man, shall give to thee thy (everlasting) life; . . . the Divine Envoy of Truth shall give to thee the diadem of the Light;——ka,[4] she shall give

---

[1] *i.e.*, where the life comes to its haven and mooring-place after the world's storms.

[2] See note 4 on page 123.

[3] *or*: gifts; we hear more of these in Chapter Six.

[4] I have not traced this broken name of the Angel of the Garland; the six first letters are missing here.

thee thy garland of renown (MP. 22 : 12-19).
Light your lamps, ... O Sons of Joy, ...
and keep watch on the Day of the Bema for
the Bridegroom of Rejoicing, and receive
the holy Light-Rays of the Good Father[1]
(MP. 37 : 25, 30—38 : 1).

5. Hail, resplendent Bema (MP. 24:20)!
Hail, Day of Rejoicing, the blessed Bridegroom! See, our lamps are ready; see our
vessels are full o oil![2] ... Hail, Gate of the
Light, Straight Way of Life, good Shepherd
of his sheep, the Souls' Hope of Life! Hail,
Tree of Knowledge that is in the midst of this
host of trees,[3] whereof when we were blind[4]
we ate and saw! ... Hail, O Rising of the
Dead,[5] the New Age of the Souls that has
stripped us of the 'Old Man' and put the

---

[1] *i.e.*, of Mani, reflecting spiritual sunlight on his children.

[2] An allusion to the parable of the five wise and five foolish virgins in Mt. 25 : 1-13.

[3] A jealous deity (*i.e.*, demon) forbade Adam and Eve to eat of this one Tree (Gen. 2 : 16-17), lest they see the 'nakedness' of physical matter and aspire to the glorious robes of the spiritual Heaven.

[4] *i.e.*, blind to the Truth, as was First Man when he fell into the power of the demons, and as were we until enlightened by the Master.

[5] *Cf.* Jn. 11 : 25, but of course there is no notion anywhere in Manicheism of a physical resurrection, only the spiritual awakening from an interior soul-death.

'New Man' upon us[1] (MP. 25:15-17, 3-8, 12-14)! Hail, Mind of the Father, Garland of Renown of the Ages,[2] the Holy Spirit who scans the 'All', the Father's Perfect Love! Hail, Rejoicing of the Gods, the Angels' Inner Repose, the whole Will of the Powers of the Light, the Trust of the Kingdom's Sons (MP. 24 : 23-28)! This is the purity of the Messenger of the Light, ... of the Saviour Christ, ... of the Spiritual Advocate, ... of the Father's Love; this is the purity of the Good Faith, ... of Perfection, ... Patience, ... Wisdom and Godliness; this is the honour ... of Fasting, Prayer and Almsgiving, ... of blessed Poverty, the honour of Humility and Kindliness (MP. 33 : 10-23)!

6. Blessed art thou, great Instrument of the Word,[3] upright Bema of the great Lawgiver,[4] the Seat of the Fathers of the Light

---

[1] St. Paul made great use of this metaphor in Eph. 4 : 22-24 and Rom. 6 : 6.

[2] *or*: Aeons. It is the garland of glories round God (*cf.* GMP 13 : 2).

[3] The Instrument like a 'waterwheel' devised to raise Souls— *i.e.*, the spiritual *sādhanas* of developing virtue.

[4] *or*: Judge; *i.e.*, Mani himself.

who are far from error, the Basis of the sweet Victory that is full of Wisdom! Hail, Bema of Victory, great Sign of our City,[1] joyous and shining Garland of the victorious Souls but judgment and conviction of the sinners [2] (MP. 8:6-12)! Thou art the blessed Root, thou art the strengthening of the Luminaries, thou art the Gift of the Air, thou art the manifesting of Light's victory! . . . Thou art the Medicine of the healing of our wounds, . . . thou art the one that crushes evil while thou placest a garland on godliness; thou art the one that purifies the Light from darkness; thou art the one that gives rest to the Souls (MP. 26 : 9-11, 21, 24-26)!

The great festival which closed the month of penitential fasting and opened a new year of joy and hope was held, like Easter, in commemoration of the Master's ascent from the darkness of the tomb of the body into the glorious brightness of the risen state. A five-stepped platform adorned with flowers, a portrait of Mani, and a copy of his Scriptures, was set up in every church; before it the faithful kept vigil with confession and prayer. In the joyful morning they received from the Messenger sacramentally present there a total absolution of their sins and the blessed assurance of his perpetual help and presence. With what love and ecstatic joy the Manicheans kept this holy festival we

[1] *i.e.*, of the Kingdom of Light, as in GPM 77 : 1.
[2] A similar contrast is in GPM 17.

can surely see in these very early passages; it was to them all that Easter has ever been to Christians. Coming in the hopeful season of early spring, it was at at once linked with the reviving life of nature; absolved and pure, lit with the certainty that he who has gone on high will raise those who trust in him, the faithful Soul entered on the life of the newborn year in overpowering joy and confidence.

39. Love Divine

1. Love is the Father of Greatness who dwells in His glorious Land; *in*[1] it the whole Godhead has revealed Itself.[2] These two are a single living Body; the Father and His Love, for He has given Himself alone for everything while He was in His Aeons;[3] on this account also the Father, the Lord of All, was called 'Love', because He has given the victory to His Aeons and His Limbs (Keph. 156 : 1-7).

2. Again, the beginning of all the Righteousness and the Divinity[4] which dwell in the holy Church has also been named 'Love', the Church being strengthened thereby. Both

---

[1] *or*: through.

[2] A beautiful sentence: Copt. *ṅta tmentnoute tēres ouōnh abal ṅhētef.* *Cf.* the citation from the Syr. 'Gospel of the Seventy' in a Turfan fragment: "What love you have for God, realise it fully", *i.e.,* experience it, live it *through*, to the end.

[3] Hermes stresses that God can only *be* God because of this ceaseless act of love-ful giving (*cf.* GH 10 : 2).

[4] *or*: godliness.

of these, the Mind and the Church, form one Body also because the Messenger gives himself *up* only for his Church. For this reason too the Church calls him also 'Love', *as* it is written: " There is no love greater than this, to make one *give himself* to death for his neighbour's sake ".[1] Again, he the beginning of the Righteousness is 'Love' of the Church bodily and spiritually; in the body—here in the Church; but in the spirit—in the Height which is above (Keph. 156 : 7-19).

As is God, pouring out His life in many Emanations to redeem creation, so is the Messenger, giving his life for his Church. And this is Love—to give oneself to the uttermost for others; that is why the name of 'Love' is shared by God and His Messenger.

---

[1] A direct quotation from Jn. 15 : 13, the slight verbal variation may suggest mediation through some apocryphal Gospel.

CHAPTER FOUR

THE CHURCH OF THE LIGHT

Here we have a brief outline of the ideal life held out before the general body of believers, the greatness of both Elect and Hearers, the glory of continuous effort for the Church, and the promise of eventual triumph.

40. Who Are the Elect?

1. My Lord (Keph. 147 : 19), thou hast appointed the degree of the Perfect and separated them from those who are in the world;[1] thou hast assigned a task to each one of them in the yoke of Jesus (MP. 4 : 27-29)!

---

[1] The choice which settled the rank of a believer could be made only with the aid of grace; probably Mani himself, so long as he was in the body, used to choose and guide those who were to rule and teach his churches. It has been suggested that the 'Elect' were rather those who could distinguish and separate the 'Light' from their food, as the *hamsa* (swan) of Indian tradition can separate water from milk, truth from the illusory.

2. The first righteousness which the man must practise in order to become truly righteous is this:[1] He must make himself celibate and pure; and gain for himself also the 'repose of the hands',[2] that he may keep his hand away from (hurting) the 'Cross of the Light';[3] and thirdly, the purity of the mouth —he must cleanse his mouth from all flesh and blood[4] and not even taste the name of wine and intoxicants at all (Keph. 192 : 7-13).

3. Again, the second righteousness he practises is this: He must assume *grace* and wisdom and faith, so that he may give his

[1] Here come the famous three Seals: Augustine writes: "By the mouth we are to understand all the sense organs in the head, by the hands all bodily actions, by the breast all lustful tendencies. . . . The symbol of the mouth implies refraining from all blasphemy" (AMM. 19-20).

[2] This does *not* mean idleness, but abstaining from hurtful activity.

[3] A technical term for all the field of nature and of embodied life, wherein the Light-Sparks have been confined, tortured, crucified. Manicheans carried this non-violence to a degree which, to Mazdeans, would seem wicked, for the true 'Elect' "does not hurt even demoniac creatures" (T. II. Toyoq). I suspect a Jain influence in this extremism of non-violence.

[4] "In its passage upward as vapour from earth to heaven (the Light-Spark) enters plants because their roots are fixed in the earth, and so gives fertility and strength to all herbs and shrubs. From these animals get their food, and where there is sexual intercourse fetter the member of God in the flesh and . . . entangle it in errors and troubles. . . . Some portion of that divine part escapes in the eating of vegetables and fruits, . . . so when the soul has left the flesh the dregs are utterly filthy and the soul of those who eat flesh is defiled" (AMM. 36-37). So far Augustine.

wisdom to every man who shall hear it from him; while through his faith he must give the Faith to those who belong to the Faith; through his *grace* he must grant grace with love and clothe them therewith, so that he may unite them with himself[1] (Keph. 192 : 16-21).

We learn from AnNadim that it was the conscience of the Manichean himself that decided his rank in the Church. Those who could live the higher life took the vows that made them the 'Elect'; those too weak for this remained in the lower grade of the 'Hearers'. The famous 'Three Seals' are here well explained: they involve vows of chastity, non-violence (but not of inaction!), and bodily purity; in addition, the Elect is pledged to teach the brethren, to inspire them with the courage of his own faith, and to shower unitive love upon them all.

41. The Glory of the Elect

1. The Elect are themselves Gods, standing up to the image of the Gods;[2] the Divinity also that has come down in them and has come to them from on high has dwelt in them, and (so) they have done the

---

[1] Negative piety is not enough; the Elect must work to spread the Faith by his own wisdom, tact, cheerfulness and love, so that the unity of the Church—the 'Column of Glory'—may be formed on earth.

[2] *i.e.*, approaching their likeness.

will of the Greatness[1] (Keph. 219:34—220:3). The Light-Mind . . . puts a great Spirit on the Elect; therefore you find him actually standing on the earth while in his heart he rises, coming up to the Father, the God of Truth. . . . *Again*, he descends by means of his insight[2] and his meditation[3] and goes down to the world of Darkness from which the Darkness erupted; his heart runs and welcomes everything[4] (Keph. 100 : 1-2, 7-14), The Good and the Evil dwell in every man . . .; the Saints carry a great burden on their shoulders . . . (for) they stand in the body which is not their own, . . . since the 'Old Man' dwells in their body also[5] (Keph. 220 : 16-18, 21-22 ; 221 : 15).

2. At the time when thou seest them quarrelling and angry of heart, do not doubt

---

[1] Mani shows the sinfulness of criticising flaws seen in an Elect, on whom lies the great strain of living in two worlds at once—in Heaven among the Gods and on earth among men. Hindus specially will appreciate this warning against any kind of criticism of the Guru, who incarnates God's will.

[2] *i.e.*, *sbō*; the word may also mean 'imagination'.

[3] *i.e.*, *makmek*, the concrete mode of thinking.

[4] *i.e.*, he willingly, for our sake, accepts these human limitations.

[5] They too are human, fallible, for none are free from sin (*cf.* GPM 38 : 2). The 'Old Man' is expelled only by Perfection, after death.

them or despise them or withdraw from them. ... See, thou abidest in all these sins; the Saints look at thee when thou doest them, yet they do not dishonour thee or hate thee, nor do they withdraw from thee or even say: "So long as he sins in this way I shall not be a teacher to him." Nay, they *even* welcome *thee* lovingly and gently; they speak with thee in God's wisdom, instructing thee (Keph. 220 : 10-11; 26 : 32); they say to thee: "Thou art our brother, thou art our kinsman who shall journey with us to the Land of Light!" Look, then; thou seest how great is the love they have for thee, they bear for thee as comrade; so this is proper for thee, to love *them* also and to honour them [1] (Keph. 221 : 2-7).

3. Now at the time when I leave the world and enter the House of my People,[2] I shall gather to that place all the Elect who have believed in me,[3] I shall draw them to myself —every one of them: I shall not leave one of

---

[1] In Man. I. 23 we read: "As the eye is beloved to the foot and the hand is to the mouth, so also and in the same degree is the Elect beloved to mankind."

[2] *i.e.*, the 'native land of the Soul', the Land of Light, where the Fathers dwell (*cf.* GPM 4 : 3).

[3] *Cf.* Jn. 14 : 3.

them in the Darkness at the time [1] of his coming forth (from the body).[2] This is why I say to you: "Let everyone who loves me love all my sons, the blessed Elect, because I am with them, I the only one."[3] Why? Because my Wisdom is spread in them all, the great Glorious One dwells in all of them; and everyone who loves them and walks [4] with them by means of his alms, shall live and conquer with them and escape out of the world of Blackness [5] (Keph. 166 : 4-16).

Such souls are truly divine in their inward nature, even when, momentarily carried away by the impulses of the flesh which they too must share with us, they may seem to fall away and to betray the lofty ideal. They are like a bridge, a ladder, joining earth to Heaven; and as they are gentle and forgiving to our frailties we too must hold for them unwavering love and reverence, even when we see their weaknesses. Mani promises, as Jesus did before, that he will take the Elect to himself when he returns on high to the Kingdom, adding that those who love them are united with himself—so close is the union between the Lord and his 'human members'.

[1] *or*: moment.
[2] None who, for his sake, have undertaken the 'yoke' of self-abnegation will be allowed to fall back from the heavenly way.
[3] *Cf.* Jn. 14 : 15 and 15 : 12.
[4] *i.e.*, shares (in the 'treasury of merit').
[5] *i.e..*, of Darkness, thus entering the glorious Realm of Light, our "abiding City in the age to come".

42. Hearers of the Wisdom

1. The first duty of the Hearer which he does is Fasting, Prayer and Almsgiving.[1] Now the Fasting in which he fasts is this, that (Keph. 192 : 29-31) the real faithful Hearer keeps fifty fasts . . . on the fifty Sundays of the year (Keph. 233 : 2-4) *and rests from the works of the world* [2] (Keph. 192 : 32-33). He controls also their purity,[3] restraining himself from the desire of his wife, keeping his bed pure by means of celibacy all the Sundays. He is *frugal* in his diet, nor does he defile his food with the *taint* of fish and the whole pollution of flesh and blood;[4] further, on the Sundays he eats nothing defiled. Also he guards his hands from hurting and tormenting the Living Soul [5] (Keph. 233 : 5-11).

Now this is the Prayer, that he must pray to the Sun and Moon, the great

---

[1] *or*: compassion (Copt. *tmentnae*).

[2] *i.e.*, abstains from worldly activities, a sort of Sabbath rest.

[3] *i.e.*, the purity of the Sunday fasts.

[4] Manicheans were always strict vegetarians in every land and century; "nor do they use the milk foods because they are milked or sucked from an animal's living body" (Aug. de Haer. 46).

[5] Skt. *jīvātma*; Pers. *grēv-jīwandag*, *i.e.*, the Light-Spark confined in all living and 'non-living' matter.

Luminaries[1] (Keph. 192:33—193:1). The times of Prayer are followed (?) by him; he keeps them, he comes daily to the Prayer, hourly and daily, all the hours of Prayer will be kept,[2] with his fasts and his alms which he gives on all the days of the year (Keph. 233 : 12-16).

The Alms is this, that he must make an offering of *food* through[3] the Saint, and piously give it to them[4] (Keph. 193:2-3). *The* Alms will be reckoned to his good, the Fast that he has kept, the cloth that he has put upon the Saints;[5] and thereby they daily

---

[1] Prayer was to be uttered facing the sun or moon or, when they were invisible, the Polar Star. But GPM 25 shows that it was not to be addressed *to* them; they are honoured as the means of salvation, the Saviour is God and His Messengers; idolatry would be a great sin.

[2] Regularity in Prayer is essential if it is to be of use.

[3] *or*: in; the offering goes through them to God.

[4] *i.e.*, the Elect. "If anyone refuses to give pious respect to the Elect, he will be punished for generations and transferred into the bodies of Hearers until he render many deeds of piety" (H. 9).

[5] The offering to the Elect of food (*miyazdā*) was to set them free to consecrate, purify and release the Sparks of God's immanent Light in the vegetables, fruits, juices, etc.; the necessary yearly robe might also be given. Augustine has in his *de Haeresibus*, 46: "Now they say the Powers of God not only carry out the same purifying and freeing of the Good from evil through the whole world and from all its elements, but even His Elect ones through the foods they take. And they declare God's Subtance to be surely mixed up with those foods and with the whole world: which they think are purified in His Elect by that kind of life wherein the Elect of the Manicheans live as more holy and excellent than their Hearers."

share a communion with them in their fasting and their good deed [1] (Keph. 233 : 16-19).

2. *The* second work of the Hearer which *he* does is this, that the man should give to the Righteousness [2] a son of the Church, or his relative *or* family-member; or he should rescue one who is in trouble; *or* buy a slave and give him to the Righteousness [3]—so that every good (deed) which this one whom he has given, . . . that Hearer who *gave him* has a share therein (Keph. 193 : 4-11).

3. Thirdly, that the man should build a dwelling-place or found (?) a temple,[4] so that it may become for him a part of Almsgiving in [5] the holy *Church* (Keph. 193 : 11-14).

---

[1] *or*: merit. The doctrine of the 'Treasury of Merit' in the Church, as in GZ 46 : 6. This does not, however, exempt the individual from having to earn his own liberation by grace-assisted effort; Copt. *ṅsekoinōnē nemeu ṅhētes hen tounēstia men pouagathon*. The idea of the Treasury is also found in Taittiriya-brahmana 3 : 10 : 11 : 2 and in Samyutta-nikaya 3 : 14, we are told. *Cf.* Dātastan-i-Dēnik: *hān i hamēṣak sūt ganj andar*, "in the Treasury of perpetual profit".

[2] *i.e.*, to Religious life, as an Elect.

[3] Each must at least provide his own successor in the Church Militant; if he cannot himself become an Elect, he must try to find at least one of his slaves selfless enough to take up this 'yoke'.

[4] *lit*: place (*topos*).

[5] *or*: through.

4. When the Hearer fulfils these three great duties ... which he makes into a gift to the *holy* Church, ... he has in **him** a great love, together with a share in every grace and good deed in the holy Church; **he** shall find many graces (Keph. 193 : 14-22). Afterwards he is cleansed ... according to the measure of his works,[1] he is purified and bathed and adorned. After that, he is moulded into a Light-Image,[2] and he soars up and reaches the Land of Rest, so that where his heart is, his treasure also may be there.[3] ... At the time of his coming forth, he departs and reposes in Life for evermore (Keph. 234 : 3-9, 18-20).

The special duties of the ordinary believer are: (*i*) to keep the purifying fasts and avoid cruel food and activities, (*ii*) to pray regularly to the two redeeming Lights—the Father (reflected in the Sun), and the Christ or Messenger (symbolised by the Moon), and (*iii*) to offer food daily as alms for the Elect who, like *sannyāsis* in India, have abandoned 'gainful' occupations. At the same time he should strengthen the Church by giving a relative,

---

[1] His personal purity and brightness depend on his own efforts, not on the merits of the Church as a whole, though he may—being pure—share the glory of his brethren also.

[2] *i.e.*, the image of the Light-Maiden who appears at death, making the merits of his own heart and conscience visible in beauty (*cf.* GZ 43 : 2, GPM 75 : 1).

[3] An almost exact quotation from Mt. 6 : 21 or some parallel.

a friend or a slave for its service and a building for its worship and other needs. These pious acts, faithfully performed, gradually purify the Soul and lead it upwards to the Light.

43. The Greatness of the Hearer

1. The wise Hearer [1] *is he* who like juniper-leaves *brings to others* much profit, like a farmer who sows seed *freely* in many furrows (M 101 H). Some Hearers are like the evergreen juniper, whose leaves are shed neither in summer nor in winter. So too in persecution and freedom (of religion), in good days and bad, under the eyes of the Elect or out of their sight, the pious Hearer is constant in charity and faith [2] (M 171). *The Hearer who bears* witness *to the Religion is like a ripe* fruit *hanging on a big* tree, *he shines* like a *spark running over* the firewood, *or he is* like a speck *of light in the sky giving out its* radiance. (M 101 A).

2. The Hearer who *is warmed by the fire* of piety *is like a man who took his friend to* a well; one *was on the* shore of the sea, one in the

---

[1] *niyoṣāg. Cf.* the Buddhist word *śrāvaka*, with the same meaning.
[2] Sogh. *pd xw'r' 'wt dy jw'r.*

boat. *Now he who was on* shore towed him who was *in the boat,* while he who was in the boat *guided him on the* sea*shore* upwards to *the well.*[1] *The Hearer who is* like *this is* like a pearl *that adorns the* diadem *on the King's head, like a bright lamp shining in the* church, like a man who *offers* fruits and flowers *to the Elect, and then* they praise *him as a* fruitful tree (M 101, 911). (But) the Hearer *who neglects the Scriptures*[2] is like the branch of a fruitless *tree; his life is* fruitless (?) *and vain;* and blessed are the Hearers *who seek the* fruit which grows out of pious deeds![3] ... The Hearer who *shares his* knowledge is like a man who threw rennet (?) *into* milk; it became hard not *liquid;* the part that was changed *became* heavy at first, just as a *man seen at* first is honoured *and he* may shine *for* about six days (M 101 A, E).

3. The Hearer who gives alms *to the Church* is like a poor man[4] who gives[5] a daughter to

[1] They help each other mutually—the one by his labours in the field to produce food for the Elect, the other by his prayers and guidance.

[2] *or:* Precepts.

[3] Sogh. *qērdagān.*

[4] *'aṣkōḥ mērd.*

[5] *or:* presents.

the King; he reaches great honour (M 101 F). Then the King is pleased with her and keeps her in his harem and has *several* sons by her, *who grow up strong and handsome.* The sons who were born to that poor man's daughter *become Kings of the land in turn* (M 221). The alms[1] in the body of the Elect is purified in the same way as a *man's rags*, which *have been exposed* to heat[2] and wind, *change into* beautiful clothes *which* on a clean body turn here and there in the breeze[3] (M 101 F.)

4. The Hearer *obeying the Precepts is* like a *man who* prepares an image of the King cast in gold, *to whom* the King gave presents. The Hearer who copies a book is like a sick man who gave his *weapons* to a *healthy* man. The Hearer who presents a daughter to the Church[4] is like *the man who took* a pledge, who gave his son to a *teacher to* learn *how to serve his* father—a pledge[5] *is the maiden daughter to this* Hearer (M 101 A.D).

[1] *rawāngān.*
[2] *lit:* fire.
[3] Here we have an allusion to the strange doctrine so ridiculed by Augustine.
[4] *or:* Religion (*dēn*). As prescribed in GPM 42 : 2.
[5] *i.e.,* investment, bringing ample profit.

5. *How* numerous *are the virtues of* the Hearer (M 101 N.)! The very Assembly of the Hearers resembles this good land which takes to itself the good seed, ... because it is that which accepts the holy Church; it cares for her and gives her rest in all its works and all its sufferings. .... Where there is no Hearer, therein the holy Church has no rest; ... the Hearers are themselves the resting-place of the holy Church (Keph. 218 : 1-2, 4-10. 29-30).

In spite of the very large amount of restoration which I have been forced to carry out in this important passage, it is clearly a vivid picture of the high ideal held for the Manichean in his daily life. It sums up as a total sincerity in thought and word and deed, and a faithful performance of obligations. Such a Hearer is indeed a tower of strength to the Church; the Elect could do little if behind him there were not many to maintain his work by their faithfulness and their selfless service of his needs.

44. The Perfect Hearer

1. Now the sign of that perfect Hearer ... who does not return again to a body [1] ... is this: Thou findest the wife in the house

[1] Though, living in the world and so committing many acts of violence and desire, the Hearer must normally expect rebirth again and again, one who simply lives to exhaust his *karmas*, without desires or possessiveness, may attain the immediate liberation normal to the Elect. A purely Indian thought.

with him is just like the stranger, his house also passes with him like the inns, while he says: "I dwell in a house rented for some days and months!"[1] His brothers and relatives are counted by him as seeming to be strangers who need him and travel with him on the road while he *journeys*. Perhaps (?) they will *soon* separate from him and each one *go his own way*. Gold and silver and the *earthenware* vessels *for the* house are to him like borrowed utensils; he takes them and they serve[2] him, afterwards he gives them (back) to their owner; he does not set his heart and his treasure on them. He has uprooted his thought[3] out of the world and set his heart in the holy Church; at every moment[4] his thought is fixed on God. But he who surpasses all this, in whom there are care, anxiety and love for the Saints, he looks after the Church as (after) his (own) house—nay, more

---

[1] This is a favourite thought among Iranian writers: Copt. *eiouēh hen ouēi apscar pros henhooue men henebete.*" *Cf.* the Urdu: *Is jahān meṅ hai basēra chand rōz*; "there are but a few days in this world", which is like an inn.

[2] *lit*: follow (Copt. *ṣemṣe*) ; *or*: "and they are made use of by him".

[3] concrete thinking (*makmek*).

[4] *i.e.*, always.

indeed than his house; he has set his whole treasure in the Elect, men and women. . . . This is the sign of those Hearers who are not (re-)embodied (Keph. 228 : 22, 15, 22-31; 229 : 1-10, 19-20).

2. Again there are others retaining celibacy and keeping all flesh far from (their) mouths, being daily ready[1] for fasting and prayer, helping the Church with alms as far as comes to their hands. In them the wickedness[2] is dead,[3] the steps (?) of their feet are turned to the Church more than to their house; their heart is always on it. Their sitting and their rising[4] is like that of the Elect; they have put away all matters of the world out of their heart. . . . Now such a man, the mind fixed in the holy Church, *gives wholly his* heart at every moment, with his gifts and *fasts* and reverences, and the graces which benefit his life, to the holy Church for those who come into the Church;[5] . . . he rejoices

---

[1] *or*: prepared, almost 'eager'.

[2] *lit*: wicked deed.

[3] *i.e.*, they no longer commit actual sins; frailties may remain.

[4] *i.e.*, both when at rest and when active.

[5] He does not care to accumulate merits for himself, but gives away whatever he may earn for the helping of weaker members.

exceedingly over these and loves them, putting his whole treasure on them (Keph. 229 : 20 —230 : 5).

Mani here clearly teaches that the perfect Hearer will share all the abundant blessedness of the Elect. He too will be freed from the pains of recurring birth into the dark 'Sea' of Matter. He who lives in the world detached, who forms no binding links with relatives or properties, who keeps the mind wholly on God and the welfare of His Church, who perfectly adheres to the code of his state of life—is in fact, whatever he may seem in name, already himself one of the Elect and destined to certain liberation once the physical body has dropped away.

45. Mystical Unity of the Church

1. (You ask:) " Whence is this great joy I have on account of the wisdom that I spread *abroad*, that it is greater in my mouth at the time I express it than at the time when it lies in *my heart*? "[1] Thou thyself art in joy because of it, but the other who hears it from thee also rejoices on its account and is enlightened by it, he gains through it an enduring power (Keph. 205 : 20-25). The wisdom

For we human beings are not *separate* but a living unity, so that we may share each other's good and ill.

[1] The common experience is that by teaching we learn, by giving away we are enriched, by making others happy we find a deeper happiness for ourselves.

which the man preaches, speaking it from his heart, ever increases more and more;[1] its greatness and its glory redouble at the time when the beauty and the brightness of the Word are revealed to the (inner) eye of the hearer, . . . while you (yourself) wonder[2] over what you utter[3] (Keph. 206 : 23-29).

2. This is why I say to you, my brothers and my beloved: ["Take trouble, exert yourselves and preach to the Souls to grasp the hour to themselves while there is time for their repentance[4] (and) to do good while there is time, before the Gate is closed and the Souls are turned back from before the Gate of Life[5] and become share and property of the Enemy.[6] (Keph. 165 : 18-23). The glory,

---

[1] Two similes are given in the context: the mother's joy in her babe is greater after his birth because others can share in the joy of admiring him; the fire latent in the wood gives warmth, use and light only when released, and not so long as it is hidden away —so too knowledge is of value only when brought out for the use of others.

[2] or: marvel.

[3] Many a writer has been amazed when he sees what the pen in his hand has written.

[4] Cf. "Now is the accepted time, behold now is the day of salvation!" in Rom. 6 : 2.

[5] Cf. Mt. 25 : 10, Lk. 13 : 25.

[6] Cf. GPM 87 : 2.

victory and merit[1] are greater for the preacher building the Church than that of the brother who goes into his (own) heart and shuts himself off alone and builds only himself"[2] (Keph. 196 : 7-10).

3. He who communes with Hearers who are in the Knowledge and helps them, he surpasses all these Kingdoms,[3] . . . because all these Kingdoms do not know God's Truth since they serve (?)[4] the desire of the world and are anxious about livelihood (Keph. 189 : 23-27). So for this reason must *he* give them[5] alms and commune[6] with them; *he* gives it to the Holy Spirit who dwells in them, and in turn the Holy Spirit will grant his grace before his true Father, and the Father of Truth shall in turn repay his loan on the last day.

[1] *lit.* good.

[2] Even the world-denying of the Manicheans was no cowardly evasion of duty, but a self-liberation that others might in turn be freed.

[3] The context names several great empires: Babylon and Persia, Rome, Ethiopia and 'Silis'—the last of which I do not know; could it be China (Sinim?) or Sūristān (Ch. *Sou-lin*), the area around Ctesiphon near Mani's birthplace?

[4] The word is unknown: Copt. *epeidē sebelē ṅtepithumia m̀pkosmos*.

[5] *i.e.*, to the Elect.

[6] *or*: shares (*koinōnē*).

For it is the Holy Spirit himself who dwells in these Saints [1] (Keph. 189 : 31—190 : 6).

4. We too, my beloved, let us rejoice in this joy, rest in this rest from everlasting to everlasting (MP. 136 : 10-11); the whole dawning of the Light wherein the Gods rejoice, . . . the blossoms of fadeless beauty (MP. 1 : 16, 19), these are exactly the flesh and blood of Jesus [2] (BM. 254)! O Jesus, . . . thou art the living Wine, the son of the True Vine ; give us to drink living Wine from thy Vine. . . . Thou invitest us, thou hast broached for us a *new* Wine; those who drink thy Wine, their heart rejoices over it, they become intoxicated with thy love, and gladness is spread over their *bosoms*; they think of Those above and arm to fight against the Dragon [3] (MP. 151 : 6-7, 13-16). The Vine is the Church, we are the branches (?) laden with fruit;[4] again, the Winepress is the Wisdom,

---

[1] Quite a Christian idea: good done to the Elect is really done to the Holy Spirit, to God Himself, and earns reward from Him (cf. Mt. 25 : 40).

[2] Equally the Catholic doctrine of the Mystical Body, a Sacrament.

[3] *Cf.* GPM 33 : 1. To be aware of love for God *is* to fight for His cause against all evil in the world.

[4] An obvious allusion to Jn. 15: 5.

God's Chosen Ones[1] the treaders (MP. 76: 6-8);
O Soul, ... thou art the five-branched Vine [2]
which is the food of the Gods, the nourishment
of the Angels (MP. 181 : 19, 34-38)!

5. The Church is a garland for which they
gather in every corner (MP. 166 : 11-12);
(we) gather in the blossoms daily and weave
a royal garland and give it to all the Saints.
... Gay lilies, gay roses, let us put them with
one another; holy hearts, holy minds, let us
build into a Church! It is a New King who
comes, let us build also a new house! The
new house is the 'New Man' the New King
is the Light-Mind [3] (MP. 153 : 9, 14-21),
the Ruler of the Church (M 738)! Let us
moor, let us moor to the Father's Love, ...
to the haven of peace, ... to compassion, ...
to kindliness; let us moor, let us moor to love
for God and love for men (MP. 177 : 21-27)!
Jesus is a Ship, blessed are we when we sail
on him (MP. 166 : 11)!

Mani explains the joy derived from his realisation
that the Church is one, and that happiness lies in

---
[1] *i.e.,* the Elect.

[2] The five faculties of the mind—memory, reasoning, meditation, contemplation, imagination—given various names in the various languages of our texts. This is the Five-pointed Star.

[3] Worked out more fully in GPM 63.

sharing with fellow-members all one has of the truth. The very attempt to teach another deepens one's own understanding and unveils new aspects hitherto unseen. He calls them, then, to constant joyful effort to spread the Gospel they have known, so that millions may benefit by the holy life and reward of bliss that it proclaims. It is noteworthy how Mani insists on the greater value of this sharing than of a selfish contemplation apart from the welfare of the world. God is in the brother; He cannot be found by turning from the brother to the self alone.

So all may enjoy this happiness of the apostolic life whereby they become one with the Lord Himself, Messengers of the Light in a gloomy world. It is to build the holy Kingdom of God, in the world around as in the heart within each one, that men are called by the Messengers to form the Church.

46. Prayer for the Religion

We are men of rest, let no one impose toil on us;[1] Jesus whom we seek is he on whom we have taken (our) model (MP. 170 : 16-18)! Let the wise be cured and restored, the kindly have joy and happiness (BM. 51)! The Messengers of the Light,[2] glorious and kindly, ... let them stand by this true Religion,[3] and guard, keep and preserve (it) pure! And with the Shield of Light, and the Buckler of the

---

[1] Copt. *anan henrōme ṅte pemtan, ṁpōrte laue ouah hise aran.*
[2] *prēstagān rōṣanān.*
[3] *dēn yōzhdaḥr.*

faithful, and the efficient Spear may they repel ... and keep afar all the enemies of Righteousness ... until the end of time! So may it be [1] (S 7)! May new blessing come and from (God) Zrwān a new reform upon ... the spirits of this world, so that He may accept our holy Religion [2] (M 4 A.)

That this labour may prevail, that God may bless the efforts of all who strive to build up His Church, that it may be strong and safe from all the assaults of evil, as a mighty rock stands firm against the beating of the waves—is the prayer of all the faithful.

47. Its Glorious Future

1. If [3] you strengthen yourselves and hold to one another and in one time [4] stand on this living Truth which has been visible to you, then all of you from small to great can conquer the Sin which opposes you.[5] But if you divide on this Truth ... what may not happen? ... You will be both split up

---

[1] This interesting prayer reads: *u pad 'ispar 'ī rōṣan u magn 'ī havistīgān ūd pād nēzag nēv 'ī razmyōz padīyizand ... ūd dūr kūnānd ō vispān dūṣmēnūn 'ī rāstīh ... dā ō abdūmīl 'i zamān. Ōh bēh.*

[2] *Dēn yōzhdahr.*

[3] or: when.

[4] *i.e.*, unanimously.

[5] Knowledge that fellow-believers are fighting the same battle gives us courage and success.

by it and also subdued under Sin's hand, and you will be *humbled* also under all its Powers that oppose you. (Keph. 128 : 18-27).

2. My brothers, let us purify ourselves from all pollutions, for we do not know the hour when the Bridegroom shall summon us[1] ... and we shall inherit the Kingdom (MP. 154 : 8-9, 12). The world shall be full of glory, ... the whole earth shall contain the righteous: those of the land shall dwell in peace, there being henceforth no Rebel any more, no name of sin which shall again be uttered; the Rich Ones of Light[2] shall rejoice on every side without anything of grief (MP. 207 : 10-15).

3. (Then) the temples of this world's Gods (shall) become dwellings of the Elect, and the holy Church of the Congregation shall greatly increase—they shall sit in the palaces of Kings (MH. 26 : 11-14); the churches and the houses of the Hearers shall be like schools of instruction;[3] you will find them singing psalms and hymns (MH. 30 : 30-33), ... the little girls

---

[1] *Cf.* Mt. 24 : 44.
[2] *i.e.*, those rich in Light, the righteous ones.
[3] For teachers will always be busy there.

learning to write while singing psalms and reading.¹ Always it is the voice of the Righteousness that shall speak out in the time *of prayer*; . . . then shall the daily wickedness cease among them (MII. 31 : 6-8, 16-17). At that time they shall fulfil all the Commands, small and great, exactly as they are written.² There shall be love dwelling in all their hearts; . . . the Elect shall love each other, and no one shall ever think of wickedness; brother shall look at brother, sister at sister, with a friendly expression ³ (MH. 29 : 15-18; 30 : 4-7).

Union is strength; so long as each strives in harmony with his fellows for the welfare of the whole, so long will the Church be strong and prosper, so long will the error of the Evil One be held at bay. The time will come for the consummation of the ages, when the Church will enter into glory and shine wondrously above and on the earth; let us see that we deserve to share the joy and honour of that victory. It is full of pathos that the confidence of the early Manicheans,

---

[1] A pleasing picture of the importance, very rare in those days, given by Manicheans to girls' education. There is nowhere any trace of inequality between the sexes in Manichean texts. This passage reads: Copt. *kacen ṅkoui ṅlilaue ṅshime euji-sbō ashei euerpsale euōs*.

[2] This rather suggests that in the writer's own days there were already Elect who did not strictly adhere to the law; cf. Mt. 24 : 12, 1 Tim. 3, and the passage quoted in GMC pp. xl-xli.

[3] The text goes on: " not as now in this world ".

misled perhaps by the lull in persecution which followed Innai's curing of the King and by their intense and living faith, looked to an earthly triumph of the Church. The apocalyptic glories of a wholly perfect human life, so often dreamed of by devotees of every faith, have still evaded us; their light, like twinkling stars on a dark and moonless night, yet beckons us on to further fields of venture in dark faith.

CHAPTER FIVE

THE WAY OF RIGHTEOUSNESS

In greater detail we now learn how the Soul came into its present dismal bondage to the flesh, how it is summoned by the Messenger of God to free itself, and how, faced with the certainty of death and the futility of all things earthly, it resolves to tread the path to freedom and calls on God for aid. The teacher then outlines that path and the qualities needed for its treading; he inspires the pilgrim to face the suffering righteousness has always demanded of those in the world. Steady perseverance, unshaken by the wavering moods; self-control through bodily abstention, prayer and poverty; and a perfect harmlessness—the whole summed up by 'Pity' and 'Sincerity'—form that path, and enable the Divine Mind to transform, transmute the whole nature into the likeness of the Divine in all five aspects of the mind. A final exhortation to brave and steady effort, and the Soul arises and steps out boldly on this ancient path, intent to realise the Light in every speck of her inner being, liberating it also in all she may contact during life down here.

48. The Fall of the Soul

(The Soul says:) "I am the Father's Love,[1] being the Robe clothing thee (MP. 116: 26-27);

---

[1] The Soul is, in fact, the Vohumanāh, the Love-Mind of God, which has clothed itself in the personality for incarnation at God's

I was a Prince wearing a crown among the Kings; I knew not how to fight, belonging to the City of the Gods.¹ From the time that the Hated One cast an evil eye on my kingdom, I left my Fathers resting, I came and gave myself to death for them. I armed myself, I came out with my First *Aeon*; he went out (and) I fought; he came in (and) protected me. Thou didst agree with me at that time, saying: 'If victorious thou shalt receive thy garland!' I conquered in the first battle, (but) yet another struggle arose for me (MP. 117 : 3-18). I put on error and oblivion;² I forgot my being and race and kinsfolk, not knowing the door of the place of prayer to Him and of invoking Him—I became an enemy to my Father (Keph. 96 : 2-5), I was made to drink the cup of madness, I was made to rebel

---

will (*cf.* GPM 73 : 1). Her identity with the 'Robe' may be compared with the thought in Bardaisan's great Hymn, and with *Voice of the Silence* 1 : 58: "Thou canst not travel on the Path before thou hast become that Path itself"—and that realisation is the fullness of the treading thereof.

¹ *Cf.* GPM 2 : 4; "Every soul, yes, every living moving creature, partakes of the substance of the Good Father" (H. 8); Gk. Abj. 7 condemns the teaching that "human souls are consubstantial with God and swallowed up by Matter"—as in GPM 3 : 1, 3.

² *Cf.* GPM 3 : 3.

against my own Self.[1] The Powers and the Authorities entered, they armed themselves against me (MP. 117 : 21-23).

As in the "Hymn of the Soul", so too here the Soul recalls its own origin in God and the glorious Kingdom it renounced on setting forth to do God's will in liberating the pure Pearl of Light from the land of Egyptian darkness and its dragon guardian. In order to live in 'Egypt' at all, the Soul has to disguise itself as a native of the Dark Realm; and then, deceived by its own appearance, it fancies itself a child of Earth, forgets the glory it has laid aside.

49. The Body is a Prison for the Soul

1. Ever since they bound me in the flesh I forgot my divinity (MP. 117 : 19-20); like a bird in a snare, so too am I *while in the* body of death (MP. 95 : 20-21), the dwelling of the robbers, . . . over which everyone has wept (MP. 70 : 1-2). *The* Mind itself *is* great and exalted, but it becomes crooked and petty because of [2] this small contemptible body [3] (Keph. 99 : 28-29), causing me to be dull and drugged and to lose all my senses

---

[1] A striking identification of "my own Self" with the King of Light against whom the Rebels 'rebelled' in GPM 2 : 2, 20: 2, *etc.*

[2] *or* : in relation to.

[3] The thought is like that of Hermes and the Platonists.

THE WAY OF RIGHTEOUSNESS 159

(BM. 38). I am not sick at heart over the bodies, but over the treasure of the Living Ones that is lodged in them[1] (MP. 218:24-26), (for) they are called the slaves of the flesh of death [2] (MP. 111 : 8-9).

2. The body prevents the Soul from rising; it is a prison and a heavy penalty for the Soul [3] (Bir. Ind. 1 : 55); it is the gateway of all the hells and the road to all rebirths [4] (BM. 26). While we are in the body we are far from God,[5] rest has not overtaken us because we are lodged in it. There is none who can glory [6] while he has still an hour in this prison, there is none who can be confident while in the midst of the sea and he has not yet reached port, for he does not

---

[1] The body itself is not the evil; it is our imprisonment therein which saddens the thoughtful.

[2] *Cf.* St. Paul's "body of this death" (*i.e.*, mortal body) in Rom. 7 : 24.

[3] Ephrem says: "If the Darkness has perfidiously schemed to give the Soul this prison so that it may not go out of it, . . . it is to do harm to it (the Soul)."

[4] Because rebirth is made possible and inevitable by bodily desires.

[5] Another Hermetic thought; *cf.* the Hymn A. and M. no. 231: "Here in the body pent, absent from Him I roam."

[6] *or*: boast.

160 THE GOSPEL OF THE PROPHET MANI

know the hour when the storm will arise against him [1] (MP. 135 : 21-28).

3. The care of my wretched [2] body has intoxicated me with its drunkenness; [3] ... many are the pains [4] I have endured while in this house of blackness [5] (MP. 152 : 14, 19) —this body that we wear is the creature [6] of the Darkness (MP. 159 : 31). In fact,[7] it is the devils' palace and the land of demons; it is also a dense forest, a marsh of weeds and rushes, where all evil birds and beasts associate, and venomous insects, lizards (?), and vipers secretly gather [8] (BM. 20). Sin raised this body . . . out of the five bodies of the Darkness and organised it, but it derived its Soul from the five Bright Gods and bound it in the five limbs of the body (Keph. 95 : 14-17). He it was . . . who, having

---

[1] *Cf.* GY 37A: 1. Only death ends the danger of a falling away from righteousness, so none should be called a saint before that.

[2] *or*: poor, the French '*misérable*'.

[3] Metaphorical, of course; it is the inebriation of having forgotten Spirit; *cf.* GPM 50 : 1.

[4] *or*: troubles (Copt. *hise.*)

[5] *i.e.*, dark house, the body.

[6] *or*: product.

[7] *or*: originally.

[8] *i.e.*, all bad thoughts, lustful desires, hates, jealousies, etc.

completed such a den and dwelling as this, snared and arrested the Light Natures, and hid himself behind while **the demons** preached to the Soul and continually led it (BM. 90) to all evil deeds and all sins of desire (Keph. 95 : 25-27).

4. (But) in vain does it disturb the everlasting King of Bliss;[1] it will at last be burned and shut up in the eternal dungeon [2] (BM. 26), (for) the Soul that is therein is the First Man, (and) the First Man who conquered in the Land of Darkness, it is he who today will also be victorious in the body of death. The Living Spirit who gave the First Man help, it is he who today is the Spiritual Advocate[3] (MP. 160 : 1-5) — this whole universe, above and below, is in the image of the human body . . . of flesh[4] (Keph. 169 : 29-31).

[1] In the original stands 'Nirvāṇa', the Buddhist term.

[2] *Cf.* GPM 87 : 3—the two forms of final destruction.

[3] The First Man and the human soul are parallel; the First Man came from God in GPM 3 : 2, and as the 'Twin' or 'Higher Self' he is identified with the creative living Spirit of GPM 18. His victory ensures the final victory of the Soul.

[4] A suggestive dictum; *cf.* the Hermetic "As above, so below." Copt. *pikosmos tēref psantpe men-psampitne ṣoop aḥrem pine m̄psōma m̄prōme . . . n̄te tsarx.*

5. With tears I now humbly pray and implore that I may leave this poisonous fiery sea of my fleshly body, wherein the surging waves and foaming billows never cease for a moment (and) sea-monsters rise and dive again to swallow ships and boats [1] (BM. 19). My Lord Jesus, do not abandon me, be an Evoker of Light and bewitch (?) them until I pass them by [2] (MP. 117 : 25-28)! My true Light, illumine me within, then; lift me, for I have fallen down, and give me a hand to the Height with thee. Be not far from me, O Physician with the medicines of life [3] . . .— heal me of the grievous wound of lawlessness (MP. 152 : 20-23)! See, I have shown my wounds, it is thine (to) give thy cures (MP. 147 : 64-65)!

This is the fate of almost every soul encased in the dull armour of the flesh, shut in by its heavy walls away from the brightness of the living Light of spiritual freedom. We cannot enjoy freedom fully while we live in that jail; so long as the physical body endures, there

---

[1] This will remind every student of Skt. literature, such as King Kulaśekhara's *Mukundamāla*, by its close parallel with the favourite description of *samsāra* (worldly life).

[2] As Jesus bewitched the Powers on his downward way, so that they could not recognise or hinder him.

[3] *i.e.*, vital remedies. The Taoist *Houen-yuan-sheng-ki* calls Mani the " dew of immortality and supreme King of Medicine ".

can be no total liberation or permanent happiness. This body has ensnared us by its needs, its endless desires and fears; never can it enter into the bliss that belongs to its captive, the Soul. For like all else derived from the demon of darkness its destiny is destruction, while the Soul is of eternal Light and endless Glory. Patterned as the body is in exact imitation of the Macrocosm, it can hold the Spirit captive only until death has shattered its ' walls ' of flesh, just as the universe itself will cease to be when all the Light therein has been liberated thence. The Soul realises this and earnestly cries for a speedy release from this enchaining body, so that it may soon enter the glorious liberty of the Light. It is Jesus, the holy Messenger, who was himself able to overcome the flesh and rise to his native heaven, who can aid us in this great effort to be free.

50. The Awakener's Call

1. I heard a Physician's cry, the voice of an Exorcist [1] coming to me (MP. 220 : 26-27): "Awake, bright Soul, from the drunken sleep wherein thou hast fallen [2] (M 4)! O man in whose hands there is wealth, [3] why art thou

---

[1] In other religions derived from Babylonia, the Saviour also holds these titles, and in the Syriac Church (*cf.* Ign. Eph. 7 : 2). He is also called Life-giver, Light and Lamp.

[2] An old Babylonian Tammuz text: "Thou art slumbering in an overwhelming sleep" (168 Rev. 9), and the Zarathushtrian fragment M 9 says: "Heavy in the drunkenness wherein thou slumberest, awake and behold me!" to which the Soul replies: "I, I am the tender painless son of Sröshāv, I am mixed and behold suffering. Take me out of death's embrace." *Cf.* also Odes Sol. 29 : 4, and countless other scriptures.

[3] *or*: the richness; *i.e.*, the treasure of Life and Light.

slumbering in this sleep? ... Wherefore wilt thou not rise betimes to give glory to the Great Lives [1], ... before the Accuser has come forth and sat down beside the Judge *and he hears the* Accuser's word and *thou* art taken away and flogged (?) [2] (MP. 222 : 5-17)? The Gods are spread over the world [3] so that they may answer any call (MP. 147 : 24-25). O my brothers (MP. 204 : 9), lift up your eyes to the land of Light; you shall see the Friend of the Righteous [4] standing beyond this world, you shall see the Great of Glories [5] from whom every Soul *has come* forth (MP. 219 : 24-28) in the beginning, and they shall also return to the Light and ascend to it in the end (Keph. 63 : 14-15).

2. O Soul, where art thou from? Thou art from on high, thou art a stranger to the world, sojourner for [6] men on the earth; [7] on

---

[1] *Cf.* the passages from Andal's *Tiruppāvai* already cited.

[2] This 'Accuser' is the great Adversary, the Satan, referred to also in Mt. 5 : 25 (*cf.* GJ 50).

[3] Copt. *apto*; *i.e.*: the cultivable land.

[4] Probably the 'Beloved of the Lights' of GPM 16.

[5] *i.e.*, the Father of Greatness, the All-Glorious (*cf.* GPM 1 : 2; 13 : 1).

[6] *or*: among?

[7] Copt. *ṅto ouṣemmo apkosmos remṅciale apto harōme*; *cf.* GPM 35 : 1.

high thou hast thy houses, thy tents of joy (MP. 181 : 20-25)! Thou art an alien (here), housed in a defiled body of the earth! . . . The days of thy life flee away from thee; why dost thou vainly waste thine eagerness on earthly things and put behind thee all those *of heaven*? Thou hast spent thy life sunk in the anxieties and cares of the world, wearing thyself out only by means of pains and griefs! . . . For how many days, then, dost thou ignore what thou doest in ignorance, while thou toilest all thy time to nourish thy bodies —yet thou hast not worried, wretch[1], in what way thou mayest be saved! Thou dost weep and shed tears for a son or a friend when he dies; yet the thought of thine own departure does not enter thy heart (MP. 82 : 15-16, 9-14, 16-23)! Thou hast made the world a harp for thyself, continually making music[2] (MP. 118 : 15)!

3. O Soul, . . . thou art the sheep that has wandered in the desert; thy Father seeks thee, thy Shepherd looks for thee

---

[1] *or*: poor thing.

[2] *i.e.*, looking on life as a jest, a mere amusement, while " Life is real, Life is earnest ".

(MP. 181 : 19, 30-33); O despised Noble, thy King searches after thee! Where are thy angel garments, thy unaging robes? Where are thy gay garlands, thy crowns that do not fall? Who has changed for thee thy fair beauty, the fashion of thy kinsmen, the seal of thy Fathers (MP. 146 : 39-48)? Move thyself, O Soul watching in the enduring chains, and remember the ascent into the joyful Air, for a fatal (?) lure is the sweetness of this flesh (MP. 52 : 17-19), the body full of darkness (MP. 53 : 4)! Drink of the water of memory,[1] throw away the forgetfulness! The wounded one who desires healing, let him come to the Physician (MP. 57 : 20-22)! O Soul, do not forget thy Self, nor faint, nor eat (out) thy heart! See, the Ships [2] are moored for thee, the Ferries are in the harbour; take thy cargo aboard and sail away to thy homes" (MP. 147 : 32-37)!

Jesus then comes and, like Hermes in his missionary sermon (GH 8), summons the Soul to rise, shake off its chains and aspire with confidence to heaven whence comes its help. He reminds the Soul of its

---

[1] The antithesis and antidote of the 'cup of madness' in GPM 48.

[2] *or*: transports, *i.e.*, the (spiritual) Moon and Sun.

THE WAY OF RIGHTEOUSNESS 167

glorious origin, its tremendous destiny and lovely heritage, awaiting its renunciation of earth's pains and duties. Nothing has real value but the effort to be free, yet for so long it has sought vain pleasures in the life of the world and of personal desires. Now the Liberator has come, and the hour for freedom has dawned if the Soul but wake to its opportunity. With courage and determination the path to liberty must be entered on and trodden to the end.

51. Death is Inevitable

1. Everything that happens to man, be it wealth . . . or even poverty, . . . his sickness and his health, it happens to him through the Zodiac(al Sign) and the Star in which he was born[1] (Keph. 122 : 12-15). The temporal contacts of a family, . . . how far do they differ from that of staying at a traveller's inn? Crowds of people stop and rest together for a night; in the morning they part and return to their own lands[2] (BM. 102). Man is born a naked shape, and he will die like that;[3] . . . in spite of his love for the

---

[1] Here we have a definite assertion of Astrological destiny.

[2] The oft-used Iranian metaphor, so beloved of Muslim poets; cf. GPM 44 : 1.

[3] So several Western Saints have chosen, like St. Francis of Assisi, to die, naked, on the bare ground.

flesh-body he must give it up at last; . . . all the riches and treasures . . . we do not wish to part with will be taken away at the end (BM. 98, 96).

2. Take to yourself the words of truth, O men who love God, that the world is nothing, there is no gain at the end of it (MP. 63 : 21-23). Do not be a friend of this beauty that shall be totally destroyed, decayed and melted like snow in the sun. . . . All things of this earthly life are fleeting, they vanish *from our sight* like *fallen* rain before the *midday* sun (M 91 : 33-35). Renounce the world's possessions *and embrace the* peace of poverty (MP. 79 : 9-10)! Our Lord Mani is a north wind blowing upon us so that we may put out with him and sail to the Land of Light (MP. 193 : 4-5)! Come, Souls, to this Ship of the Light! (M 4).

> The futility of an earth-centred life is here pointed out in the usual way; life is short and death is sure. Who really cares for us? At the last we must leave all things behind. So it is better to leave them now, to face life as it really is, stripped of all its fleeting trinkets, and enjoy the peace and power of " my Lady Poverty ", stayed on the eternal strength of the Liberating One. The reference to the influence of Astrology here is of some interest; Mani was educated in ' Chaldea '.

52. The Soul Resolves

1. The two Sources of the Light and of the Darkness have natures absolutely distinct [1] (CRER. 1) ; I have learned . . . what is the King of Light who is the Tree of Life, and also what is the Darkness which is the Tree of Death (MP. 66 : 25-28) ; I have put the Law of the Darkness behind me, while I have adopted the Law of the Light (MP. 68 : 13-14). I repent in the presence of the God Majesty of Law [2] (T. II. D 260), I have thrown out of my eyes this sleep of death which is full of error [3] (MP. 75 : 31—76 : 1).

2. When again the evil became worse, I lifted up my eyes to the Land of Light; a Man called down to the world, saying: " Blessed is he who shall know his Soul ! " [4]

---

[1] *Cf.* GPM 1: 1 and App. I 4: 1.

[2] Seemingly the Turkish equivalent far the ' Righteous Judge ' of GPM 76.

[3] " By the Great Calamity one has the distaste to separate from the body; in the Flaming Abode one makes the vow of trying to escape; one wearies the body to save the (Bright) Nature; the holy Doctrine is firmly established " (CRER. 2 b). This is parallel to the awakening of Tammuz and his loosing from bonds in the Liturgies, p. 140, and the awakening in the Mandean John-Book 52-53. It is an obvious metaphor for spiritual conversion.

[4] Surely equivalent to the Gk. " *Gnōthi seauton* " (know thyself); in Copt. *neitef ṁpetāernoie ṅtefpsukhē*.

So I am troubled at heart about my Soul, lest it faint and stray and become even worse (MP. 219 : 17-22). O my Father, my God, my Saviour, my King, I will be a champion for Thee, I will myself go forth and fight. O my Maiden, my Beloved, the Living Fire, I shall give myself for thee, I shall *give* my body to death for the sake of thy body, and give my fair beauty for the sake of thy beauty [1] (MP. 148 : 25-30) ! I will untie the knot of worldliness, the bond of action will I break; I will lead the one gone astray, heal the long incurable diseases of passion, and open (men's) eyes to the Wisdom ! On every side I will become a bestower of joy on those who have come to sorrow [2] (T. II. D. 260) !

Realising the vanity of this earthly show, the Soul makes its free choice of spiritual reality, puts away the lure of the Darkness to pursue the eternal Light, resolves to break the link with earthly things, and to do all it can to cure others also of the disease of Ignorance which afflicts us all.

[1] Here the Soul speaks as did the First Man in the earliest crisis of the revolt of Evil.

[2] This is a beautiful outline of the ideals of true spiritual life, equal to the best we have from any sources elsewhere.

53. And Appeals for Aid

1. Hither for health,[1] O Rouser of Sleepers and Shaker of the Drowsy, who art Awakener of the Dead ! . . Hither for health, O Rescuer of the Chained and Physician of the Wounded (M 28)! Thy cures are not of this world, thy healing is from the Land of the Living (MP. 221 : 2-3)! Where is the welling of thy mercies that thou hast left me to extend my prayer?[2] If my voice has reached thee, then how has thy mercy delayed?[3] If I have turned towards thee a little, thou shouldst have turned much to me! . . . I have wearied (of) knocking for thee; O Doorkeeper, open for me the door; I will not stem my tears, O Mighty One, unless thou wipe away my sin (MP. 188:5-9-11-12)! O great Saint,[4] I am a new and lovely Robe that has been wholly soiled with filth by the demons; please wash and cleanse it with the water of

---

[1] *i.e.*, Come here, that I may be strong and happily active.

[2] *lit*: let me be long in my prayer (Copt. *je akhaat aiōsek hentalitē*).

[3] *Cf.* the pathetic appeal in GY 76 A: 1. Does not God promise that He will even anticipate the prayer of His devotee?

[4] *i.e.*, God, the King of the Light.

Righteousness,[1] so that I may attain the sublime body of joy and pure limbs (H 71)!

2. I am a shining Lamb,[2] son of the Great Saint,[3] and with streaming tears and crying I implore (help) in my sufferings. The jackals, wolves and many savage beasts have seized me suddenly and carried me away from the Branch of the Good Light.[4] Grant great mercy: please take me in adoption, put me among the soft and gentle Flocks of the Light, and admit me to the hills and woods of the Religion,[5] roaming and sauntering always fearless on the fair mountains [6] (BM. 65-66)!

3. Hither for health, true Word, great Lamp and vivid [7] Light (M 28), my true Guardian, . . . Firstborn of the Father of the Lights, watch over me! . . . While I am in the midst of the Sea, O Jesus, be a guide to me! Do not abandon us lest the waves ravish us; when I utter thy Name over the Sea it

---

[1] *or*: the Law, *i.e.*, Skt. *dharma*.

[2] *or*: Lamb of the Light; so too Tammuz is called "the lamb put in the power of the underworld" (Liturgies p. 296: 14).

[3] *i.e.*, God, the King of the Light.

[4] *i.e.*, from contact with God and His Glory.

[5] *or*: the Law.

[6] Is this a memory of the prophecies of 'Deutero'-Isaiah?

[7] *lit*: much.

stills its waves¹ (MP. 151 : 4-5, 8-11)! Guide my eyes² lest they look an evil look,³ guide my ears lest they hear a *flippant*⁴ word, guide my nostrils lest they smell the odour of desire, guide my mouth lest it utter slander, guide for me my hands lest they minister to Satan,⁵ guide for me my heart that it do no evil at all,⁶ guide my spirit for me while it is in the midst of the storm-tossed Sea, guide my 'New Man' while it wears the mighty Image,⁷ guide my feet lest they walk in the way of error, (and) guide my Soul that *it be not stained by* sin (MP. 150 : 22-31)!

4. O Tree of the Nature of Life, ... most high imcomparable King of wondrous Medicine,⁸ ... the ever-thriving precious Tree ... whose fruits are always fresh with

---

¹ This seems to recall Mt. 8:26, Jesus himself stilling the waves.

² *lit*: place of considering—*i.e.*, sense of sight.

³ *lit*: wink in an evil wink.

⁴ This broken word reads ṣ—; I have restored as *ṣouit*, vain, trifling.

⁵ *i.e.*, the Enemy, the King of Darkness, Ahrimēn or Shumnu.

⁶ *or*: to the 'All', *i.e.*, the universe, or 'Cross of Light'.

⁷ *lit*: statue; *i.e.*, while the reformed converted heart is still fashioned in the shape of God's purity.

⁸ His Medicine is the 'Living Wine', the medicine of Life, as in Ign. Eph. 20: 2 and the Syr. Acts of Thomas, etc.

sweet fadeless dew [1]—whoever eats them will for ever leave the stream of worldliness [2]— (while) its fragrant perfume spreads around the world; . . . send down the springtide of the great Law to fertilise the ground of my Soul and let the flowers and fruits of my Soul flourish [3] (BM. 72-74, 31)! Teach me the way to Life,[4] and I shall come to thee rejoicing, *let* (me) dwell in Thine Aeons, Thy bride-chambers of Light (MP. 197 : 4-5)!

But this great work cannot be done alone, so the Soul calls on the Divine Saviour who has roused him from the dream of worldliness to purify him from all pollution of the flesh, to drive away from him the countless enemies of his peace who preyed so long upon him, and to protect him from passions and thoughts that would drag him down again. There is a fine prayer for the control of all senses and their organs, and that grace may refresh and vivify the whole nature, so that it may blossom forth in the flowers of virtue and the ripe fruits of righteous deeds.

54. The Way to Life

1. Well, in three . . . things consists [5] Perfection: in the Commandments and the

---

[1] *or*: unfading immortality.
[2] *lit*: birth-and-death (Skt. *samsāra*).
[3] *or*: ripen.
[4] Such phrasings make it almost certain that the Manichean Psalmist knew and loved the Hebrew Psalms (*cf.* Ps. 119: 33).
[5] *lit*: is.

Wisdom and the Love,[1] for all the men of God attain Perfection through these. ... For this reason let us pray and beseech[2] Him who has chosen us that He may make us perfect (MP. 38 : 18-21, 24-25).

2. Keep yourselves far from magic arts and the sorceries of the Darkness,[3] for the man who shall learn them and practise them and realise them, finally where the King of those of the Darkness shall be bound with his Powers, they shall bind also in that place the soul of him who has played with[4] them and walked in the magic arts of the Error (Keph. 31 : 25-30).

3. Wisely and skilfully strengthen yourselves around the body's gates[5] lest the Sin that dwells in the body[6] prevail over you and bear away your Light from you and extinguish it in place after place[7] and shatter it everywhere in every way. So then let not this be

---

[1] *i.e.*, Ethics, Knowledge, Devotion.

[2] *lit*: implore a prayer to.

[3] Mani's own homeland was saturated with sorcery from history's dawn.

[4] Copt. *politeue*: pass life in, live familiarly with (*Polotsky*).

[5] *i.e.*, the senses and their organs.

[6] *Cf.* St. Paul in Rom. 6 : 12.

[7] *or*: here and there.

allowed to happen to you,[1] but be men watchful and strong in your Truth. Be prepared from everything to everything,[2] so that your rest and your end[3] may be with Him for whose Sign and Hope you watch (Keph. 144: 2-12)!

4. Be ever firm and strong in keeping the Precepts and the Rites; . . . give alms (and) practise fasting, . . . worship, praise and recitation. . . . Sing and chant the words of the Religion[4] without break or stop, . . . read and study eagerly, discriminate with your wisdom and accept the pure Commands. . . . Always be clean and pure in the deeds of body, mouth and mind; . . . also earnestly practise kindly deeds, be gentle and amiable, bear humiliations, and purify all (your) roots. . . . (Follow) good rules and habits and determine to rest your minds in the Place of Liberation; leap with joy and stand firm by the Right Religion[4] (BM. 113-114, 258-259)!

[1] Copt. *mē genoito oun atre-pei šōpe m̄mōtne.*
[2] Copt. *šōpe etetnsebtait abal hemptēref ṣa ptēref.*
[3] probably hendiadys for "your final rest".
[4] *or*: Law, Righteousness.

5. All these are the remedies for the Light-Sparks[1] (BM. 259); if thou doest these things and sleepest not, thou shalt go up and see the Land of Light. . . . If indeed thou truly fastest,[2] thou shalt be taken in to the Garden;[3] if thine eyes do not glance evilly,[4] thou shalt be seated under the Garden's shade; if thy mouth speak truly, they shall show thee their image;[5] if thy hands are pure (?) from *violence*, the pleading of thy *speech* shall be heard;[6] if thy heart stands firm, *they will lift thee up* and stand thee in their midst; if thy feet walk in the way of Truth, *they will* make thee one of them [7] (MP. 225: 3-14).

As a part of the way of life leading to perfection, there is a special warning against the black arts to which Babylonia had so long been addicted. A

---

[1] *lit*: Light-bodies.

[2] *lit*: thou makest fast in the fast.

[3] The Garden of Light, wherein is the Tree of Life, is the bridechamber of the Father-Mother nuptials, the mystic Marriage of the Soul—an old Sumerian concept. The temple of the God is the House of Life; it has a grove tended by the King as gardener.

[4] *lit*: wink.

[5] Copt. *hikōn*. The truthful shall see the Divine Beings.

[6] *Cf. Light on the Path*: "Before the voice can speak in the presence of the Masters, it must have lost the power to wound."

[7] Another fine summary of the spiritual life.

constant watch on all the senses lest they open the door to many evils, a faithfulness in the commandments, devotion to study of the holy books, prayer, purity in deed, word and thought, kindness and humility—does not every religion teach this way? Perhaps Mani laid a greater stress on a monastic chastity and self-control, for only the pure in heart can come to see God and live in His lovely Garden of the Light. Asceticism and righteousness is *the* way.

55. Courage under Suffering

1. All the blessed ones who have (ever) been have borne these pains, down to the Glorious One, the beloved Jesus our Lord (MP. 142: 10-11); every man of God who has (ever) been, male, female, all have suffered, down to the Glorious One, the Messenger Mani. Even our Lord Mani himself was given the Cup to drink,[1] he took the likeness of them all,[2] fu'filled all their signs. How many of his disciples also received the same as[2] their fathers! My brothers, we too have our share of sufferings, we shall join with them in the suffering and rest in their rest (MP. 143: 15-21)!

[1] The same metaphor as in Mt. 20: 22-23.
[2] *i.e.*, resembled all of them, became like.

2. It is good for us to be silent (MP. 134: 28); let us not think in our heart that our God is forgetful of us (MP. 150:19), (for before us) all hardships will disappear like gloomy shadows before the glorious Sun (BM. 194). Our Father's Covenant, the profit and the loss, is shared among us; we are true sons, the heirs of their fathers (MP. 143 : 22-23)!

3. There is nothing at all that is free from suffering which will rest at its end;[1] even the very seed that is sown finds no way to live unless it dies,[2] but through its death it lives and gives life also. Let us too strengthen ourselves, my brothers, for see, the Rest has come to us that we may receive the blessing of all these things we have spoken of, and dwell together in the glorious Land of the Light! For there is no hater, no enemy, no rival (?) henceforth, but it is peace and joy and life for evermore (MP. 143 : 24-31)! Let the bridechamber keep festival, for the Bridegroom is at hand [3] (MP. 150 : 18)!

---

[1] *Cf.* the saying: "No Cross, no Crown!".
[2] A very close parallel with Jn. 12: 24.
[3] *Cf.* Mt. 9: 15.

But all who thus renounce the world are hated by the world; persecution soon falls on them, and wicked men do all they can to force them from this narrow path into the broad worldly road that leads to destruction. When the great Messengers have suffered, we too must surely suffer. So we must bravely face whatever comes, strong in the memory of Divine aid and in the joyful knowledge that even death will avail only for our final liberation and lead us the more swiftly to everlasting Life and Light.

56. Fluctuating Moods

1. Many are the ships that have gone down after they came near to mooring at the quay;[1] plenty of houses have fallen after the parapet[2] had been reached! So too is it with this, my brothers: there is a Soul that shall fight at first, and (then) the storm rises against him and the waves seize on him[3] (MP. 165 : 18-22).

2. Sin arouses from time to time its disorders in the body; . . . there is a time when Sin lifts itself up in its foolishness, annoys the understanding,[4] embarrasses the man's wisdom and good sense, causes the truth to be

---

[1] *lit*: bank, shore.
[2] *lit.* garland-course, *i.e.*, the decorated parapet.
[3] *Cf.* GPM 49 : 2.
[4] Copt. *makmek*.

confused in him,[1] and (then) he utters stupid words. . . . The Powers of the Light . . . give the Enmity a chance to offend, and they work their will *for* a while, and then they are seized (Keph. 94, 97).

3. At the time *when the* body is disturbed, thou art disturbed by means of the aspects (?)[2] of the lower ones,[3] the coarse parts [4] which enter thee in the food *and* the eating. Again at the time when the aspects (?)[2] of the higher ones are favourable to thee and also the food that has entered thee is refined and clean, . . . both overflowing with Light and Life, while also the dregs in it are few and the badness in it scanty, . . . thy heart is (then) found steady in its place, while thy thought is pacified from the confusion.[5] . . . . (Then thou sayest:) " My wisdom and the lecturing are sweet to me while my heart is drawn towards the fasting

---

[1] *or*: turns the truth in him to doubt.

[2] Copt. *lihme*, an unknown word; its sense is suggested by several other astrological passages in this book, and seems clear.

[3] *i.e.*, the lower tendencies of the planets, which according to Chaldean astrology always war on the Soul's higher aspirations.

[4] *lit*: limbs.

[5] Of course this doctrine that impure food corrupts the mind and soul is in frank contradiction of Jesus (Mt. 15 : 11); it has a somewhat Indian flavour.

in which I fast; I do not wish to give up praying, ... nor do I desist from repeating psalms; ... I welcome my brothers to me kindly, because I live in steady discipline,[1] ... my soul itself rejoicing in the Wisdom and the true Knowledge, ... while my thoughts too are *gay*, my body being light upon me, ... and I am restful in happiness of mind (Keph. 213-216)!"

At times it seems easy, at times the hardest thing to do, to cling to living out this resolve. Sometimes the evil hidden deep down in the Soul stirs and wakens its foul yearnings for the renounced delights of the past. These disturbances are caused by the changing aspects of horoscopic planets and the taking in of impurities in food; when we are under good aspects and our food is pure and scanty, then the religious life seems natural, and the heart overflows with joy in brotherly affection and the contemplation of spiritual things. This is another reason for purity in diet.

57. Fasting

1. "What shall I do with this lion that is always roaring?[2] What shall I do with this seven-headed serpent?"[3] Take to

---

[1] or: well-ordered way of life (*Polotsky*).

[2] *i.e.*, the desires of appetite, greed for foods of various kinds, the lion of Nemea.

[3] *i.e.*, sex passion, always eager to take new forms, and so resembling the Hydra overcome by Hercules, whose labours are clearly in the psalmist's mind here.

thyself[1] Fasting and thou shalt strangle this lion, lo, Virginity and thou shalt slay this serpent (MP. 149 : 22-25)! This is entirely the purpose[2] of keeping a fast, . . . *for* seven Angels are born from the fast of every one of the Elect (Keph. 193 : 29-32). Those who have no power *to fast* daily, they too (may) fast on the Sunday, and they also share *in the merits*[3] and the fasting of the Saints by means of their faith and their alms[4] (Keph. 191 : 31— 192 : 3).

2. Just as (finally) the Fire swallows this world with mighty wrath and relishes it, even so does this fire that is in the body[5] swallow the outer fire that comes (to it) in fruit and food and enjoys it (M 35). The fire that dwells in the body, its work is eating and drinking, but the Soul thirsts continually for the Word of God[6] (MP. 40 : 29-30). A man

[1] *i.e.*, adopt.

[2] *lit*: work.

[3] *lit*: deeds. We find again the doctrine of the common treasury.

[4] Fasting and Alms are always closely associated.

[5] In Skt. texts also the digestive powers are called a fire.

[6] The same contrast is found in GZ 36 : 2; the 'Word of God' *is* good deeds and kindliness.

must not put out his hand and hurt this Living Cross [1] recklessly and greedily, ... but when you have to [2] eat it, do not eat it recklessly with revelling, gluttony [3] and greed, but eat it (only) in great hunger and drink it in great thirst, and from it derive nourishment for your bodies [4] (Keph. 213 : 3-5, 8-12).

Spiritual refinement is now enquired into. *Fasting*: The body's hunger is an insatiable flame, but the Soul's nature is to long for God. So the bodily appetite must be controlled, being fed only what is necessary to keep it alive until the Soul has been purified from mental defilement; those who can fast even more intensely will benefit the more thereby. For the body that is overpampered, fed too luxuriously, easily turns astray into the violation of its chastity, and plunges wildly downhill into the precipice of lust and greed and wrath, besides inflicting needless suffering on nature.

[1] *i.e.*, all Soul held in Matter, especially in the plant kingdom.

[2] *or*: are about to.

[3] *or*: luxuriousness.

[4] " They consider all things ensouled—even the fire and the water and the air and the plants and the seeds. For which reason those who are perfect among them neither break bread nor cut vegetables, but even openly abuse those who do this as murderers; yet they make use of what are cut and broken" (T). Ephrem also speaks of " those who did not wish even to break the bread from fear of hurting the Light which is mixed there ", and Hegemonius tells of a quaint apology they offer to the spirit thus injured when they make use of comestibles (9). Faustus then naturally finds everything to be a sacrament and avows: " We attribute the same sacredness to the bread and wine that we do to everything " (AF. 20 : 2). The Omnipresent God *is* everywhere.

58. Prayer

Now indeed he, the man, stands up and washes in the flowing water or something else, and he turns towards the greater Luminary, standing. . . . Now as for the first prayer it is at noon,[1] and the second prayer between noon and sunset, and the night prayer three hours after **that** (N. 333 :.14, 26-27). He who sings[2] a psalm is like those who weave a garland, while those who answer after him are like those who put roses in his hands[3] (MP. 47 : 15-17). For this reason let us pray (MP. 38 : 24), let us all sing together (MP. 37 : 26), let us set before us joy, the sign of God,[4] and let us do away with

---

[1] There seems to be an error here, for there are *four* obligatory daily prayers, the first of which was at sunrise. Three others were optional.

[2] *lit*: says.

[3] Certainly, as Alberry points out, a reference to the liturgical practice of chanting these beautiful psalms in the Manichean churches. Christian antiphonal chanting is similar.

[4] Faustus says well: " I look on myself as a reasonable temple of God if I am worthy to be so, and I consider Christ His son as the living image of His living Majesty; and I hold a well cultivated mind to be the true altar, and pure and simple prayers to be the true way of paying Divine honours and of offering sacrifices " (AF. 20 : 3). Hermes (GH 43 : 2) shows a like aversion to pomp and ritual.

grief, which is the sign of the Darkness [1] (MP. 38 : 30-32)!

Continually dwelling on its goal, the Soul will speed more swiftly thither; regularity and joyfulness in Prayer soon uplift the heart to the Source of every joy, which is God Himself, the eternal King of Light.

59. Holy Poverty and Almsgiving

1. My brothers, let us love poverty, and be poor in the body but rich in the spirit; and let us resemble the poor making many rich, as having nothing (yet) possessing the universe.[2] What shall we do with gold and silver? Let us love God; His Light is power, His Wisdom the wise (one) (MP. 157 : 5-10)!

3. The living Alms receives *to itself* affliction for a while, and *then* rest comes to it for evermore through the Saints [3] (Keph. 212: 33 —213: 2). Moreover, at the time when these

---

[1] Here we see well the essential optimism of a religion which to the superficial mind might seem pessimistic—that the world is evil, and so the soul can be happy in God, who is everywhere.

[2] *or*: everything (the 'All'). St. Francis, the Poverello, might have been speaking here! Nowhere is the noble thought more forcibly, more charmingly expressed: Copt. *Nasneu, ṅten mere tmentheke, tenerhēke henpsōma remmao hōf henppneuma; tenerthe ṅnihēke eneire ṅoumēṣe nremmao, hōs ementen laue enemahte ajenptēref.*

[3] The soul imprisoned in the very matter of the offerings is released by its intimate contact with the Elect, on being eaten or drunk by them.

Alms reach the holy Church they are saved thereby and are purified and rested by its means; they come out thereby and go to the God of Truth in whose name they have been given.¹ So again it is the holy Church which is resting-place for all these Alms that rest therein; it is this alone that becomes for them a door and a vehicle to that Land of Rest (Keph. 217 : 13-20).

Those who are encumbered by little of this world's goods can be most truly rich in happiness, strong in independence, able to spread God's light and wisdom to all. So it is good to give generously of what we have, for even the very things we give are thus consecrated, uplifted, transmuted into the Light for whose sake they have been given. They support the Church and help it to do good works, so by its merits are themselves set free, refined, exalted by the noble use to which they have been put; the Light in them is released and enabled to merge in the unbounded Light of God. St. Augustine, his materialistic mind being unable to understand a pantheism nobler than its own dualistic concepts, found here only a fit cause for mockery, which sometimes became vulgar and almost obscene.

---

[1] "If food consisting of vegetables and fruits comes to the Saints, . . . by means of their chastity and prayers and psalms, whatever is excellent and divine in it is purified, and so it is wholly perfected in order to restoration free from all hindrance to its own kingdom" (AMM. 36). "The Life escapes in the mastication and digestion of the food, so that only a particle remains in the excrement" (AF. 6 : 8). This seemed merely funny, if not blasphemously foolish, to Augustine. Yet the doctrine follows legitimately on the beliefs that God is pervading all things, and that contact with the Saints purifies.

60. True Harmlessness

1. The word that wounds is this: When a man speaks a word for the sake of[1] the killing of a man or the killing of beasts or the killing of trees and the ' Cross of Light ', the lying word, and that of anger and that of anger and that of fury, or a corrupt and viciously (?) obscene (word), or a quarrelsome word that one flings at his brother—this is the hurtful *word* (Keph. 211 : 9-14). For this is Anger, that thou findest occasion to desire [2] an evil deed *wherein there* is sin (Keph. 198 : 2-3).

2. It is proper for man to look on the ground at the time when he walks on a road,[3] lest he tread with his foot on the ' Cross of Light ' and destroy the plants; it is specially for the worm,[4] lest he tread on it and kill it with his foot. (Keph. 208 : 17-20). But it is

---

[1] *i.e.*, to bring about—slander, accusations, etc.

[2] It is the motive that makes an act good or bad.

[3] Probably this comes from the Jains, who even to this day avoid by elaborate precautions the possible injuring of small creatures; "If a person walks on the ground here he injures the earth, and if he moves his hand he injures the air; and the air is the life of men and living creatures " (H. 9)—an obvious exaggeration. It is the creatures on the ground and in the air which should not be hurt, if possible, not the elements themselves.

[4] *or*: serpent—a less likely meaning here.

I who forcibly [1] say to you that every man of the righteous Elect who walks on a path for the sake of God's work, or if he walks on the earth, even when he crushes with the sole of his foot the 'Cross of Light', he has no sin therein,[2] but his whole path is a garland and a palm-leaf, because he does not walk in his own desire, nor does he run for the sake of gain and frivolous things when he treads on the earth and the 'Cross of Light' (Keph. 209 : 12-19). It shall not bear resentment against [3] thee with hatred and anger, for it knows that thou walkest on it for rest and healing, to preach for it . . . (and) to reveal its mysteries (Keph. 210 : 26-29).

True gentleness is less in action than in motive. The unintentional causing of pain cannot be a sin, as the Jains have supposed; sin lies in the reckless and purposive infliction of suffering on others, even the most humble. It is good to watch carefully while walking, lest we carelessly hurt some tiny creature of our loving Father—ant or worm; but when we have to travel on the work of the Church and not our own, even the pain we may thus accidentally inflict becomes

---

[1] *lit*: with a loud voice, *i.e.*, positively.

[2] Because the motive is now to work for their final liberation; this makes all the difference. In the context Mani speaks of the lifelong gratitude of the patient for the use of the surgeon's knife in cutting away the cause of a more dangerous and agonising pain.

[3] *or*: be vexed with.

a blessing to the Soul, the Light-Spark, in the crushed insect or blade of grass. Because our motive is the liberation of *all* imprisoned Soul, the very contact with us at that time releases the Light in the dying creature, and it is grateful for that pain to us, as is the patient to the surgeon for his healing knife.

61. A Sure Path

Pity and Sincerity[1] are, for all the Saints of the past and also of the future, the essential foundation[2] of brightness, the wonderful Gate which lets (them) see everywhere; they are also the Straight Path one walks upon, keeping to one side the length of the great sea of troubles in the Three Worlds.[3] Among lakhs of men rarely is even one found to walk in this Path![4] Were there any who devoted themselves thereto, thanks to this Path they would be born in the 'Pure Land',[5] would

---

[1] *i.e.*, humane kindliness to others and a total integrity of the self. We here come very close to the Confucian portrait of the 'Superior Man' (cf. GC 26, etc.).

[2] *lit*: base and root (Ch. *ki-tche*; Turk. *töz-yiltiz*).

[3] Probably the Skt. *trilokam*; Mani usually speaks of the 'eight worlds'. In Chinese we read *san-kiai*.

[4] The thought occurs in almost every scripture, and in daily life! "Many are called, but few chosen!" E. g., "One in a thousand will be found, and two in ten thousand, for the accomplishing of the first mystery": *Pistis Sophia*, pp. 354-355.

[5] Ch. *tsing-t'ou*, the Mahayanist 'Sukhāvati' among the 'Pure Land Sect' of Japan; in it can enter nothing that defiles or corrupts; cf. Rev. 21 : 27.

free and save themselves from penalties, and would at last without fear rejoice for evermore in calmness and tranquillity (CMT. 68).

Summing up the whole Path in two words, the Manichean would choose Compassion and Integrity for its definition—a wholehearted sincerity in thought and word and deed; a perfect harmlessness inspired by sympathy and love. Through these the Soul can avoid the miseries of being subject to passion, and come to the sweet joy of eternal peace. But how few try to hold to these!

62. Sincerity of Heart

1. Blessed is the man whose heart does not condemn him;[1] the faithful man of God judges himself willingly.[2] ... If perchance thou wouldst give a lesson (to others), do it (thyself) before thou hast given it (MP. 40 : 31-32, 6). Do not adorn thyself outwardly and be found rotten[3] in thy inward parts[4] (MP. 189 : 11-12); do not strive after pleasing men and then become an enemy to God; ... do not give rest to thy body and

---

[1] *Cf.* 1 Jn. 3 : 20-21. Note that it is the conscience which really judges.

[2] *lit*: gives his judgment to himself alone, *i.e.*, does not judge others if he can help it.

[3] *or*: wasted away, destroyed.

[4] *Cf.* Mt. 23 : 25-29.

then pay the penalty with thy Soul [1] (MP. 40 : 18-19, 21).

2. (Mani says:) " My brothers, love me with your heart, do not flatter [2] me with your lips; the children of the lip are blotted out, the children of the heart remain! Do not be like the pomegranate whose rind is gay outside . . . while its inside is full of ashes (?); . . . do not be like the tombs of corpses, which are indeed whitewashed outside but are inside full of carrion; . . . do not be like horse-saddles, for outside indeed **they** wear fine trappings [3] . . . while inside they are full of straw (?) ! . . . For my sake be like a jar of wine, placed firmly on its stand, for while the outside is a piece of earthenware, there is a fragrant wine inside " [4] (MP. 220 : 1-24)!

The vital importance of Sincerity is further stressed: it is a total one-pointedness towards the goal, a complete freedom from every kind of hypocritical outer show. Outside it matters little what we seem, so

[1] What profit in gaining the whole world and losing the Soul? (cf. Mk. 8 : 36).

[2] *lit*: please.

[3] *lit*: Babylonian (cloth), an echo of Babylon's traditional luxury.

[4] It is pleasant to have here the *positive* form for the so negative denunciation by Jesus of the hypocrites of his day.

long as we are really *pure* within and rich with the fragrance of a true righteousness devoted to the liberation of the One Light everywhere.

63. The Work of the Light-Mind

1. The Light-Mind,[1] who is the Awakener of those who sleep, the Gatherer in of those scattered abroad [2] (Keph. 44 : 11-12), (is) the Father of all the Messengers, (Keph. 35 : 22) who chooses all the churches (Keph. 36 : 1-2). The Physician of the Souls, he is the Light-Mind, (and) this is the 'New Man'.[3] The caustic medicines are the Precepts, while the cooling medicines are the Absolution [4]—he who would be healed, see, of two kinds (are) the medicines of Life (MP. 40 : 13-16)!

2. There is a mighty power dwelling in this body; . . . it is very terrible with great cunning [5] until the Light-Mind finds how to

---

[1] " Christ . . . is Mind, . . . that which is known and that which knows " (AL. 24)—a dictum which sounds almost Indian! He reveals truth to Hermes.

[2] *Cf.* " In all am I scattered, and whencesoever thou willest thou gatherest Me; and gathering Me thou gatherest thyself " (Gospel of Eve).

[3] Ch. *sin-jen.*

[4] *lit*: forgiveness of sins. It is painful to know the Commands we have so poorly kept, and delightful to know that our failures have been condoned and put away.

[5] *lit*: wisdom.

13

subdue this body and to drive [1] it according to his will (Keph. 94 : 17-22). (Then) the Light-Mind [2] comes and finds the Soul *a captive in the flesh*; . . . he frees the Soul's limbs and makes them free from the five limbs of Sin,[3] . . . (and) those he chains [4] (Keph. 66 : 7-9, 22-25).

3. Because he loathed the five craggy and dangerous earths [5] of the Darkness, he flattened and overwhelmed them; he began by removing the brambles and all the poisonous weeds, and burned them in fire. . . . Then, being armed with the sharp Axe of Wisdom, the Messenger of the Light . . . felled the five kinds of poison trees . . . of death (CMT. 49, 58, 49, 52).

---

[1] *or*: sail, wound.

[2] "He called an Envoy, a storehouse of life which is the Mind, . . . and sent him forth: . . . 'Dig up their land with the spade and overturn the fragrant roots; . . . aid the Righteous and plant thy Trees in the world.' . . . Then he armed himself and at once girt himself, the Son of the Lights; . . . he dug up the fragrant roots and took them, . . . he helped his Righteous, (and) he planted his Trees in the world " (MP. 208 : 11—209 : 4).

[3] *i.e.*, the five aspects of the Soul, as corrupted by evil. See the accompanying table of the Five Dark Trees.

[4] "When they had made all these things and established the universe, imprisoned the five kinds of demons and chained them by means of the third great Bright Powers . . .—the five Bright Sons of First Reason, and the Bright Sons of Pure Spirit, then 'Call' and 'Reply', as well as Srasha."

[5] *Cf.* AnNadim in App. I 4 : 8.

DARK

LIMBS	ROOTS	TRUNKS	BRANCHES	LEAVES	FRUITS	TASTES	COLOURS	ELEMENTS	PRISONS
Thought	Death	Violence	Irritation	Dislike	Division	Insipidity	Slander	Ether	Bones
Feeling	Hypocrisy	Neglect	Hesitation	Violence	Torments	Greedy Lust	Resistance	Wind	Nerves
Reflection	Lust	Laziness	Violence	Envy	Mockery	Greed	Sensuality	Light	Veins
Intellect	Anger	Stupidity	Hypocrisy	Unintelligence	Contempt	Ambition	Scorn	Water	Flesh
Reason	Stupidity	Forgetfulness	Slow-thinking	Self-complacency[1]	Luxuriousness	Jewellery	Gluttony	Fire	Skin

[1] Ch. *Kou-ying*: lit. looking at his shadow.

BRIGHT

LIMBS	ROOTS	TRUNKS	BRANCHES	LEAVES	FRUITS	TASTES	COLOURS	ELEMENTS	PRISONS
Thought	Pity	Joy	Happiness	Popularity	Stillness	Reverence	Firmness		
Feeling	Sincerity	Faith	Respect	Vigilance	Studiousness	Love of Reading	Calm Joy		
Reflection	Contentment	Good Thought	Courtesy[1]	Truthfulness in Action	Speech	Talk on Religion	Sociability		
Intellect	Endurance of wrong	Total Calm	Patience	Discipline	Fasts and[2] Hymns	Zeal in Practices	Energy		
Reason	Wisdom	Discernment	Religious Discussion	Skill in Debate	Eloquence	Teaching Power	Sweetness of Speech		

[1] Ch. *Wei-yi*: lit. imposing rites, or manners.   [2] Raising to the 'Column of Glory.'

THE WAY OF RIGHTEOUSNESS

4. He took his own precious Trees ... of Life ... of five kinds,[1] shining, pure and unexcelled, and he planted them in the soils of the First Nature. He sprinkled these precious Trees with the water of immortality, and they produced fruits which give deathlessness (CMT. 58, 64, 58).

5. He arranges[2] the limbs of the Soul, builds them, polishes them and organises them into a 'New Man', a son of the Righteousness[3] (Keph. 96 : 25-27). He evoked the Aeons of Peace in whom there is no waning and decrease; ... he established treasuries[4] of Life, and in them set up living Images ... which never perish[5] (MP. 203 : 9-11, 14-17); then over the five kinds of precious luminous

---

[1] *i.e.*, the five pure aspects of the Soul, as listed in the accompanying table.

[2] *or*: organises, constructs.

[3] *i.e.*, the 'Christ in You', who replaces the 'Old Man', the fallen Adam enslaved to sin. "God makes man when the Inner Man is renewed in God's image" (AF. 24 : 2). The process is fully described by Richard Rollo, *The Mending of Life*, and Walter Hilton, *The Scale of Perfection*, and many other works by Catholics on Ascetic and Mystical Theology; e.g. St. John of the Cross.

[4] *or*: chambers, homes.

[5] Are these the living portraits of disciples, whereof C.W.L. speaks in his *The Masters and the Path*?

terraces he lit five precious Bright Lamps that last for ever [1] (CMT. 51).

6. The 'New Man' becomes King through [2] his love, his faith, his perfection, his patience, and through his wisdom. [3] His King again, *who is the* Light-Mind, *is* King over the 'All'; [4] he reigns over it according to his will (Keph. 97 : 19-23). (So too) the Light-Mind ... comes and shines in the world and *chooses* the holy Church, ... and parts the Light from *the Darkness and separates the Truth* from Lawlessness (Keph. 80 : 33—81 : 1). O Mind that conquers Matter, spread thy mercy over my spirit (MP. 59 : 11-12) !

Now for a moment we look at how the Illuminator, Guru or Messenger of the Light, who is really the awakened Light-Spark within the man himself, proceeds in his work. First come the precepts in the Scriptures, reproving and consoling, and then the repression of the inner 'demon' and the steady uprooting of the heart's lawless tendencies. This results in the purifying of the life and the change of

---

[1] " He hung up the five Powers of Darkness in the Five Lights, the Sons of Men, for the whole Enmity is fastened and fettered in them " (Keph. 89)

[2] *or*: reigns in.

[3] These five qualities correspond with the 'Roots' in the accompanying table. Such consistencies between lists in Chinese, Persian, Coptic, Syriac, Greek, Latin texts, show how faithfully the Manicheans guarded the details of their faith, even where technical names may have varied somewhat.

[4] *or*: the universe, everything (Copt. *ajem ptēref.*)

vices into virtues ; and these are carefully cultivated until they come to fruition. Thus the 'New Man', of whom St. Paul also speaks, takes power in the Soul and manifests the five Divine qualities within it, and equally in the wider field of the Church and society.

64. Five Kinds of Masters

1. Sometimes the soldiers of the 'Old Man'[1] ... are defeated ; then the religious thought of the Kindly Light[2] ... enters the Town[3] of the wonderful Pure Thought ; in the stately Hall found there it places a Seat for the Law and instals itself there. ... When the Kindly Light moves in the Town of Thought, it should be known that this Master preaches the Right Law wonderfully ; he delights in speech about the Three Eternals[4] and the Five Greatnesses[5] of the Great Light.[6] and he fully develops all thoughts by means of his supernatural intuition.[7] In his preaching of the Law he then stresses Pity (CMT. 39-40).

[1] Ch. *kou-jen*. St. Paul uses the same phrase.

[2] *i.e.*, the Light-Mind, or even God Himself; Ch. *houei-ming fa-siang*.

[3] Ch. *tch'eng* (enclosure).

[4] *i.e.*, Light, Power and Wisdom.

[5] God's five Splendours; Ch. *ta ming san-ch'ang wou-ta*; cf. GPM 1 : 2.

[6] *i.e.*, *Vazurg-Rōṣan Narēsaf*, God the Supreme.

[7] Ch. *shen-t'ong*, probably the Skt. *abhijña*.

2. When the Kindly Light moves into the Town of Feeling, ... this Master is pleased by talk of the bright Palaces of the Sun and Moon,[1] and he fully develops majestic power; ... then in his preaching of the Law he stresses Sincerity (CMT. 41).

3. When the Kindly Light moves into the Town of Reflection, ... this Master delights to speak of Obedience,[2] the great Servant, and by means of his supernatural intuition he fully develops silence.[3] Then in his preaching of the Law he stresses Contentment (CMT. 42).

4. When the Kindly Light moves into the Town of Intellect, ... this Master is pleased to speak of the Five Lights,[4] and by means of his supernatural intuition he fully develops ....[5] Then in his preaching of the Law he stresses the Endurance of Wrong (CMT. 43).

---

[1] Called the ' First Gate of the Kingdom ' ; cf. GPM 25.

[2] Text: Srōsharay, Ch. Su-lu-sha-lo-yi (Pers. Swyr-lu-ṣa'-l'ai). We meet Sraosha in Avesta texts; he is Obedience, one of the three Judges of GZ 38 : 2, called there strong and holy. The name may mean: Sraoṣo-aṣyo, like the King who judges affairs. He is called the 'Great Servant' (Ch. ta-siang) and represents the Column of Glory, the Perfect Man, the Church.

[3] Ch. mo-jan; AnNadim calls one member ' Discretion '.

[4] Ch. wou-ming—the Five Bright Elements.

[5] The word is missing from the text.

5. When the Kindly Light moves into the Town of Reason, it should be known that the Master is pleased to talk of the Messengers of the Light, past, future and present; and with his supernatural intuition he develops the power to be invisible or visible. Then in his preaching of the Law he stresses Wisdom. So, then, he who is wise in the study of such a Master knows at once in which Realm the Kindly Light is found (CMT. 44).

As there are five aspects, principles, of the Soul, so there are five kinds of Saints, each manifesting specially the quality of one of the aspects—Thought, Feeling, Reflection, Intellect and Reason, or however we may prefer to translate these terms. By observing the ways of one of the Elect we can see which of these is at the time illumined by the Divine Light, and by following his example kindle the flame in the corresponding aspect of our own Soul.

65. Exhortation to Spiritual Effort

1. O man of God, thou hast come on [1] to the Road; do not fall, for the Gods have desired thee; thou hast been called, *do not* fail to hear. Look back no more—they do not keep account of what is past, (so) do not

---

[1] Copt. *akpeh ṅsoohe*; i.e., been set right.

think of what thou hast forgetfully done.¹ Strain thyself forward, and God will not turn thee away; but if thou slacken, thou shalt receive suffering (MP. 164 : 20-26). Be thou zealous for God, . . . do not flinch within thyself (MP. 165 : 30-31)! Do not prefer the life of this body to this everlasting Life; put the fear of God in thy heart, and thou shalt live without suffering ² (MP. 82 : 27-29). If thou hast resolved to love Me, then I will put on thee the Robe of Glory and the Garland of *Victory*, because thou hast believed in ³ the Truth (MP. 53 : 12-14) O how great is the joy that is prepared for the Perfect ⁴ (MP. 64 : 2), the King's Bride (M 20)!

2. My brothers, do not slacken in doing good by night and by day,⁵ for what the man plants is the same as what he shall reap ⁶ (MP. 52 : 3-5). I myself left the Land of Light

---

[1] This refers to the repentent convert, whose act of faith and surrender blots out the past. Copt. *elak ekiarme apahou, maubi ōp men-netauouine, m̂pōrmeeu anetakeitou*: cf. GPM 89.

[2] This is no promise to escape the suffering shown inevitable in GPM 55; it is the pain of failure, of sin and darkness, which is now destroyed. Other suffering is joy in the light of eternal bliss.

[3] *or*: trusted to.

[4] Apparently an echo of Isa. 64 : 4 and 1 Cor. 2 : 9.

[5] Night is put first, because slackening is more likely at night.

[6] The 'law of *karma*', echoing 2 Cor. 9 : 6 and Gal. 6 : 7-9.

and of eternal Bliss, and for your sakes I have come here, bringing these Trees (of Virtue) which I would plant in your holy multitude. ... Each one of you must plant these Trees in his own pure heart, that he may let them thrive and grow tall. ., . If now you would realise in yourselves the pure fruits of the great Incomparable Light, you must welcome all the precious Trees and let them have all they need. Why so? Because, good people, it is by means of the fruits of these Trees you will be able to free yourselves from the Four Afflictions,[1] and all embodied beings will be saved from worldliness[2] and come at last, ever victorious, into the Realm of unmoving Happiness (CMT. 92)! (For) he who sows his soul with good seed finds the return again, Eternal Life in the land of the Gods (Man. III. 11).

3. See, my beloved, do not be enticed[3] by the forms of this Ruler,[4] the Root of *all*

---

[1] Ch. *sseu-nan*. The Gnostics (FFF. p. 347) listed these as Fear, Grief, Doubt and Supplication; the Chinese list is not known, but Mani is so close to the Gnostics it may well have been the same.

[2] *or*: birth and death (Skt. *samsāra*).

[3] *or*: deceived.

[4] The Pistis Sophia was trapped by the beauties assumed by the Powers of Matter.

the erupting wickedness and the Camp of every hatred. But protect yourselves from his tricks and his evil ideas [1] that dwell in your body, [2] lest they mix with [3] you and ruin your gentleness [4] and lead your truth astray into a lie. But be you zealous and perfect before the Mind of Truth who has shown himself to you, so that you *may be true* of heart and be drawn up on high and inherit Life from everlasting to everlasting (Keph. 79 : 1-12).

4. Because all the Souls that arise in human flesh and (then) vanish are led to the great Aeons of the Light, and there is a resting-place for them there in [5] the Aeons of the Greatness. As for you, my beloved, try [6] every means that you may become good Pearls and be assigned to Heaven by the Light-Diver [7] when he comes to you and leads

---

[1] *or*: impulses.

[2] This is the 'Sin' that lurks in the body and wars with the 'New Man'.

[3] *or*: contaminate.

[4] *or*: sweetness.

[5] *or*: through, by means of.

[6] *or*: wrestle (?)

[7] The Light-Mind that comes down into the Sea of Matter (*samsārasāgara*) to rescue Souls. The context is the moving story of Mani and the Ugly Saint (see his Life in our Introduction, §11).

THE WAY OF RIGHTEOUSNESS

you *to the* great Supreme Merchant, your Rest in Life for evermore (Keph. 204 : 13-22).

5. You are the Sons of the Day *and* the Sons of Light [1] (Keph. 163 : 30-31); fight yet a little while, O Sons of Light, and you will be victorious; he who evades his burden will lose his bedchamber! ... Support one another, my brothers, do not flinch at all; we have a God who cares (for us), He will help us in *His* compassion. It is Jesus who has helped me, he will help you, my beloved [2] (MP. 58: 24-26, 17-19)! Be yourselves Refiners and Saviours for your Soul which abides in every place, [3] that you *may lead it* to the dwelling of the Fathers of the Light . . . in the New Aeon [4] in the Place of Joy (Keph. 77 : 18-21)!

---

[1] *Cf.* 1 Thes. 5 : 5 and Eph. 5 : 8, a very close parallel: *ṅtōtne ṅṣēre m̀phooue men-ṅṣēre m̀pouaine*; Thes. reads: *ṅthōten hanṣēri ṅte-phouōini nem hanṣēri ṇte-piehoou*, and allowing for dialect differences this is practically verbatim.

[2] Though these are the words, not of Mani himself but of a converted Manichean, once Christian, they are consistent with Mani's own identification of Jesus with the revealing Angel-Twin, when he calls himself " the Apostle of Jesus ".

[3] Note this noble doctrine of self-help, combined once more with a true pantheism of the omnipresence of Soul: Copt: *ṅtōtne hōttēne ari henrefsōtef men henrefsōte ṅtetṅpsukhe tettēk aretes hem ma nim*.

[4] The 'New Heaven and New Earth' of Rev. 21 : 1, and the ' Renewal ' of GZ 50 : 4, GPM 12 : 4 and GH 35 : 2.

6. The crowd [1] have erred because they look to a distant day, *but* let us today do good (MP. 162 : 15-16), so that our way (may) be radiant once again . . . and we may be fearless wherever we may . . . go (BM. 207)! Let us not slumber and sleep until our Lord changes us, [2] his garland on his head (and) his palmleaf in his hand, wearing the Robe of his glory—and all of us enter the bride-chamber and reign together with him (MP. 193 : 8-12)!

Now the Soul is awake, taught, resolved; it remains only to exert to the utmost to attain the goal of freedom. This is won through detachment from the world (*vairāgya*) and attachment to the Messenger or Guru (*i.e.*, to God: *śraddhā-bhakti*), with a steady perseverance in the spiritual life (*abhyāsa*). Mani explains that his mission is to sow the seed of these in every heart, but that each must labour that the tender seedling may grow into a mighty tree bearing luscious fruit, and so each Soul will be freed from the misery of fleshly life by a 'ceaseless awareness', an unresting watch on the lower tendencies that again and again drag it down to earth. All Souls are destined to achieve (GMP 12:4), but each may aspire to a brighter glory, as stars differ from each other in their splendour. Those who make real effort may be sure of Divine aid ever ready at their side; to procrastinate is foolishness, for *this* is the ' accepted

---

[1] *or*: majority.

[2] *or*: transports, carries us over.

time'; today we must work at refining ourselves and glorifying the inner self, to blow its tiny 'spark' into a vast and brilliant flame.

66. The Soul is Righteous Now

1. Fair is a holy Soul that has taken the Holy Spirit to herself (MP. 174 : 19), fair is the Dove that has found a holy Pool; it is Jesus who flies into the heart of his faithful one (MP. 161: 7-8)! See, the Gods rejoice over him because he has become one like them;[1] it is the Soul that is safe [2] from stain [3] who can proceed to the presence of God [4] (MP. 150: 13-14).

2. I withdrew far from the world, I left my parents behind, I turned to the Lord who is greater than the heaven and the earth. . . . I did not do the body's will (MP. 93 : 19-22), so I found the Land of Light, I made my way to the City of the Gods, I communed with the Righteous while I was in the body [5] (MP. 95: 28-30). For I removed myself from

---

[1] See the close parallels throughout GP; the idea is quite Egyptian, like so much else we find in these Coptic Psalms.

[2] *or*: healthy, free.

[3] *i.e.*, spotless, flawless like a pure Pearl.

[4] The pure in heart will see God.

[5] The great value of saintly contacts is well known to all religious thinkers and practicants.

the bitter *waters*,[1] I came to port even before the sea became stormy,[2] . . . I put off the vain garment of the flesh, being safe and pure; I made my Soul's clean feet confidently trample on it;[3] I stood in line with the Gods who are clothed with the Christ (MP. 99 : 12-13, 27-30), for I am a God (and) a servant (of) God[4] (MP 75 : 5)!

The Soul that has thus deified herself by her own unremitting effort against the lower tendencies of the flesh, abstaining from carnal desires and ever seeking the company of Saints, becomes glorious and radiant even before escaping from the body; after death she goes straight to God, whose nature of pure Light she already shares.

---

[1] *i.e.*, sensual emotions and sex-contacts; sweet at first, but very bitter in their results because they dim the glory of the Light and destroy all peace of mind.

[2] *i.e.*, before the passions of growing youth came on, in early manhood.

[3] *Cf.* the Agraphon spoken to Salome: " When you shall tread on the vesture of shame " and so conquer sex, then shall the Truth be known.

[4] Closely parallel to the Visishtādvaita-like ending of GP 70 : 3: " The King is indeed God, and the son of God." One, yet distinct.

CHAPTER SIX

LIBERATION OF THE LIGHT

That same death of the body, which seems a ceaseless dread or terror to the worldly when attached to the body of flesh and its delights, is an ecstatic expectation to the spiritual man. The body may feel pain in its own dissolution, but the Soul rejoices at the sound of its Liberator's approaching steps and bids the sorrowing friends around rather to share its joy. At the same time the Soul knows it needs the mighty Guru's help at this moment also, and with passionate earnestness calls him to take her across the river into the bright Realm of God; her confidence bases on her knowledge of mutual love and a devotion that has never wavered, so that now between them there is the perfect intimacy of heart-union.

To the prayer of the dying the Lord responds with sweet assurances, and joyfully the Soul escapes from the prison of the flesh, the evil thoughts that always inhere therein flee away, and the angels of love and piety welcome her home. They take her safely through the judgment of the ' Lords of Karma ', while she sings with joy at her victory over death and enters into the eternal paradise of bliss, where all the righteous live in endless joy.

67. The Agony of Death

1. One[1] too must die at last; . . . like *a shadow* of his body he lies down, his goods remain withheld (from him).[2] . . . Ten thousand demons come, black foggy demons hover around, the darkness of night presses *on the dying*, oppression comes to them; sitting on the breast, **the demons** make them dream[3] (T. II. D. 169).

2. A false hairy hoary demoness[4] comes, the hailcloud is like her (in colour); provided with *hideous* brows, her look is like a bloody *butcher* (?),[5] her blackened teats are like a nail (in sharpness). A grey cloud rises out of her nose, from her throat ascends black smoke; her breast is wholly compact with a myriad snakes, her *hair* is a viper; her finger is altogether *sharp and venomous*. . . . She seizes

---

[1] Not only *others* must be ready for the body's end, but every single one of us.

[2] *i.e.*, those properties that were so dear to him on earth cannot go with him now: cf. GZ 36 : 3.

[3] Torturing memories of lost chances, cruel and blasphemous actions done, filthy thoughts encouraged and given rein.

[4] This may be Humāmah, the demoness of Arrogance, or Āz, the Envy-demon: the description tallies with that of the evil conscience in GZ 40 : 2-3.

[5] This word *bcana* is not known elsewhere; from the context it may mean a 'slaughterer' or the like.

on the erring Soul; beating on its head, she thrusts *it* into *hell*. The demons found in hell seize *it*, the evil demons come, they take it to themselves. There you see many *dark* spirits, to implore *whom when* near to death is purposeless[1] (T. II. D. 169, 178).

Each man, naturally, while he faces with equanimity the death of his friends, shrinks from the thought of his own, imagining all kinds of terrors must lurk in the dark hour of the inevitable end. Those whose conscience is troubled by evil memories may easily be afflicted then with ghastly visions and the dread of the horrible hell which haunted his mind in early childhood.

68. The Righteous is Called

1. See, I have safely finished my voyage (MP. 73 : 7), my own hour has already come. They summon me (MP. 72 : 30-31): "O Soul, lift up (thy) head and go to thy Fatherland (MP. 182 : 11-12)!" I depart from your midst and I go away to my true home[2] (MP. 72 : 31-32). I have cleansed myself in the washing of immortality by the hands of the Saints;[3]

[1] Refuting the idea that a mere deathbed conversion from fear of punishment may avail the Soul.

[2] Naturally enough, the Soul's true home is Heaven whence she came and whither she returns: " *Qui vitam sine termino nobis donet in patria* ", as St. Thomas Aquinas sings.

[3] This *may* refer to a baptismal rite on the deathbed, such as Mani, with Chaldean antecedents, is said to have used, while

(now) they summon me to the bride-chambers of the Height, and I will go up clothed in the Robe[1] (MP. 76 : 9-12).

2. I will go up to the Nature of Excellences[2] (MP. 76 : 21), I will pass away up to the skies and leave this body on the earth.[3] The trumpet sounds. I hear (it)! I am being called up to the Immortals! I will throw away my body on the earth from which it was assembled. Ever since I was in my early childhood I have learned to walk in God's Path; let no one weep for me—neither my brothers nor those who produced me; my true Fathers, those who are from on high, they love my Soul, seek after it! My Soul's enemy is the world, its wealth and the love of it; all life hates godliness. What am I doing while I am in the place of my foes[4] (MP. 75 : 13-24)?

insisting on the far greater value of a spiritual and inner cleansing during life.

[1] The 'Light-Vesture' of the Gnostics; it is the innate divinity of the Soul now manifesting outwardly.

[2] *i.e.*, the Good Tree, the King of Light, spoken of in GPM 1 : 2; 13 : 1.

[3] Sharply contrasting the different destinies of the two parts of man as known down here; cf. GP 23 : 3.

[4] A striking passage: Copt. *pbios těref maste ñtmentnoute, eireu eisoop henbma ñnajaje.*

But those whose conscience is clear, who have always longed for God and chosen the Light rather than the deeds of Darkness, look to death rather with delighted hope, for they are going home to join their long-lost Kindred in the land of joy and radiant peace. They feel no sorrow at the passing of all earthly things, but rather rejoice to be free from their entangling lure.

69. He Comforts his Friends

1. The life and death of everyone is in his own hands[1]—as for us, let us live; what is all the crowd to us (MP. 158 : 6-8)? What have we now (in common) with the world?[2] Arise, let us go to our Aeons![3] Where are our Light-Crowns that never fall at all?[4] Let us wear our Garlands that do not fade eternally (MP. 154 : 15-18)!

2 The Living Kingdom shall once again appear, the Love of God, the White Dove[5] (MP. 156 : 25-26); the Kingdom is Love, this White Dove—it is not gold and silver, it is not eating and drinking (MP. 158 : 8-9)! The

[1] Man chooses his own destiny—to walk on the narrow path to Life, or on the wide way to ruin; cf. GY 20 : 4.

[2] Like the Hermetists (cf. GH 49 : 2), Manicheans were almost always a small minority; their standards were too high for the masses. Copt. *ahran menpmēṣe tēref . . . ahran tīnou menpkosmos*?

[3] *i.e.*, to our Divine qualities, parallel to the Twelve great Maidens, who represent the Virtues of God Himself.

[4] *Cf.* GPM 80 : 5; or: never never fall.

[5] The gentle Dove, white because pure, is often taken as a symbol of God's Spirit, *i.e.*, of Love.

Kingdom is Joy and Peace and Rest (MP. 154: 13); see, (it is) within us;[1] look, (it is) without us; if we believe in it we shall live therein for evermore (MP. 160 : 20-21)! My brothers, come in through this narrow Door[2] and let us comfort one another with the word of Truth (MP. 156 : 5-6)!

3. See, the Bridegroom has come! Where is the Bride who resembles him? The Bride is the Church, the Bridegroom is the Light-Mind; the Bride is the Soul, (and) Jesus is the Bridegroom[3] (MP. 154 : 3-7)! If he rises in us, we too shall live in him; . . . if we believe in him, we shall transcend death and come to Life[4] (MP. 159 : 23-26).

Death for such is a happy hour, and the dying calls on those he has to leave behind to share his joy at entering the spiritual realm, where there is union with the beloved Lord whom he has faithfully served on this dimly lighted world. Knowing the Land of Light,

---

[1] Not only within, as in Lk. 17 : 21, but all around; to know this is to be always *in* the Kingdom, to be eternally one with it.

[2] *Cf.* Lk. 13 : 24.

[3] This may profitably be compared with Catholic doctrine on the Mystical Body, e.g. the Encyclical of Pius XII, and with all the writing of the mystics—also with those of Sufis, Sikhs, and Vaishnavas. God is Love, and to know Him is to *love* Him. There is no other way to express it.

[4] The birth in our own hearts of the Living Christ is the certainty of our spiritual 'resurrection' and 'ascension'. As He, so too we.

which is Spirit, is within as well as outside himself, the dying realises that he goes to no alien environment but rather merges in what is already one with himself, and so is eternally full of confidence, restfulness and peace.

70. And Prays for Help to Jesus

1. O great 'Call' who has wakened this soul of mine from slumber (HR. II. 62), O Merciful filled with mercy, the Saviour of those who are *his own*[1] (MP. 112:8-9), I worship thee ! I have called upon thee with an innocent voice because I know that thou art the Rescuer of Souls (MP. 65 : 31-32) ! Stretch out thy Right Hand to me, and I shall leave the things of the body behind me (MP. 69 : 6-7) ! Come, I implore thee, draw me up out of (the) Underworld [2] of the Dead (MP. 67 : 15-16) ! Let not the demons frighten me and the Fury with her fearful face,[3] because I have not served the Error but have passed my whole life nourished in thy Truth (MP. 84: 21-22) ! (Now) save my soul from this (state of) life and death (M 311) !

[1] How can those who reject him be saved by him?
[2] *lit*: the hidden (place)—Amente; *i.e.* Hades, "the Unseen".
[3] *cf.* GPM 67 : 2.

2. See, my faith clings[1] fast to me; see my alms that I have done in thy name; see, my prayers and my zeal demand that I receive grace upon me![2] A robber was saved upon the cross only because he confessed thee;[3] . . . cleanse me from all my sins, for I too have hung upon thy Hope (MP. 49: 20-24, 27-28)! Behold, I am coming out of the body of death; . . . now do I call on thee, O Saviour: "Come to me in the hour of my need (MP. 50 : 11, 15)!" Show me thy Maiden[4] at the *moment* of my departure from the 'All' (MP. 112 : 9-10); let me too be worthy to see thy Maiden for whose sake I have toiled, and her three Angels also who are with her, who bring all the Gifts of the faithful one (MP. 66 : 22-24)! My holy Father, let me see Thy Likeness that I saw before the universe was created,[5] before the Darkness

---

[1] *lit*: stands.

[2] One who follows the way taught by the Messenger can claim his help and demand to be saved by him.

[3] See Lk. 23 : 42-43.

[4] The Soul's perfect purity, which appears to the Righteous in GZ 43 : 2-5, is itself a reflection, a gift of God's own immaculate Self, called in GPM 27 the 'Maiden of the Light'.

[5] Is this an echo of Jn. 17 : 5?

dared to stir up envy against Thy Aeons.[1] On that occasion indeed did I become a stranger to my Kingdom;[2] I have cut its root and have come up victoriously on high (MP. 79 : 24-28).

3. O my prayers and my fasts and my virginity which I have perfected in thy name (MP. 51 : 26-27), Jesus my Light (MP. 87 : 16), this is the moment of my death when I have need of you (MP. 50 : 16-17)! Yoke for me speedily my soaring chariots (and) my horses—which are my holy fasts, my prayers to God, and my almsgivings![3] Take me swiftly in to the Land of those of the Glory (MP. 111 : 23-26)! O Mighty One, crown me! Take me on thy wings, O Eagle, (and) fly with me to the skies![4] Put my white Robe upon me, take me in as a gift to thy Father (MP. 188 : 19-22)!

[1] The revolt of GPM 2 : 2 and 19.

[2] Only to defeat this revolt did the Soul come down from heaven and so was alienated from God and Spirit, contaminated by the enclosing Matter.

[3] Surely a telling metaphor, based on the Sun-chariot of Mithra or Phoebus-Apollo (GZ 22 : 1), or on the fiery chariot of Elijah (2 K. 2 : 11).

[4] Closely parallel to GP 31. But the mystical state of Rapture is usually compared with an Eagle snatching the Soul on high; see Consummata's beautiful account in Fr. Raoul Plus's story of the mystic's life.

4. O eternal Victor, I call to thee; hear my cry, Compassionate! Let thy Members cleanse me, and wash me, thou, in thy holy waters and make me spotless,[1] even as I (really) am![2] Lo, the time has drawn near that I should return to my homes! Thou art the Way, thou art indeed the Gate of eternal Life, O Son of God, my Saviour, who has taught me to wear his holy Precepts[3] (MP. 59 : 24-31)! Open to me, O Tree of Life; O Tree of Rest, open to me! Open thine essences[4] to me, and I shall gaze upon the face of the Saints! Open to me thy halls, for my heart has swooned after thy bliss! Open thy gardens to me, and my spirit will receive (their) fragrance (MP. 154 : 22-29)!

The Soul implores her Saviour, the Master, Jesus, to guard and guide her through the approaching crisis, putting all her trust in the memory of a life lived in union with Spirit, into whose realm she is now

---

[1] This is the Mandean *massiqta*, the baptism of the dying, an older rite in Chaldea—not to avoid later sins which could not be absolved, as in the alleged case of Constantine. Cf. GPM 68:1.

[2] The *real* Self is ever-immaculate; it is only a superficial, a seeming defilement which we see.

[3] *i.e.*, adopting his way of life, 'putting on the Christ'; as Paul might well have said.

[4] *or*: being. In union with God, we can really see the Saints, for they are invisible to those who are not themselves one with them. "Only the saint can know a Saint."

about to pass. May all dark and gloomy evil thoughts give place to the quiet happiness of this blessed memory, personified now as the lovely Maiden of his righteousness! And may the joyful consciousness this brings become a fiery chariot to waft the liberated Soul towards the skies, there to be glorified for evermore as Victor!

71. Having always Preferred Him to the World

1. Come, my Saviour Jesus! Do not abandon me (MP. 51 : 4), help even me ! I have depended on thee, victorious stiller of the fear of death through the Cross[1] (MP. 53 : 30-32)! Jesus, it is thou whom I have loved! . . . See, the glorious armour [2] of thy Commandment wherewith thou didst gird thyself, I have put it on my limbs; I have fought against my foes (MP. 51 : 5-10)! I have subdued youth,[3] running in thy virtue, O Christ; . . . I have forsaken the defilement of intercourse, have put on me this purity thou desirest [4] (MP. 88 : 27-30); the murderous snake, foe of virginity,[5] I have not listened to

[1] Could any Christian have spoken with greater fervour?
[2] The 'armour of light' of Rom. 13 : 12 and GPM 3 : 2, called 'righteousness and peace' in 2 Cor. 6 : 7 and Eph. 6 : 11.
[3] *i.e.*, youth's passions, such as sex desire.
[4] Catholics too hold that Christ loves chastity and virginity.
[5] Psychoanalysts have shown how often the snake recurs as a symbol of sex desires.

his laws and his lying words (MP. 60 : 18-21).
I have not even tasted the pleasure of the
bitter sweet (MP. 55 : 27), nor have I meddled
with the intercourse of the flesh, for it is a
thing that perishes (MP. 86 : 31-32), nor have
I let the fire of eating and drinking rule over
me [1] (MP. 55 : 28-29).

2. Show to me thy face, O holy and un-
sullied [2] Radiance, . . . my true gracious
Physician (MP. 61 : 27-29)! I am thy sheep,
thou art my good Shepherd! [3] Thou didst
follow me and save me from the destroying
wolves; I listened to thy words and walked in
thy laws, I became a stranger in the world [4]
for thy Name's sake, my God (MP. 60: 26-29)!
(Yet) thou didst not leave me in want, . . .
for I was given food and drink because of thy
Name (MH. 2 : 3-4)

3. I have touched the world and known it
that there is not a scrap [5] of life in it (MP.
223 : 24-25). I have wandered over the whole

[1] *Cf.* GPM 57 : 2.

[2] *or*: immaculate.

[3] *Cf.* GPM 50 : 3.

[4] *i.e.*, turned away from worldly loves and ways.

[5] *lit*: little toe.

world and witnessed all the things that are therein, (and) I have seen that all men vainly run about,[1] ... for they have forgotten the God who came and gave himself to death for them [2] (MP. 51 : 11-16). The strangers with whom I mingled, they never knew me; they tasted my sweetness [3] and wished to keep me with them; I was life to them, but they were a death to me! I tolerated them,[4] and they wore me as a garment on themselves [5] (MP. 54 : 19-24)!

4. My Lord, when I saw these things I took thy Hope and strengthened myself upon it, I did not refuse thy yoke which thou didst lay on me, thy good Precepts which thou gavest me I have fulfilled, my Saviour; I did not let my enemies put out thy Lamps of Light [6] (MP. 51 : 17-22)! I have despised the world to give life to my Soul, I have forsaken the things of the flesh and been content with

---

[1] This definitely seems to refer to Mani's own experience.
[2] Surely this refers to Jesus, the 'God' who died on the Cross.
[3] *i.e.*, exploited me.
[4] *lit*: bore up under.
[5] *i.e.*, used me as a cover for their own actions.
[6] *Cf.* the Agraphon: "Do not put out the light which has shone forth in you." These may be the 'Lamps' of GPM 63 : 5.

220 THE GOSPEL OF THE PROPHET MANI

those of the Spirit [1] (MP. 63 : 28-29). I have known the 'Cross of Light' that gives life to the universe,[2] I have believed in it that it is my beloved Soul which nourishes everyone, whereat the blind are offended because they are ignorant of it [3] (MP. 86 : 27-30).

5. Since I found my Saviour I have walked in his footsteps; never have I in the least [4] hung back, so as to receive this Garland (MP. 63 : 33—64 : 1); *the* gay *trees* that blossom and are full of *fruit I have* given thee, my husbandman: namely, Prayer, Fasting, Alms, Love to thy *children* (MP. 91 : 8-10). My 'Inner Man' is like thee in his form, my 'Outer Man' receives grace through the Word [5] (MP. 173 : 19-21). I have constantly practised in thy holy Wisdom,

---

[1] The Soul says. "Go away, you of the Hebdomad; go, attend to your snares, . . . and let your snares attend to you. Go, sink down in the madness, and fall into the fire that is kindled: I am not of the sons of the world that I should fall into the snares and be caught; I am a *scion* of the Living Ones, an entire Lamp of Light (MP. 211 : 6:13).

[2] Copt. *ettenho ṁptēref.*

[3] *i.e.,* I have known myself to be the same indwelling life in everything; those who do not know this despise subhuman life as inferior, to be ruthlessly exploited and misused.

[4] *or*: at all, at least.

[5] The inner self is in God's image, the outer man lives by His commandments.

which has opened my Soul's eyes to the light of the Glory and let me see the hidden and revealed things, those of the Abyss and those of the Height (MP. 86 : 23-26)!

6. O Light-Mind, the Sun of my heart *that gives* my Soul the things of the Light, thou art my witness that I have no comfort save in thee (MP. 173 : 14-15)! I have heard every voice, (but) no other voice save thine has pleased me (MP. 154 : 31), for it is thou alone whom I have loved from the beginning to the end (MP. 87 : 9-10)! Since my childhood it is thou to whom I have given thanks; I have forsaken everything (MP. 91 : 22-23)—I do not know the day when they vanished. . . . *I have left behind* my beauty for the sake of thy Name (MH. 3 : 5-7), I have stood firm in thy Name, O Aloneborn[1] (MP. 91 : 23-24)! I have accepted thy sweet yoke in purity (MP. 55:30-31), I have borne thy yoke, have bound my *limbs* to thy Cross (MP. 92 : 5-6); I have made myself pure for thee according to my power, O King of Saints (MP. 89 : 30)! It is thou to whom I have given my Soul (MP. 91 : 27), for thou art

---

[1] *i.e.*, Self-existing, *not* 'only-begotten son'.

the hidden Joy of thy children[1] (MP. 92 : 19-20)!

It is only the knowledge of a devoted life on earth, faithfully clinging to righteousness in this hard environment, which can give this confidence. The Soul knows that she is the Lord's, because she has always striven after Him and renounced the flesh; how then could the Lord fail to receive her to Himself, when He has always watched, protected, nourished her through the years? Seeing for herself the vanity of this fleeting, *unreal* world, the Soul has long ago made her choice of the beloved Lord and tried to live without hurt to the Soul hidden in every form, while cultivating all virtues in herself. Now she is sure of the Master's blessing, and confidently prays for His active aid.

72. The Bride to her Spouse

1. Jesus, my Light whom I have loved, take me in to thee! I have trusted to the knowledge of thy Hope which called me to thee (MP. 85 : 23-26), take me up to thy homes, Jesus my Spouse! . . . Pick me ripening on the pleasant bush of the Church; I am a gay[2] fruit, pure since I was small[3]

---

[1] What beauty, what deep experience in love lie behind these words! Copt. *ṅtak petaiti atootek ṅtapsukhē, je ṅtak pe preṣe ethēp ṅte nekṣēre.*

[2] *or:* ripe, flourishing.

[3] A charming conceit, worthy of St. Thérèse. Copt. *jalet eiraut hentbō etnatme ṅtekklēsia, anak oukarpos efraut eitoubait jen ṅtamentkoui.* It is almost exactly the phrasing used by little Maria of Padova.

(MP. 58 : 3, 9-11)! I am a Tree in thy Light-Orchard (MP. 175 : 8); *my lamp* shines like the Sun; I have lit it, O Spouse, with the good oil of purity (MP. 80 : 13-14).

2. My Bridegroom, Saviour, cleanse me in thy waters[1] . . . that are full of grace (MP. 79 : 29-30); wash me in the dew-water[2] of the Column of Glory (MP. 103 : 35)! I have become divine again as I was (at first),[3] . . . . I have set myself to please thee to the end (MP. 58 : 28, 5)! Make even me worthy of thy holy bridechambers (MP. 62 : 13-14) *that are filled with* Light[4] (MP. 79 : 17-18), for I have loved thy Saints like thee thyself, my Saviour (MP. 62 : 14-15)!

3. Jesus Christ, receive me to thy bridechambers (MP. 79 : 19), that I may chant with those who sing to thee; add me too to the number of those who have conquered and have received their garland (MP. 117 : 29-31).

---

[1] *Cf.* GPM 70 : 4.

[2] *i.e.*, sweet dew, immortality (cf. Skt. *amritam*),

[3] Copt. *aiernoute ñtahe ñkaisap.* *Cf.* GPM 70 : 4.

[4] The Bridechamber of Light is common also in Ephrem. the Gk. and Eth. Acts of Thomas, and the Chaldaic and Nestorian liturgies: e.g.: " The King's son has built for his bride a glorified bridechamber " (*genōna*, a protected retreat, like a walled garden).

Let me rejoice in all the bridechambers, and do thou give to me the crown of the Saints (?) (MP. 80 : 20-22)!

So great is her confidence, born of lifelong unity of will, that the Soul really feels the Master to be her Spouse, and in an overflowing ecstasy of love she longs for an even closer union with the Beloved, and for the total purifying that can alone make such perfect union possible. Who could read these glowing words without a memory of St. Gemma Galgani, Sri Krishna Chaitanya, St. John of the Cross, the 'Little Flower'? Mysticism is a grace deeply planted in the human Soul everywhere, the crowning glory of ages of longing for the Lord.

73. The Lord's Reply

1. As I was saying these things weeping, the Saviour called to me (MP. 93 : 25) and spoke with me, . . . and my spirit[1] was exalted[2] (T. II. D. 178); Jesus, the King of Saints (MP. 61 : 9), the true Light of the Faithful (MP. 62:6), in a sweet voice answered me, saying, " O blessed righteous man, come forth (MP. 50 : 18-19)! Ascend, thou Soul, and alarm thyself no more; death is vanquished, and the longed-for *bliss has now* drawn near. . . . I have come, I who will redeem from

---

[1] or: ego (Per. *grīv*), *i.e.*, the personal self.
[2] *i.e.*, with joy at his reply.

evil, cure the pain, and make peace in thy heart; I shall give thee all thou hast desired of me, and restore thy place in higher splendour[1] (M 91 : 24, 14-15)! Be not afraid (MP. 50 : 19)! I am thy Higher Self,[2] a security and seal; thou art my body, a garment *I have put on* in order to terrify the Powers, while I (myself) am thy Light, the original Effulgence[3] (T. II. D. 178)! Arise in a joy free from sorrow, and I will lead thee! Do not sit in fatal[4] apathy; turn thyself round and see the embodied beings, *how they wander* in misery . . . and are certainly reborn in all shapes[5] (M 91 : 29-32)!

2. "I have heard thy prayer, O blessed Soul; it is I who will give to thee the reward of thy good deeds (MP. 113 : 14-15)! For in this *world* thou didst abstain from killing, thou didst feel compassion on the lives of all creatures, so that thou didst neither kill them

---

[1] I will restore to the original glories, but as it were on a higher plane.

[2] Text has '*Manvuhmed*', the Vohumanāh, Light-Mind, or Higher Mind; cf. GPM 75 : 1, GZ p. li, etc.

[3] *ūt az ḥēm tō rōṣan 'ispēxt ḥasēnag.*

[4] *lit*: death-bringing,

[5] This sight will encourage and spur on to the final effort needed for freedom from material bonds. The doctrine of Reincarnation.

nor eat of their flesh[1] (T. II. Toyoq).[2] Comfort thyself, stem thy tears, beloved! Good is the profit of thy treasure, for thou hast laid the foundation of thy tower upon the Rock of Christ,[3] hast kindled thy lamps . . . with the oil of faith;[4] thou hast cared for the widows, clothed the orphans, endured the persecutions for the sake of the Name of God, the Giver of rewards, the Granter of grace (MP. 53 : 21-26)! Thy prayers and fasts have become a crown upon thee (MP. 54 : 3); victory and salvation (to thee), O garlanded Soul who has fulfilled her Father's desire (MP. 85 : 16-17)! Now step forward to the fragrant wonderful Garden where there is eternal joy (T. II. Toyoq);[2] come and rest henceforward in the Land of Light, O Soul that lovest God (MP. 85 : 17-18)!

3. "Fear not, I am thy Guide in every place [5] (MP. 50 : 19-20); I will open before thee the door in every heaven and cleanse thy

---

[1] *i.e.*, kept the 'Seal of the Mouth', and so preserved bodily purity—and purity in the mind; cf. GPM 42 : 1. The influence of diet on the lower passions seems, in fact, to be beyond argument.

[2] Quoted from W. B. Henning: Soghdian Tales, in BSOAS, 1945.

[3] *Cf.* the parable in Mt. 7 : 24, and also Mt. 16 : 18.

[4] *Cf.* the parable in Mt. 25 : 4, and GPM 72 : 1.

[5] *Cf.* Isa. 41 : 10, 13.

way in fearlessness and *without trembling*. I will establish thee in strength,¹ clothe *thee* in radiance, and lead *thee* to the place of the blessed regions; . . . there shall I show the beauties of the King of Light, of all the Angels and the Gods; . . . I shall show thee the Father, eternally the Sovereign, and lead thee up in pure raiment before Him! I will show thee the Mother of the Light, and thou shalt for ever be at peace in the praised joy (M. 91 : 16-17, 39, 18-19)! I am thy Light, thy beginningless Illumination (T. II. D. 178).''

How can a loving Lord, a Bridegroom, ignore His faithful lover's appeal? At once the response comes to her cry of faith and aspiration: " Put away all fear, you belong to Me, I will never leave you; the good that you have done for others I will do for you, and I will take you to be for ever with Myself in the infinite joy and beauty of the visible presence of the Father and Mother of the Light.''

74. The Soul Breaks Free

1. When I heard my Saviour's voice, a Power clothed all my limbs ² (MP. 50 : 21); (I said to him:) " I have received thy words, O my Father; stretch out to me now thy

---

¹ Words familiar to members of a certain Order.
² *i.e.*, every part of the nature—mental, spiritual, physical.

Right Hand, so that when the seven demons[1] before me see they may flee afar from me (MP. 108 : 17-18)!"

2. (Then after that) the seven frightful demons [1] departed from me, their foul hands being also empty of my blood, their heart being further laden with grief and sorrow because they had been unable to inveigle me into the nets of pleasure—for I have never been a slave of the outrage-working wickedness (MP. 103 : 29-33). See, I have subdued the Darkness; see, *I have put out* the fire of the eruptions (MP. 55 : 6-7), their bitter walls I have destroyed, and battered down their gates (MP. 50 : 22-23).

With a cry of joy the Soul breaks the bonds of the body and comes forth free into the new life, its dark and anxious tormenting thoughts scattering on every side before the joyous confidence the Beloved's words have strengthened in the heart.

75. Deathbed Scenes [2]

1. In the time of **his** departure, when the Light-Form [3] (Keph. 41 : 11) that appears to

---

[1] Possibly the seven planets, whose power over man ends with the death of his physical body.

[2] This account may be compared with that of Mani's own death, as told in the passages used for our Introduction.

[3] *i.e.*, the Maiden, the parting Soul's personified merits.

everyone about to leave his body, after the example of the Image of the Messenger [1] (Keph. 36 : 12-14), comes forth before **him** and separates **him** from the Darkness to the Light (Keph. 41 : 12-13), the Higher Self [2] rises out of all dark embraces (M 284). The blessed glorious Man has mysteriously become —in his likeness, in his form, in his love, in his holy Maiden who is the Maiden of Light —the Father's Soul [3] (Keph. 84 : 17-20). This Light-Form pacifies the man by the Kiss [4] and its quietness [5] from the fear of the demons that (would) destroy his body; through its appearance and its image, *the* heart of the Elect who leaves his body is calmed (Keph. 41 : 13-16). At whatever time he dies, ninety-nine thousand [6] girl-Angels will come to meet him with flowers . . . and a golden litter,[7] and

---

[1] *i.e.*, Mani's own Light-Maiden, who came to escort him home.

[2] Text: *Manuhmed*; cf. GPM 73 : 1.

[3] *i.e.*, "The blessed . . . has become . . . the Father's Soul (Copt. *prōme m̄makarios . . . afšōpe . . . tpsukhē m̄piōt*)"—another hint at a final deification of the Soul, even in Manicheism.

[4] The kiss of peace and union, whereof much is said in the Kephalaia.

[5] *lit*: rest (Copt. *hrak*).

[6] The text reads 80 plus—the last part being broken away.

[7] This is the shining chariot of GPM 70 : 3.

speak thus to him: " Fear not, righteous Soul ! " . . . And his own merit [1] will come before his face like a divine virgin Princess, immortal *and lovely*, a flowery *wreath* upon her head; she herself will set him on his way [2] (T. II. Toyoq).

2. (Thus) the glorious Deity of Righteousness [3] comes to the Soul with the three Gods who are He Himself [4] (T. II. D. 175), the three great glorious Angels who come with him —the one holding in his hand the prize of victory, the second bringing the Light-Robe,[5] (while) the third is the same who holds the diadem, the crown and the wreath of Light [6] (Keph. 36 : 14-18). Then the Angel

---

[1] *or*: action (*karma*).

[2] *Cf.* GPM 70 : 2. She does for the Soul as Jesus does for Adam (GPM 10 : 4), and the Living Spirit does for the First Man (GPM 4 : 3). The righteous Parsi sees the same vision.

[3] *i.e.*, the " God of the Majesty of Law ", the Judge.

[4] The three Angels of GPM 70 : 2, who bring the rewards in hand.

[5] In the old Parsi texts, *paimōgh 'ibrāzāgh*, the gift of Vohumanāh; in *Kauṣītaki Upaniṣad*, the Brahma-garment given by the Apsarases. In *Bundahiṣn* Vayu puts on a " robe which was golden, silvery, bejewelled, and adorned with all colours of many tints " —the same as the Robe in the Hymn of the Soul—a largely Iranian poem. The Mandeans also speak of this Robe—the heavenly body (Skt. *sūkṣma śarīram*).

[6] Widengren tells us that the ' bishops ' of Manicheism were also in life invested with a Robe, a Diadem and a Garland.

who holds the prize of victory stretches out to him the right hand and draws *him* out from the abyss of his body, and embraces [1] him with the Kiss and the Love.[2] That Soul worships her saviour who is this Light-Form. Now at the very moment when *he dies*, he perfects (himself) and awakes in conformity with *God's will* (?) in the House of the Living and the Gods, Angels, all the Messengers and the Chosen Ones,[3] and he receives the *shining* garland of glory in everlasting life (Keph. 41 : 17-25), (and) puts on the raiment of divinity (M 284).

As the radiant Soul steps out of the dark encumbrance of the flesh, she is welcomed by the smiling Judge—a happy conscience—and the Angels who bring her rewards; she is robed and crowned with the glory of her well-won victory.

76. Individual Judgement

1. (The glorious Deity of Righteousness)[4] sends **the Soul** to the Judge of the Dead . . . (and) the just Judge seizes the

---

[1] *lit*: receives in (herself).
[2] *i.e.*, the kiss of love, or the loving kiss, a hendiadys.
[3] *i.e.*, the Kingdom of the Light, God's Paradise; cf. GPM 80.
[4] These words have been reused from the context.

confused Soul which appears as in a mirror.[1] It is set down in the Balance [2] . . . its merit [3] is *apparent*, its evil deed *revealed* . . .; the deeds done by itself appear—the majesty of the Earth and Water [4] is unhappy, the splendour of the Fire and Water [5] weeps, the brightness of Plants and Trees wails aloud (T. II. D. 175 : 5; 173, 178) ! On that day of danger no bribe or gift or pleading (can) avail ; the Father's Image, the Maiden of the Light, is the (only) one to help upon that day [6] (M 727) ! Those near the King are the Righteous (M 47).

2. If the Balance rises, his (good) deeds *will overcome* his sins committed *and* will *raise him to the Garden of the Light* [7] (T. II. D. 173).

---

[1] *i.e.*, reflected perfectly and clearly revealed.

[2] An Egyptian (?) touch, or as in GZ 38 : 2, perhaps itself ultimately derived from Egypt, like so much else in religious thought and expression.

[3] *i.e.*, action, *karma*, deserts.

[4] *i.e.*, the 'Light Cross', the Light imprisoned in the 'Elements'.

[5] Possibly this is an error for Air, the fourth element.

[6] *i.e.*, the nature of the man's own being, his own merits, alone helps him to face the judgment of his own conscience.

[7] " The souls of the Elect, when they have left their bodies, unite with the Column of Glory in order to reach the Light that is above the heavenly sphere ", says Shāhpūr ibn Tāhir (Shahrastāni, 2:422).

Those indeed who are doers of good, to them He rewards the good deed according to their goodness, ... He gives them the Kingdom of Light and makes them heirs in everlasting Life (Keph. 223 : 10-13)—they will be forgiven because they have forgiven (others), but they will atone for every sin they have committed[1] (S 9). Woe to it, the empty (Ship) that comes empty to the Customs-House,[2] they shall ask it when it has nothing to give! Woe to it because there is nothing on board! It shall be roughly treated as it deserves and sent back to rebirth[3]—it shall suffer what corpses suffer (MP. 218 : 3-7)!

3. " O Gods, to You must I appeal; all Gods, in pity take away the sins from me (M 4)! Wipe away our iniquities, the scars that are branded on our Soul (MP. 47 : 10)!

---

[1] Forgiveness of the sin does not exempt from the need to make amends; cf. GZ 46 : 8.

[2] Customs officers appear in the Mandean *Ginza* and *John-Book*: " Woe to the empty one who is standing empty in the house of the Customs officials "—a close parallel. The Mandean liturgies explain 'empty' as having no merits or sweetness, *i.e.*, not acting as a good Merchant. The old Syr. Acts of Thomas also uses the metaphor, which is probably Chaldean.

[3] " The souls of the dead, if they are wicked or not purified, are made to pass through various changes, or suffer punishment yet more severe " (AF. 20 : 21).

We have controlled our lightless Earth [1] we have known and understood our Body and our Soul (Man. III. 6)."

"Lift up thy face, beloved, and look upon my face! See how I gaze at thee with no (such) evil look in my eyes as I stare at the sinner when he is brought to my judgment and found guilty (MP. 104 : 27-30)! Mayest thou live for evermore (M 43)!"

"Hail, righteous Judge, strong Power, the Path of Truth, clear Mirror [2] separating the acquitted and the condemned! Clothe me in thy Robe, give me the Garland and the Prize (MP. 83 : 21-24)! I have lived ever since I heard thy sweet voice, O true Judge, O Glorious One (MP. 104: 31-32)!"

How can such a Soul dread the baring of its every thought and act before the conscience, before the 'lords of Karma', who ensure exact return, a precise effect for every cause? It is only the wicked and cruel Soul who must dread the accusation of all it has injured, the misused creatures, the broken flowers and trampled ants. The righteous one is fearless there, confidently awaiting the reward of her kindness, gentleness and purity. A prayer for final absolution is answered with kindly assurances, and the Soul, acquitted, goes on towards her eternal home.

---

[1] *lit.*, seized: (Turk: *tuidumuz yaruqsuz yirimizin.*)
[2] *Cf.* the Mirror in GPM 35 : 4 and that in GPM 76 : 1.

77. Joy of the Freed Soul

1. My Lord, the joy of thy sweet cry has made me forget life,[1] the sweetness of thy voice has made me remember my City [2] (MP. 53 : 27-28); I myself again have received the three holy Gifts which the three holy Angels extend to me (MP. 108 : 19-21); from Light-Mind [3] and the Divine Teacher have come a fresh Garland, a new Diadem, and a shining Robe (M 31). I ran to my Judge; he set the garland of glory upon me, he put the prize of victory in my hand, he clothed me in the Robe of Light, exalted me over all my foes (MP. 50 : 23-26). See, joy has overtaken me through thy Right Hand [4] that came

---

[1] *i.e.*, livelihood, worldly life (Copt. *bios*).

[2] *i.e.*, the true Native Land of Light where we have " our abiding City ".

[3] Text, *Vahmān*, or Vohumanāh, who is *Yišōʿ qanīg rōšan*, Jesus the Maiden of Light; he receives the Righteous into heaven, and is God's Great Mind (*Vahuman-vazurg*, almost Skt. *Paramātman*) and at the same time the mind or self in each individual. So in BuBb p. 27 : 329-330 we read: " We glorify the Great Vahman whom you have arranged in the heart of the good-souled ones " (*i.e.*, the Hearers; cf. GPM 63 : 5). S 7 says: " May the procession of the Vahmans of Light ascend in purity to the dwellings of immortality"; here the Great Mind (Copt. *pnac ñnous*, Syr. *haunā rabbā*) is the same as the Column of Glory (Syr. *estōn ṣūbḥā*) and the Perfect Man (Parth. *mard ispurrigh*).

[4] The usual metaphor for giving help.

to me (MP. 153: 4)! I embrace¹ you, O Gods,. Angels of glory who are in the Land of Light (MP. 69 : 17-19)! Henceforth no longer shall I be a Prisoner, a Slave (Man. III. 25)!

2. I have found the Ships—the 'Ships' are the Sun and the Moon—they have transported me to my City; . . I have found the Haven—the 'Haven' is the Commandment! I have set my foot on the Path—(and) the Path is the Knowledge of God² (MP. 168 : 5-8, 1-4)! Ferry me to the Sun and Moon, O Ferryboat of Light ³ that hovers ⁴ over these three earths (MP. 81 : 10-12)! Disperse the dark cloud that is before my eyes, that I may be able to cross rejoicing to thine honoured dwellings. I have contrived ⁵ to see thy Light, so I have no concern with the Darkness⁶—therefore let no one weep for me; see, the Gates of the Light have opened to me⁷

¹ *or*: greet, kiss.

² *i.e.*, true Gnosis.

³ This must be the Column of Glory whereby the Soul is raised to the Moon, then to the Sun, and finally to the Light-Kingdom.

⁴ *lit*: rests; *i.e.*, it waits for us.

⁵ *lit*: attained.

⁶ Copt. *sji ce arai en hapkeke.* Cf. Jn. 14 : 30. How can darkness co-exist with light?

⁷ before me. This is a constant refrain in the Pyramid Texts. (GP).

(MP. 62 : 21-26)! I rejoice as I ascend to my Father with whom I have conquered in the land of darkness;[1] O my great King, transport me to the City of the Angel-Gods (MP. 50 : 27-29), take me in to the homes of joy—for I am thine!—and count into my hand the reward of my many contests (MP. 101 : 29-31)!

3. I rejoice, I rejoice for eternity of eternities (MP. 168 : 16-17)! I worship Thee, O Father of the Lights, and I bless you, O Aeons of Joy, and my brothers and sisters from whom I have been far away and have found again once more (MP. 85 : 13-15)! I have become a holy Bride [2] in the peaceful [3] Bridechambers of the Light; I have received the gifts of the victory (MP. 81 : 13-14).

> She knows the way, the doors fly open, the heavenly ships of salvation land her on the shore, the clouds of ignorance and doubt disperse—the Soul steps out boldly, singing, in her overwelling ecstasy. Free, free for all eternity! Free from every hindrance to a perfect union with the beloved Spouse, long dimly visioned during the faithful service of ages in the dark Abyss that now lies behind!

[1] *i.e.*, the body. It is victory *in* the body that earns spiritual bliss.
[2] Treated here as a masculine noun—for it is sexless.
[3] *or*: restful, still, quiet.

78. Depart, O Manichean Soul!

1. Victory and salutation,[1] O busy Soul that has finished her fight and subdued the Ruling Power, the body and its passions[2] (MP. 57 : 27-28)! Today thou art called to dwell with the Angels because thou hast left behind thee (MP. 64 : 30-31) the hunger and thirst of death.[3] . . . Hereafter thou hast become free of anxiety, for thou hast abandoned the house of care, the body of death, and hast flung it before the face of its enemies[4] (MP. 70 : 22, 29-31). Thou hast swiftly gone beyond the authority of the flesh, thou hast ascended like a swift bird into the Air of the Gods [5] (MP. 64 : 18-19)!

2. Thy wares [6] which thou hast produced, look, they have gone before thee—a part of

---

[1] Copt. *jro menio*.

[2] Copt. *pathos*; *or*: feelings, affections.

[3] *i.e.*, the desires which lead to death, physical and spiritual, and to rebirth later on.

[4] In Mani's own death the same idea recurs: *vide* Introduction. In Ephrem, Christ wears the same armour as the defeated Adam, *i.e.*, the physical body; in an Epiphany hymn we find: "He put on the armour, triumphed and was crowned; he left the armour on earth and was raised." Cf. also Odes of Sol. 22 : 3.

[5] Again we are in the atmosphere of the Pyramid Texts (GP).

[6] These are the soul's good deeds, brought home as 'talents' rom its trading in the world, together with God's gifts.

them following after thee, a part of them overtaking¹ thee; rejoice then, being glad as thou steppest before the Judge ² (MP. 70 : 18-21)! He will appear to thee . . . with a face that is full of joy; he will also cleanse and purify thee with his pleasant dewdrops,³ he will set thy foot on the Path of Truth and furnish thee with thy Light-wings like an eagle becoming distant as it soars forth into its air (MP. 100 : 27-30)! Go *now* aboard thy Ships of Light and receive the *Garland of Glory*⁴ (MP. 55 : 11-12) and the Gifts of Light from the Judge's hand (MP. 57 : 29)!

3. Look, the Ship has put in for you: Noah is aboard,⁵ he is steering—the Ship is the Commandment, Noah is the Light-Mind (MP. 157 : 19-20), he who comes and puts on the Saints (Keph. 89 : 23). Embark your wares, sail with the windy dew⁶ (MP. 157 :

---

¹ *i.e.*, preceding. The idea is also in the Qur'ān (GI).

² *Cf.* GPM 76 : 3.

³ *lit*: water of dew, *i.e.*, the purifying draught of ambrosia, immortality.

⁴ *or*: glorious garland.

⁵ If Manicheans were really so hostile to the Old Testament as we are often told, how can we account for this identification of Noah with the saving Light, the Messenger?

⁶ Could this mean rather the 'dewy wind'? It would make better sense, the immortal Spirit. Copt. *erhōt mentiōte ṅteu*.

20-21); return to thy kingdom and rejoice with all *the Aeons* (MP. 55 : 12-13) and rest thyself (MP. 57 : 30)! Thy defence is Christ, for he will welcome thee to his Kingdom (MP. 54 : 10), he will bring thee to the haven of peace (MP. 78 : 23-24)!

4. Walk on rejoicing; thy troubles [1] today have passed. See, thou hast moored to the harbour of peace (MP. 163 : 27-28)! Now shalt thou have thy fill of the joyous Image of Christ,[2] so go thy way victoriously to thy Light-City! Thou art glad that thou hast mingled with the holy Angels, on thee is set the seal of thy glorious purity! Thou art happy that thou hast seen thy Divine Brethren [3] with whom thou shalt dwell in the Light for evermore (MP. 64 : 12-17). Thou hast reached thy Light-Suburb wherein is neither hunger nor thirst; [4] implore thy Father for a grace on our

---

[1] *or*: pains—the bondage in flesh, and all its implications.

[2] So Mani told his disciples on his last journey to 'gaze their fill' at him. What we think of intently, specially at the end of life, we become.

[3] *i.e.*, the spiritual kindred of the Light Realm.

[4] *Cf.* the hymn: "Looking for home on Zion's mountains—No thirst, no hunger there!" based on Isa. 49 : 10 and Rev. 7 : 16.

LIBERATION OF THE LIGHT   241

behalf;¹ do not leave us to be desolate ² (?) (MP. 70 : 22-25)!

Sensing the bliss on which the dying Soul has entered, even his friends on earth now take up her song and urge her onward, swiftly, swiftly to the everlasting Abode. Death is left behind, the flesh is overcome, consecrated to decay, the Soul's righteousness has gone ahead to smoothe her path into heaven where all lovely Angels wait to welcome the returning pilgrim, the exiled ' Prince ', as she draws near to receive the Father's kiss and to take her throne.

79. Jesus Takes Her Home

1. The Ship of Jesus³ has come to port laden with garlands and gay palms; it is Jesus who steers it, he will put in for us till we embark; (it is) the Saints whom he takes on, the Virgins whom he accommodates (?). Let us make ourselves also holy that we may make

---

¹ *lit*: some grace upon us. "May it happen to us together that we may be included in his Merchandise and rejoice with all the Aeons; may we be counted among those of the Right Hand, and inherit our Kingdom; and may we live with our Kinsmen from everlasting to everlasting" (MP. 202 : 18-22).

² This shows that Manicheans believed in the intercession of departed Souls for those left on the earth.

³ *i.e.*, both the Moon, and the Church, wherein Jesus dwells as Saviour. Ephrem (IV. 601 : 15) calls Jesus a "skilful Shipmaster, bringing out his treasure", *i.e.*, the Soul; and "his Ship is the Moon" (GPM 7 : 1). In Babylonia the Moon-god was a Ship sailing over the skies, and Ishtar sails in a Ship to rescue Tammuz. Widengren quotes (p. 102) from Assyria: "The rope of the Ship is at the quay of Life".

our voyage to *the Air* (?).¹ The Ship of Jesus will make its way up on high, it will add its cargo to the shore, and return for those who are left behind; . . . it will take them (also) and bring them home to the Haven of the Immortals (MP. 151 : 31—152 : 7).

2. How great a lover of men thou art, O Jesus the First Rose of the Father! How gentle thou art (MP. 151 : 24-25), my true Bridegroom!² Glory to thee, O Christ of the Bridechambers of the Light (MP. 102 : 31-32)! I worship thee, O Image of my Master which I have loved before I ever saw it, but because of its fame whereof I heard I kept myself holy³ that I might be worthy of it! . . . Draw now the veil of thy secrets until I see the beauty of the joyous Image of my Mother, the holy Maiden who shall sail with me until she brings me to my City⁴ (MP. 84 : 24-26,

[1] Augustine says bitingly: "while the good souls are placed in ships and sail through heaven to that imaginary Region of Light for which they died fighting"; but does Christianity tell us anything more true, or consoling to the sorrowing soul, in the hour of death? It is so easy, so childish, to scoff at others.

[2] Obvious is the devotion behind this cry: (Copt. ṅtek oumairōme ṅouēr, Iēsous, tsarep ṅourt ṁpiōt, ṅtek ouhelcēt saouēr . . . papatseleet ṁmēe).

[3] *lit*: watched over myself being holy.

[4] First he sees the Ideal of the Saviour, and then he purifies himself till he can see the ideal of his own perfection.

30-32)! Embark me on the Ship of the Saints, let them put in quickly for my Soul[1] (MP. 95 : 26-27)!

We are once again reminded of Mani's deep love for Jesus, planted in his disciples, when we read these glowing words. He is the Shepherd, the Guide of Souls, the Pilot of the homeward bound; it is he who, in the Ship we by metaphor call the Moon, plies to and fro between the earth and heaven, carrying the unceasing freight of aspiring Souls, the Ferryman of the old Pyramid Texts (GP 34) to the Ship of Re', the Sun (GP 37). Relying on this gracious Saviour, the Soul knows well she cannot miss the road to glory.

80. The Land of Light

1. My Father is the glorious, ... the glad Light, the glad and blessed Light (MP. 203: 3-5), self-existent, eternal, miraculous (M 178)! No height or dimension forms a limit and measure[2] *where all* is Light and no place is dark, where all the Illumined[3] and the Messengers of Light reside; it is in

---

[1] The essential optimism of Manicheism is shown by these words of Shahpur ibn Tahir (Shahr. 2 : 422): "The spirits of those involved in error enter into the bodies of living beings and pass continuously from one to another until they are purified of their sin; whereupon they are united with the Light above the heavenly sphere". Few indeed are *eternally* lost, as many Christians averred.

[2] How can there be a boundary to the omnipresent? Yet with strange inconsistency Mani visualised a boundary on the side of darkness, below; cf. App. I 3 : 1; 4 : 3.

[3] *i.e.*, the Race of Light, called in this text, the Buddhas.

brief the Home of the Adorable of the Light [1] (BM. 265-266)! In height it is beyond reach (?), nor can its depth be perceived (M 178); there Light is omnipotent, and *all* is clean and pure, eternally happy, calm and quiet (BM. 266); no enemy and no injurer walk this Land (M 178)!

2. In the unsurpassed World of Light, the many lands of subtle and wondrous nature . . . are like grains of sand (in number). . . . These many countries have precious diamond soil, radiating light downwards from the dim past until now and to everlasting time . . . with countless miraculous hues illumining one another (BM. 270-271, 276). (That world), its divine pavement is of a diamond substance that does not shake for ever (M 178); whoever is allowed to live in that land will be eternally free from every care and sorrow [2] (BM. 268).

3. In that land are spacious gardens and parks, stately and clean, . . . without dust or

---

[1] *i.e.*, Zrwān or Äzrua, the Father of Light (*Pidar Rōṣan, Bārist 'i Rōṣan;* Ch. *Ts'ing-tsing kwang-ming she-kiai ming-tsouen*—" the Venerable of the Light of the pure Light-World ").

[2] The spiritualist sources of Drayton Thomas, etc., and the Mahayanist scriptures, closely agree with this account.

LIBERATION OF THE LIGHT 245

screen, . . . broken tiles and gravel, brambles, thorns and all unclean weeds; . . . the country is rich and fertile (BM. 299, 302, 299, 281). All good things are born from it: adorned graceful hills wholly covered with flowers most excellently grown, (and) green fruitbearing trees whose fruits never drop, never decay, and never become wormed (M 178). A strange unique fragrance, . . . spreading like a vapour, pervades the whole world, . . . and the wonder of perfumes is perfected when the Saintly masses [1] walk about. . . . In this realm all glorious blossoms may be gathered; . . . floral crowns are verdant, nor ever fade or fall (BM. 299, 301, 280, 283). Fountains flow ambrosia that fills the whole of Paradise,[2] its groves and plains (M 178). From a hundred streams, rivers, seas, and fountain-heads the deep and clear Waters of Life are all fragrant and wonderful, . . . tasting like veritable nectar; . . . in them *one* will neither drift away nor drown (BM. 290, 304, 290).

[1] *i.e.*, the countless hosts of the redeemed.
[2] The word is the 'Bahisht' of GZ; *i.e.*, the 'better place'.

4. The Saints live safely and are always happy (BM. 291); they go to the heaven of Light where the Gods dwell, and are at peace. They receive as their nature the original Splendour of the radiant Palace, and are joyful; they put on the shining Robe, and live for ever in Paradise[1] . . . They are calm in quietude and know no fear. They live in the Light where they have no darkness, in endless Life where they have no death, in Health without sickness, in Joy without sorrow, in Charity without dislike, in the company of friends where they have no separation (M 737, 178). (They) are fully fed without want (BM. 304) on unlimited ambrosial food, wherefor they bear no toil or hardship (M 178); (their) foods are all (like) sweet dew [2] (BM. 281), manna of the Land of Light, . . . our resplendent City, . . . the home of the blessed ones (MP. 136: 38, 40, 43), countless mansions and palaces, thrones and seats that remain perpetually for ever and ever (M 178), trees of fragrance, fountains

---

[1] The word is the 'Bahisht' of GZ; *i.e.*, the better place.

[2] *i.e.*, ambrosia—the subtle inbreathing of vitality from the immortal airs everywhere pervading.

filled with life, all the holy mountains (and) the trees that are green with Life (MP. 136: 45-48)!

5. Those Saints are pure, humble and ever gay in body (BM. 285), in a shape that is not brought to naught,[1] in a divine body where there is no destruction; . . . in appearance they are lovely, in strength powerful (M 178), light,[2] ever clean and pure; . . . free from weariness, . . . their diamond frames need no sleep, . . . never becoming feeble and old; . . . very subtle and wonderful (BM. 284-285, 312, 314), their brightness never darkens (M 178). Light shines on them, and their bodies become splendid and translucent; . . . light is within and without, . . . radiating great brilliance limitless in extent . . . for evermore (BM. 277-278, 314). Their robe of joy is a finery that is never soiled, set with jewels of seventy myriad kinds (M 178). All the glorious clothes they wear are delightful, not fashioned with the work of hands, . . . fresh and clean, incorrupt despite much wear.[3]

---

[1] *i.e.*, changeless, incorruptible.

[2] Because weight derives from gross matter, which does not exist there.

[3] So too the clothes of the Israelites in the wilderness did not wear out during the forty years.

(Their) crowns, with ornaments of hanging jewels, can never perish, nor be taken from whoever has once put them on [1] (BM. 279, 282).

6. Their wondrous bodies roam in many temples, wherever they may desire; . . . wherever one wanders freely, all is peaceful and smooth! . . . There no temples or halls, palaces or cells were built by hands, and yet they are strong;[2] no craftsmanship was needed, they were instantly completed by the Law. . . . Wonderful breezes, blowing and waving, are all delicious, mild and pleasant, spreading all around in the ten directions,[3] gently touching the jewelled towers and pavilions, and constantly moving the lovely bells, small and big, to music (BM. 319, 325, 308, 305).

7. Ever honest and true are the minds and thoughts of the Saints, . . . enlightened and with wondrous kindness, . . . freely

---

[1] Because they are a part of their very nature, the glory of the Soul itself.

[2] Houses, gardens, etc., are produced by the very thought of the glorified Soul, in the beauty which his own acts have merited. The process is well described in modern Spiritualist books.

[3] Up and down, to the four Cardinal points, and to those between, the north-east, north-west, south-east and south-west.

LIBERATION OF THE LIGHT

enjoying body¹ and mind in the sweetly scented air (and) counting neither years nor months, nor hours and days, . . . (being) void of birth and death **and** mundane love. . . . All who live there are unstained by ignorance, passion and desire; . . . how can they be pressed or hurried by rebirth?² . . . They relax in mind and move at will unhindered . . . more swiftly than the wind, . . . (for) they are not as heavy as a feather. . . . By nature they are not forgetful and short of memory, but they totally see everything . . . in the boundless world as if looking in a bright mirror.³ . . . Merciful and generous, they exchange sympathy; . . . (they) are of one mind, harmonious.⁴ . . . In response, (Saints) appear in

---

¹ *i.e.*, of course, the subtle refined 'spiritual body' which alone exists there—the astro-mental bodies of the Theosophists.

² This does not deny the possibility, but only the urgency of rebirth—which depends on physical desires. When there is no 'stainful desire', how can birth in a gross and filthy body, born from lust, take place—save as a pure Messenger of the Light? Mahendra's wife said to him: "Do not speak that word! We never speak of it, for if we expect to be soon reborn it happens so, and this is far better—we none of us want to go back to earth." Naturally!

³ All authorities speak of the power to move with the speed of thought and to see earthly events at will.

⁴ *Cf.* GH 29 : 9, a very close parallel. But if it were untrue, it could be no heaven, for it is disharmony that fashions hell and makes our lovely earth unhappy.

the ten directions¹ unchecked;² . . . every thought and feeling reached, and all intentions of the mind, are mutually shown and seen (BM. 287, 286, 330-331, 272-273, 292, 278, 286, 292, 273, 293, 318). They are all in agreement and concord, . . . rejoicing and being glad in the Glory (?), filled and abiding in everlastingness (MP. 203 : 22-25).

8. Whatever has sprung from the precious soil gains the power to see and hear, to feel, know and watch the unequalled King of Infinite Bliss,³ and to . . . praise . . . the Great Saint's authority. . . . Chanting hymns, their wondrous voices are clear and lovely, all peaceful and calm, harmoniously vibrating wondrous echoes from above and from below —which of themselves and ceaselessly spread around the monasteries,⁴ . . . (which) are clean and holy, . . . comfortable to live in, . . . without troubles and calamity. . . .

---

[1] Up and down, to the four Cardinal points, and to those between, the north-east, north-west, south-east, south-west.

[2] So too our later authorities claim that spirits can see other spirits almost instantaneously at will.

[3] The greatest joy of all—the Beatific Vision that only a perfected love can know.

[4] *i.e.*, separate dwelling-places, for some there also delight in a solitary retreat among Nature's glories for contemplation.

Light (BM. 309, 321, 328, 335, 332, 329), clouds of brightness dropping dew (?) and life (MP. 203 : 17-18), fills all things; life is eternal and ever full of peace (BM. 329).

This vivid and detailed description of the 'Summerland', agreeing closely with those from every other source (see *e.g.* Antony Borgia's *Life in the World Unseen*, 1954), seems to show that its first author, the Apostle Amu (Ammōs), had himself a personal experience of its delights. We may note here how he stresses the continuing personal life of the redeemed, sharing bliss on spiritual planes of a subtle radiant matter with their fellows in perfect understanding and brotherliness, free from limitations of time and space, pillowed in exquisite natural beauties, and eternally delighted by the presence of the beloved and adored King of All. It is indeed, as the Spiritualist has sung: "a land upon whose blissful shore there rests no shadow, falls no stain; where those who meet shall part no more, and those long parted meet again". The "heavenly Jerusalem to which our hearts aspire"— how can words created for our earthly needs serve to describe the abundant blessednesses of its loveliness?

81. The Triumph of a Holy Death

1. Who can see, my brothers, and return to earth and make known to all men the glory I have received today? . . . For I have found the reward of my toil (MP. 93 : 25-28, 30)! See, I have brought my Ship to the shore; no storm has risen against it, no

wave has snatched it away! . . . . I was heading for shipwreck[1] before I found the Ship of Truth; a divine tacking was Jesus, who has given me a hand.[2] Who then shall be able to tell of the Gift that came? A grace overtook me, (but) there is no one who can say it[3] (MP. 63 : 13-14, 17-20).

2. I have left the garment[4] on the earth, the senility of diseases that I had; I have put upon me the immortal Robe (MP. 81 : 8-9). I have taken my washed clothes, my robes that grow not old; I have rejoiced . . . in their gladness, have rested in their rest (MP. 155 : 10-12).

3. O Saints, rejoice with me, for I have returned again to my beginning[5] (MP. 155:9), the Path of Light has stretched for me right up to my first City (MP. 80:29-30), it has victoriously given me into the hands of the *Angels*, and they have escorted me *to my*[6] Kingdom (MP. 52:1-2). See, the Maiden's

---
[1] *lit*: was about to be shipwrecked.
[2] *i.e.*, he helped me.
[3] *or*: an unspeakable grace overtook me.
[4] *i.e.*, the gross physical body; *cf*. GPM 70 : 1.
[5] *or*: source; *i.e.*, the heaven-world whence I came.
[6] Perhaps we should read " to His kingdom ".

light has shone on me, the glorious likeness *of the Truth*, and her three grace-giving Angels.[1] The gates of the skies have opened before me through the rays of my Saviour and his glorious Light-Image (MP. 81 : 3-7)! Christ my Bridegroom has welcomed me to his bride*chamber*, (and) I have rested with him in the Land of the Immortals; *my* brothers, I have received my garland (MP. 63 : 3-5)! O excellent pain that I have suffered! O my end which has had (so) happy an issue! O my everlasting possession (MP. 81 : 15-16)!

And so at last the Soul, about to enter on her everlasting bliss, looks back once more on the friends left behind upon the gloomy earth. Telling of her happiness so far as words can reach, touching on the wordless glory of the spiritual marriage now attained, she encourages the poor delaying ones to " look upward to the skies, where such a light affliction shall win so great a prize ". Indeed, the burden of the short day on earth is not worthy to be mentioned before the wonder of the glory that lies beyond the tenuous translucent veil of death. Who then can fear the change? Who among the Manicheans could shrink from the brief pains of martyrdom? Rather they rushed upon it, singing like a bird that finds the cage door opening to the sweet air of fragrant freedom blowing above the trees!

[1] *Cf.* GPM 70 : 2.

CHAPTER SEVEN

THE END OF THE WORLD

And here indeed we might have ceased. Yet Mani, obedient to the curiosity of his age about the final scenes of our humanity, drew aside a little the veil that drapes the future. We glimpse the fulfilment of the purpose of creation, when all the Light that can possibly be redeemed from contaminating Darkness has been freed and together forms the Perfect Man, the " fullness of the stature of the Christ ", perfectly reflecting the Father as His ' Image '. Then comes the final settlement of things; those Souls which by their own deliberate will, strengthened by ages of repeated choice, have preferred to adhere to Darkness and to spurn the Light, go where they desire to be—in the Darkness—and share its fate of eternal ruin; while those—the overwhelming majority, almost all—who have sought and loved the Light are merged therein. Mani therefore implores his hearers to choose the blessed Light and so be safe for evermore, entering upon the unimaginable bliss of everlasting union with God, the Source of all Goodness.

82. The End is Near

The time draws near when the Light-Body shall be freed from (its) fetters, the forces of

Light and Darkness will be separated evermore, and so will the doers of good and their evil foes. The universe—heaven and earth, and *the countless* dense and close *things*—will be properly dissolved and freed by the pitiful Adorable One; the demon races will be put into the dark prison for ever, and the Race of the Illumined [1] will leap for joy and return to the Realm of Light (BM. 232-234). Then *shall* the light go to the Light,[2] . . . while darkness (MP. 215 : 24-25) shall fall and henceforward never rise again (MP. 212 : 5); (it shall) be blotted from its place (MP. 215 : 26).

Mani warns the world that its days are limited and the end is hastening on, when the Darkness and the Light, Evil and Good, will be finally and altogether separated once again (cf. GPM 12 : 2).

83. The Last Statue [3]

1. At the time when all the Light in the universe has been purified and refined (Keph. 165 : 6-7), Jesus the Child,[4] who is the Image

---

[1] *lit*: Buddha-family.

[2] The Spirit returning to God who gave it; *cf.* Eccl. 12 : 7.

[3] Copt. *pandreias ṅhae*, a technical term for the perfect Image of God to be revealed at the 'End'.

[4] So called because he is born in the faithful heart (*cf.* Gal. 4 : 19).

of the Living Word¹ (Keph. 92 : 7-8) in his two persons (Keph. 35 : 28-29), who is the Call and the Hearing that lie in the Elements (Keph. 81 : 2-3) which are mingled (Keph. 54 : 11)—it is he who makes a separation between the good and the bad² (Keph. 81 : 3-4).

2. Again at the end (Keph. 81 : 4) he *joined* with them, he stood up in silence, he drew up the *Light-Sparks* until the *final* moment when he should awake and stand in the Great Fire, and gather his own Soul to himself³ and form himself into this Last Statue (Keph. 54 : 11-15), which is the last Hour of the Day, the time when the Last Statue will go up to the Aeon *of* the Light (Keph. 165 : 9-11).

3. And thou shalt find him purging and refining out of himself this impurity which is foreign to him, but the Life and the Light that are in everything *he* gathers in to himself

---

¹ *i.e.*, the Logos, almost in a Johannine sense, because Jesus, this 'Perfect Man', perfectly fulfils God's word.

² *Cf.* Mt. 25 : 32.

³ The mystical gathering in of the scattered members of his Body to form the perfection of Humanity divinised; referred to in many Gnostic works.

and builds his body thereof.[1] When this Last Statue is complete in all its limbs,[2] then it shall emerge and come down in that great struggle through the Living Spirit, its Father [3] (Keph. 54 : 15-22).

Uniting the Master who awakens and the Pupil who listens and obeys, the ' Perfect Man ', the Mystical Body of Christ's universal Church in every creed, now comes to birth and stands forth as the silent Judge. Those who love the Light are then in Him; those who cleave to the Darkness because they love the deeds of darkness are left outside (Jn. 3 : 19) and will inevitably perish in the Fire that burns away all dross and delivers the gold in perfect purity.

84. Perfect Justice will Prevail

1. The great Judge (Keph. 35 : 25) who sits in the Air judging all men (Keph. 80 : 30), *his* tent is set up in the Air under (?) *the* Great Wheel *of the* Stars [4] (Keph. 35 : 26-27) —there is no partiality in his law, no turning in his righteousness. He knows (how) to forgive the one who has sinned and repented, (but) he has no dealings with one who may

---

[1] *lit*: builds it upon his body.

[2] *or*: parts.

[3] So called because it is made up out of the living beings created by Him.

[4] *i.e.*, he judges all acts done under the horoscopical influences.

come to his feet and implore him; he does not forgive the one who is of two minds[1] (MP 45 : 27-30).

2. No one will be able to hide from him when he searches out the deeds that each one has done and repays them according to their deserts (MP. 49 : 14-16), **so** he who has something good let him put his trust in his deeds (MP. 81 : 29-30)! Let us not neglect ourselves and keep to our own regret[2] (MP. 45 : 31-32)

There can be no possible injustice in this final settlement, for each must inevitably go to its own nature; the gold can never be burned, nor can the dross survive that fearful flame. Nor can the Judge be deceived, for being within the secret crevices of the very heart, an infallible memory, he knows everything and pitilessly brings the truth to light.

85. Signs of the End

1. Thou seest how near it has come to the end of the world; the lifetime of men has come to a fraction, their days have decreased, their years have become fewer, for the Life and the Light that were in the world in the first

---

[1] *i.e.*, hypocrite. Jesus also was most stern with such.

[2] *or*: fail in our hearts through our own neglect. There is no outer judgment, but the inescapable judgment of our own hearts.

generations were more than today's[1] (Keph. 146 : 9-14). Those who are born today in these last generations are small and stunted in lifetime, and they are also born each one in a single womb, scarcely two or less or more, while they are also ugly in their appearance, small in their size, and weak in their limbs. Their ideas and thoughts are filled with wickedness; ... in old age they waste away[2] their lifetime with sufferings, also death comes to them swiftly.[3] (Keph. 147 : 10-17).

2. When that *immortal* Light is led up to the Gods, then will both the zenith and the nadir of heaven be brought together, for the Custody of Splendour[4] will seize the topmost heaven, which exactly matches the lowest, and it will become loosened from bond and order.[5] ... Then will the Third Envoy[6] *come* from the Vehicle of the Sun to the combined

---

[1] So in the first ages the 'Patriarchs' could live for nearly a thousand years, and now few indeed survive a hundred.

[2] *or*: spend.

[3] This old idea of the degeneracy of the aging world is met also in GH 34 : 5-8.

[4] Text has '*Pahragbed*', an equivalent name.

[5] A very close parallel with GPM 12 : 2.

[6] Text has '*God Mithra*', an equivalent, the deity in the Sun.

region, and a Shout will be raised,[1] . . .
(and) in the Moon and the Zodiacal Signs [2]
and the Stars a great Sign will become manifest[3] . . . the whole world will get the news
(simultaneously). . . . Afterwards *will come*
the God of the Realm of Wisdom,[4] he who is
the First . . . Knowledge,[5] and just because
of the sorrow upon sorrow and *distress* upon
distress[6] he will send down Wisdom and
Knowledge (M 472-473).

3. Then *will appear* the Kingdom of *the God
of* Wisdom; . . . those Gods who are in all
the regions of the heavens and the earths—
the Supporter, the Light-Adamas, the Glorious
King, the King of Honour (and) the Custody
of Splendour [7]—and who are revilers of the

[1] This is parallel, of course, to the Cry of GPM 4 : 3 and 73 : 1, *cf.* Revelation of Thomas.

[2] Text reads 'Zodiac'.

[3] Some believed that this 'Sign' was that all the planets would come close together and form a Cross in the sky (*cf.* Mt. 24 : 30).

[4] *i.e.,* Jesus, who is to return as Judge at the end; Islam kept the same idea derived from Christianity. He is called the God of the New Kingdom (*nōgsahr-yazd*), because he initiates the new age.

[5] *i.e., pratūmīn khrad*; Ch. *Sien-yi.*

[6] *Cf.* Mt. 24 : 21-22, and countless parallels in apocalyptic everywhere.

[7] These names are given in the text as Mānbed, Visbed, Zandbed, Dahībed and Pahragbed—the equivalents.

demons, will bestow a blessing on that Realm of Wisdom, and the men *who are righteous* will become Rulers in the Kingdom (M 473).[1] They shall themselves see him, the Image of the Light, all rejoicing and being glad over him. . . . Desire shall depart far from them with also the other kinds of temptation. . . . When they wish they shall clothe themselves with their body and gain the victory over it, and they shall find the way from it to the Kingdom of Life made smooth [2] (MH. 39 : 12-18). They will pay *homage* and receive him with joy . . .; but the man who is a worker of Greed, *along with* the evildoers and the perverters (?) of men . . . will be filled with remorse (M 473).

The steady decline in human nature, the weakening of the body, the lowering of its moral standards, show how near the crisis is to us, when the clear eye of the Sun, of Mithra the all-seeing Lord (GZ 22 : 4), will shine forth and illuminate every dark corner of all lives. Then will dawn the glorious Day of that Church, the Mystical Body of the universal Christ, the Logos of the 'All', the God of Wisdom, and the long night of wickedness will hasten to its close.

---

[1] *Cf.* Mt. 19 : 28.

[2] Implying that the redeemed may take incarnation when they will, but they are never again under the control of their bodies, and may re-enter the spiritual realm easily.

86. The Universal Judgment

1. And then the God of the Realm of Wisdom [1] will send Envoys to the East and the West; they will go and gather mankind [2] —the Helper (?) and also the Hearers; while the evildoers, with those of like malice, *will come* before the Lord of Wisdom. ... *Moreover* the demons will go into his presence, *offer* homage and *carry out his* command. ... They will rush in and speak thus: "We are imitators of our Gods, and everyone *believes* in this doctrine that we taught mankind, but they will go on in the love of evildoing!" [3] Further, the Elect who may not believe in Religion, he too will sell himself to them. At that time, when things in the world become like this, *the Righteous* and the *Pretenders* alike *will be arraigned* both on earth and in heaven (M 473).

2. Then the Righteous shall say, "O our Lord, if (we have) hidden (anything) we shall say it now in thy presence!" To them the

---

[1] *i.e.*, Jesus.

[2] *Cf.* Mt. 24 : 31, et al.

[3] *Cf.* Lk. 13 : 26. Even missionary work is not enough.

God of the Realm of Wisdom[1] shall make this answer, " Gaze on me and be happy[2] (M 475), my brothers and my limbs (Keph. 213 : 3)! For hungry and thirsty was I and you gave food and drink, I had become naked and I was clothed by you, bound was I and was freed by you; I was caught and I was released by you, and I became a stranger and homeless (?)[3] but I was taken by you into the house." Thereon they, the Righteous (and) the Helpers,[4] shall prostrate[5] and then speak thus: " O Lord, thou art a God and an Immortal whom neither Greed nor desire (can) vanquish, who becomes neither hungry nor thirsty and on (thee) distress never comes. When was it that we (did) this service?"[6] Then shall the Lord say to them, " Whatever you have done you have done to me; To you I shall give the reward of Paradise! " (He shall give) them great joy (M 476-477). Those whom he has called to the Kingdom

[1] *i.e.*, Jesus.
[2] The very sight of the Lord is itself the happiness of Paradise.
[3] Text: *ūd ūzdēh vā qārdāg būd ḥēm, ōtān ō qadag padtriftī* (?) *hēm*.
[4] *i.e.*, the Hearers, who support the Elect on earth.
[5] Text: *ōyṣān 'ī dēnvarān ḥiyārān namazh barand*.
[6] *Cf.* Mt. 25: 37-38.

of Light, his Righteous and his Virgins, he has made them like the Angels [1] (MH. 38 : 15-16).

3. The 'Goats' who stand at his left hand [2] shall see the Hope that he has given to those on his right; their heart shall rejoice for a moment, while they think that the victory of the 'Sheep' will come to them also.[3] Then he shall *turn to* those who stand to the left, and speak and say to them: "*Away* from me, accursed ones! Go to the Fire *made for* the Enemy [4] and his Powers, for I have hungered and thirsted, but (?) never has one of you given help to me (MH. 38 : 16-23)!" [5] He will (then) put Angels in charge of the sinners and they will take them into keeping and (throw) them into

---

[1] *Cf.* GY. 107 : 3. "Then shall their bodies be changed into the likeness and image and honour of the holy Angels, and into the power of my holy Father's Image. Then shall they be clothed with the Robe of eternal life out of the Cloud of Light which has never been seen in this world—for that Cloud comes down out of the highest realm of the heaven from my Father's Power; and that Cloud shall compass with its beauty all the spirits who have believed in me": *Revelation of Thomas*.

[2] *Cf.* Mt. 25 : 33.

[3] So too when they see the Angels on their deathbed; cf. App. I 9 : 3.

[4] or: Adversary; in our Bible, 'Satan', or the 'Devil'.

[5] *Cf.* Mt. 25 : 41-43.

hell (M 477). As for 'Death' the Enemy,[1] he will enter *the* chain in the dungeon of the souls of the deniers and blasphemers who have loved the Darkness, . . . and there shall be dark night on them (Keph. 165 : 11-14).

Following closely the lines already traced in Mt. 25, Mani in the usual metaphorical language we have seen in other Scriptures (*e.g.*, GH 29 : 8, GI 52-56, GMC 49, GZ 49-51, GGS 23-24, GY 100-107) sketches the scene when good and wicked stand side by side, to learn in public the fate that each individual soul has earned. None can escape that awful tribunal, and some whom men may have deemed impious and godless blasphemers while on earth will there be found transformed to angels because through kindly deeds of charity they, being atheists, yet waited on and served the Lord.

87. The Fate of the Wicked

1. God too is a Judge of the Souls *who* obey the Adversary and do what is evil, not believing in the Truth, . . . and He condemns them through their deeds (Keph. 222 : 30—223 : 1), because they are *cut off* and excluded from the Last Statue[2] (Keph. 150 : 3-4) when the *universe*[3] shall be dissolved

---

[1] So called because Evil leads to death; cf. Rom. 6 : 23.

[2] This is punishment enough, to be cut off from the perfection they were created to attain.

[3] Copt. *kosmos*—i.e., the organised creation designed for a certain end, which is now achieved.

(Keph. 52 : 16) and all things destroyed, and the Great Fire be let loose (Keph. 102 : 33-34) and the Last Statue be formed *out* of the remains of all things (Keph. 75 : 24-25). The souls of the deniers and blasphemers shall weep (Keph. 149 : 30-31) when the Last Statue comes down therein; ... then shall they cry aloud that they are cut off from the company of this great Statue and remain behind for ever.[1] ... For from this time there is no rest for them ... who shall go in to this Darkness and be chained with the Darkness as they have desired and loved, and put their treasure in its keeping (Keph. 150 : 9-12, 16, 6-8).

2. He does not take them to Himself at their end, but they become the *portion* of the Enemy whom they have loved.[2] ... God Himself has not done them any wrong, but it is themselves alone who are against them; it is their own actions which condemn them and throw them to the hell of burning

---

[1] "They were to be cut off from their own kingdom and bound f or ever in the Mass (*bōlos*) of Darkness" (AF. 21 : 15).

[2] This is their conscious will, so there can be no remedy from outside their own will; the evil spirits too gravitate to their own 'loves', as Swedenborg also tells us.

(Keph. 223 : 2-3, 7-9); the wicked justly come to hell through the venomous beast's[1] wickedness (M 544) (and) through the disease of pollution (S.J., p. 121).

3. The Light shall withdraw to its place and ascend and reign in its Kingdom,[2] while the Darkness *falls* and is taken into the Grave[3] *with all its children*, and they shall be chained with it (Keph. 75 : 25-28), binding with them [4] the Darkness, the Enemy, who has lifted himself against the Light from the beginning (Keph. 104 : 27-29). The souls of all the sinners who have been condemned through their deeds ... are fastened to the Enemy (Keph. 105 : 2-5) in the Grave—its masculine and feminine [5] (MH. 41 : 6-7); the masculine shall be parted from the feminine and bound in the 'Lump'.[6] ... This final

---

[1] *i.e.*, the 'Dragon', the ancient enemy of God and King of Evil.

[2] *Cf.* GPM 82.

[3] This is the 'bottomless pit' of Rev. 20 : 3; it was dug by the Great Builder, or Architect.

[4] *i.e.*, with the chains.

[5] *i.e.*, Ambition or Arrogance, and Lust or Greed, the two chief demons manifesting the nature of Evil.

[6] Copt. *bōlos*, the shapeless mass or clod of filth, the dregs from which no further Light can be distilled. Also called *sphaira*, Globe.

'Lump' shall be densified¹ (?) when all forms and images are enclosed² in it (Keph. 105 : 31-32, 5-7); the Globe shall sink down by its (own) weight *to the Abyss, the Abyss* will (also) sink down (M.H. 40 : 23-24) for all eternity;³ . . . whereas the feminine shall be thrown into the Grave (Keph. 105 : 14,32-33).

4. The Light shall be purified and separated from the Darkness by means of that Great Fire (Keph. 104 : 3-4) wherein the universe will be dissolved and all things be destroyed, and perish in that Great Fire⁴ *which* shall burn them in fourteen *hundred and sixty-eight* years (Keph. 75 : 20-23).

Lest any blaspheme against the terrible fate of the incorrigibly wicked, Mani assures us that it is their own deliberate choice to stand apart from the Mystical Body 'which alone can exist in God's high Heaven.

[1] Copt. *selce*, an unknown word.

[2] *or*: included.

[3] *lit*: to eternity of eternities.

[4] *Ch.* "The violent greedy and poisoned fire" (*tch'an-tou-monghouo*). AnNadim gives the same figure, whereas Hegemonius reports that he has not in his texts found the duration. I do not know the significance of this number 1468; it may be 'mystical', as $IHCOYC = 888 = 87 = XIT\Omega N$; so the Vestment ($\chi\iota\tau\omega\nu$) is a symbol of Jesus; and $CIM\Omega N$ (76) + $IX\Theta YC$ (77) = 153 (fishes) in Jn. 21 : 11; Simon contacting the 'Fish' (*i.e.*, Jesus) catching many fishes. Such play with Greek numerals, and Hebrew, was a delight in those ages, as Eisler has shown in his *Orpheus the Fisher*; cf. the number 666 in Rev. 13 : 18.

There is no injustice; they too are happy, enjoying the Darkness they have preferred and the depth of the bottomless Abyss where it must evermore be held enchained so that the Light be free from aggression.

88. The Messenger's Appeal

1. Not one of all the Messengers has wished to receive his recompence on the earth, but they have spent all their time in trouble, welcoming sorrow and crucifixion [1] in their body so that they might save their souls [2] from that dream [3] *and* ascend to this Rest for evermore (Keph. 150 : 27-32). From the time I came to the world I have had no joy in it because of the holy Church which I have chosen in my Father's name. I have freed her from the slavery of the Authorities, [4] and placed the Light-Mind in her; every time I see her in trouble and persecution that afflict her through her Enemy, I shall feel pity for her. [5] I have no other grief, save this for the souls who neither accepted the Hope nor

---

[1] Doubtless in the wider sense of all kinds of torture and pain.

[2] *i.e.*, the souls of human beings.

[3] *or*: error, wandering (Copt. *sõrme*); it may be almost 'illusion'.

[4] *i.e.*, the Rulers of the body, the planets which generate evil passions in the heart.

[5] Manicheans must often have found courage in such a promise.

strengthened themselves with this strengthening and this steadiness [1] *of Truth*; for they shall come out and wander [2] and go off for ever to the hell. For this reason only I grieve for them, that they have not accepted repentance or been reconciled with the Right Hand of Peace and the Grace which I have brought out from the Father (Keph. 148 : 8-20).

2. Hear my words that I speak to you: Cling to [3] the deeds of Life, endure the persecutions that come on you, strengthen yourselves through these commands that I have given you, so that you may escape from that second death,[4] and avoid this final fettering wherein there is no hope of life, and be saved from the sorry end of the deniers and blasphemers [5] who have seen the Truth with their eyes and (yet) have turned away from it. They shall come to this place of punishment wherein there is no day of life, for the Light which illumines shall be hidden from them and they

[1] *lit*: standing up.

[2] *i.e.*, come from the body, only to take rebirth again and again.

[3] *lit*: hold yourselves in to.

[4] Doubtless as in Rev. 20: 14; cf. GH 28: 2.

[5] Constantly we find these two classed as the greatest of sinners. Islam also considers the *kadhdhabīn*, who deny God's revelation and make Him a liar, as beyond hope after death.

shall not see it again;¹ the air and the wind shall be withdrawn from them, nor shall they get breath of life in them from this time; the waters and the dews shall be taken away from them, nor shall they taste them any more (Keph. 106 : 5-18). Because they have not known the Kindly God, they will writhe (?) and burn in hell² (TM. 3 : 6).

Mani tells us how his loving heart has always yearned for the salvation of every Soul and grieved over those who tragically turned from his Message and the Father of the Light. So too has every Prophet grieved and striven every way (cf. Lk. 19 : 41) if only to rescue a single Soul for the blessedness of devotion to Righteousness.

89. None of the Faithful Perish

1. The Messenger of the Light, who comes at the (right) time and puts on³ the Church (and) human flesh, and acts as Leader within the Righteousness⁴ (Keph. 36 : 3-6), chooses the forms of his whole Church and frees them, both those of the Elect and those of the

---

[1] Having turned away from it, how can they see it any more?

[2] Life is to *know* God (cf. Jn. 6: 40 and GH 29: 3); the ignorance of Him is itself a dreadful hell (cf. GH 29:12-13).

[3] *i.e.*, assumes responsibility for, identifies himself with.

[4] *i.e.*, the 'Imām' or '*Arkhēgos*' of the Religion.

Hearers (Keph. 225 : 1-2); he dives down into the deep oceans of water[1] (T. II. D. 93 b) and pulls them out of the jaws of the deep[2] (M 502). As for them, they do not stray again, but they are only drawn to the rebirths and toil,[3] afterwards **they come** to the Angels' hands; . . . then the Angels make their way with them to the places wherein they are to be refined. For no Hearer ever at all goes on account of his deeds to the hells, because of the Seal of Faith and Knowledge which is stamped on his Soul[4] (Keph. 225 : 27-29, 10-14).

2. Only when they *guide* the man into the Truth, and he accepts the Knowledge and the Faith and begins to fast and prays and does good, at that time these new works which he has done—the fasts, . . . the prayers . . . the alms he has given to the Saints—all these things *are a purifier* and redeemer of his first works in

---

[1] *i.e.*, the sea of worldliness; Phl. *zād-mūrd*; Ch. *sheng-sseu-hai*.

[2] As the Diver recovers the 'pearls' in GPM 65: 4.

[3] *or*: pain (Copt. *hise*).

[4] So too many Catholics once believed that no one validly baptized would be lost. Rebirth was the worst that could happen to a Manichean, for the Seal of Gnosis—which could never be taken away—made impossible the hell which consists in not knowing or loving God.

every place where they may be found[1] (Keph. 225 : 30—226 : 6). Now it is the power of that Hearer to release all his deeds (from impurity) by himself alone while he is in his body. . . . From the first day that he has forsaken the first error in which he used to be, and has taken the Right Hand of Peace,[2] has been convinced and taken his stand on the stairway of the true Hearership[3]—in the hour he receives this grace[4] and believes this way, these first fasts which he has kept ascend and are welcomed into the Light-Ship of the Night[5] . . . out of the heaven and the earth and the trees and the (creatures of) flesh, . . . with this first fast and this first prayer, the beginning of all his (good) deeds (Keph. 226 : 25-27, 7-13, 17, 19-20).

Not even one who turns, be it the dying thief on the cross, to the Light and tries to follow it, can ever be

---

[1] His later good works purge away the evil out of all he did before his conversion to the Faith.

[2] *i.e.*, has accepted the reconciliation with God and Righteousness conferred by Manicheism.

[3] *i.e.*, has set out to live truly as an ideal 'Hearer' (cf. GPM 42—44).

[4] *or*: gift.

[5] His good deeds go up by the 'Moon' to the Light-Kingdom, and so he becomes a saviour of the Light-Sparks imprisoned in them.

lost in the gloomy Darkness. There may be ages of purgatorial wanderings through births and deaths, but the Angels whom he has even once invoked will follow him through all, urge him to noble deeds of piety, and so bring him at last to the consummation of all delight in Paradise.

90. The Path of the Redeemed

1. The Souls who come up and discover *the* holy *Church . . . for the sake of the* Hope(?) *abandon* everything; it is Reflection that *inspires them.* They raise themselves up to *the Column of Glory which* is the Intellect; they lift themselves up to the Insight, which is the First Man *who* dwelt in the Ship of the Night; from the Insight they raise themselves up to *Thought,* which is the Envoy dwelling in *the* Ship of the Day. And he, the great glorious Thought, brings (?) them in to the Mind— which is the Father, the God of Truth, the Great Mind of all the Aeons of Glory (Keph. 20 : 21-31). (There) the Souls of the Righteous are garlanded and they ascend gloriously on high with the Angels (MP. 81 : 23-24), the Father shall not thenceforth hide from them [1] (Keph. 103 : 28-29).

---
[1] Because in the Light-Realm He is always visible to the souls of Saints, their supreme joy and glory (cf. GPM 80 : 8).

2. So then your Souls must embark on those Ships of Light, (singing:) " Rejoice, O Perfect Man,[1] the holy Path leading up on high, the clear Air, the Landing-place [2] of everyone who trusts in Him![3] Open to me Thy secrets, and take me to Thyself from the affliction! . . . Let me be worthy of my three Gifts: the Likeness (MP. 83 : 25-31) **or** Light-Form which the Elect and the Hearers assume when they bid farewell to the world (Keph. 36 : 10-11), Love, (and) the Holy Spirit (MP. 83 : 31-32)!"

Step by step, gradually purifying all the five aspects of the Soul, the aspirant travels inward, upward, by the ancient Path towards the great All-Father, the Divine Mind in whom we all subsist, and there enters on his infinitely glorious destiny. Joy, joy be with us as we go aboard the shining Ship that bears us home, as we enter the Church established by the Messenger of God's Light, and manfully strive to keep the Precepts that guide us on our way!

---

[1] *i.e.*, the Column of Glory, which we are told is composed of prayers and adorations and all good deeds, and so leads the Soul upward to the Light of the human Saviour, *i.e.*, the ' Moon '.

[2] *lit*: mooring-harbour.

[3] One who trusts in, loves, an Ideal is sure to reach it some day.

CHAPTER EIGHT

EPILOGUE

The liberated Soul now pays due homage to the Divine Liberator for bringing her life to full fruition. The reader in his turn then prays for the same great service to be done to him, having thrown himself with passionate devotion at the Liberator's feet. Knowing this Liberator is no other than God Himself, the infinite King of Light, he then adores that Unutterable and blesses the holy names of all His Emanations, until his heart dissolves in ecstasy at His infinite loveliness and greatness. After a final prayer for eternal liberation from the deserts of exile, he is dismissed with a closing exhortation so to live that he may be worthy to enter on the longed-for Peace and Joy.

91. Thanksgiving to Mani

1. Let us worship our good Father and honour the *mighty* Saviour, for he has revealed everything, has taught us everything, has spread them (all) before us; he has given us the knowledge of the Beginning, he has taught us the mysteries of the

Middle, together with the Final separating and the destruction of the universes which were prepared for the bodies and the Spirit. Our Father, our Messenger has not let us lack (any) of them; so long as he was in our midst he gave us a hand, helping us greatly; even on the very day of his departure he left his good for the orphans and the widows [1] (MH. 7 : 9-19). Crowds have witnessed of him, all the Messengers have spoken of him, the Prophets have preached about him; his fame is spread abroad in all the world, his principle is in all the religions (MH. 8 : 1-4).

2. O Father, true outleading God,[2] we bless thee, the adored of Souls granting vision and commandment.[3] Blessed, blessed art thou, thou good instructing God! Through thee we travel together (?) by means of the blessed vision of words of prayer (T. II. D. 178 : 4). Thou, our Father, art the Root of all the wisdoms (Keph. 176 : 30); through

---

[1] Remember Mani's counsel to the disciples at Pargalia (Life, (§18); Manicheans were as devoted to corporal charity as Christians, but their few numbers forced them to rationalise a strict limitation of it to among themselves.

[2] *i.e.*, leading Souls out of darkness into Light.

[3] *i.e.*, the Knowledge (Gnosis) and Ethics.

the Father's will, O beloved, thou hast spread out over us this mighty gift of thy Knowledge (MP. 31 : 23-24), thou hast preached to all of us thy Wisdom, thou hast taught us what used to be, what are, and what shall be;[1] thou hast rescued [2] us from the Darkness (MP. 13 : 6-8). All the mysteries have been fulfilled in thee, our Father [3] (MP. 18 : 3) (and now) all thy churches are fulfilling thy mystery; we today give our rose like these fruitful trees,[4] that it may become for us a garland and thou mayest place it *upon us* (MP. 21 : 7-10).

3. O *mighty* Power, Wisdom full of Life, first-born great Commander! God of *our life*, my Lord Mani, our Lord of dear kindness, who out of pity *didst assume* a worldly appearance manifesting before us the visible Sign,[5] Perfect Living Word, clothe us in the *Robe of Light* (T. II. D. 178 : 4)! O glorious Mani, great God (and) Saviour,[6] thou art entire

---

[1] *i.e.*, the Three Moments—past, present and future.

[2] *lit*: made us healthy, *i.e.*. cured us. It is a disease.

[3] *Cf.* GPM 36 : 3.

[4] The flower of the heart is compared to actual roses offered liturgically in the church.

[5] *i.e.*, showing the Signs of a true Messenger (cf. GPM 31).

[6] Copt. *pnac ñnoute psōtēr*; the deification is now complete.

Absolution, the Preaching of Life, the Envoy of those on high (MP. 8 : 30-32)! The Three Wheels [1] glorify thee, the Wind and the Water and the Fire, which daily ascend from the Abyss (MP. 144 : 32—145 : 2). The Love that died is this Sheep that was chained to the Tree; the Shepherd searching after it is the revealing Wisdom (MP. 172 : 24-25); thou dost not weary, O Wisdom, thou dost not give in, O Love (MP. 171 : 25)!

4. We bless thy Light-Twin, [2] Christ the author of our good (MP. 42 : 22-23), (namely), our Lord Mani, the Spirit of Truth who (is come) out from the Father, . . . the Advocate whom Jesus has sent [3] (MP. 20 : 15-16, 21), the great Conqueror, our Lord, our Light, who has given his loved ones the victory (MP. 13 : 25-26)! Thou hast come in peace, O new Sun of the Souls

---

[1] They probably stand for the three 'chariots'—prayer, fasting, and charities—which raise the Soul to the 'Column of Glory'.

[2] *i.e.*, Equal in the Light. In his Acts the 'Twin' of Thomas is Christ; the Twin is often feminine, as in the case of '*Sophia*', wisdom, in MP. 11 : 15. Pistis Sophia also speaks of her Twin, apparently involved in her descent.

[3] See Jn. 14 : 16-18, 26. To his disciples Mani certainly was such a 'Comforter', and he certainly explained to them all they found obscure in the earlier Faiths. His claim was *not* a lie, as Augustine pretended, being unable to lead this harder path.

280 THE GOSPEL OF THE PROPHET MANI

(MP. 20 : 22-23); we trust in thy mercy, for thou quickly turnest and showest pity (MP. 71 : 1-2)! Thou shinest, O cheerful Image in the Sun's likeness, thou Leader of the Truth of the same form as the God Zrwān (BuBb 29 : 390-394)!

5. Thou hast spoken out all the mysteries to us, O Giver of the streams [1] (?) of all the revelations, and we give thee thanks, our Father, with great admissions [2] that thou hast spoken to us frankly about everything. Thou hast given us great outpourings [1] (?) of the Knowledge, so that we may give a share in them to these who listen to us [3] (Keph. 244 : 15-20). This is the only gift we have to satisfy thee with, that we confirm ourselves in thy Faith and abide in thy Commands and agree in thy Word which thou hast spoken to us [4] (Keph. 102 : 9-12).

We have followed Mani's thought reflected through his devotees so far that perhaps many of us will join with fervent sincerity in these words. Even

---

[1] The word is broken; I have conjectured *nnhrousis* (Gk. *rhusis*) from the last three letters.

[2] *i.e.*, thanks, acknowledgments.

[3] Naturally those who have freely received will freely give—and that can best be done by a holy life according with the teaching.

[4] *Cf.* GPM 47 : 1.

those specially attached to other of his great Brethren cannot but recognise the greatness we have glimpsed in them shining equally in this ' Apostle to the East '. He revealed the nature of this universe as divided between Good and an Evil in revolt, and showed us how to choose the Good and cleave to it until we are refashioned in its image, able to share its eternal blissfulness when once liberated from earth's last stain. How can we show our gratitude for this immeasurable blessing, save in using it—treading the Path thus opened out before us, helping our brothers too to find the way, and ourselves walking thereon to the end.

92. Total Surrender

1. My Liberator in(to) the praise of the lovable God, holy Mani, come among God's three Sons[1] (M 4)! Thou art the Advocate whom I have loved since my childhood;[2] thy Light shines out in me like the lamp of light,[3] (for) thou hast driven away from me the forgetfulness of the Error,[4] thou hast taught me to bless God and His Lights (MP. 56 : 17-20)! O gentle God, think of this son of the Mind (?), the Hearer, the afflicted Soul which has answered thee! . . . Come, God, look on

[1] *ad hre Bag-puhrān*; i.e., Zarathushtra, the Buddha and the Christ.

[2] *lit*: smallness (Copt. *mentkoui*).

[3] *or*: a lighted lamp.

[4] i.e., the illusion, that is, forgetting our real spiritual nature and thinking our interests are those of the body which is our foe and prison.

me, *thou art* my Help in this time *of need* (M 4)! O holy Mani, Light-bringer, make peace in me and rescue my Soul from this worldliness[1] (M 38) (by means of) the complete Seal of my hand and mouth and thought[2] (M 32)!

2. Now forgive me my *offences*, let my weeping turn to jubilation, let thy most glorious Power[3] watch over me until I come out of my body. . . . I am not faithless (?) towards thee, be not harsh[4] towards me! . . . Thou art the Lord, I am *thy servant; put away* from before thee all my sins which I have committed secretly and in the open (MH. 5 : 16-24)! Let the great Brightness[5] come and cause the Path to be lit before me, let thy three Angels bring to me thy Garments, thy Crowns *and thy Garlands;* let my way be restful,[6] let a door open before me into the Column *of Glory by the law* of the Judge of

---

[1] *lit*: birth-and-death, the Skt. *samsāra*.

[2] *pad mūhr 'ispūrīg cē man dast rūmb ūd andēṣiṣn*.

[3] *i.e.*, the Angel-Twin who was always helping and strengthening Mani himself through life.

[4] *lit*: in a badness.

[5] *i.e.*, the Light-Form of merit, the 'Maiden' who takes the Soul on to the upward path; cf. GPM 75 : 1.

[6] *i.e.*, calm, still, unhinde

Truth, let me cross over in the Ships of Light and *rest for evermore* (MH. 6 : 19-26)!

3. Thou art the Lord, the authority is in thy hand, . . . thou hast chosen my Image and set it free, . . . thou art the Root of Good [1] (MH. 3 : 24-25,27). Thy love is with me, . . . my body whose lord I am! . . . I have no one greater than thou; thou art more honoured than my father, I have *loved thee* more than my mother, thy friendship (?) was in my heart more than my brothers and relations [2] (MH. 2 : 12-13, 15-18).

4. Look, my Soul is given into thy hand; I have received my whole *life* from thy grace; I have let it drink the milk of thy spirit, thy scriptures and thy mysteries have brought me up;[3] since the start of my life thou hast sealed me with thy Hope and thy Name. . . . See,

---

[1] Identifying Mani with God Himself, the original Source of Goodness of GPM 13 : 1. How is *this* blasphemy, if it is 'faith' when the Christian speaks of Jesus?

[2] An Iranian love-declaration reads (TM. 383 : 20-23) "Thou hast come like a Father, our kind Physician, thou hast stood up like a Mother, thou art helpful as a Brother, thou hast come into the state of being a Son." The phrase "Kind physician (*biziṣkmōn kerboghor*)" is explained in *die Stellung Jesu* (p. 121): "a doctor for him who becomes senseless through the disease of the flesh-body; and he himself beeame an oculist for the blind and an aurist for the deaf." His medicines are the teaching.

[3] *i.e.*, have nourished me.

my head is under thy burden;[1] see, my neck lifts up thy fruit; see, my eyes look at *thy beauty*, ... my ears listen to thy word! ... my heart is a throne *whereon thou art seated* (MH. 4 : 6-10, 17-20, 27). Look, my feet are on the Path of thy truth *along with* thy great host; let me belong to the van of thy host, let me not be of its stragglers! *Strengthen with thy grace my* body and my spirit, for I rely on thy Name, do not let me down![2] ... *The* three gates[3] of my body *shall* be *opened* by the most glorious Key;[4] ... look, thou hast paid the price of my spirit; it is thou who art the good Lord of my spirit unto eternity of eternities (MH. 5 : 5-9, 11-16). From eternity to eternity thou art my God[5] (MH. 1 : 19)!

It is only by a whole yielding of the petty personality, a full dedication of the self to the treading of this Path, to the love of the enlightening Master, the Light-Messenger, which can avail us for that treading of the way. The faithful Manichean therefore gives himself in full and glad surrender to his Lord, that he

---

[1] *i.e.*, I have accepted thy 'yoke'.

[2] *mperia-totek nsōi*, in Coptic.

[3] Very unusually, the Latin word *porta* is used here for 'gate'.

[4] *i.e.*, the master-key, Truth.

[5] In Copt, *jen-anēhe ṣa-anēhe ntak pe panoute*—a tremendous saying, equal to St. Thomas' wonderful avowal in Jn. 20 : 28—"My Lord and my God!"

may be purified and led tenderly by the hand to his eternal Home.

93. The Eternal Infinite

1. Let us gather together, my brothers, and understand who is God, the Hidden One who is revealed,[1] the Silent One who also speaks (MP. 171 : 26-28)! Now who, my brothers, is worthy of all glory? It is the Father of Greatness who is worthy of all glory, the King, the God of Truth, the Exalted One of the Height, He of the bottomless Abyss, He of the unfalling crowns, He of the unfading garlands (MP. 133 : 1-7)!

2. O Repose of the 'All',[2] we give Thee glory—the Father of Greatness, the Glorious King, the Sun in His Aeons, the mighty Crown-wearer, the Father of all our Race, the God of all the Gods, the Good Tree that has given no evil fruit, the Father whose sons are many, the Watcher who guards His tower, the sleepless Shepherd, the Helmsman who does

---

[1] or: manifested.

[2] or: Rest of the Universe. Augustine's lovely impassioned cry: "Thou hast made us for Thyself, and our heart is restless till it rests in Thee!" (Lat. *Fecisti nos ad te: et inquietum est cor nostrum donec requiescat in te*). This is the very nature of man, whose happiness can be found only in the infinite Abyss of God, nothing less can satisfy his heart.

not drink,[1] the King and God of Truth, He of the unfading crown (MP. 136 : 13-27)!

8. O Lord, Thou art Alif the first, and Ta the last has come together in Thee,[2] and so Thy beneficent will has been fulfilled. All the Gods and Rulers, the Light-Deities and the Righteous give praise with many a 'Holy!' (M 78). Holy, holy, holy to Thy hymned Sovereignty! Holy, holy, holy to Thee, Father! Holy, holy, holy to Thy chosen Name! Holy, holy, holy to Thee, Father, holy, holy, holy (M 75)!

4. Thou art, Thou art, Thou art! Thy years shall not cease!

Holy, holy, holy to Thee, O Amen, King of the Aeons![3]

Amen, pleasant Ships that will land us at our Haven!

Amen, sweet Dew that gives sweetness to all the fruits!

---

[1] *lit*: get drunk. A revealing comment on the habit of drivers—even as sometimes in our own days!

[2] The Beginning and the End, Source and Goal, are now united, and the Light has merged again in Light, 'Alif' and 'Ta' are the first and last letters of the Syrian alphabet; cf. Alpha and Omega in Greek. Text reads: *Aalef naxvēn ō, Khudā'ī, ūd Tā 'ustōmēn pad tō angad.*

[3] *or*: Ages.

Amen, this unsetting Sun, the Lord of all the dawning-places!

Amen, Moon filling the measure which yet never wanes!

Amen, the Perfect Day wherein there is naught of night!

Amen, the crowned King who remains in His Kingdom!

Amen, this holy God who is garlanded by [1] His Aeons!

Amen, this lofty Light who shines forth in His loved ones!

Amen, this mighty Power who gives strength to the Elements!

Amen, the true Wisdom who gives teaching to the Souls!

Amen, this Holy Spirit who also gives life to the Spirits!

Amen, this beloved Son who has given himself to death for us!

Amen, the gentle Father who embraces us with His Love!

Amen, this gracious Mother who gives Her Milk to us! [2]

---

[1] *i.e.*, surrounded by; cf. the Sun in the twelve Zodiacal Signs (?).
[2] *or*: pours on (?) us, (Copt. *arōn*).

The Father, Son, (and) Holy Spirit—this is the Perfect Church![1]
Let us answer to the Amen!
When I utter the 'Amen', doors of the skies are opened;
O psalmist of the Sky, Amen, to whom they make music! (MP. 190 : 7-28).

Love, adoring gratitude to the Teacher, yes; but to God alone be all our worship, for He alone is wholly deserving of all we can say or give, of all that we can ever be. The very utterance of His mystic Name opens the door to His very Presence and fills us with adoration of His holiness and love, in whatever form.

94. Is Endless Love and Sweetness

1. God, God, God! Lovely is God, God, God! God, my (?) God! God[2] (MP. 164 : 11-12)! I dived to the depth of the Abyss wishing to comprehend Thy depth; I swam

---

[1] In Coptic the first three 'Amens' are spelt with a prefixed 'h' —I do not know why, but they seem to refer to the reigning Father, the redeeming Son, and the Immortal Spirit pervading all. Similarly, the hymn ends with the Trinity in reversed order, adding the Mother of Life; and the central portion also seems to refer by veiled epithets to the same Three Persons. So it is a sort of Triple Trisagion. The Church is a sort of incarnation of that Trinity.

[2] This ecstatic and untranslatable cry reminds the student of Guru Arjun's passionate style; it too seems a kind of Triple Trisagion. Copt. *Noute noute noute, nese noute noute noute, noute panoute noute!* Cf. GGS 41 : 3; 18 : 1.

in the breadth of the Sea wishing to comprehend Thy breadth! Who can comprehend Thee, and who is able to understand Thee, my Lord[1] (MP. 120 : 13-17)? What light shall I find and compare it with Thy fragrance (MP. 118 : 27-30)? Where is there a gracious Mother to compare with my Mother, Love? Where a kind Father to compare with my Father, Christ? What honey is so sweet as this Name, Church[2] (MP. 158 : 25-27)?

2. My Mind has not ceased thinking of Thy wonders;
My Thought has not swerved from searching Thy secrets;
My Insight has not moved from aspiring (?) in Thy mysteries;
Nor has my Counsel swerved from seeking after Thy marvels;
My Intention have I sent up desiring to comprehend Thee, my Lord[3] (MP. 126 : 3-12)

---

[1] Here too we find a likeness to the burning devotion of the Sikhs; Cf. Acts of Thomas.

[2] Because 'Church' is the Holy Trinity manifested as the 'Perfect Man'; it is also the 'Column of Glory' by which the Soul enters into Light. See GPM 93 : 4.

[3] Thus all five aspects of the Soul (Copt. *nous, meeu, sbō, sajne,* and *makmek*) are absorbed in God, aspiring to His deepest Being.

I have tasted a sweet taste; I have found no
   sweeter than the Word of Truth!
I have tasted a sweet taste; I have found no
   sweeter than the Name of God!
I have tasted a sweet taste; I have found no
   sweeter than Christ!
Taste and realise that the Lord is sweet[1]
   (MP. 158 : 20-24)!

Who can tell of His infinite power and loveliness (cf. GGS 55, etc.)? Who can think of anything so sweet, so good, so great as He? The redeeming Christ, his maternal Love, and the Church fashioned by the union of the two—here have we another Trinity to love and adore! Never in all the ages can we come to an end of God's infinite wonders, or the richness of His love, His wisdom and His power. All the faculties of the Soul will be for ever happily absorbed in penetrating them, deeper and deeper, yet never finding boundary or limit through all eternity!

95. Mani's Last Message

1. " O gracious Father, kindly Prince, countless myriads of years have now passed since we were separated from Thee! We yearn and long to see Thy luminous and living Face! Unstained we roam forth in Thy power, unstained we come (again) to stand before

---

[1] An almost exact quotation of Ps. 34 : 8.

EPILOGUE 291

Thee!¹ It is true we have not altogether been able to fulfil Thy will, but now be merciful to us, O gracious and royal God; we would forget our sorrows, we would live in the joy of eternal Love!"²

Often repeat such prayers; the Great King will then unveil and show His radiant Face; then will all things change, and you will live eternally in Joy and Love (S 174)!

2. And now I bid you, Hearers (M 135), my beloved ones: Do you walk at least with a true heart on this Path of *Righteousness* that I have shown to you (Keph. 81 : 13-15). Bear in mind my Precepts and *my Words*, that Straight Path and True Image³ that I have shown to you, namely the Holy Religion (M 135). Judge by a true law like a righteous judge; let brother speak truly with his brother, so that at the time when you come forth and receive the victory . . . you may rest in

---

[1] Coming and going, we are always, in our real self, immaculate Light.

[2] Among all the prayers from various Faiths and in various languages, I do not think I know any more adequate, more beautiful than this. It contains all we need to ask, all that we can have to say—for having God Himself what else can we lack? He is all in all.

[3] *or*: mould, pattern—*i.e.*, the perfection of humanity.

these resting-places for evermore (Keph. 81 : 15-20) with Him for whose Sign and Image you watch (Keph. 144 : 11-12). Strive through that Image, so that you may join me in the everlasting Life (M 135).

3. Thereupon all the Hearers became very joyful and happy because of the divine Words and priceless Precepts which they had heard from the Messenger, the holy Lord Mani. They paid the choicest homage and received the blessing (?)[1] (M 135). Prostrating themselves, they . . . joined their hands, saying: . . . . " Now we shall not let ourselves be negligent; we shall at all times take care to watch over the precious unsurpassed Trees, so that they may have all they need. . . . We shall use this Cord of Light and throw it into the vast Sea, in order to remove and save ourselves and set ourselves in the precious Ships. . . . We have heard of the Gate of the Wonderful Law; . . . our heart has been able to open itself and understand; . . . we have been enabled to walk in the Straight Path! " . . . Thus, when all the members of the Great Assembly had heard this holy

[1] An unknown word *'bznw* (*abzēnō* ?).

Scripture, they accepted it with faith as the Law, and cheerfully put it into practice [1] (CMT. 94, 96, 98, 100).

So we end our 'Gospel' with a beautiful, almost Indian, prayer expressing the Soul's ancient yearning for freedom from the endless chain of births and deaths, so that it may at last know the boundless bliss of the eternal vision of our Father's love. In return, Mani pledges that such prayers must certainly be granted; he bids us walk patiently upon the path of self-purification which alone can lead us to that glorious Goal, and so with words of faith and blessing he bids us farewell. The sincere Hearers then pledge themselves to make full use of the Light he has brought for them and to be faithful to the Faith until the end.

---

[1] We conclude in the auspicious way common to Buddhist Sutras: cf. also GH 43.

APPENDICES

APPENDIX I

FRAGMENTS OF THE SCRIPTURES

1. The Coptic Summary of the Myth

1. When the Holy Spirit came, he revealed to us the path of Truth, he taught us that two Natures exist, that of the Light and that of the Darkness, separate from one another since the beginning. While the Kingdom of the Light exists in five Greatnesses, namely the Father and His twelve Aeons, and the Aeons of the Aeons, the Living Air, the Land of Light, with the great Spirit breathing in them (and) nourishing them with His Light—the Kingdom of Darkness exists in five storehouses, namely the Smoke and Fire and Wind and Water and Darkness,[1] their Counsel[2] creeping in them, moving them, and *inciting* them to make war on one another.

2. Now then, as they were warring on each other, they dared to make a raid on the Land of Light,

---

[1] *i.e.*, foul air, burning fire, storm-wind, drowning and poisonous water, and gloomy darkness.

[2] Copt. *sájne*; the word sometimes means plan, plot.

thinking in themselves that they would be able to conquer it. But they do not know that what they have thought against it they will bring down upon themselves.

3. There was a host of Angels in the Land of Light, having the power to come out to subdue the Enemy of the Father,[1] who was pleased that He should send Himself through His Word to subdue Rebels who desired to raise themselves over the one higher than they. Like a shepherd who shall see a *lion* coming to destroy his sheepfold: for he plays a trick and takes a lamb and sets it as a decoy that he may catch it thereby, for by means of a single lamb he saves his sheepfold, (and) afterwards he heals the lamb that has been wounded by the lion.[2] The same is the method of the Father, who has sent His strong Son, and he in turn produced from himself his Maiden furnished with five powers[3] so she might give fight against the five abysses of the Darkness.

4. *When* the Watcher (?)[4] had stood up in the boundaries of the Light, he showed them his Maiden who is his Soul; they moved themselves in their abyss wishing to lift themselves upon her, they opened their mouth desiring to swallow her. *He* controlled

---

[1] But He would not send any of them, preferring to sacrifice a part of Himself; cf. GPM 3 : 1.

[2] The simile may not much appeal to our minds; it seems cruel.

[3] *i.e.*, the five Elements, or Bright Gods.

[4] Probably the Great King of Honour (cf. GPM 5 2).

her power,[1] he spread her [2] over them like nets over fishes, he made her [2] rain down upon them like purified [3] clouds of water; she [2] thrust herself into them *like* a piercing lightning, she [2] crept within them and bound them all unawares. When the First Man had *finished* his war the Father sent His second Son; he came and gave a hand to his brother out of the Abyss.

5. He [4] established this whole universe out of the mixture of the Light and the Darkness that had occurred. He spread out all the Powers of the Abyss to ten heavens and eight earths, he enclosed [5] them in this universe together; [6] he made it both a prison for all the Powers of the Darkness, while it is also a place of purifying for the Soul that had *plunged* (?) into them.[7] The Sun and the Moon were established, were placed on high, *so that* they might purify the Soul; the refined part they daily carry *up* on high, while they sweep out *the* dregs . . . mixed (?), they convey *it* above and below.[8]

6. This whole universe standing firm for a while as a great Building is being built outside this universe.[9]

[1] *or*: source (?) (Copt. *arkhē*).

[2] *i.e.*, the Soul, a part of God.

[3] better: distilled.

[4] *i.e.*, the Living Spirit—but all these Divine Aspects are essentially *one* God.

[5] *or*: included, confined.

[6] *lit*: at one time.

[7] Even the foul prison is used eventually to purify the Soul.

[8] *i.e.*, part upwards, part downwards.

[9] The eternal spiritual world is 'outside' this ordered Cosmos of Time and Space.

In the hour that that Builder shall finish, the universe shall be all dissolved and set on fire, so that it may be smelted away. All life, the remnant of the Light which is in every place, he will gather to himself and fashion of it a Statue; while as for the Counsel of Death, the whole Darkness, he shall gather it in and make it into a picture of its own self,[1] it *and* the *slaves* of the Ruler.

7. The Living Spirit comes in a moment; . . . he will give hand to the Light, but the Counsel of Death and the Darkness he will confine in the storehouse [2] that was established for it, for it shall be bound therein for ever. There is no means of binding the Enemy save this means; for he shall not be received to the Light because he is a stranger to it, nor again can they leave him in his land of Darkness, lest he should wage a (new) war greater than the first. A new Aeon will be built instead of this universe, which shall dissolve that the Powers of Light may reign within it, because they have done, have fulfilled, the Father's whole will, they have subdued the Hated One, they have *trampled* on him for ever.

8. This is Mani's Knowledge; let us worship him and bless him. Hail to everyone who shall trust in him, for he is the one who shall live with all the Righteous (MP. 9 : 2—11 : 23).

---

[1] Copt, *neferzōgraphē mmaf mmin mma*.

[2] This is the 'Lump' (*bōlos*) of grossest matter, antithesis of the 'Last Statue' of radiant spiritual perfection.

2. From " The Fundamental Epistle "

1. MANI, by the providence of God the Father, Apostle of Jesus the Christ:

2. These are healthful words from the perennial and living Source,[1] which he who first hears and believes them, then guards what they teach,[2] shall never be subject to death but will enjoy eternal and glorious life. Happy indeed may he be deemed who has been initiated in this divine Gnosis,[3] whereby he will be liberated and abide in everlasting life!

3. May the peace of the Invisible God and the Knowledge of the Truth be with the holy and most dear brothers who believe in the heavenly Precepts and at the same time fully keep them! May also the Right Hand of Light guard and save you from every evil assault and from the snares of the world! May the pity of the Holy Spirit open the depth of your heart and let you see your soul with your (own) eyes![4]

4. Dearest brother Patteci,[5] on that whereof thou hast written to me saying that thou desirest to know how the birth of Adam and Eve took place—whether

---

[1] Lat. *haec sunt salubria verba ex perenni ac vivo fonte*—*i.e.*, from God the Source of Life.

[2] Lat. *deinde quae insinuant custodierit*; Jesus promised thus in Jn. 6 : 40.

[3] Lat. *qui hac divina instructus cognitione fuerit.*

[4] Note the Trinitarian form of this beautiful blessing; the ' Right Hand ' is the Saviour, *i.e.*, the ' Son '.

[5] Probably Mani's Apostle Fattaq, here clearly different from Mani's own father, who bore the same name.

these were brought about by a word or firstborn from the body, thou shalt be answered as is fitting. For it is recorded and reported of these by most in various scriptures and revelations in different ways: so that the truth of this matter as it actually was is unknown to almost all peoples, and even to those who have long and much discussed it. For if it had come to them to know clearly about the generation of Adam and Eve, they would never have been subject to corruption and death.[1]

5. Necessarily then there are many things to be remembered beforehand in order without any ambiguity to attain to that mystery. Whence, if you please, hear what existed first, before the creation of the world, and after the conflict was stirred up, so that you may be able to separate the nature of the Light and the Darkness.

6. Well, then, in the beginning there were these two Substances separated from each other. And a certain God the Father was holding the Empire of the Light—eternal in one holy Origin, magnificent in power, true in His very nature, ever rejoicing in His own eternity, containing in Himself Wisdom and the Vital Senses by means of which even He comprehends the twelve Members of His own Light,[2] namely the abounding Riches of His own Kingdom. Now in each of His Members are hidden thousands of untold and immense treasures. This same Father, sovereign in His

[1] For they would not have identified themselves with this gross physical and sensual body.

[2] *i.e.*, the Twelve Aeons, or Maidens, surrounding Him.

glory and incomprehensible in vastness, has blessed and glorious Aeons united with Him, to be estimated neither in number nor in extent, with whom the same holy and illustrious Father and Producer lives, nothing existing either poor or weak in His splendid realms. His most glorious realms indeed have been so founded on the bright and blissful Earth that they can neither be moved nor ever overturned by anyone.

7. Now just adjoining one part and side of that bright and holy Earth was the Earth of Darkness, deep and immense in size, wherein dwell fiery bodies, namely the poisonous races.[1] Here were infinite darknesses emanating from the same Nature, countless with their own offspring. Beyond which there were filthy and muddy waters with their denizens, inside of which terrible and violent winds (prevailed) with their own ruler and the fathers. Next the fiery and corruptible region, with its own leaders and peoples. Finally, at the centre, a people full of mist and smoke, wherein was residing the horrible Chief and Leader of all, having around him countless chieftains, of all of whom he himself was mind and source.[2] Now these were the five natures of the pestiferous Earth, while these races inhabiting those five natures were fierce and destructive .... (AFE. in PL. 42).

8. Indeed, the Father of the most blessed Light knew the great impurity and ruin which would erupt

[1] Lat. *ignea corpora, genera scilicet pestifera.*
[2] Mani here reverses the usual order, beginning with the smoke.

out of the Darkness to threaten His holy Aeons, unless He opposed (to them) some extraordinary Divinity, outstanding and mighty in strength, by which He could at the same time overcome and destroy the Race of Darkness, on the extinction of which perpetual quietude would be ensured for the inhabitants of the Light. . . . (NB. 42).

9. The Ruler of Darkness . . . with crooked motives spoke to those . . . friends of his, the other Rulers of Darkness . . . who surrounded him: " What does this greatest Light which rises seem like to you? You see how it moves the Pole (of heaven) and overturns most of the Powers![1] For this reason it is right you should remit to me as much as you have of the Light in your control to command; thus I shall produce an image of that Great One which has appeared in glory, by which we shall be able to reign, free from the life of darkness (known) hitherto!"

10. After hearing this and long discussing it together, they thought it most proper to concede what they were asked. For they did not hope always to retain that Light, so they found it better to offer it to their Ruler, in no way giving up hope to reign with him when that was done.

11. So then, how they handed over that Light which they held is (now) to be considered. Now this is scattered all through all the divine scriptures and

[1] *i.e.*, upsets the whole organism of the horoscope. So it is the liberated man *rules* his stars and is free from their control.

heavenly mysteries: to the wise it is not at all hard to know how it may be put, for it is clearly and openly known by the one who has truly and faithfully wished to understand (it).

12. As the bulk of those who had gathered were of both sexes, namely females and males, he forced them to pair off together; in this coupling some sowed, others were made pregnant. But the offspring were like those who had begotten, being the first(born) receiving most of the parents' strength.[1]

13. Taking these as a royal tribute, their Prince was satisfied and, as we see done even now, the nature of Evil shapes the formation of bodies, taking up power from them, so indeed the aforesaid Prince, accepting (his) friends' offspring with the senses of the parents (and their) prudence, at the same time devoured the Light and procreated with them in (the act of) generation. Then, having gained full power from such a food, wherein was not only the strength but rather the cunning and depravity of the parents' savage Race, he called to him his own mate,[2] issued from that same Race to which he belonged.

14. Now having paired with her he sowed among other things the abundance of ills he had swallowed; and he also added something of his own thought and strength, so that her sense might form and describe all those (elements) which he had spread abroad. His

---

[1] *or*: qualities.
[2] Their names are elsewhere given as Ashaqlun and Nebroel. They are the demonic progenitors of the (physical) body of man.

partner received these as a soil excellently prepared usually accepts the seed. For in her were built up and hatched the images of all the heavenly and earthly powers, so that she might obtain the likeness of the whole universe which was being formed   (NB 46).

15. In fact, the Enemy, who believed he had crucified the Saviour, the Father of the Righteous,[1] was himself crucified, at the time when one thing was done and another shown. Thus the Ruler of the Darkness was nailed to the Cross and the same with his friends wore a thorny crown and had a purple robe; he also drank the vinegar and the gall, which they imagined a certain one, the Lord, to have drunk. And all that he seemed to bear was (really) inflicted on the leaders of the Darkness, who were also wounded with rods and the lance [2]   (FE. 28).

16. Those souls who for love of the world have let themselves wander from their own first bright Nature and have become foes to the holy Light [3] and openly armed themselves to ruin the holy Elements, and have submitted to the Fiery Spirit, and have even by their cruel persecution imprisoned the holy Church and the Elect included in it who observe the heavenly Precepts, will be shut out from the bliss and the glory of the holy World, and because they have let themselves be

---

[1] So called because they learn from and are converted by him.
[2] *Cf.* the hymns in GPM 34 : 6 and in the Acts of John (GG).
[3] *Cf.* GPM 48.

ruled by Evil,[1] they will continue in the same Race of Evil—that peaceful Earth and the immortal regions being forbidden them. What then will come to them when they have thus fettered themselves by wicked deeds, so that they are estranged from the life and liberty of the holy Light? They cannot then be received into those peaceful realms, but will be confined in the horrid 'Lump' aforesaid, on which moreover a guard must be set. Whence also the same souls will cling to those things they have loved, being left behind in the same 'Lump' of Darkness, seeking that out for themselves by their own deserts. For they have neither cared to know these coming things, nor withdrawn from the same when time was given   (FE. 5).

(*Many other fragments are quoted or alluded to throughout polemic literature, but not referred by name to this Epistle.*)

3. Severus on the "Two Sources"

1. At the beginning were Two Principles, Good and Evil, Light and Darkness also called Matter. Each of them was uncreated and beginningless, both the Good that is Light, and the Evil that is at the same time Darkness and Matter, and they have nothing in common with one another. The Good is a Tree of Life; it occupies the regions of the East, West and North; the Evil is a Tree of Death (and) it occupies the Southern regions.[2] The difference between the Two Principles is as great

[1] *Cf.* GPM 87 : 2.
[2] In Iranian thought the evil land was pictured as in the North; Mani reversed this, for in Babylonia the South was the demons' world.

as between a King and a pig—the one lives in the places suited to him, as a royal palace; the other like a pig wallows in the mire, feeds and delights in decay, or squats like a serpent in its lair. Like him, this pig and this serpent are born of themselves.

2. As for the things which exist perpetually and without beginning, each of them exists of its own nature. That is how the Tree of Life exists, which is there adorned with all its beauties and splendours, which is filled and clad with all its good things, firm and stable in its nature. His Earth contains three regions: that of the North which is outside and below, the East and the West, outside and below—and beneath it there is nothing which could be plumbed or taken up by Him in any of these regions, but infinity is outside and below. There is no body outside, around or below infinity, nor in any one of these three regions, but He is of Himself below and outside at the North, the East and the West, and in these three regions nothing surrounds Him or encloses Him. But He is in Himself, of Himself enfolding His fruits in Himself, and the Royalty is in Him. He is not in the Southern region, and that because He is hidden in what is its bosom. God has, in fact, surrounded this place with a wall[1]—and this wall is autophyte, that is, self-subsisting.

3. His Light and His beauty are not visible,[2] so as not to give occasions for desire to the Evil Tree that is

---

[1] *Cf.* GPM 11.

[2] *i.e.*, to the Rulers of the Darkness, until its own disorderly violence carried it up out of its own realm; cf. GPM 3 : 1.

in the South, and lest it be a cause for its excitement, torment and exposure to danger. But He is enclosed in His Glory, and because of His Goodness He gives no occasion but He is protected by His Justice. And He is in this Glory, in being altogether continuously in the nature of His Greatness in the three regions.

4. Now by its (very) nature the Tree of Death has no life, nor has it any fruits of Goodness on any of its branches. And it is ever in the Southern region, and it too has its own place, namely that which is above it.

5. The Tree of Death is divided into a great number (of branches); war and cruelty are among them; they are strangers to peace, filled with complete wickedness, and never have good fruits. It is divided against its fruits, and the fruits against the Tree; they are not united with what has borne them, but all produce corruption because of the corruption of their state; they are not subject to what has borne them, but the entire Tree is bad. It never does any good, but is divided against itself, and each of its parts corrupts what is near to it.

6. Now these things refer to Matter, to its fruits and its members; but the chance of ascending to the worlds of the Light was given them by their Revolt. Indeed, these members of the Tree of Death did not know each other and had no idea of each other, for each of them knew nothing more than its own voice and they saw (only) what was before their eyes. When one cried, they heard; they perceived that, and hurled themselves impulsively towards the

sound—they knew nothing else. They were so excited and impelled, one by the other, as to reach the frontiers of the glorious World of Light.

7. When they saw that admirable and splendid spectacle, which is far superior to their own, they joined together and plotted against the Light in order to mingle with it. Because of their madness they did not know that a mighty and strong God dwelt there; thus they tried to rise and to lift themselves because they had never noticed who God was. But because of this blessed world they threw a frenzied look, and they thought it would become their own.

8. Then all the members of the Tree of Darkness, with its corrupting Matter, rose up and ascended with the many Powers whose number cannot be told. Now these members differed: some indeed had hard bodies and were of infinite size; others, incorporeal and intangible, had a subtle tangibility like the demons and ghostly apparitions.[1] After raising itself, all Matter ascended, with its winds, its tempests, waters, demons, phantoms, its Rulers and Powers—all earnestly seeking how they could enter into the Light.

9. Because of the disturbance roused from the depths against the World of Light and against the holy fruits, it was necessary for a fragment of the Light to come and mingle with these Wicked Ones, so that by means of the mixing the foes might be captured and there might be peace for the Good, and that the Nature of the Good might be preserved, this blessed

---

[1] *Cf.* GPM 2 : 3—" demons and phantoms and fire and water '"

Nature having been saved from the fire of Matter and of the destroying corruption; that on the other hand the Lights be freed from Matter by the Power which had been mingled therein, so that Matter should be destroyed and the Tree of Life be God in all and over all.

10. In the World of Light, indeed, there was no burning Fire which could be thrown against the Evil, no sharp Iron existed, there were no drowning Waters nor any other such evil thing. Indeed, all is Light and a noble region and one could not injure (in) it. But there was this problem: that after being dispersed by the fragment detached from the Light, the enemies should stop their rush and be taken by means of the mingling. (*From Alfaric's French.*)

4. AnNadim on the Two Realms

1. The source of the universe is Two States,[1] one of them Light and the other Darkness, each of them separated from the other. Now the Light is the immeasurable First Good, and that is God, the King of the Gardens of the Light;[2] and He has five members: Dreaming[3] and Knowledge and Reason and

[1] Ar. *kōnēn*, cognate with the Syr. *kynyn*, source, used in GPM 1 : 1.

[2] Ar. *mālik jannāni 'nNūr*. Qur'an also speaks of Heaven as the Gardens, an Iranian idea, or possibly from the 'Garden of Eden', Chaldean.

[3] *Alḥalm*. Or it may be *alḥilm*, patience. The idea may however rather be the imaginative faculty of the mind. Note the variations here from the usual Greek and Coptic lists. Both Imagination and Memory (Ar. *alghaib*) are relevant.

Memory and Understanding; and five others, spiritual, and these are: Love and Faith and Integrity[1] and Courage and Wisdom. In His purity He is this Eternal, and with Him derive Two Eternals, one of them the Air, and the other the Earth. Now the members of the Air are five: Dreaming and Knowledge and Reason and Memory and Understanding; while the members of the Earth are Space,[2] and Wind and Light and Water and Fire.

2. Now the other Principle, well, that is the Darkness, and its members are (also) five: Fog[3] and Conflagration, and Hot Wind and Poison-Liquid and Gloom.

3. And that Principle (of Light) borders on the Dark Principle; there is no keeping apart between them, for the Light touches the Darkness on its border.[4] There is no end of the Light above it, on the left hand or the right,[5] nor is there end to the Darkness below it, nor to the left hand and right.

4. And out of this Dark Earth Satan came into being: not that there are the Two Eternals in his substance, but in their elements his essences are eternal. Then these essences gathered together out of its elements, so it was formed into Satan—his head like a

---

[1] *i.e.*, Sincerity.

[2] *or*: Zephyr; it is the still Air, unmoved by any disturbance.

[3] Copt. *haqnôs*, 'Smoke'.

[4] "The state of these two original creations is perpetual and altogether contiguous just like sunshine and shadow, and no demarcation or gap exists between them" (SGV. 51-52).

[5] *i.e.*, to North (viewed as *up*), East and West.

lion's head, and his body like a dragon's body, and his wings like a bird's wings, and his tail like a fish's tail, and his four feet like the feet of a beast of burden,[1] (329 : 3-13).

5. The Light-Earth has five members: Space and Wind and Light and Water and Fire; and the Light-Air has five members: Gentleness and Knowledge and Intelligence and Penetration and Intuition: all these ten members which belong to the Air and the Earth are the ' Greatness '.

6. Now that shining Earth possesses a body, is bright, beautiful, radiant, and sunrise reddens over it—the purifying of its purity and the beautifying of its bodies: form by form and beauty by beauty, generosity by generosity,[2] purity by purity, joy upon joy, light upon light, strength upon strength,[3] aspect upon aspect, goodness upon goodness, elegance upon elegance; also gates upon gates, towers on towers, palaces on palaces, homes on homes, gardens upon gardens, trees upon trees, and branches upon branches, having twigs and fruits! The joy of this view and lovely light is in plentiful colours, some of them better and more flowerlike than others, and clouds upon clouds and showers on showers.[4]

[1] *Cf.* the description of Ahrimēn, the Evil Spirit, in GPM 29 : 2.

[2] *i.e.*, lavishly pouring out its gifts.

[3] *lit*: durability.

[4] *Cf.* the account in GPM 80. In the hot dry lands known to Islam, clouds and showers indicate great joy and freshness.

7. And that Light-God in this World is an eternal God. Now the God in this Earth has twelve Greatnesses called the Maidens;[1] their bodies are like His body, all of them wise, intelligent. The Greatnesses are called the strong Working-Architects, and Space is the life of the world.[2]

8. The Earth of Darkness . . . has depths and abysses and regions and coverts and ruins and thickets and bushes—an earth broken up, ramifying, rough, and erupting Smoke from towns on towns and from rubble on rubble; and it erupts Fire out of towns on towns, and produces Gloom from towns on towns. Some of these it has lifted over others, and some parts are lower. And the Smoke which is produced from it, well, it is (at) fever-heat; death erupts from the bottom[3] of an abyss, its foundation, out of plenty of Dust and the elements of the Fire and the elements of the Hot-Wind strong and dark, and the elements of the heavy and dark Water. The Light-Earth is close above that, while this is below. For one of them there is no limit in the matter of height, nor (for) the Darkness in the matter of depth.[4] (332 : 10-26).

---

[1] They are the Victories, Virtues, Bright Hours, and Buckets of GPM.

[2] *i.e.*, vitality is drawn in from the surrounding still air.

[3] *lit*: source.

[4] What a vivid picture of 'Hell'! It agrees closely with spiritualistic accounts.

5. The Soul is Aroused [1]

1. He [2] was sent and came hurrying and rejoicing to the First Man to tell him the news; he came and knocked at the gates and cried: "Open quickly, and I shall tell thee the news! . . . Rise up, O good shepherd, take the lamb from the wolf's mouth, [3] and I shall tell thee the news!"

2. "Who art thou, for my doors are closed? Give a sign, and I shall open to thee, and thou shalt tell (me) the news!"

3. "I am the son of the Father's Son; it is the Father's Son [4] who hast sent me to tell thee the news. Open, open quickly! Open the closed gates that the news may be told to thee!"

4. As the gates were about to open, he was found (already) inside the door, eager to tell him the news of the (skies). The First Man found him at his side; he rejoiced and said to him: "Tell me the news! What does my Father do, the Father of the Lights, who makes *me* delay altogether outside Him? . . . What

---

[1] From one of the Psalms of Herakleides I have taken this, greatly abbreviated, as an example of how Manicheans delighted to retell in poetic expanded form incidents from the great Myth of the Soul; it may be compared with GMP 4 : 3.

[2] *i.e.*, the 'Call' of the living Spirit, an emanation from the Great Builder.

[3] *i.e.*, rescue the soul from the devouring passions; this must be done by the Soul itself, at least in intention, before it is able to 'open' and 'hear the news' of Heaven. Passions deafen the Soul with their clamorous din.

[4] Actually 'grandson', as shown in Note 2.

do the Twelve Aeons do, whom I left surrounding the Father? . . . What does the Mother of the Living do, whom I have left together with her other Brethren?" . . . The First Man is rejoicing as he asks, he says to him, "Tell me the news!"

5. Now the Call again answered: "I came forth when they were together, . . . I came forth when the Aeons were together, being a garland round the Father. They sent me when the Father was rejoicing at being in the bridechamber of the Land of Light, that I might tell (thee) the news. . . . I was sent while the Mother was watching, her Brethren being together with her. . . . I came when the City [1] was calm and the citizens were rejoicing and glad; . . . I came from the House of Joy; I have brought you the joy as I came. I came from the House of Plenty; I have brought Plenty as I came to you. See, this is the news! I came while the Mother was looking for thee, her Brethren being also there with her. Let us go! They await thee, they are at the Border (?), they are expecting thee![2] See, the whole of God has come; [3] call thou, (and) He will answer thee. They are laden with wreaths and palms to give to thee, the Captain! See, this is the news!

6. "The Air is set over the Smoke, . . . the Breeze guards the king of the Storm, . . . the Light is set over the king of the Darkness, . . . see, the Waters

---

[1] *i.e.*, the Land of Light, the Spirit-World.

[2] Copt. *maran, seahe arak, sehentstetas, sesamet oubĕk.*

[3] Copt. *eis pnou'e tēref afei*; the Soul is only a fragment of Divinity.

have confined the king of the fatal Flood, the Maiden, the living Fire, has become mistress over the Land of Darkness!¹ Look, we have laid waste the Land of Darkness, we are waiting with the garland for thee! . . . Receive the news!

7. " Let us go! They await thee! The Light has surrounded the Darkness! Let us go; they await thee! They are on the Border (?), they are expecting thee! . . . See, those who are to help thee are waiting for thee, their hands are open to embrace thee, they are laden with wreaths and palms to give thee, the victorious Captain! Take the news!"

8. The Envoy heard the good news, he took it to the one who had sent him. The Fathers of the Light came to help their beloved; they helped the First Man, (and) he cried out before him rejoicing: " Look at me! Look at my wares!"² Great was the joy that ensued when the First Man was in their midst laden with garlands and palms! (MP. 197-202).

6. From " The Treasure of Life, Bk. VII "

1. Then that blessed Father, who has the Bright Ships for residence and habitation or greatnesses, with His usual kindness brings to His vital substance aid, by

---

¹ *i.e.*, the five Bright Elements have conquered the five Darknesses, evil is overcome, the Soul is now free to enter the Realm of Light (cf. GPM 71 : 1-3).

² *i.e.*, merits, the profit of spiritual trading with the 'talents' given by God; cf. GPM 76 : 2 and Mt. 25 : 15, 27-29.

which it is withdrawn and freed from impious attachments and difficulties and torments.[1] So by His invisible signal He transforms those of His Powers[2] which are held in this most brilliant Ship,[3] and makes them appear to the hostile Powers which have been allotted to the various regions of the skies. As these consist of both sexes, males and females, He orders the aforesaid Powers to appear, some in the form of unclad youths to the hostile race of females, some in the shape of dazzling maidens to the opposite tribe of males—knowing all those hostile Powers would be most easily captured because of an innate mortal and most unclean longing for Himself, and be enslaved by the same most beautiful forms which appear, and in this way be dissolved.[4]

2. Now you must know that this same blessed Father of ours is indeed the very same as His Powers,[5] whom He for an inevitable reason changes into the inviolate likeness of boys and maidens. But He makes use of these as it were His own weapons, and by means of them fulfils His own will. The Bright Ships[6] are indeed full of these divine Powers, which are arranged

---

[1] Lat. *fert opem qua exuitur et liberatur ab impiis retinaculis et angustiis atque angoribus suae vitalis substantiae.*

[2] *or*: Virtues, Qualities.

[3] *i.e.*, the Sun.

[4] *or*: destroyed, setting free the imprisoned Light, or Life.

[5] God cannot be separated from His Qualities; it is *His* beauty which captivates and defeats the sensual powers of Matter.

[6] *i.e.*, the Luminaries, Moon and Sun.

opposite the infernal races as the equivalent of a partner, and which with alacrity and ease carry out in the same moment what they have planned. So then, when reason has required them to appear to the males, the same holy Powers show their Image in the form of most beautiful maidens; again, when it has come to women, putting aside the shapes of maidens, they show the shape of unclad boys.

3. Now at this alluring sight their ardour and desire increases, and in this way the chain of their worst thought is loosed, and the Living Soul that was held in the members of the same (demonesses), being by this event released, escapes and is mixed with its own purest air;[1] where, being cleansed inwardly, the Souls ascend to the Bright Ships which have been made ready for them to embark and cross over to their own country. That indeed which up to now [2] carried the stains of the hostile race descends bit by bit through burning and heat [3] and is mixed with the trees and other plants and all the seeds, and is coloured with various hues.

4. And, this done, out of that great and most brilliant ship the figures of boys and maidens appear to the opposite Powers that live in the skies and have a fiery nature; and, being loosed by that beautiful sight, the part of Life which is held in their members

---

[1] *i.e.*, the desires are sublimated to the highest each one can attain, and so the Soul transcends the realm of passion and rises to Heaven. Transmuted lust becomes spiritual Love, conquered sin the road to perfect virtue.

[2] *or*: still, hitherto.

[3] *i.e.*, passion and vehemence.

is led down through the heat on to the earth. In the same way also, that most high Power which dwells in the Ship of Living Waters[1] appears to these Powers whose nature is cold and wet, and which are allotted to the skies, in the likeness of boys and holy maidens, through his own messengers. He also appears to those who are females in the form of boys among them: but to the males (in the form) of maidens. By this changing and variation of the divine and most beautiful persons, then, the Rulers of the wet and cold root,[2] male or female, are dissolved, and that which is vital in them escapes;[3] while what will remain is loosed and led down on to the earth through the cold and mixed with all earth's species[4] (NB. 14).

7. The Work of the Great Builder[5]

1. Then the Lord of the Seven Climes[6] and the Mother of the Righteous began to plan how to arrange

[1] The Moon is the seat of Jesus as Saviour of men.

[2] *or*: Race.

[3] *lit*: flees.

[4] In its present form this story is not attractive to our minds, but we must try to understand its deeper meaning: that God wins even the lower nature of men to Him by a sight of His beauty—which is all beauty everywhere, and that men tread the path to Him over the ashes of their own dead selves and vanquished passions.

[5] This account from Soghdian, derived from W. B. Henning's article in the BSOAS, 1948, may well be compared with the Arabic account in GPM 11; both seem to be from the same Syr. original; they describe the Zodiacal circle of 360 degrees (stalls) in twelve Signs, each of 30 degrees, six on each side (*i.e.*, six 'male' and six 'female' Signs).

[6] Sogh. *avtkyṣpy xwt'w*, *i.e.*, Lord of the World, the Living Spirit.

this world. Then they began to fashion it. First they made five Carpets;[1] there they seated the Holder of Custody.[2] Under that they formed ten firmaments (and) set up one magic twelve-faced Lens;[3] there they seated a Son of God as Watcher,[4] so that the demons could do no harm in all the ten firmaments. Furthermore **they** evoked forty Angels, who hold the ten firmaments upraised.

2. In each firmament they fashioned twelve Gates; they constructed four more Gates in the four directions right where those Angels stand. The thickness of the ten firmaments is a hundred thousand parasangs; (that of) their air again is ten thousand parasangs.

3. To each of the twelve Gates that are in each of the firmaments they constructed six Thresholds, to each Threshold thirty Bazaars; in each Bazaar (there are) twelve Rows, (and in each Row two Sides); to the one Side they made 180 Stalls, (and) 180 to the other Side. In every Stall they chained and confined *yakshas* (and) demons, the males apart from the females.

[1] *or*: mats, beds—which are the Wheels of the Wind, Fire and Water wrapped up in the five 'haplōmata' (*maṣkbē*) referred to by bar Khoni. The word *fasba* here used is cognate with Per. *farasp*, tapestry, says Henning.

[2] Presumably the 'Holder of Splendour' or 'Custody of Splendour' is meant by this.

[3] Sogh. *myj*; *i.e.*, the "Wheel that lies in front of the King of Honour" (Keph. 36), to which are attached the roots of all things. In it he can therefore see all that goes on everywhere. "The Wheel is like a great Mirror" (Keph. 88 : 31); it contains twelve 'types'. This word may be Phl. *mycwk* and Per. *mizu*, lentil, says Henning.

[4] Probably the Great King of Honour.

320 THE GOSPEL OF THE PROPHET MANI

4. Thereupon the All-Maker [1] called the Lord of the Firmaments; [2] they seated him on a throne in the seventh heaven, and made him the lord and king over all the firmaments. Then they fashioned below the ten firmaments a rolling Wheel and Zodiac. Within the Zodiac they fettered those that were the most wicked, vicious and rebellious of the demons of the Darkness. They made the Twelve Signs and the seven Planets rulers over the whole Mixed World, and set them in opposition to each other.[3]

5. From all the demons that had been imprisoned in the Zodiac, they wove to and fro the roots, veins and links; [4] in the lowest firmament they bored a hole and suspended the Zodiac from it. Two Sons of God [5] were set as Watchers by them, so as continually to control (?) the Upper Wheel (M 178: *Henning*).

8. The Vivification

1. An agitation [6] was made by the death-giving demons [7] for the help of their own spirit; [8] and out of

---

[1] *Višparkar*, the Demiurge *Viśvakarman* in Skt. books.

[2] Called here *Smān-khṣedh*.

[3] Chaldean astrology regarded all planets as malevolent, all zodiacal signs benevolent.

[4] *i.e.*, planetary and zodiacal aspects.

[5] Probably the Glorious King and the Light-Adamas.

[6] Phl. *āṣōb*; Skt. root, *kṣubh*; cf. *āsōbgarēft*, making disturbance. I owe these notes largely to Jackson's edition.

[7] Phl. *dēvān oṣgarān*.

[8] Phl. *vēṣ grīv*; cf. Skt. *grīvā*, bosom; Ch. *ńik-liu*, vital element.

the corruption[1] of the demons and the pollution of the fiends he caused this defilement to be made, and introduced himself into it. Afterwards out of the five Elements,[2] the armour of the Lord Ohrmizd,[3] he extracted (?) the good Soul[4] and bound (it) in the defilement. He made it like one blind and deaf, senseless[5] and debauched, so that it did not know the first origin and source[6] of itself; it was he who made its defilement and bound the silent[7] (?) Soul in prison. Demon, fiend, and every witch tormented that prisoner; he immediately bound the Soul and mocked (it) in the defilement, he made it hateful and wicked, hostile and malicious.

2. *But* Ohrmizd the *Lord* pitied it *and all* Souls, and into *the bodies* of men caused it to descend on earth;[8] he washed it (free) of the wicked Greed[9] and made it a being endowed with sight,[10] and showed

[1] *nns*, cf. *ninēsānd*, filth.

[2] Phl. *ac panzh amahrāspandān*; the five Bright Gods of Syr., perhaps the same as the Ameshaspentas of Mazdeism; Ch. *moholoṣapen*.

[3] Av. *Ahuramazdāh*; Turk. *Xormuzta*; *i.e.*, the 'First Man' of our texts.

[4] Phl. *giyān*.

[5] Phl. *abēūṣ*; cf. Urdu *bēhōṣ*, unconscious.

[6] Phl. *nāf*; first 'navel', and then 'kindred'.

[7] or: uncomplaining (Phl. *vīdrāī*; cf. New Pers. *darāy*, conversation).

[8] Because like the Cosmos, the Body itself can be used to purify the Light through resisting its darknesses.

[9] Phl. *Āz 'i darvānd*. She is called the 'mother of all fiends', and in Turkish: shameless and insatiable (totüncsüz). Ch. *T'an-mo*, Ar. *Ḥirṣ*; she is the pair of Lust (*Avarzog*; Copt. *Epithumia*; Ar. *Ṣahwah*).

[10] Phl. *ūṣ kērd ast caṣmgāh*.

it clearly everything that was and will be; he quickly made plain to it that Ohrmizd did not make the defilement of the body, nor did he himself cause the Soul to be bound.[1]

3. He brought about the wise Soul's resurrection,[2] which is a good mercy; it believed in the Gnosis of Ohrmizd, the good Lord. All and every advice and command, and the Seal of Love,[3] he made it most zealously embrace; its defilement of death was removed, and it became eternally free and was led up to Paradise,[4] to that Realm of the Glorious Ones (S 9: *Jackson*).

9. AnNadim on the Religion

1. **Mani** said: He who desires[5] to enter the Religion[6] must examine himself, and if he sees he can control Passion and Greed,[7] and (if) he leaves off eating meats and drinking wine and sex-contact, and gives up offending (?) Water and Fire, and sorcery and idolatry[8] (?), then he may enter the Religion.

---

[1] *Cf.* the story in GPM 10:3.

[2] Phl. *ristahēz*; a spiritual rising from the state of the 'born dead' (*zād-mŭrdā*) of worldliness, not a physical rising of the corpse.

[3] Three 'Seals' are moral and four are doctrinal; cf. the Buddhist 'Seals' of body, voice and mind (*kāya vāk-citta*).

[4] Phl. *ūd ūl ahrāft ō Vahišt*.

[5] *or*: intends.

[6] *i.e.*, to become of the Elect, the 'Religious' of Manicheism.

[7] *i.e.*, Āz and Avarzog, against whom he has so long successfully fought.

[8] Ar. *arRiyā'a*.

2. But if he has no control over all that, then he does not enter the Religion. Now if he loves the Religion and (yet) cannot control Passion and Greed,[1] then he must take opportunity to protect the Religion and the Elect, and before his vile acts he will have seasons wherein he detaches activity [2] and (acquires) kindness and night prayers and pleadings and askings. And if that makes him happy in his eagerness and his death, then his form becomes the 'Second Image' in the Column [3] (of Glory). . . .

3. Mani enjoined on his followers ten Rules on the Hearers, and they are obeyed: . . . Now the Ten Rules (are): giving up the worship of idols, lying, possessiveness, killing, adultery, theft, the teaching of heresy, sorcery and persistent worry (that is, doubt of the Religion and looking for the Hope) and sloth in the work (that is, forgetting the prayer).[4] (332:28—333:12)

10. AnNadim on the Three Kinds of Death [5]

1. When death comes to the Righteous,[6] the First Man sends him a Bright God in the form of the Sage,

[1] i.e., Āz and Avarzog, against whom he has so long successfully fought.

[2] i.e., intervals when he is able to check himself.

[3] He forms the lovely 'Maiden' of virtue, who guides him on the road to Paradise.

[4] St. Benedict calls worship "God's work" (*opus Dei*).

[5] This, from Arabic, may usefully be compared with our Coptic and Turkish versions used in GPM 67-76.

[6] i.e., the Elect.

the Guide, and three Gods [1] (come) with him carrying the Flask and the Fillet and the Crown and the Garland—(all of) the Light; and with them comes the Maiden, the Image of the soul of that Righteous One. Then the demon of Greed appears to him, together with Lust [2] and the (other) demons, and when the Righteous sees them he appeals to the deity who is in the Sage's [3] form, and to the three Gods,[1] for help. Then they draw near to him, and when the demons see them they turn away in flight. They then take that Righteous One and clothe him in the Crown and Garland and Robe, and they give him the Flask in his hand. They go up with him in the Column of Glory to the spheres of the Moon, and to the First Man, and to the Radiant One, [4] Mother of the Living, to his first possession in the Gardens of the Light. Then his flesh remains lying there, while the Sun and the Moon and the Bright Gods draw the Power out of it—namely the Water and the Fire and the Air. So he is raised to the Sun and becomes God,[5] while the dregs of his flesh are thrown out to a hell which is wholly darkness.[6]

[1] *i.e.*, Angels.

[2] The two great demons, whom he has resisted so long.

[3] This is the 'Twin', the 'Sophia' or Wisdom, the Messenger, Jesus.

[4] As Jackson shows, this word must read *alBahiyya*, not *Nahnaha*.

[5] Another uncompromising assertion of the real nature of the liberated Soul; Ar. *fa-yirtafaʻu ilā 'ṣṣamsi wa yaṣīru ilāhān*.

[6] Having been robbed of the Light-Spark once in it, the body is now a mere corpse.

2. Now as for the man striving for and well disposed to the Religion and Innocence, who guards both these and the Righteous Ones,[1] well, when his death takes place, these Gods whom I have mentioned are present, and the demons are (also) there. Then he calls for help and relies on what he used to do for Innocence and guarding the Religion and the Righteous Ones; so they save him from the demons. But (as) in the world the likeness of the man who in his dream sees phantoms and does not cease, plunging into mud and mire, so too he does not cease in that way, until his Light and his Spirit are freed, and after the long time of his wandering about[2] he soars up into the Assembly of the Righteous Ones and puts on their Robe.

3. As for the wicked man, over whom Greed and Lust have prevailed, well, when his death draws near the demons are present with him; then they seize him, harass him and make him see horrors. Then these Gods come and that Robe with them, so the wicked man fancies they have come to save him; but they are there only to revile him, and to remind him of his deeds, and to compel the realisation that he has lost the help of the Righteous Ones. Then he does not cease to roam about miserably in the world until the time of the End, when he is thrown into hell.

4. Mani said : Well, these three paths in which human souls are grouped: one of them (leads) to the Gardens, and they are the Righteous ; and the second

[1] *Cf.* GPM 70 : 2.
[2] In various rebirths into physical bodies.

to the world and the phantoms, and they are the guardians of the Righteous [1]; and the third to hell, and that is the (road) of the wicked man. (335 : 10-29)

APPENDIX II

KHUASTUANIFT, THE HEARERS' CONFESSION

1. When we had come to know the True God and the Pure Law, 'we knew the Two Roots and the Law of the Three Times; we knew the Bright Root to be God's Garden, we knew the Dark Root to be the Realm of Hell, we knew what existed before the Earth-god was, we knew why God and the Demon fought with each other, and how Light and Darkness were thereby mixed. We knew who created heaven and earth, and how the Ruler, Earth-god, will be eliminated again and Light and Darkness thus separated; we knew what would happen thereafter. Believing and trusting in the God Zrwān, the Sun-Moon-god,[2] the Mighty[3] God, the Messengers, we became Hearers.

2. Ohrmizd the God and the Five-god[4] came down with the purity of all the Gods to fight with the Demon.[5] He fought with the malicious hosts of

---

[1] *i.e.*, the Hearers.

[2] Turk: *kün-ai tängrikä*; the two Luminaries are regarded as one —as Jesus is fused in the Christ.

[3] *i.e.*, the Living Spirit; Turk. *küclüg tängrikä*.

[4] Turk. *biş-tängrii—i.e.*, the Soul, composed of five aspects or elements. Here, rather as the Elements that made up the 'armour' of First Man.

[5] Turk. *Yäkkä*, cognate with Skt. *yakṣa*.

Darkness,[1] and then God and the Demon, Light and Darkness, were mingled. Ohrmizd the Youth-god—the Five-god and our Soul—began to fight with Sin and Demonry and became snared and entangled. All the demon-rulers came with the greedy shameless Envy-Demon[2] and with fourteen million demons united in (evil) knowledge but without understanding and sense. He himself, born and created, forgot the eternal Heaven and became separated from the Gods of Light.

3. Therefore, my God, if intending evil deeds Shumnu has led our understandings and our thoughts[3] astray to wickedness, and so we have become unwise, without understanding, and have sinned against the Root of all the Lights, against the pure Light-God Zrwān, (and so) Light and Darkness, God and Demon (became mixed; if we have said of any creature that the Demon) is (its) foundation and root; if we have said: "It lives (when) God gives life; it dies (as) God kills"; if we have said: "Good and bad, all is God's creation"; if we have said: "It is He who creates the eternal Gods"; if we have said: "Ohrmizd and Shumnu are twin brothers"—if we have sinfully, unawares becoming false to God, uttered such tremendous words of blasphemy, and have thus sinned this unpardonable sin—My God, I Raimast-farzind[4]

[1] Turk. *Smnw*, vocalised perhaps as Shumnu; equivalent to Ahrimēn.
[2] Turk. *Soq-yäk*.
[3] Turk. *ögümüzni saqīncīmīzni*.
[4] The name of the owner of the manuscript.

now repent; cleansing myself from the sin, I pray: My sin remit![1]

4. *Second.* When for the sake of [2] the Sun-Moon-god, the Gods enthroned in the two Light-Palaces, Foundation and Root of the Light of all the Messengers (and) of the Earth and (Water) they are to go to the Heaven meant for them to gather in—then their main Gate is the Sun-Moon-god; to rescue the Five-god and to separate Light and Darkness, he rolls along fully from the depth, and shines on the four corners (of the sky).

My God, if by sin we have somehow sinned unawares against the Sun-Moon-god, the Gods enthroned in the two Light-Palaces; if we have called him the true, powerful and mighty God and yet have not believed in him; if in any way we have spoken many wicked words of blasphemy; if we have said: "The Sun-Moon-god dies!"; if we have said: "His rising and setting show weakness; had he strength, then he would not rise (and set)"; if we ourselves have said: "Our own bodies were created before him"—then we pray to be freed from this second unwitting sin: Remit my sin!

5. *Third.* Because in defending the Five-god, the divine Youth Ohrmizd, (*i*) the divine Air, (*ii*) the divine Wind, (*iii*) the divine Light, (*iv*) the divine Water, (*v*) the divine Fire [3]—having fought with

---

[1] This recurrent phrase reads: *Manastar ḥirza.*

[2] or: by means of (?).

[3] Turk: *tintura, yil, yaruq, suw, oot,* the five elements.

APPENDIX II

Sin and Demonry have been snared and mingled with the Darkness, they could not go to God's Heaven and are still on the earth:[1] the tenfold heavens above, and the eightfold earths below, exist only for the sake of the Five-god; of all on the earth the Majesty, the Brightness, the Image, the Body, Soul, Strength, Foundation and Root is the Five-god.

My God, if we have sinfully in any way unconsciously hurt or caused displeasure [2] to the Five-god by a bad and wicked mind; if we have let the fourteen kinds (of members) dominate us; if, taking living bodies as our food and drink with ten snake-headed fingertips and thirty-two teeth, we have in any way angered and vexed God; if we have in any way sinned against the Dry Earth and the Wet, against the five kinds of living beings and the five kinds of plants and trees [3]—now, my God, cleansing ourselves (from sin), we pray: My sin remit!

6. *Fourth.* My God, if in any way we have unknowing sinned against the divine Yalavaci-Messengers of the Masses, against the meritorious righteous pure [4] Elect;[5] if though calling them divine Yalavaci-Messengers or pious and pure Elect we have yet disbelieved in

---

[1] Because the world arises from the mingling.

[2] Turk. *birtïmiz*, from *bir-*, murmur; so, twist, torment.

[3] Augustine writes; "*ipsam partem naturae Dei ubique permixtam . . . in omnibus corporibus siccis et humidis. . . . in omnibus seminibus arborum herbarum.*

[4] Turk. *buyanci*; cf. Skt. *puṇyā*.

[5] Turk. *dintarlarqa*.

them; if we have spoken God's word and yet have foolishly broken it; (if we have said: "The Law is burdensome to keep (?)"); if we have hindered the Law by not spreading it; My God, now we repent, cleansing ourselves, we pray: Remit my sin!

7. *Fifth.* Offending the five kinds of moving things: first, against two-legged mankind, second fourfooted animals, third flying creatures, fourth beings in the water, fifth living beings creeping on their bellies on the earth [1]—in a sinful state, my God, up to the large ones and down to the small ones; if in any way we may have frightened or alarmed them,[2] if in any way we may have beaten or struck them, if in any way we may have killed (them)—thus becoming tormentors of such living and moving beings—Now, my God, we repent, cleansing ourselves we pray: My sin remit!

8. *Sixth.* If in sinfulness we have committed the ten kinds of sin by thoughts, words (or) deeds;[3] if in any way we have invented lies; if in any way we have fabricated perjuries; if we have in any way become a liar's witness; if in any way we have afflicted the innocent; if in any way, carrying words here and there, we have made people enemies, corrupting hearts and minds; if in any way we have practised sorcery; if in any way we have killed many living moving

[1] Augustine calls these: *bipedia, quadrupedia, volantia, natantia,* and *serpentia.*

[2] The extraordinarily high level of 'harmlessness' here may be noted. I have not yet seen anything to equal it elsewhere.

[3] Turk. *saqïncïn sözün qïlïncïn.*

beings; if in any way we have been fraudulent and deceitful; if we have in any way ruined (?) the industrious (?); if in any way we have done things displeasing to the Sun-Moon-god; again, if in our first self or in this self, now that we have become Manichean youths,[1] we have sinned or erred in any way and thus brought injury and ruin on so many living beings—My God, now cleansing ourselves from these ten kinds of sin we pray: Remit my sin!

9. *Seventh.* If in sinfulness one should say: "Who is he that comes (?) to the entrance of the two poisonous roads and to the road leading astray to the gate of hell?", the first is the one adhering to false Faiths, the second worships with prostrations calling the Demon by the name of God. My God, sinfully misunderstanding and not comprehending the True God and the Pure Faith,[2] disbelieving the Messengers and the preaching of the pure Elect, trusting those who lie: "I am a man of God, I am a Preacher!", and accepting their words, we have in some way kept fasts mistakenly and wrongly given alms in any way; or if saying, "We shall gain merit", we have in any way done evil deeds by mistake; or if calling a Demon or a ghost[3] God, we have killed living and moving beings and prostrated (*i.e.*, offered animal sacrifices); or if we have submitted to a false Law, (evidently referring to the "Law of the Jews") calling (it the) Messenger,

---

[1] *i.e.*, converts.

[2] Turk. *kirtü tängrig arīgh nomugh*.

[3] Turk. *ickakkän*, the Skt. *preta*.

and worshipped it with a blessing, thus offending God and worshipping the Demon—My God, we now repent, cleansing ourselves from sin we pray: My sin remit!

10. *Eighth.* . . . (*repeats para.* 1) Four Light-Seals have we sealed in our heart; the first is Love, the Seal of God Zrwān; the second is Faith, the Seal of the Sun-Moon-god; the third is Reverence,[1] the Seal of the Five-god; the fourth is the wise Wisdom, the Seal of the Messengers.—My God, if we have (in any way) let our mind and heart drift away from these Four Gods; if we have deposed (them) from (their) places; if we have violated God's Seals—Now, my God, cleansing ourselves from sin we pray: Remit my sin!

11. *Ninth.* In our keeping of the Ten Commandments[2] it was ordained to keep perfectly three with the Mouth, three with the Heart, three with the Hand, and one with the entire Self.—My God, if knowingly or unawares, walking in the love of the physical body or following the words and accepting the plans of bad companions and chance acquaintances, friends and colleagues; or if to gain cattle and property, or swayed by stupid attachment to the world, we have broken these Ten Commandments, or been in any way found wanting or of no avail: Now, my God, cleansing from sin we pray: My sin remit!

12. *Tenth.* It was ordained to invoke daily with one mind and pure heart four Blessings: on God

[1] *or*: fear of God, piety (Turk. *qorqmaq*), mark of the Soul.
[2] Turk. *on caxşapat.*

Zrwān, the Sun-Moon-god, the Mighty God, and the Messengers. If for want of reverence or for laziness we have not uttered these Blessings well and properly; or if we have not held our hearts and thoughts on God while uttering them; if our blessings and prayers have not reached God purely; if they have been hindered and stopped: Now, my God, cleansing from sin we pray: Remit my sin!

13. *Eleventh.* It was ordained thus to offer seven kinds of Alms[1] to the Pure Faith, and it was ordained (that) the Angels[2] gathering the Light of the Five-god, the divine Call and Reply should bring us (that part of) the Light of the Five-god which was going to God for purifying—that then, much adorning ourselves, we should dress ourselves ceremonially according to the Ritual:[3] if through foolishness or because of stinting the gift of alms, we could not give the seven kinds of Alms perfectly according to the Law,[3] or if we have confined[4] in house and household the Light of Five-god that was to go to the Gods for purifying; or if we have given to those fond of evil deeds,[5] to wicked living and moving creatures, if we have thus spilled it, if we have thrown it away, sending the divine Light to

---

[1] Turk. *puṣi*, a Chinese word for food-offerings —the *miyazdā*.

[2] Turk. *fāriṣtilär*, derived from the Iranian *peri*, our word 'fairy'.

[3] The same word, *nomqa*, is used for Law, and Ritual.

[4] *badīmīz*; to store food was to hold its Light captive, a sin.

[5] Augustine makes much of this prohibition to give alms to the wicked, which Mani probably inherited from Mazdean thought, rationalising it in his own way.

an evil place—My God, now cleansing ourselves from sin we pray: My sin remit!

14. *Twelfth.* It was ordained to keep every year like the pure Elect a fifty days *vosanti*; thus it was a rule to fast with pure fasts[1] to God. If because we possess house and household, and have gained cattle and property, or are overcome by foolish attachments, or because of the greedy shameless Envy-Demon, or because of irreverent hearts, we may have broken the Fast, being fearful and indifferent,[2] weak, strengthless; if we have not fasted according to the Law and Ritual though sitting down to fast—My God, now cleansing ourselves from sin we pray: Remit my sin!

15. *Thirteenth.* Every day of the Moon-god it was a rule to pray to God, to the Law,[3] the pure Elect, to cleanse ourselves of sins and trespasses. If, strongly or powerlessly, indifferent, lax, keeping contacts with affairs, we have not gone to clean ourselves from sin—My God, now cleansing ourselves from sin we pray: My sin remit!

16. *Fourteenth.* It was ordained to sit down every year to seven *yimqi*,[4] and it was a rule to observe one month's *chakhshapat*; further it was the rule that, sitting in the Prayer Hall to observe the *yimqi*, we should pray

---

[1] *i.e.*, by preserving chastity and scrupulous cleanliness in whatever food was taken on the fifty Sundays; cf. GPM 42 : 1.

[2] *or*: weary, lax.

[3] *or*: Faith, Religion. Cf. the Buddhist Buddha-Dharma-Sangha as the triple Refuge.

[4] The word *yimqi* is unknown; it was probably the public confession before the Bema-tribunal, or the reading of Scriptures.

with one mind from the depth (?) of our heart to the divine Messenger to nullify our sins.—My God, if we could not sit down to the seven *yimqi* perfectly; if we could not keep the month's *chakhshapat*[1] in a good, pure and perfect way; if, sitting in the Prayer Hall[2] to observe the *yimqi* well according to the Law and the Ritual, we could not pray from our heart with one intent to shake off the sins of one year; if in any way there was a defect and ineffectiveness in our conduct— My God, now cleansing ourselves from sin we pray: Remit my sin!

17. *Fifteenth.* Every day how many evil thoughts we think! How many miserable words we speak that should not be uttered! How many deeds we do that ought not to be done! Through our evil deeds and wretchedness we ourselves torment our own bodies! Because body and soul we have ourselves walked in the love of the greedy shameless Envy-demon, the Light of the Five-God that we have daily absorbed in our food goes to the evil place. Because of this, my God, because of the Divine Prognostic Faith,[3] cleansing ourselves from sin we pray: My sin remit!

18. My God, we are imperfect and sinful, tormentors and malcontents! For the sake of the greedy insatiable Envy-demon—by thoughts, words and deeds —seeing with eyes, hearing with ears, speaking with

---

[1] Evidently the month of special observances terminating with the Feast of the Bema.

[2] Turk. *caidan*, often called church ' (*ekklēsia*) in the Coptic.

[3] Turk. *tängrii dinmurwa üčün*; *murwa* means ' omen '.

tongues, touching with hand, walking with legs—we long and ceaselessly torment the Light of the Five-god, the Dry and Wet Earths, the five kinds of living beings, the five kinds of plants and trees. Yes, we are imperfect and sinful! Because of the Ten Commandments, the Seven Alms, the Three Seals we bear the name of ' Hearers '—(yet) we cannot act their deeds.

19. If in any way we have sinned or erred against the Light-Gods, the Pure Law, the Man of God, the Preachers (or) the Pure Elect; if in any way we have not walked by the letter and spirit[1] of God's speech; if we have displeased the heart of the Gods; if we could not keep the *yimqi*, fasts, blessings, and commandments according to the Law and Ritual; if in any way we have been found wanting and ineffective—every day, every month, we indeed commit sins!

To the Light-Gods, the Majesty of the Law,[2] the pure Elect, we pray cleansing ourselves from sin: Remit my sin!

APPENDIX III

ANATHEMA AGAINST MANICHEISM

(*Commonitorium*, PL. 42 : 1154-1155).

1. Let him who believes there are Two Natures existing in different origins: one good, which is God,

---

[1] *or*: sound and meaning.
[2] Turk. *nomqutinga*, spoken of as Judge at the hour of death.

the other evil, which God has not created, having its own Rulers and evils which God has not created—be accursed.

2. Let him be accursed who believes that the Two Natures waged war one on another, and in that war a part of God's Nature was thoroughly mixed with the Rulers of Darkness and all the races belonging to the Evil Nature, and by them was held fast, smothered, defiled—which also make (it) believed that God's Nature is changeable and can be polluted.

3. Let him be accursed who believes a part of God is held bound and polluted in demons and in all living things and in varieties of shrubs, and is freed and purified through the food of the Manichean Elect, so as to believe a part of God is held defiled in cucumbers and melons and radishes and leaks, and in every meanest herb, and that escapes when such things are eaten by the Elect of the Manicheans.

4. Let him be accursed who believes the first man who was called Adam was not made by God but begotten by the Rulers of the Darkness, so that the part of God held captive in their members might be more firmly and fully held in the earth; and was in this way created: When the male and female Rulers of the Darkness had had intercourse and given their embryos to the Chief Ruler of the Darkness, and he had eaten all and lain with his own Spouse, he so generated Adam from her, binding in him a large part of God that had been bound in all the embryos of the Rulers of the Darkness which they had given him to devour.

5. Let him be accursed who believes the Rulers of the Darkness were bound in the sky, having confined in themselves in pains and misery the Life-Substance—that is, the part of God—and in this way it was liberated from their members: When the blessed Father, who has Light-Ships and various little dwellings, namely the Sun and the Moon, changes His Powers into beautiful women whom He sets before the male Rulers of the Darkness to lust after, and into handsome men whom He sets before the female Rulers of the Darkness to lust after, so that by this same lust the Life-Substance—which is the part of God—might be freed and purified out of their members.

6. Let him be accursed who believes the part of God which could not be freed and purified from the mixing with the Race of Darkness is to be condemned and for ever fixed to a horrible 'Sphere' where the Race of Darkness is confined.

7. Let him be accursed who believes the Law given through Moses was not given by the Good and True God, nor did the Prophets who have been in the people of Israel and are kept in the Canon of divine Scriptures in the Catholic Church speak by the Spirit of the Good and True God.

8. Let him be accursed who believes the Son of God, the Lord Jesus Christ, had no true flesh, nor did he undergo a real death and rise again from the dead, but was only a spirit without flesh, so also willed to appear that what he was not should be considered flesh—and in this way contradicts the Gospel where it

is said, the Lord himself speaking, . . . (*Lk. 24:39*), who thus so declares Christ a God as to deny the true and natural Man also.

9. Let him be accursed who believes Mani or Manicheus, who preached and taught all the above things which deserve a curse and condemnation, had the Holy Spirit, the Paraclete, when not the Spirit of Truth but the Spirit of Falsity could have taught them all.

10. And especially may the same Mani or Manicheus be accursed, who has taught and written down, and has persuaded miserable folk to believe, all the above-written impieties, with other sacrilegious and damnable fables, tending to seducing spirits and the doctrines of lying demons.

Prosper's Refutation, PL. 65 : 23-30).

12.[1] Let him be accursed who believes human souls are transferred again in other bodies or living creatures.

13. Let him be accursed, whoever says the Sun and Moon are heavenly Ships for carrying over Souls, or the Substance of God, and ascribes honour to them or something of divinity to that visible light, and not as a created thing left behind for the service of mankind and made by the Lord of heaven and earth.

14. Let him be accursed who believes all flesh—of quadrupeds, serpents, flying and swimming things, or all that are in the world—is created by not the True God but the Rulers of Darkness.

15. Let him be accursed who believes the Creed or Prayers of the Manicheans, not detesting or abhorring,

[1] Paragraphs 1 to 11 are much like Paragraphs 1 to 10 above.

or has wished to remember or utter (them) with the mouth.

16. Let him be accursed who believes human souls are of the Substance of God, and human bodies either made by or derived from the Ruler of the Darkness.

17. Let him be accursed who believes the Devil is not a good angel made by God and having fallen through pride by his own will became a devil, and declares that the same one was not created by God along with the rest of the Angels, but was always coeternal with God.

APPENDIX IV

FADING FOOTSTEPS OF MANICHEISM

1. The Bogomile Book of John

(*From a 14th c. Vienna ms. with Latin comments, printed in Benoist's 'Histoire des Albigeois', Paris, 1691:* "*This is the secret (book) of the heretics of Concorèze, brought from Bulgaria by their Bishop Nazarius; full of errors*"*. Perhaps dating from 6th or 7th century, latinized by 12th c.*)[1]

1. I John, your brother and sharer in tribulation, who shall share also in the Kingdom of Heaven— when I lay on the breast of our Lord Jesus Christ and asked him: "Lord, who is it shall betray thee?" he answered and said: "He who dips his hand with me

[1] M. R. James in "New Testament Apocrypha".

APPENDIX IV 341

in the dish, then Satan entered him and he sought how to betray me."

2. And I said: "Lord, before Satan fell in what glory did he dwell with thy Father?" And he said to me: "In such glory was he that he commanded the heavens; while I sat with my Father he ordered all the Father's followers and went down from heaven to the deep and ascended up out of the deep to the throne of the invisible Father. So he saw the glory of Him who moves the heavens, and tried to place his seat above the clouds of heaven, wishing to be like the Most High.

3. "And when he had gone down into the Air, he said to the Angel of the Air, 'Open the gates of the Air to me'; and he opened them to him. And he tried to go down further, and found the Angel who held the Waters, and said to him 'Open the gates of the Waters to me'; and he opened for him. Then he passed through, and he found all the face of the earth covered with waters. And he passed through beneath the Earth, and found two fishes lying upon the Waters, and they were as oxen yoked for ploughing, holding the whole Earth by the commandment of the invisible Father, from the west even to the rising of the Sun. Now when he had gone down he found clouds hanging which held the Waters of the sea; and he went down yet further and found Hell, that is, the Gehenna of Fire; thereafter he could not go down further because of the flame of the raging Fire.

4. "So Satan returned back and passed over the paths, and entered in to the Angel of the Air and to

the one who was over the Waters, and said to them: 'All these things are mine. If you will listen to me I will set my seat in the clouds and be like the Most High; and I will take the Waters from this upper firmament and gather together the other parts of the sea. And after that there shall be no water on the face of the whole Earth, and I will reign with you for ever and ever.'

5. "And when he had spoken thus to the Angels he went up to the other Angels, even to the fifth heaven, and spoke thus to each of them: 'How much do you owe your Lord?' One said: 'A hundred measures of wheat.' And he said to him, 'Take pen and ink, and write sixty.' Then he said to others: 'And you, how much do you owe your Lord?' They said: 'A hundred jars of oil.' So he said, 'Sit down and write fifty.' And as he went up through all the heavens he spoke thus, even to the fifth heaven, seducing the Angels of the invisible Father.

6. "And a Voice came out of the Father's throne, saying: 'What are you doing, O denier of the Father, seducing the Angels? Doer of iniquity, do quickly what you have planned.' Then the Father commanded His Angels, saying: 'Take away their garments.' And the Angels took away their robes and their thrones and their crowns from all the Angels who listened to him."

7. Then I asked of the Lord: "When Satan fell, in what place did he dwell?" And he answered me: "My Father changed his appearance because of his pride, and the light was taken from him, so his face

APPENDIX IV 343

became like heated iron and his face became altogether like a man's. And with his tail he drew the third part of God's Angels, and he was thrown out from God's seat and from the stewardship of the heavens. So Satan came down into this firmament, and he could find no rest for himself, nor for those who were with him. Then he implored the Father: 'Have patience with me, and I will pay Thee all!' So the Father had pity on him and gave him rest and those who were with him, as much as they wanted, even to seven days.

8. "And so he sat in the firmament and commanded the Angel who was over the Air and him who was over the Waters, and they raised up the Earth and it appeared dry. Then he took the crown of the Angel who was over the Waters, and of the half of it he made the moonlight and of the (other) half the starlight; and of the gems he made all the hosts of the stars.

9. "And after that he made the Angels his servants according to the form of the order of the Most High, and by the command of the invisible Father (he made) thunder, rain, hail and snow; he sent forth Angels to be servants over them. And he commanded the Earth to bring forth every beast for food, and every creeping thing, and trees and plants; and he bade the sea bring forth fishes and the birds of the skies.

10. "And furthermore he planned and made man in his (own) likeness, and commanded an Angel of the third heaven to enter into the body of clay. And he took of it and made another body in a woman's shape, and commanded an Angel of the second heaven

to enter the body of the woman. But the Angels lamented when they saw a mortal form upon them and that they were unlike in shape. So he commanded them to do the deed of the flesh in the bodies of clay, but they knew not how to commit sin.

11. "Then did the contriver of evil plan in his mind to make a Garden, and into it he brought the Man and the Woman. He commanded a reed to be brought, and this the devil planted in the centre of the Garden, and the devil so hid his plan that they did not know his deceit. Then he came in and spoke to them, saying: 'Eat of every fruit that is in the Garden, but do not eat of the fruit of the Knowledge of Good and Evil.' Again the devil entered into a wicked serpent and seduced the Angel who was in the woman's form, and (persuaded her) and worked his desire with her even in the form of the serpent. And therefore are they called devil's sons and serpent's sons even to the end of this world who work the lust of the devil their father. Again, also, the devil poured out the poison of his lust upon the Angel who was in Adam, and it begets serpent's sons and devil's sons even to the end of this world."

12. And after that I John asked of the Lord, saying: "How do men say that Adam and Eve were created by God and set in the Garden to keep the Father's commandments, and were handed over to Death?" And the Lord said to me: "Listen, John, my Father's beloved; foolish men speak thus in their deceitfulness that my Father made bodies of clay: but

APPENDIX IV

by the Holy Spirit He made all the Powers of the heavens, and holy ones were found with bodies of clay because of their transgression, and therefore were they surrendered to Death."

13. And again I John asked the Lord: " How does a man in a fleshly body begin to be in the spirit?" And the Lord said to me: " (Some) of the Angels that fell enter the bodies of women and receive flesh from the lust of the flesh; and so is a spirit born of spirit and flesh of flesh, and so is Satan's kingdom accomplished in this world and among all nations."

14. (And again I asked the Lord: " How long shall Satan's reign be on the Earth?") and he said to me: " My Father has allowed him to reign seven days, which are seven ages."

15. And I asked the Lord and said: "What shall happen in that time?" and he said to me: " From the time when the devil fell from the Father's glory he sat upon the clouds and sent his servants, even Angels flaming with fire, to men, from Adam even to Enoch his servant. And he lifted up Enoch upon the firmament and showed him his godhead, and commanded pen and ink to be given him: and he sat down and wrote sixty-seven books. Then he bade him take them to the Earth and hand them to his sons. So Enoch let his books down upon the Earth and handed them to his sons, and began to teach them to carry out the rite of sacrifices and unrighteous mysteries, and so he hid the Kingdom of Heaven from men. He said to them: 'Behold, I am your God and there is no

other God besides me.' And so my Father sent me into the world that I might make it known to men, so that they might know the devil's evil device.

16. "And then when he perceived that I had come down out of Heaven into the world, he sent an Angel and took of three kinds of wood, and gave them to Moses that I might be crucified, and now they are reserved for me. Then did (Satan) proclaim to him (Moses) and to his people his own godhead, and commanded a Law to be given the children of Israel, and brought them out through the midst of the dried-up sea.

17. "When My Father thought to send me into the world, He sent before me His Angel, named Mary, to receive me. And when I came down I entered in by the ear and came out by the ear. Then Satan, the Ruler of this world, perceived that I had come to seek and save those who were lost, and he sent his Angel, even Elijah the Prophet, baptizing with water, who is called John the Baptist. And Elijah asked the Ruler of this world: 'How can I know him?' Then his lord said: 'On whomsoever you shall see the Spirit descending like a dove and resting on him, he it is who baptizes with the Holy Spirit to forgiveness of sins; him you will be able to destroy and to save (our kingdom?).'"

18. Then again I asked the Lord, I John: "Can a man be saved by the baptism of John without thy baptism?" And the Lord answered: "Unless I have baptized to the forgiveness of sins, no man can see the

APPENDIX IV

Kingdom of Heaven by the baptism of water. For I am the Bread of Life that came down from the seventh heaven, and those who eat my flesh and drink my blood, they shall be called the sons of God."

19. And I asked the Lord and said: " What does it mean—' to eat my flesh and drink my blood '? " . . .

20. (And I asked the Lord again): " . . ." And the Lord said to me: " Before the devil fell with all his host from the Father's glory, they glorified the Father in their prayers thus, saying: ' Our Father who art in heaven . . .'; and so all their songs came up before the Father's throne. But when they had fallen, they were no longer able to glorify God with that prayer."

21. And I asked the Lord: " Why do all men receive John's baptism, but thine not at all? " And the Lord answered: " Because their deeds are evil and they do not come to the Light. John's disciples marry and are given in marriage, but my disciples neither marry nor are given in marriage, but are like the Angels in heaven." But I said: " If it be sin then to have dealings with a woman, it is not good to marry." And the Lord said to me: " Not everyone can receive this saying. . . ."

22. I asked the Lord about the Judgment Day: " What shall be the sign of thy coming? " Then he answered and said to me: " When the number of the Righteous shall be complete, that is the number of the Righteous who are crowned (out of those) who have fallen, then shall Satan be loosed out of his prison,

having great wrath, and he shall make war with the Righteous, and they shall cry with a loud voice to the Lord. And immediately the Lord shall command an Angel to blow with the trumpet, and the Archangel's voice in the trumpet shall be heard from heaven even to hell. . . .

23. "Then shall the Son of God send the evil spirits to bring all nations before him, and shall say to them: 'Come, you who said: We have eaten and drunk and received the gain of this world!' And after that they shall be brought again and all shall stand before the Judgment Seat, even all nations, in fear. And the Books of Life shall be opened, and all nations shall show forth their ungodliness. And he shall glorify the Righteous for their patience, and glory and honour and immortality (shall reward) their good works. But as for those who kept the precepts of the Angels and unrighteously obeyed, indignation and trouble and anguish shall take hold of them. . . .

24. "And the rest (of the Angels), beholding the last cutting off, shall throw the sinners into hell by the command of the invisible Father. Then shall the spirits of those who believe not go forth out of the prisons, and then shall my voice be heard, and there shall be one fold and one shepherd: and the darkness and obscurity shall come forth out of the deep of the Earth—that is to say, the darkness of the Gehenna of Fire—and shall burn all things from below even to the air of the firmament. And the distance (?) from (?) the firmament even to the depths of the earth shall be

as if a man of thirty years old should take a stone and throw it down, it would in three years barely reach the bottom, so great is the depth of the pit and of the fire wherein the sinners shall dwell. . . . And the Son of God shall walk above the firmament with His Elect, and shall shut up the devil, binding him with strong chains that cannot be loosed. . . . .

25. "And then shall the Son of God sit on His Father's right hand, and the Father shall command His Angels, and they shall serve them and set them among the choirs of the Angels, to clothe them with immortal robes; and (they) shall give them unfading crowns and seats immovable. And God shall be in the midst of them; and no more shall they hunger or thirst, neither shall the sun or any heat light on them. But God shall wipe away every tear from their eyes. And He shall reign with His holy Father, and of His Kingdom there shall be no end for ever and ever."

2. Extracts from a Catharist Gospel

(Derived from the admissions of Bavilus, a pupil of the Elect Belibasta, and used by the 'Manichean heretics' of South France in 12th-13th centuries, together with the 'Ascension of Isaiah'. It may depend on the lost 'Gospel of the Twelve', and is said by F. C. Conybeare to resemble the known traces of the 'Gospel of the Egyptians' of 2nd century).

2. . . . Thereupon the Father began to write a book, which He composed in the space of forty years.

In this book were written in detail the sufferings, losses, sorrows, poverty, infirmity, shame, injuries, envy, hatred, malice and generally speaking all the penalties which can befall men in this life. And therein it was stated that he who was willing to endure all the aforesaid penalties and to teach them also should be a Son of the heavenly Father. And when the holy Father began the book, Isaiah the Prophet began to prophesy that a Branch or Bough was to come who should redeem human souls. And when the holy Father had composed that book, He placed it in the midst of the heavenly spirits who had remained with Him in heaven and said: "He who shall fulfil the things which are written in this book shall be My Son."

3. And many of the heavenly spirits, wishing to be Sons of the holy Father and to be honoured above the rest, went up to that book and opened it; but when they read therein the penalties which he must needs suffer who should desire to come among men and uplift the human race, after reading a little in that book, they fell fainting in a swoon. None of them was willing to forfeit the glory he possessed and subject himself to the penalties of this life, in order to become the Son of God.

4. Then, seeing this, the holy Father said: "So then there is not one of you desires to be My Son?" Then one of the spirits standing by, who was called Jesus, rose up and said: "I myself am willing to be Son of the Father and to complete all things which are written in that book." Then he went up to the book and

opened it, and read therein four or five pages; and he fell in a swoon beside the book, and so remained for three days and nights. Then having awakened from his swoon he grieved much and mourned; but because he had promised that he would fulfil these things which were contained in that book, and because it was right for him not to lie, he told the Father that he himself desired to be His Son and to fulfil all things which were written in that book, however grievous they might be. Then he descended from heaven and appeared as a newly-born Boy in Bethlehem. . . .

6. After baptism by the great demon John, the devil carried Jesus hanging on his neck. . . .

8. And he was in Samaria with the blessed Peter, and there they ate bread and fishes, that is to say, God Himself and the blessed Peter did so, and from the table were taken up twelve baskets (of what remained). . . .

10. The Son of God said that a man should in no wise swear, neither by Heaven, for a man could not make one star in it small or great, nor by his own head, because a man could not make one hair of his head white or black. . . .

12. A certain woman came to the Son of God and said that her daughter was frenzied; and the Son of God placed his hand on her daughter's head and healed her—which healing was nothing else than this: that the soul of the daughter went out of her body, and that he healed the soul. For the Son of God did not free them from bodily infirmities but only from sins,

which are the infirmities of the soul. And this is why the Son of God was a good healer, because he drew souls to salvation.

13. (And he called the Jews) Pharisees, hypocrites, who stand in the gate of the Kingdom, but neither entered the Kingdom nor let those enter who desired to go in. . . .

15. He said to them that he was going to his Father and that he would return to them on a certain day which he fixed for them, between the third hour and noon, and that he would find them in the house of Simon bar Yona. And when he had said this the Pharisees appeared on the scene, together with children of the devil who were working with them, and arrested him. And all the injuries and the insults which they could inflict on him, the said Pharisees and their servants did inflict upon the Son of God, so much so that a certain leper spat in his face, but he forbore from all resentment. And when he was thus spat upon by that leper, and derided and abused, he said: "Father, I only know that I am Thy Son because Thou didst promise me this when Thou didst send me, to the end that I should be abhorred by all men, that is, that I should be a reproach to abjects among men."

16. Then after they had mocked at him and threatened him, they set him on a cross and wounded him, and inflicted many wounds upon him. And when this had been done, he himself—without death intervening, for the Son of God could not die—ascended to

APPENDIX IV

the holy Father, kneeled before Him and said: "Holy Father, in obedience to Thy will I have completed all things which were written in the book Thou didst write." And the holy Father replied to him: "Whereas thou hast done all things which I wrote in the book, thou shalt be My Son." To whom the Son answered: "Father, and what wilt Thou give, that I may give myself to my friends and to those who believe in me?" And the Father Himself replied that He was desirous that the same Power which He had given to him, he himself should be able to give in turn to his friends, and they to others, in such a way that the said Power should pass from hand to hand among the good men; and also that what he gave to them should be this: that whatever they themselves did upon earth should be done by the Father Himself in heaven.

17. These words having been uttered, he quitted the Father's presence and came down, so that on the appointed day he might appear to his friends.

18. Now although it seemed to the Jews that the Son of God was dead and that after death they had placed him in a sepulchre, nevertheless he was not truly dead, nor was he buried, though he seemed to be so. No sooner had those who buried him retired from the tomb than he appeared to a certain woman who was mourning for him. And he told her to approach him, because it was he himself whose lying in the said tomb she was deploring; he told her also that he had never been dead, nor sustained any suffering or

affliction, although Satan and the Jews had put it in his power for them to kill him and ill-treat him.

19. (Then) on that (appointed) day, when Mary Magdalene and another woman were walking together, they saw an old and decrepit man coming along, walking quickly in their direction. Then they feared exceedingly, and hid themselves in two bushes which were beside the highway. And when that old man had passed by, Mary Magdalene put her head out of the bush and called the old man, who seemed to be a stranger. Now when the old man told her that he could not wait because he had much to do, and when she pressed him to return and speak with her, he then returned to her. She asked him if he had any news of the Prophet. Then he answered: "Yes, because on the day designated to his friends he himself will be with them in the house of Simon bar Yona, between the third hour and noon." And when she asked him if this were certain, he replied: "Why, yes." Then departing from her he immediately disappeared. And thereupon Mary Magdalene knew that the old man was the Prophet.

20. And she herself, and the Prophet with her, gathered together the Prophet's friends in the house of Simon bar Yona, the apostle Thomas only excepted. Now when they were all gathered together in the said house, and already the chosen hour seemed to be passing by, Peter said to the others, who thought they had been deceived: "Either we are sinners, or we make a mistake about the day, for the Prophet is

no liar." And when they answered him that they had made no mistake about the day, Peter replied: "Then it is we who are sinners, and it is because of our sins that the Prophet comes not." And then he said to the rest: "Seeing that we are sinners, let us try to see in what way any one of you believes in him." Thereupon they composed the Symbol or Creed of the Apostles. . . .

21. And when the Apostles stood waiting for the Prophet throughout one evening, that Prophet did come in the form of Fire. And by that Fire they were all illumined, and those who were ignorant of letters became so cognisant of them that none could excel them in knowledge. It was also given them that they should talk in the tongues of all races.

22. And Thomas, who did not believe that the Prophet could come, entered and when he had come he said that as for himself he would not believe that the Prophet could come to them unless he should put his own hand in the wound. And thereupon the Prophet said to Thomas that he should put his hand in the wound. And when Thomas had done so, he said to the Son of God that he must excuse him, because he now believed that he existed, and would believe for the future. To whom the Son of God replied: "Let indulgence be shown to thee, and for the future thou shalt not be unbelieving." Thomas replied to him that he would not be.

23. Then the Son of God said to all of them: " Preach my words throughout the whole world, and

guard yourselves from false prophets who will thrust themselves among you; for as a false prophet entered my Father's Kingdom and threw it into confusion, so also will false prophets who make their way among you throw you into confusion. . . . Yet for this they shall be heavily punished, because the holy Father said: 'He that shall deceive Me, it shall be pardoned him, and he that shall deceive the Son, it shall be pardoned him; but he who deceives the Holy Spirit shall have no peace or end.'" (Then) the Son of God said to his Apostles that they should ask of him, and he would give to them. . . .

24. And this said, he divided their preaching, marking out the country wherein each one of them was to go and preach. Now to Peter he committed the Church, but Peter's authority came to an end with Peter, because the Roman pontiffs who have succeeded him lack that authority which he had, for they do not preserve and hold to the faith and the ways of the Son of God. . . . (Then) Christ distributed among the disciples fishes and a honey-comb. . . . And then he ascended into heaven, and thereafter the Apostles preached throughout the world.

25. The Son of God said when he had returned to heaven, " My little ones, be not sad on this account, because you who stand in truth and justice and not as other men shall return otherwise to my Father's Kingdom. There are three kinds of flesh: one is of men, and another of beasts, and a third kind is of fishes, which is born in the water. You, my little ones,

shall not eat of that flesh save what is born in water, because such flesh is created without corruption; but other kinds of flesh are produced with corruption and cause the flesh to be over-proud."

26. And having said the above, the Son of God said to bar Yona: "Let no one put his hand to my plough unless he wishes to grasp it firmly. For he who shall give a cup of water to my little ones shall be blessed, because he shall receive a hundredfold and more. See, therefore, if the holy Father promises us much, yet he who shall have deceived my little ones in the matter of a single *obol*, his soul shall not be worth another *obol*. . . . Where there is one who is my little one, I myself shall be with him, and where there are two, likewise, and where there are three, in the same way."

27. (Now) the twelve Apostles who descended from heaven with Christ were spiritual beings, and afterwards in the State of Samaria there were twelve baskets of fragments left over from five loaves and (a few) fishes. Those Apostles gave the said twelve baskets to twelve men, and so were created the carnal Apostles, who had the same power as the spiritual; and whenever one of the spiritual Apostles died a carnal one succeeded him.

3. Extracts from the Yezidi Books

(Long kept secret by this little-known sect of ' devil-worshippers' in the Lebanon Mountains, these books still show

traces of Manichean ancestry. These fragments dating from about 1162 and 1342 respectively, are derived from ' Quest', vol. V; they probably go back in essence to at least the 8th or 9th century.)

He who existed before all creatures is the Angel Ta'us. It is He who sent the Servant of Ta'us into this world, to separate His chosen people and to make it wise and free it from ignorance and error—and that first by oral teaching, but afterwards by means of this Book called REVELATION, a book which no stranger to the Faith may read.

I was, I am, and I shall be, until the end of the aeons, ruling as Sovereign over the creators, and looking after the interests and the doings of all who are subject to My rule. I am ready to help all who trust in Me and invoke Me in their need. I occupy all Space. I am concerned with all the happenings which by the unbelievers are called evils; but they call them so only because they do not answer to their desires.

Every age has its Ruler; but he rules according to My counsel. In every century the Leader of this world changes, and one after the other accomplishes his task. With perfect justice I let Nature carry out everything which is in conformity with her ; he who struggles against Me will earn only regret and pain. However great they be, the other Gods do not meddle with My affairs, and cannot hinder the execution of My decrees.

APPENDIX IV

The books in the hands of those who are strangers to My teaching possess no sanction, and Prophets have not written them. These unfortunates have led themselves into error, leaving the Way of Truth and beating out their own path; thus every one of their prophets abolishes what his predecessor has established. Moreover the true and the false may be distinguished by experience. My retribution threatens those who speak of My covenant (to the uninitiated).

I reserve to Myself certain things; certain things I forbid. Everything is in its time and in its place. I teach and direct in the right way all who follow My doctrine, and they find true delight in submitting to My precepts.

I requite and reward every man according to My knowledge. In My hand is everything above, on, and underneath the earth; I allow no collision of the different worlds. I do not work against their own good, especially if their good luck is for the benefit of those who blindly follow Me. I reveal Myself in one way or another to those true to Me. . . .

It is I who give, I who take back, who make rich and poor, who make man's happiness and allow his misfortune; but everything happens according to time and circumstance. None has a right to interfere with my doings or to resist Me. I send sickness and infirmity to those who refuse to obey Me, but he who tries to satisfy Me does not die like other men. I do not let anyone live longer than I have determined; but if I will I can send him back to this earth twice or thrice in rebirth.

I teach without a book. ... I punish in the other world those who resist My laws; the children of this Adam are ignorant of what is reserved for them beyond the grave. ... The rule of the worlds, the revolutions of the ages, and the overthrow of their Rulers have been preordained from all eternity. I do not resign My rights over any of the other Gods.

The four Elements, the four Seasons, and the four Corners of the world are established for the needs of the creatures. The Books of the unbelievers are received for that in them which tallies with My Law; as for the rest, it is a product of their own imagination. ... Those who patiently suffer the pains and mishaps of this world, I shall not fail to reward in one of My worlds. I desire that all believers in Me congregate into one Covenant to confront the outsiders, ... forbearing to pronounce My Name or to mention My qualities to anyone.

Bestow all possible veneration upon My Statue and upon My Image, for it will recall My memory to you—a thing you have for years left undone. Obey My ministers, for it is they who teach you of the Invisible and of all that relates to Me.

From the Black Book:

Before the earth and the sky existed, God abode on the oceans. He had made for Himself a Vessel, and in it He drifted in the midst of the seas. In the beginning God created for Himself a white Pearl, to which He gave orders for forty years. He then created a Bird, and ... (this) sat on it for forty thousand years.

Nura'il created man, the animals, the birds and the wild beasts. After that he put them into the pockets of his robe, and issued thus out of the Pearl, accompanied by hosts of Angels. Then he uttered a mighty cry against the Pearl, and instantly it broke into four parts. Out of its womb sprang the Water, which became the ocean. The noise became the mountains, and the dust became the hills, and the smoke the skies. At that time the Earth was round and without any cleft.

God created Gabri'ël in the shape of a Bird, and He put the four Corners of the world into his hands. Then He created a Ship, wherein He remained for thirty thousand years. Then He came to inhabit Lalish: He cried against the Earth, and it became solid; having become hard, it began to quake. Then He took one piece of the Pearl and put it under the Earth to strengthen it, and another piece He put on the door of the Sky to adorn it. It is in this portion of the Pearl the Sun and Moon are set. Then around these two Luminaries He scattered the powdered pieces that had been left over from the breaking of the Pearl, and they became the Stars in the firmament, the whole being suspended from the Sky.

Thereafter God ascended into the skies, condensed them, and fixed them without pillars. He made the fruit trees and plants of the earth come forth from the soil; it is also He who made the mountains rise, to make the surface of the Earth more pleasant. He locked up with a key the Earth and the abysses; He established then the heavenly Throne and placed it on the Carpet of Glory. And then He took His pen in hand and wrote down the events of creation.

Then He begat six Gods from His own Essence and from His Light, creating them in the same way as a man lights one lamp at another. The First God said to the Second: "I have drawn from the non-existing the Sky alone; ascend thou into it, and create something else." He ascended and became the Sun. Then He said the same thing to the Third, and he became the Moon. The Fourth constituted himself the Sphere of the heavenly bodies; the Fifth proclaimed himself as the Morning Star; and the Sixth changed himself into the Atmosphere. . . .

There are about 70000 Yazidis in Assyria, they say, but only a few hundreds in Persia; their numbers are fast decreasing. The word is derived from Per. *yazd*, and means 'worshippers of God'; they speak Kurdish and are noted for cleanliness; most are tillers or cowherds. Their religion is said to be, like Mani's, a synthesis of neighbouring cults.

The Angel Ta'us is the Preserving Angel, Active God, and receives their main prayers. They recognise no evil deity or hell, but carry seven 'peacock-angels' (*sanjak*) yearly round their village shrines and make an annual pilgrimage to the tomb of their Sheikh 'Adi. Theirs is a pure worship of Light, and their era dates, strikingly, to A.D. 292; they maintain a rigid caste system with a priestly caste, and seclude their womenfolk. One of their sayings is notable: "Know that (even) sincere pretensions extinguish the flame of knowledge."

INDEX [1]

1. Aspects of Deity

Aeons, 7, 13, 15, 18, 25, 28, 38, 53, (63), 65, (69), 70, 77, 83, 90, 93; Angels, 12, 16, 18-21, 23, 36, 45, 57, 70, 73, 75, 77-78, 81, 86, 89-90, 92; Column of Glory, 7, 12, 26, 28, 72, 90, 92; Diamond (Adamas) of Light, 4, 8, 21, 85; Divine (Light) Power, 3, (5), 7, 9, 12, (13, 38), 56, 74, 91-93; Father of Greatness, 1, 3-4, 6, (12), 13, 15, (24, 27), 34, (36), 39, 41, (50, 70), 93; Fathers (of Light), 4, 10, 17, 38, 48, 65, 68; Father of Truth, 45; First and Last, the, 37, 93; First Man, 3-4, 6, 10, 13, 18, 22, 31, 38, 49, 90; Five Glories, 1-3, 64; Four Days, 13; Friend of Lights, 4, 16, 35, of the Righteous, 50; the Gods, 10, 18-19, 21, 23, 38, 41, 45, 47-48, 50, 65-66, 73, 75-78, 80, 85-86, 93; God of Truth, 14, 24, (30), 41, 59, 90, 93; Great Builder, 4, 8, 12, 17; Great King of Honour, 4-5, 20, 85; Holder of Splendour, 4-5, 19, 85; Holy Spirit, 14-15, 34, 38, 45, 66, 90, 93; Immortals, 68, 79-81, 86; Judge, 20, 35, 38, 50, 62, 76-78, 84, 87, 92, 95; King of Bliss, 49; King of Glory, 4, 8, 22, 85; Living Spirit, 4-6, 8, 10, 12, 18, 31, 35, 83; Maiden, the, 70, 75, 79, 81, of Light, 8, 10, 12, 14, 27, (31), 38, 75-76; Majesty of Law, 52-53; Mother, 28, 93-94, of Life, 3-6, 10, 12, 15, 18, of Lights, 28, 73; Perfect Man, 7, 12, 26, 28, 38, 90; Sons of First Man, 3-4; Supporter (Atlas), 4-5, 8, 12, 22-23, 85; Supreme Merchant, 64, (92); Three Eternals, 64, (92); Three Servants, 8; Tree of Life, 10, 14, 28, 34, (35), 37, 52-53, 63, 70, of Knowledge, 38, of Rest, 70; Venerable (Adorable) of Light, 32, 35, 80, 82.

2. The Soul

Bright Gods, five, 5, 8, 18, 49, 64; Divinity, (38), 39, 41, 49; heart, 8, 10, 20, 24, 27, 29, 38, 41, 44-45, 49-50, 53, 56, 62, 65-66, 70-71, 74-75, 86, 95; Light-Cross, 40, (57, 59), 60, 71; Light

---

[1] It is obvious that fully to index a book of this sort is to prepare a Concordance, which is impossible; a suggestive selection of words and topics has been made here. Readers may find under a synonym any word not found in its alphabetical order. Grouping has been made in the light of the general doctrinal significance, but many words might appear with equal propriety in other Groups. The numbers refer to Text-Sections.

364 THE GOSPEL OF THE PROPHET MANI

Image, Form, 42, 75, 81, 85, 90; Living Soul, 25, 29, 36, 42; Soul(s), 3, 10, 24, 45, 49-50, 52-53, 56-57, 63, 65-66, 68, 70-72, 75-76, 78-79, 83, 87-92; its five Limbs or Trees, 3, 8, 28, 63, 71, (83), 90, 94-95; Sons, Race, of Light, 4, (12), 20, 22-23, 32, 35, (38, 48), 65, 82, 93; Twelve Virtues, Buckets, etc., 6-7, 12-13 24, 31.

3. Powers of Evil

Abortions, 9, 21, 24; Abyss, 20, 22, 24-25, 71, 75, 87, 91, 93-94; dark bodies, five, 1, 49, 63; dark earth, 1, 4-5, 29, 41, 49, (77); dark powers, 2-3, 17, 24, 27, 29, 34, (35), 47-48, 54, 73, (78); demoness, Fury, 8, 67, 70; demons, 2, 7, 10, 20-21, 29, 49, 53, 67, 70, 74-75, 82, 85-86; dragon, 21, 29, 33, 45; Enemy, foes, adversary, 1, 3, 17, 29, 32, 35, 45-46, 48, 55-56, 62, 68, 71, 77-78, 80, 82, 86-88; evil trees, 21, 24, 32, 34, (63); giants, 8, 18, 20-21; Great Spirit, 10; ignorance of Evil, 2, 29; King of Darkness, 1-3, (5), 8-9, 29, (35), 54; Matter, 1-2, 7, 9, 12, 21, 28-29, 63; Pride, 2-3, 9, 24; Rebels, 10, (18), 20, 36, 47, (48); revolt against God, 2-3, 70, 87; Rulers crucified in Sky, 5, 8, 18, (63); Sea-Monster, 49; Sin, 8, 19, 21, 24, 29, 34, 38, 41, 47, 49, 53-54, 56, 60, 63, (65), 76, 84, 87, 92; Sons of Darkness, 3, 5, 8; Tree of Death, 52, 63; Venomous Beast, 87; vices, 1; Watchers, the, 20, 93.

4. The Universe

Air, 11-12, 21, 35, 38, 50, 78-80, 84, 88, 90; astrological aspects, 56; Building, the, 17-18, 34, 36; cloud, 29, 67, 77, 80; cold, 7; creation, 5, (10, 23), 24, 28, 70; day(s), 13, 28, 34, 38, 40, 43, 50, 65, 76, 80, 83-85, 88, 90-91, 93; dew(drops), 28, 38, 78; dry, 8, 27; dust, 15, 80; earth, 2, 8-10, 12, 15, 20-21, 23, 29, 34, 36, 38, 41, 47, 50, 60, 66, 68, 76, 81-82, (85), 86, 88-89; earthquake, 22-23; eight earths, 5, (8, 11, 28); elements, five, 3, (5), 34, 83, 93; Fire, 1-2, 5, 8, 12-13, 22, 24, 29, 34, 43, 52, 57, 74, 76, 83, 86-87, 91; Five Vaults, 23; Four Supports, 23; ground, 60; heat, 7, 43; macrocosm, 5, 12; microcosm, 5; mountains, 20-21, 35, 53, 80; New Aeon, Earth, 8, 12, 17, 38, 65; night 38, 51, 58, 67, 89-90, 93; river(s), 34, 37, 80; sand, 15, 80; sea, 18, 21, 26, 32, 34, 36, 38, 43, 49, 53, 61, 66, 80, 94-95; sky, heaven(s), firmament(s), 5, 8, 10-11, 20-21, 28, 34, 43, 66, 68, 70, 73, 80-82, 85, 86, 89, 93; smoke, 1, 67; soil, 34-35, 63, 80; Sphere, 5-6, 21, 38, 87; stars, 5, 35, 51, 85, wheel of, (18), 84; storm(y), 49, 53, 56, 66, 81; seventh heaven, 20; Seven Columns, 21; streams, fountains, 22, 28, 35-36, 53, 80, 91; summer, 43; ten heavens, 5, (19); Three Columns, 23; three earths, realms, 22, (23), 35, 61, 77; three heavens, 19; Three Wheels, 8, 18, 22, 91; ,Three Times, (13), 37, 64, 80, 91; Water, 1-2, 8, 12-13, 22, 28, 34, 37, 53, 58, 63, 66, 70, 72, 76, 80, 88-89, 91; wave(s), 38, 49, 53, 56, 81; wet, 8, 27; Wind, 1, 8, 12, 22, 43, 51, 78, 80, 88,

INDEX 365

91, of Life, 37; winter, 38, 43; year(s), 15, 20, 38, 42, 80, 85, 93, 95; Zone, the, 18, 24.

5. Animals

Bird, 49, 78; cattle, 5; dog(s), 3, 10; Dove, White, 66, 69; eagle, 29, 70, 78; elephants, 10; fish, 29, 42; flesh (and blood), 21, 24, 28, 34, 38, 40, 42, 44-45, 49-51, 63, 65-66, 71, 73-74, 78, 89; goats, 86; honey, 94; jackals, 53; lamb, 32, 53; leopards, 10; lion, 10, 29, 57; milk, 43, 92-93; sheep, 28, 34, 38, 50, 71, 86, 91; snakes, etc., 3, 32, 42, 57, 67, 71; tigers, 32; venom, 8, 32, 67, 87; wild, beasts, 4, 32, 49, 53; wolves, 32, 53, 71; worm, 38, 60, 80.

6. Plants

Branch, 28, 43, 45, 53; flower(s), blossom, 28, 31, 38, 43, 45, 53, 71, 75, 80; fragrance 35, 53, 62, 70, 73, 80, 94; fruit(s), 1-2, 13, 21, 28, 34-37, 43, 45, 53, 57, 63, 65, 71-72, 80, 92-93; fruitful trees, 13, 28, 31, 37, 43, (45), 53, 71, 80, 91; garden(s), 10, (35), 54, 70, 73, 80; garland(s), 13, 16, 34, 36, 38, 45, 48, 50, 58, 60, 65, 69, 71-73, 75-79, 81, 90-93; incense, 34; juniper, 43; leaves, 38, 43; lilies, 45; plants, 5, 8, 28, 32, 34-35, 60, (63, 65), 76; pomegranate, 62; Roots, Natures, Sources, Two, 1, 5, 9, 12-13, 21, 30, 32, 41, 52; rose(s), 28, 45, 58, 79, 91; sap, 28; seed, 34, 43, 55; 'sweet dew', immortality, 13, 35, 53, 63, (68), 78, 80, 88, 93; trees, 1, 8-9, 21, 28, 31-32, 37-38, 43, 60, 63, 65, 71-72, 76, 80, 89, 91, 95; Two Trees, 1, 13, 29, 93; Vine, 28, 45; wine, 28, 40, 45, 62.

7. Fall of the Soul

Accuser, 50; body of darkness, 3, 49, of death, 49, 70, 78, Soul fettered in, 3, 6, 24, 49-50, 63; care, anxiety, 44, 49-50, 65, 78, 80; death, departure, 10, 17-18, 29, 35, (37, 41-42), 49-51, (53), 55, 67, 69-71, 73, (75), 76, 78, 80, 85-86, 88, 90-92, 95; desire, lust, 3, 8, 21, 24, 27, 29, 35, 45, 49, 53, 60, 73, 80, 85-87; dregs, 12, 24, 56; eating and drinking, 56-57, 69, 71, 86; Error, 29, 35, 38, 48, 53-54, 70, 89, 92; fire of digestion, 22, 57, 71; food, 42, 45, 56-57, 71, 80, 86; forgetting, 3, 36, 38, 48-50, 77, 80, 92; Four Afflictions, 65; intoxication, 40, 45, 49-50; killing, 5, 21, 29, 34, 38, 57, 60, 73; madness, cup of, 48, water of, 38; Matter contaminates Soul, 3-5, 9, 12; pain, sorrow, etc., 4, 6, 12, 24, 28, 32, 34, 36, 38, 42, 46-47, 49-50, 53, 55, 58-59, 61, 65, 73-74, 76, 78, 80-81, 84-86, 88-90; passion(s), 2, 78; penalty, 49, 61-62; rebirth, 44, 49, 73, 76, 80, 88-89; relations, family, 9, 10, (20), 27, 31, 41-44, 47-48, 50-51, 56, 60, 77-78, 92, 95; robber(s), 34, 49, 70; slave(ry), 42, 49, 74, 77, 88; sleep, spiritual, 10, 25, 36, (49), 50, 52, 54, 63, 65, 80; sorcery, magic, etc., 29, 32, 49-50, 53-54; wife, 42, 44; womb, 28, 34, 85; World,

366 THE GOSPEL OF THE PROPHET MANI

the, 21, 24, 26, 28-32, 34-35, 40-42, 44-47, 50-51, 53, 57, 63, 66, 68-69, 71, 80, 86, 88; worldliness, birth-and-death, 52-53, 65, 80, 92.

8. Artefacts of Man

Armour, 3, 22, 28, 31, 36, 71; Axe, 32, 34, 63; balance, 38, 76; Bema, 34, 38; boat, 43, 49; book(s), Scripture, 30, 34, 36-37, 43, 92, 95; buckler, 46; chambers, 15, 17-18; chariot, litter, 24-25, 70, 75; Cross, 34, 36, 70, 71, (91); crown(s), diadems, 3, 6, 34-36, 38, 43, 48, 50, 69-70, 72-73, 75, 77, 80, 92-93; Customs-House, 76; door(s), 24, 28, 36, 48, 53, 59, 73, 92-93; drums, 35; flutes, 35; gate(s), gateway, 11, 24, 32, 38, 49, 54, 61, 74, 77, 81, 92, of Law, 95, of Life, 45, 70; gold and silver, 13, 44, 58, 69; harbour, port, etc. (38), 45, 49-50, 56, 66, 77-79, 90; harp, 13, 35, 50; house(s), 35, 44-45, 47, 49-50, 56, 78, 86; iron, 2, 29; ladder, 28, 38; lamp(s), 38, 43, 53; 63, 71-73, 92; lutes, 13; medicine(s) 28, 35, 38, 49, 63; mirror, 35, 76, 80; moat, 11, 35; oil, 38, 72-73; palace, 32, 35-36, 47, 49, 64, 80; parapet, 56; prison, 17, 20, 49, 82, 86; Robe, garment(s), etc., 6, 28, 30, 34, (42), 43, 48, 50, 53, 65-66, 68, 70-71, 75, 80-81, 91-92; schools, 47; shield, 8, 46; spear, 8, 46; stairway, 28, 38, 89; temple(s), 42, 47, 80; tomb, 30, 34, 62; treasure(s), 28, 32, 42, 44, 49, 51, 73, 86; treasuries, 28, 63; trumpet, 68; wall(s), 11-12, 28, 31, 35, 74.

9. Agents of Salvation

Advocate, 14, 38, 49, 91-92; Answerer, Reply, 4, (34), 83; Apostles, 34, 36; awakening, 10, 22, 28, 36, 50, 52, 63; baptism, 26, 38; beauty, 9, 24-25, 27-28, 31, 37, 45, 50-52, 71, 73, 79, 92; Call, Shout, 4, 18, 34, 36-37. (50, 52, 65, 73, 77), 83, 85, (86); Church(es), 13, 21, 26, 28, 30, 34, 36, 38-39, 42-45, 59, 63, 69, 72, 88-91, 93-94; dive, 89, 94, Light-Diver, 65; Envoy's Image, 12, 18-19, (21), 22, 24, (70, 95); Envoy, Third, 6, 8-9, 12-13, 18, 24, 85, 90; Faith, 6, 14, 25, 28, 31, 35, 38, 40, 43, 63, 70, 73, 89, 91, 95; Ferry, 7, 32, 50, 77; Flock(s), 12, 32, 34-35, 53; forms, male and female, 8-9, 35; Grace(s), 26, 33-34, 38, 40, 42, 44-45, 70-73, 78, 81, 88-89, 92; Hope, the, 28, 30, 34, 38, 54, 70-72, 86, 88, 90, 92; Kindly Light, 28, 64; King(s), 1, 13, 24, 28, 30-31, 34-35, 43, 45, 47-48, 50, 52-53, 63, 71, 73, 77, 80, 93, 95; Law, Religion, 29, 32, 34-35, 38, 43, 46, 52-54, 64, 71, 80, 86, 92, 95; memory, water of, 50; Messenger(s) (of the Light), 13, 19, 21-23, 28. 30, 32, 35, 37-39, 46, 55, 63-64, 75, 80, 86, 88-89, 91, 95; Mind, Light-Mind, (3), 13-14, 26, 28, 31, 33, 35, 37-39, 41, 45, 48, 63, 65, 69, 71, 77-78, 88, 90, Moon, 5, 7, 10, 12, (13), 25, 31, 42, 64, 77, (79), 85, (89-90), 93; Name, the, 34-36, (40, 47), 53, 59, 70-71, 73, 92-94; pearl(s), 13, 34, 43, 65; Physician, 28, 49-50, 53, 63, 71; preaching, 34, 45, 49, 60, 64, 91; Prince, noble, 36, 48, 50, 95; Prophets 31, 91; psalms

INDEX 367

and hymns, 7, (35), 47, 56, 58, 80, 93; Redeemer, 10, 28, 89; resurrection, 28, 34, (37), 38, (69); revelation, 2, 4-5, 8, 18, 22, 24, 30-32, 34, 45, 60, 91, 95; Right Hand, 4, 18, (49), 70, 74-75, 77, 88-89; sacrificing love, 36, 39, 48, 65, 71, 88, 93; Saints, 13, 28, 35, 41-42, 44-45, 59, 61, 68, 70-73, 78-81, 89; Saviour, 28, 35, 52, 65, 70-75, 81, 91; Seal, 25, 38, 50, 78, 89, 92; Sects, religions, 29-30, 34, (91); Shepherd, 28, 32, (34), 35, 38, 50, 71, 91, 93; Ships (of Light), 7-8, 12, 18, 24-25, 28, 32, 34, (38), 45, 49-51, 56, 76-79, 81, 84, 89-90, 92-93, 95; signs, characteristics, (6), 14, 25, 29, 31, 34-35, 38, 44, 51, 54-55, 58, 85, 91, 95; Sun, 5, 7, 10, 12-13, (19), 24-25, 28, 31, 35, 37, 42, 51, 55, (58), 64, 71-72, 77, 85, 91, 93; Twin, Comrade, 28, 35, (41), 91; Word(s), the, 18, 33, 35-36, 38, 45, 53, (56), 57, 60, 69, 71, 74, 83, 91, 94-95.

10. Spiritual Life

Almsgiving, 38, 41-42, 44-45, 54, 57, 59, 70-71, 89; beloved, 16, 28, 36, 38, 45, 55, 65, 73, 91, 93; Commandments, Precepts, 14, 34-35, 38, 43, 47, 54, 63, 70-71, 77-78, 86, 88, 91, 95; disciples, 30, 34, 55; Elect, the, 14, 31, 34, (40), 41, 43-44, (45), 47, 57, 60, (66), 75, 86, 89-90; "Faith and Morals", (10, 14, 30, 91); fasting, 14, 38, 42, 44, 54, 56-57, 70-71, 73, 89; forgiveness, absolution, 38, 63, (65), 76, 84, 91; good deeds, 7, 30-31, 42-43, 45, 54, 65, 73, 76, 84, (88), 89; Hearers, the, 14, 42-45, 47, 86, 89-90, 92, 95; Illuminates, 31, 80, 82; joy, happiness, 13, 17, 25, 28, 31-32, 35-38, 45-46, 54-56, 58, 65, 69, 71, 73, 77-78, 80, 82, 85-86, 88, 95; merchandise, wares, etc., 4, 7, 28, 50, (76), 78-79; New Man, 38, 53, 63; Old Man, 38, 41, 64; orphans and widows, 73, 91; path(s), 22, 25, 28, 53, 60, 68, 76-78, 81, 90, 92, 95, Straight Path, 34, 36, 38, 61, 95; peace, rest, repose, 3-4, 25, 28, 32, 36-38, 40, 42-43, 45-49, 54-55, 59-63, 69, 73, 78, 80-81, 87-89, 91-93, 95; pity, compassion, 4, 10, 19, 28, 37-38, 45, 61, 64-65, 70, 73, 88, 91; poverty, 38, 51, 59; prayer, 6, 14, 32, 38, 42, 44, 47-48, 53, 56, 58, 70-71, 73, 89, 91, seven prayers, 4; repentance, 34, 45, 84, 88; righteousness, 10, 34-35, 39-40, 42, 46-47, 53, 63, (75), 84, 89, 95; road, 44, 49, 60, 65; silence, 15, 28, 55, 64, 83, 93; sincerity, 6, 31, 61, 64; stranger, alien, (32-34), 35, 44, 50, 70-71, 83, 86; study, 47, 54, 64; Three Seals, 14, Victory, 3, 6, 13-14, 16, 25, 31, 34-35, 38-39, 45, 48-49, 65, 70-71, 73, 75, 77-78, (81), 85-86, 88, 91, 95; virginity, purity, 6, 14, 33, 38, 40, 42, 44, 54, 56, 70-72, 78-79, 86; voice, 4, 10, 29, 47, 50, 53, 70-71, 73-74, 76-77; war, fight, etc., 1-3, 8, 12, 17-18, 28, 33, 45, 48, 77-78, 83; way, 53-54, 60, 65, 70, 75, 85, 89, 92.

11. Final States

Bride, 69, 77; bridechambers, 53, 55, 68, 72, 77, 79, 81; Bridegroom, Spouse, 28, 38, 47, 55, 69, 72, 79, 81; City, the, 7, 38, 48,

368 THE GOSPEL OF THE PROPHET MANI

66, 77-81; end of the world, 12, 21, 85, (87, 91); Fatherland, 68; Garden of the Light, 76; Grave, the, 12, 87; hell(s), 10, 49, 67, 86-89; Kingdom, 28, 35, 38, (45), 47-48, 69-70, 76, 78, 81, 85, 87, 93; Kingdom of Light, 1-2, 34, 36, 38, 41, 50-52, 54-55, (59), 65-66, (70), 73, 76-77, 80, 82, 86; Knowledge of God, Gnosis, 10, 28, 33, 36, 45, 56, 77, 85, 89, 91; Last Statue, 12, 18, 83, 87; Love, 14, 28, 38-40, 42, 44-45, 47-48, 51, 54, 59, 62-63, 65, 68-69, 71-73, 75, 79-80, 86-87, 90-95; 'Lump', the, 12, 87; Native Land, 32, 35; perfect(ion), 28, 38, 40, 54, 63, 65, 91; return, 7, 32, 50, 78-79, 81-82, 95; separation of Light and Dark, 5, 7, 8, 11-12, 24, 26, 32, 38, 63, 75-76, 80, 82, (83), 87, 91; Wisdom, 6, 13, 22, 27-28, 30-38, 40-41, 45, 54, 56, 59, 63-64, 71, 85, 91, 93.

12. Proper Names

Adam, 9-10, 21, 24; Ambition, 12; Amen, 34, 93; Ashaqlun, 9; Aurentes, 30; Babylonia, 30, 36; Buddha, the, 30; Christ, 14, 28, 30, 36, 38, 66, 71-73, 78-79, 81, 91, 94, descends, 10, 34; Eve, 9-10, 21-22, 24; Gushtasp, 30; Hindus, 30; India, 30; Ioel, 10; Jesus, 22, 28, 30, 34-36, 38, 40, 45-46, 49, 53, 55, 65-66, 69-73, 79, 81, 91, the Child, 28, 34, 83, Immanent, 10, 28, 34, 37; in the Moon, 12, 28, the Radiant, 10, 13, 28, 38, 70, 72, Son of God, 34-35, 70; Jews, 34; Judas the Iscariot, 34; Judea, 34; Manbed, 23; Mani, 14, 30-31, 35-37, 51, 55, 62, 91-92, 95; Mazdean, 30; Mithra, 24; Nahashbet, 3, the First Aeon, 48; Nebroel, 9; Noah, 78; Paradise, 35, 80, 86; Persia, 30; Satan, 34, 53; Shitil, 30; Visbed, 21; Zarathushtra, 30; Zrwān, 30, 35, 46, 91.

13. Special Doctrines

Alms purified by Saints, 43, 59; docetism, 10, 34, 91; God is wholly Good, Matter, Evil, 1-2; intercession by Saints, 78; *karma*, 38, 65, 73, 76-77, 81, 84, 87; sharing of merits, 41-42, 45, 55, 57; universalism, 12.

14. Similes

Bitten man, 3, 8; borrowed utensils, 44; branch of fruitless tree, 43; farmer, 37, 43; inn, 44, 51; iron in fire, 29; hair in dough, 8; lightning, 4; man and vomit, 8; nail, 67; night, 5; pearl in King's crown, 43; poison in cake, 3; raging lion, 10; rain before sun, 51; raincloud, 67; river, 37; saint with demons, 10; shadows before sun, 55; sharp sword, 4; sick man, 43; snow in sunlight, 51; sun, 37; swift bird, 78; thunder in clouds, 29; two Kings, 1.

BIBLIOGRAPHY

A. Chief Source-Books

C. W. Alberry, A Manichean Psalmbook, Pt. 2, 1938; *Prosper Alfaric*, Les Ecritures manichéennes, I-II, 1918/9; *Gustav Flügel*, Kitāb al-Fihrist, 1872; *A. E. W. Jackson*, Researches in Manichaeism, 1931; *Migne's Patrologies:* P. G. vols. 1, 10, 18, 39, 42, 83, 94, 103; P. L. vols. 32, 42, 65; *F. W. K. Müller*, Handschriften-Reste in Estrangelo Schrift aus Turfan, I-II, 1904, Soghdische Texten, I-II; *S. D. F. Salmond*, The Acts of Archelaus, 1882; *Addai Scher*, Corpus Scriptorum christianorum orientalium curantibus, LXVI, 1912; *R. Stothert*, St. Augustine On the Manichaean Heresy, 1872; *Schmidt-Polotsky-Böhlig*, die Kephalaia, I, 1940.

Andreas—Henning, Mitteliranische Manichaica aus Chinesisch-Turkestan, 1932/4; *A. von le Coq*, Türkische Manichaica I-III, aus Chotscho, 1912; *W. Henning*, Ein manichäisches Bet-und Beichtbuch, 1937; *C. W. S. Mitchell*, S. Ephraim's Prose Refutations of Mani, Marcion and Bardaisan, 1912; *C. Salemann*, Manichäische Studien I, 1911.

B. Doctrine

Sir Thos. W. Arnold, Survivals of Sassanian and Manichaean Art in Persian Painting, 1925; *F. C. Burkitt*,

The Religion of the Manichees, 1925; *Arthur Lloyd*, The Creed of Half Japan, 1911; *E. B. Pusey*, St. Augustine's Confessions, 1946; *R. Reitzenstein*, das iranische Erlösungsmysterium, 1921, das mandäische Buch des Herrn der Grösse, 1919; *Torgny Säve-söderbergh*, Studies in the Coptic Manichean Psalmbook, 1949; *Georg Widengren*, The Great Vohu Manah and the Apostle of God, 1945, Mesopotamian Elements in Manichaeism, 1946.

W. Bousset, Hauptprobleme der Gnosis 1907; *Franz Cumont*, La Cosmogonie manichéenne; Recherches sur le Manichéisme, 1908; *G. Flügel*, Mani, seine Lehre und seine Schriften, 1862; *K. Kessler*, Mani: Forschungen über die manichäische Religion, I, 1889; *H. Pognon*, Inscriptions mandaïtes des Coupes de Khouabir, 1898/9; *H. J. Polotsky*, Abriss der manichäischen Systems; *Schmidt-Polotsky-Ibscher*, Ein Mani-Fund in Ägypten, 1933; *Waldschmidt-Lenz*, die Stellung Jesu in Manichäismus, 1926; *O. G. Wesendonk*, die Lehre des Mani, 1922.

C. Related Studies

J. H. Bernard, The Odes of Solomon, 1912; *A. A. Bevan*, The Hymn of the Soul, 1897; *E. A. Wallis Budge*, The Paradise of the Holy Fathers I-II, 1907; *R. H. Charles*, The Book of Enoch, 1912; *Mark Lidzbarski*, Ginza, der Schatz, 1925; das Johannesbuch der Mandäer I-II, 1905/15; *G. R. S. Mead*, Fragments of a Faith Forgotten, 1906, The Gnostic Crucifixion, c. 1907, The Hymn of Jesus, c. 1906, The Hymn of the Soul, 1909, Pistis Sophia, 1921; *Matthew Norberg,* Codex Nasaraeus; *A. Resch*, Agrapha, 1906; *C. E. Sachau,* Albiruni's Chronologies of Ancient Nations, 1879, India, 1879; *Carl Schmidt*, Koptisch-gnostische Schriften I, 1905.

D. Articles by the following scholars

W. Bang, A. A. Bevan, Chavannes-Pelliot, A. von le Coq, Robert Gauthiot, W. C. Henning, A. E. W. Jackson, K. Kessler, F. Legge, G. R. S. Mead, V. Minorsky, H. J. Polotsky, S. H. Taqizadeh,

in the following Journals

Bulletin of the School of Oriental and African Studies, 1935, 1942-1943, 1945, 1948; Journal Asiatique, 1911, 1913; Journal of the American Oriental Society, 1910 ff.; Journal of the Royal Asiatic Society, 1909, 1913; Le Muséon, vols. 36, 38, 44, 46; The Quest, vols. 1-7; Z.D.M.G. vols. 82, 90, etc.

and Articles in these Encyclopedias:

Catholic Encyclopedia, Encyclopaedia Britannica, Encyclopaedia of Islam, Hastings Encyclopaedia of Religion and Ethics (by *A. A. Bevan*), and the New Schaff-Herzog Encyclopaedia (by *K. Kessler*).

THE WORLD GOSPEL SERIES

(*Uniform with this Volume*)

EACH Volume of this Series contains a Text made up of selected passages from the recognised Scriptures of the Religion under study, carefully arranged in logical order into topical Sections. Most of these passages have been newly translated in simple words from the original languages for this Series, after carefully consulting the work of earlier scholars. Each Section is followed by an illuminating Commentary, special points in the Text being further elucidated by short Footnotes.

To each Volume is prefixed a scholarly Introduction —describing the life and times of the Founder of the Religion, giving a brief Outline of its historical background and development through the centuries, together with important studies on special doctrines of the Religion and on the various literary sources drawn upon for the Text. Valuable features in each Volume are a Synopsis that gives the central thought of the various Sections of the Text, and a Catechism wherein, to aid comparative studies, the questions are, as far as possible common to all the Religions. In a few pages the essential drift of the whole Volume is printed at the beginning, and its central keynote appears in scriptural words on the title page. The usual Index, Bibliography, etc. are supplied, and in several Volumes special Appendices facilitate historical or doctrinal study.

In every case, orthodox opinion of the adherents of the faith is made the basis of rendering and understanding the Texts, and an attempt is honestly made to view the Religion as from within its own fold, factually and without criticism or comparison.

Vol.
1. THE GOSPEL OF ISLAM, based on a new translation of the *Holy Qur'ān*, expounding the simple world faith of the Prophet of Arabia.

2. THE GOSPEL OF CHINA, based on translations of the Four great Classics of *Confucius and Mencius*—a noble ethic reared on contemplative philosophy.

3. THE GOSPEL OF HERMES, based on the *Hermetic Literature* of the few centuries before and after Christ—an important system of Western Yoga and Theosophy—with an Appendix of parallel texts from all over the world.

4. THE GOSPEL OF JESUS, based on a new translation from the *Synoptic Gospels* and Agrapha of Synoptic type, critically judged as giving the most reliable portrait of the Man Jesus—Jewish ethicist and parabolist.

THE WORLD GOSPEL SERIES

Vol.
5. THE GOSPEL OF ZARATHUSHTRA, based on the *Avesta* and *Pehlevi Scriptures*, with a new translation of the *Gāthas*—the noble Religion of the Holy Prophet of Iran.

6. THE GOSPEL OF THE MYSTIC CHRIST, based on a new translatton of the *Gospel of St. John* and several Apocrypha—the spiritual life of the Divine Man, the 'Christ in You', and the Mystic Path to Him.

7. THE GOSPEL OF NARADA, based on a new translation of the *Nārada Pāncarātra*, and *Nārada Bhakti Sūtras*—typical of the Vaishnava Faith of pure Devotion, with an account of Sri Rāmānujāchārya's philosophy in India.

8. THE GOSPEL OF THE GURU-GRANTH SAHIB, derived from the *Sikh Scriptures* newly translated from Gurmukhi, with a new rendering of the *Japji*—the manly Religion of Active Devotion.

9. THE GOSPEL OF THE PYRAMIDS, newly translated from the Ancient Egyptian Hieroglyphs of the *Pyramid Texts*, oldest surviving scriptural texts in the world—proclaiming immortality and the glory of the Divine Initiate King. With an Appendix of newly translated Texts of the same date, and a history of Egypt from the start to the Pyramid Age.

Vol.
10. THE GOSPEL OF ADVAITA, newly translated from *Yoga Vasishta, Ashtāvakra Gita, Sri Sankaracharya's* works and other standard books, to illustrate the *Māndukyopaniṣad*—direct realisation of universal oneness. With an Appendix to show the same vision in modern saints of India and in the West.

11. THE GOSPEL OF ISRAEL, newly translated from the Hebrew of the *Old Testament* of the Jews, and the Greek, Coptic etc., of certain non-canonical books added as an Appendix—the Religion of ethical union between God and His faithful People.

12. THE GOSPEL OF THE PROPHET MANI, the forgotten Religion: newly translated from many languages, here for the first time brought together from many lands between China and Provence —with a life of the martyred Prophet of the first great eclectic Theosophy and its later history, and several important Appendices.

13. THE GOSPEL OF THE GNOSTICS, based on surviving books like the *Pistis Sophia*, the two *Books of Iēu*, and hymns, etc., preserved by the hostile Christian Fathers, here first brought together—showing the value of such mystical revelations even in our own day.

Vol.
14. THE GOSPEL OF MAHAYANA, derived from Sanskrit, Japanese and Tibetan works, giving the essence of the inner teachings of the great Lord Buddha as preserved in the Northern School.

15. The Gospel of the Light, proclaimed by the Mandeans of ancient Chaldea.

16. The Gospel of the Desert, the mysterious devotional '*Odes of Solomon*', full of beauty and joyous thrill.

17. The Gospel of the Spirits, revealed in our own days through a few of the higher mediums.

18. The Gospel of the West, based on great Mystics like St. Teresa, St. John of the Cross, and Dionysius.

19. The Gospel of Egypt, as taught in the days of her Imperial greatness.

20. The Gospel of the Sufis, passionate devotees of Muslim lands.

21. The Gospel of the Ṛṣhis, enshrined in timeless Vedas and Upanishads.

Vol.
  22. The Gospel of the Buddha, found in Ceylon's great Hinayana Scriptures.

  23. The Gospel of the Stoics, pagan teachers of humanitarianism and pure altruism.

  24. The Gospel of the Tirthankaras, the preaching of the Jain ascetics.

  25. The Gospel of the Behais, universal brotherhood taught by Iran in our own days.

  26. The Gospel of Sri Krishna, as revealed in the Sri mad Bhāgavatam and the Bhagavad Gita.

It is also proposed to sum up the entire Series with an Abstract Volume, containing the essential teachings of all these in brief, entitled

  27. THE WORLD GOSPEL.

ALSO AVAILABLE FROM THE BOOK TREE

THE BOOK OF JUBILEES, Translated by R. H. Charles. This rare and important holy book sheds new light on Judaism and early Christianity. It was written sometime between 250 BC and AD 100 by one or more Hellenistic Jews, and reflects a form of Jewish mystical thought at around the time of Christ. It retells much of the Old Testament story, but includes additional material not mentioned in the Bible. It also relies heavily on *The Book of Enoch*, which was, like this book, translated from the Ethiopic text. It covers Adam and Eve, the Fall of Man, Cain and Abel, the fall of the angels and their punishment, the deluge foretold, the ark and the flood, the tower of Babel and confusion of tongues, evil spirits, corruption of the human race, God's covenant, the Messianic Kingdom, Jacob's visions, prophetic dreams, and Moses, among other interesting topics. **224 pages • paper $18.95**

THE BOOK OF JASHER: A Suppressed Book that was Removed from the Bible, Referred to in Joshua and Second Samuel, translated by Albinus Alcuin (800 AD). According to some sources, this book was once the original start of the Bible. We know that it was once part of the Bible, being referred to in Joshua and Second Samuel. *The Book of Jasher* survived the burning of the Alexandria Library in about 389 AD due to a fast acting custodian. Albinus Alcuin later found this work and did the original translation of it from Hebrew in 800 AD. It was later suppressed but rediscovered in 1829, when it was once again suppressed. Only now has it reemerged and we hope that it will become widely available and judged properly for its value. Note: A 63 page version is in circulation, but is a proven forgery. **304 pages • 6 x 9 • perfect bound • $24.95**

THE LOST BOOKS OF THE BIBLE OR THE APOCRYPHAL NEW TESTAMENT, assembled by William Hone. Translated by William Wake and Jeremiah Jones. First published in 1820 under the title The Apocryphal New Testement. These documents were written soon after the death of Christ, during the early days of Christianity. Yet when the Bible was compiled near the end of the fourth century, these texts were not included and were suppressed by the church. **295 pages • 6 x 9 • paper • $24.95**

THE BOOK OF ADAM AND EVE or The Conflict of Adam and Eve with Satan, Translated by Rev. S.C. Malan. This book reveals the life and times of Adam and Eve after they were expelled from the Garden of Eden, up to the time when Cain killed his brother Abel. It covers where they went, where they lived, and their various troubles and temptations, including those coming from Satan. This is an interesting book because it provides one with more information to work with beyond the standard Biblical account. The work includes a number of helpful notes by the translator, issued for clarification, and they appear consistently throughout the text. **256 pages • 6 x 9 • paper • $21.95**

To order call 1.800.700.TREE 24 hrs. OR visit www.thebooktree.com